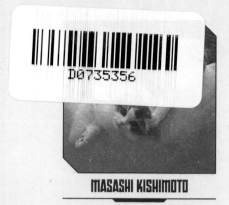

MASASHI KISHIMOTO

Master Daruma has a real-life model. The model's name is Latte, the one on the right up there.

AKIRA OKUBO

It's always exciting when I get to read Kishimoto Sensei's written draft of each week's chapter. I hope that you enjoy the finished result too.

SAMURAI 8
THE TALE OF HACHIMARU

02

SHONEN JUMP Manga Edition

Story MASASHI KISHIMOTO
Art AKIRA OKUBO

Translation/STEPHEN PAUL
Touch-Up Art & Lettering/SNIR AHARON
Design/JULIAN [JR] ROBINSON
Editor/ALEXIS KIRSCH

SAMURAI8 HACHIMARUDEN © 2019 by Masashi Kishimoto, Akira Okubo
All rights reserved.
First published in Japan in 2019 by SHUEISHA Inc., Tokyo.
English translation rights arranged by SHUEISHA Inc.

The stories, characters and incidents mentioned in this publication are
entirely fictional.

Printed in the U.S.A.

Published by VIZ Media, LLC
P.O. Box 77010
San Francisco, CA 94107

10 9 8 7 6 5 4 3 2 1
First printing, May 2020

viz.com

shonenjump.com

SAMURAI 8
THE TALE OF HACHIMARU

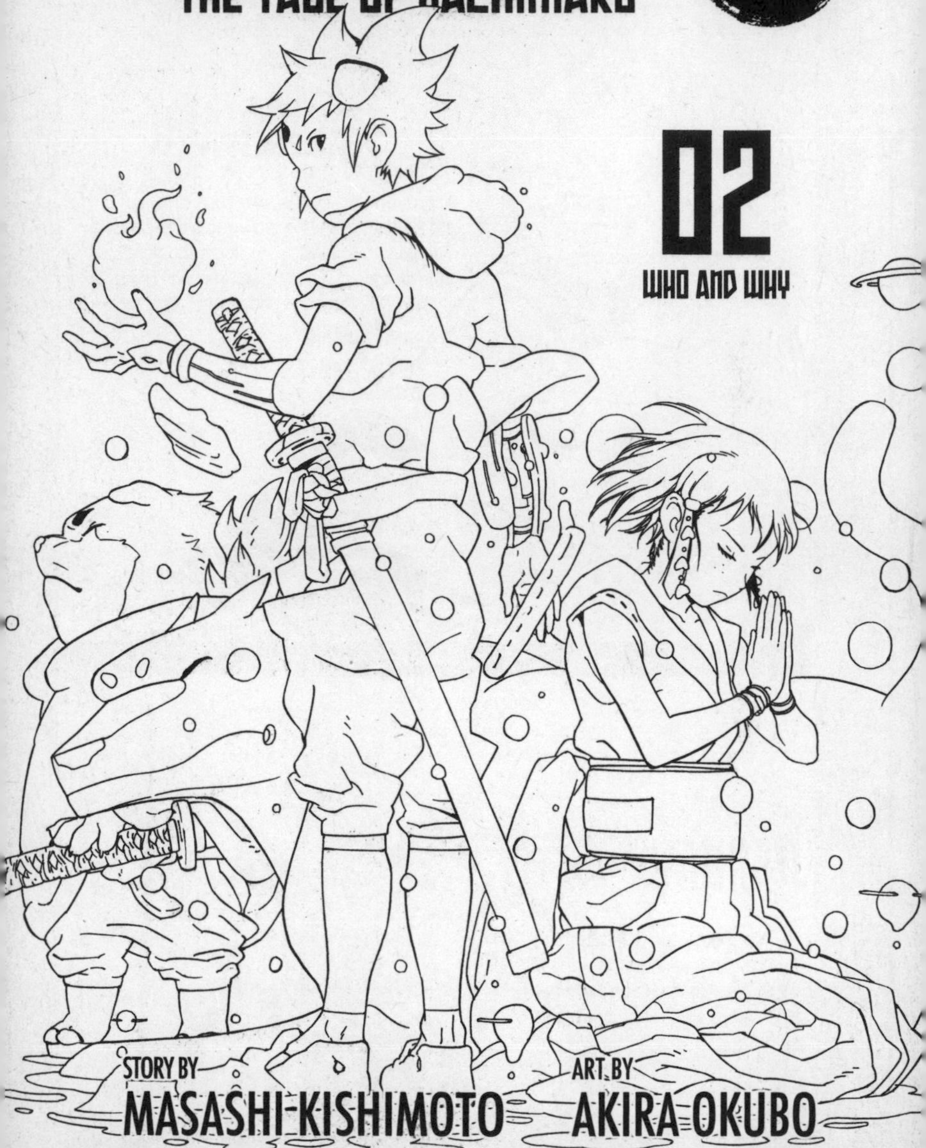

02
WHO AND WHY

STORY BY
MASASHI KISHIMOTO

ART BY
AKIRA OKUBO

THE TALE OF HACHIMARU

CHARACTERS

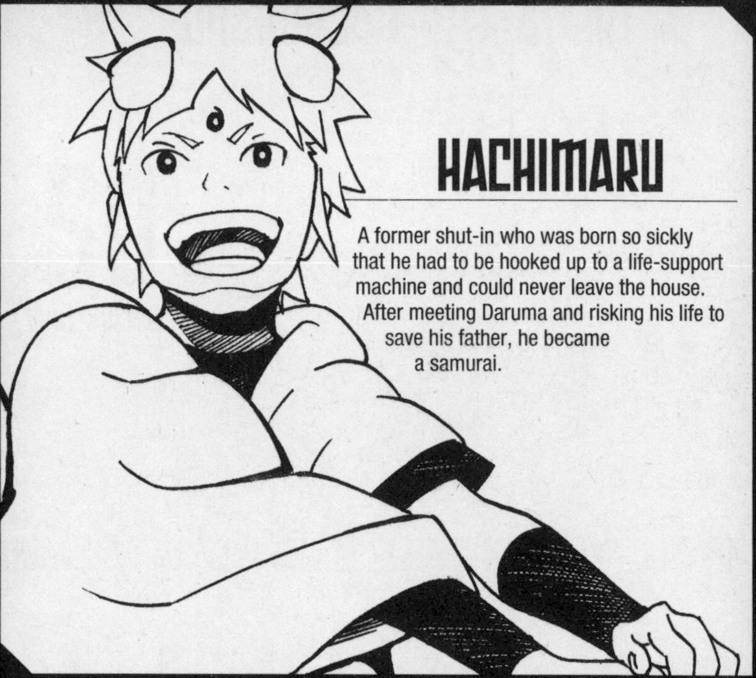

HACHIMARU

A former shut-in who was born so sickly that he had to be hooked up to a life-support machine and could never leave the house. After meeting Daruma and risking his life to save his father, he became a samurai.

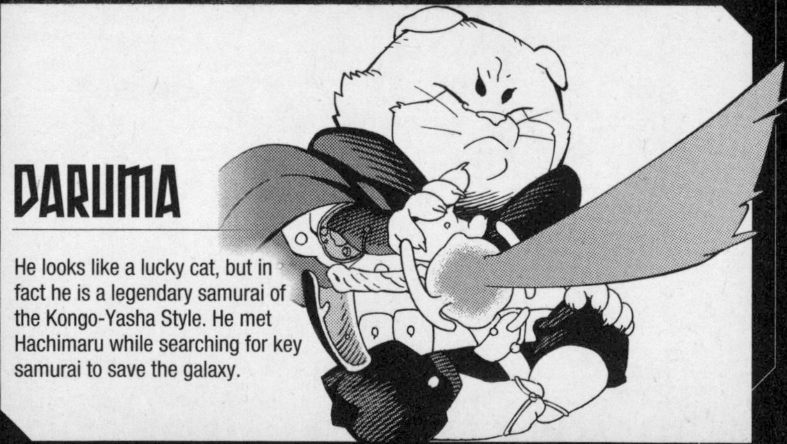

DARUMA

He looks like a lucky cat, but in fact he is a legendary samurai of the Kongo-Yasha Style. He met Hachimaru while searching for key samurai to save the galaxy.

SAMURAI 8

HACHIMARU'S FATHER

Cares for his son to the point of being overprotective. Seems to know a surprising amount about samurai...

HAYATARO

Hachimaru's Pet Holder, who is now his Key Holder. Says "meow" despite being a dog type.

WHAT IS A HOLDER?
A lifeform(?) that inhabits this galaxy. Their name changes based on their role: Pet Holder, Guard Holder, etc. Ones who serve a samurai master are called special Key Holders.

ANN

A young princess in training. She lost her Locker Ball, which is necessary to complete the samurai ritual.

STORY

Hachimaru is a boy with a weak body. He can't survive without being hooked up to a life-support device, and believes his dream of becoming a samurai will never come true. But one day, he meets Daruma, a samurai in the body of a large, round cat. Daruma likes Hachimaru, but he's unable to see samurai heroism within the boy. A ronin captures Hachimaru's father and forces Hachimaru to commit seppuku. Hachimaru does, but the warrior god Fudo Myo-o sees his heroism and grants him new life as a samurai. Now that he can move about freely, Hachimaru travels with Daruma to undergo samurai training. Meanwhile, a princess in training has lost her precious Locker Ball...

SAMURAI 8
THE TALE OF HACHIMARU

02

WHO AND WHY

CONTENTS

07	ENCOUNTER	001
08	TAKE IT SLOWLY	029
09	TOGETHER...	049
10	TARGET ACQUIRED	071
11	HOW DARE YOU	091
12	WHO AND WHY	111
13	I SAW A HERO	135
14	FATHER'S SECRET	155
15	HACHIMARU'S CALLING	175

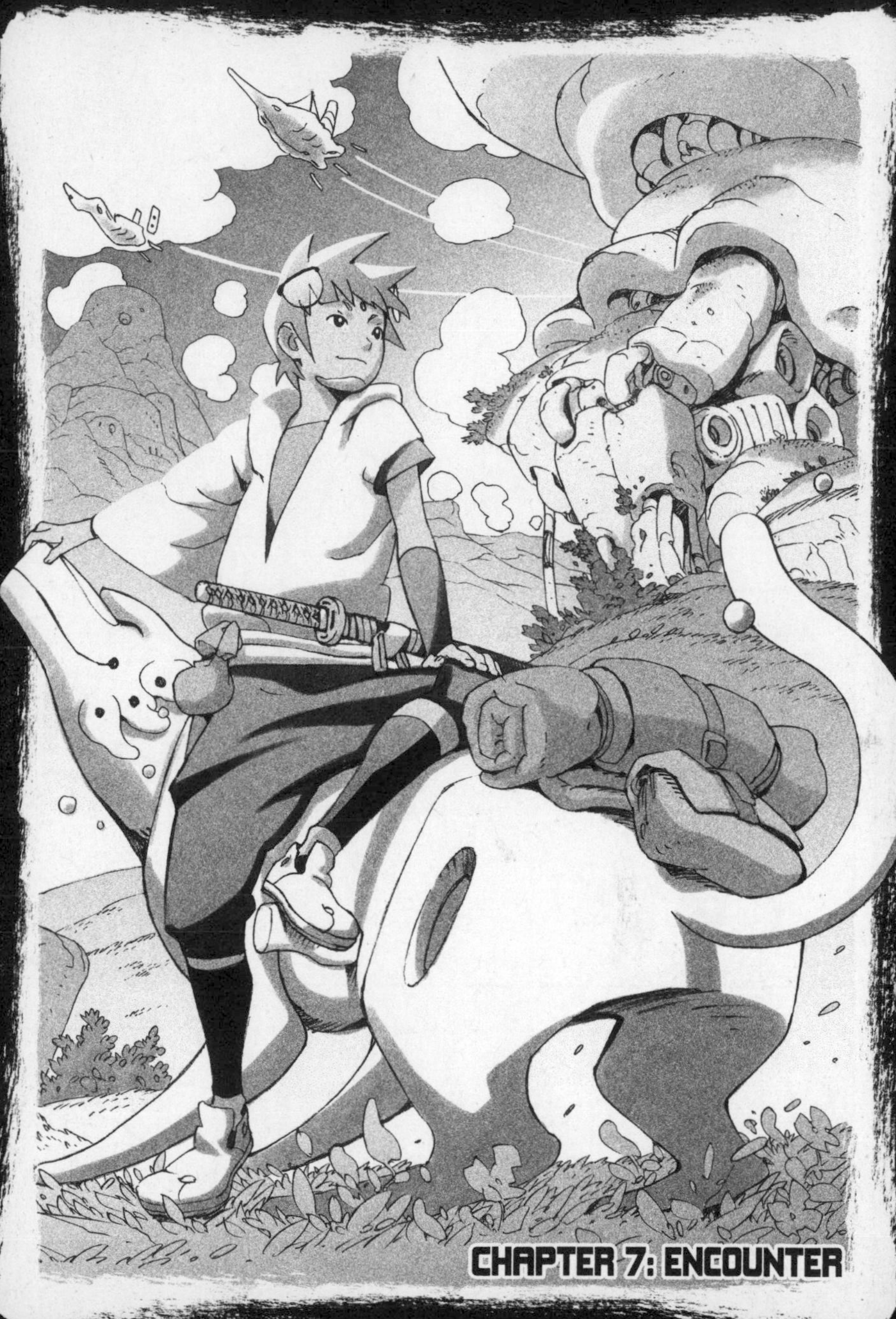
CHAPTER 7: ENCOUNTER

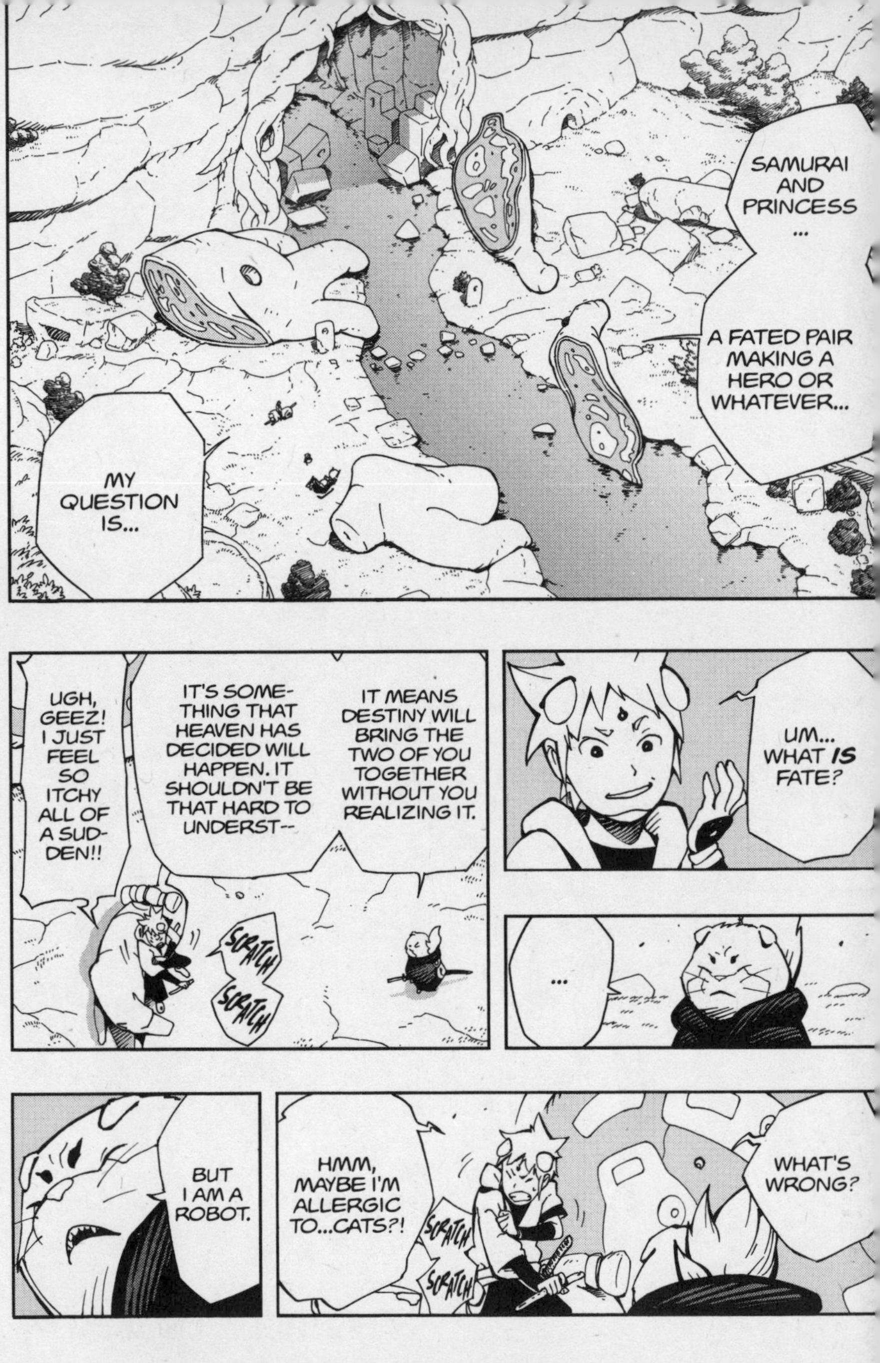
SAMURAI AND PRINCESS ...
A FATED PAIR MAKING A HERO OR WHATEVER...
MY QUESTION IS...
UM... WHAT *IS* FATE?
...
IT MEANS DESTINY WILL BRING THE TWO OF YOU TOGETHER WITHOUT YOU REALIZING IT.
IT'S SOMETHING THAT HEAVEN HAS DECIDED WILL HAPPEN. IT SHOULDN'T BE THAT HARD TO UNDERST--
UGH, GEEZ! I JUST FEEL SO ITCHY ALL OF A SUDDEN!!
SCRATCH
SCRATCH
WHAT'S WRONG?
HMM, MAYBE I'M ALLERGIC TO...CATS?!
SCRATCH
SCRATCH
BUT I AM A ROBOT.

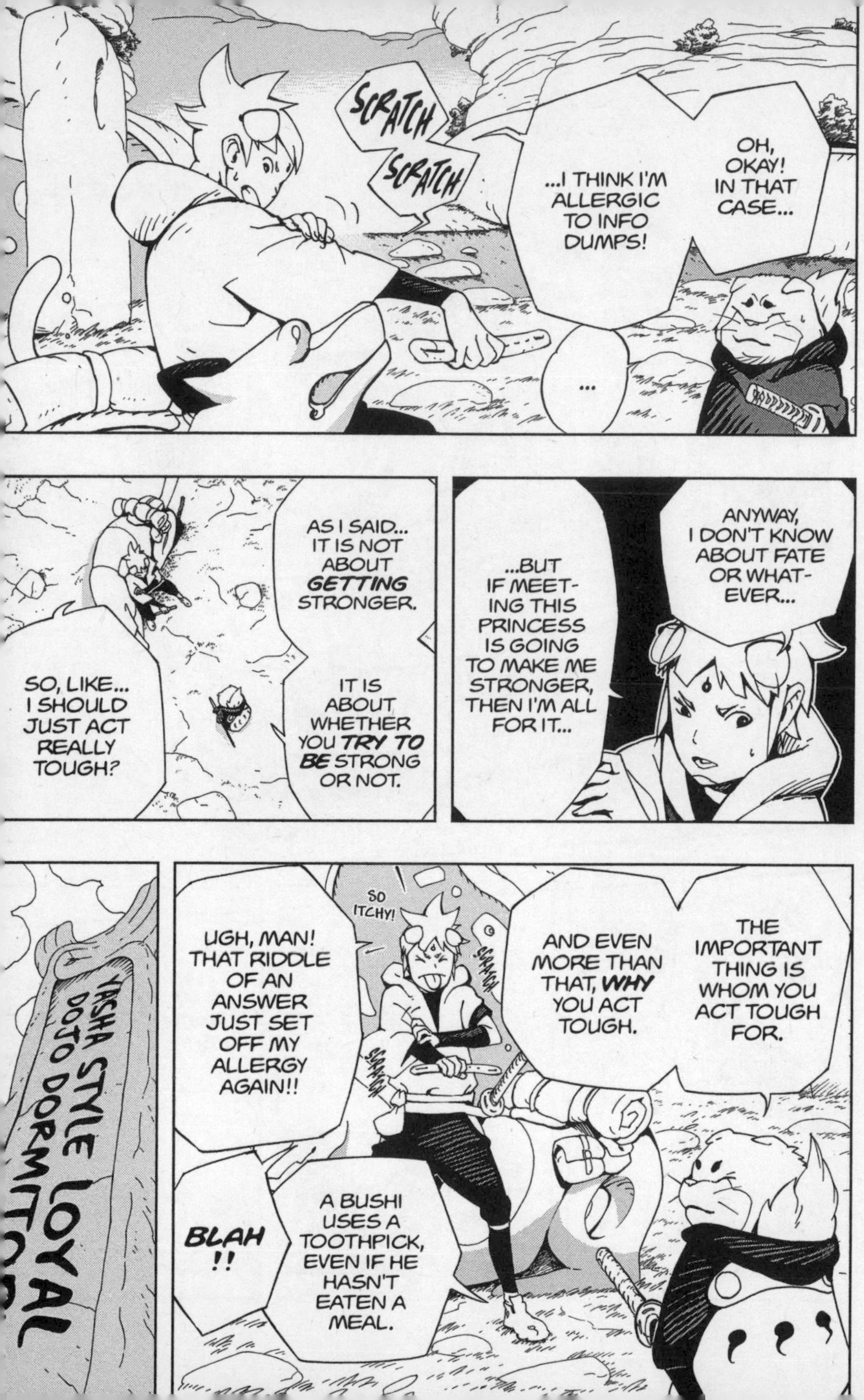
OH, OKAY! IN THAT CASE...
...I THINK I'M ALLERGIC TO INFO DUMPS!
SCRATCH
SCRATCH
...
ANYWAY, I DON'T KNOW ABOUT FATE OR WHATEVER...
...BUT IF MEETING THIS PRINCESS IS GOING TO MAKE ME STRONGER, THEN I'M ALL FOR IT...
AS I SAID... IT IS NOT ABOUT *GETTING* STRONGER.
IT IS ABOUT WHETHER YOU *TRY TO BE* STRONG OR NOT.
SO, LIKE... I SHOULD JUST ACT REALLY TOUGH?
THE IMPORTANT THING IS WHOM YOU ACT TOUGH FOR.
AND EVEN MORE THAN THAT, *WHY* YOU ACT TOUGH.
SCRATCH
SO ITCHY!
UGH, MAN! THAT RIDDLE OF AN ANSWER JUST SET OFF MY ALLERGY AGAIN!!
SCRATCH
A BUSHI USES A TOOTHPICK, EVEN IF HE HASN'T EATEN A MEAL.
BLAH!!
YASHA STYLE DOJO DORMITO
LOYAL

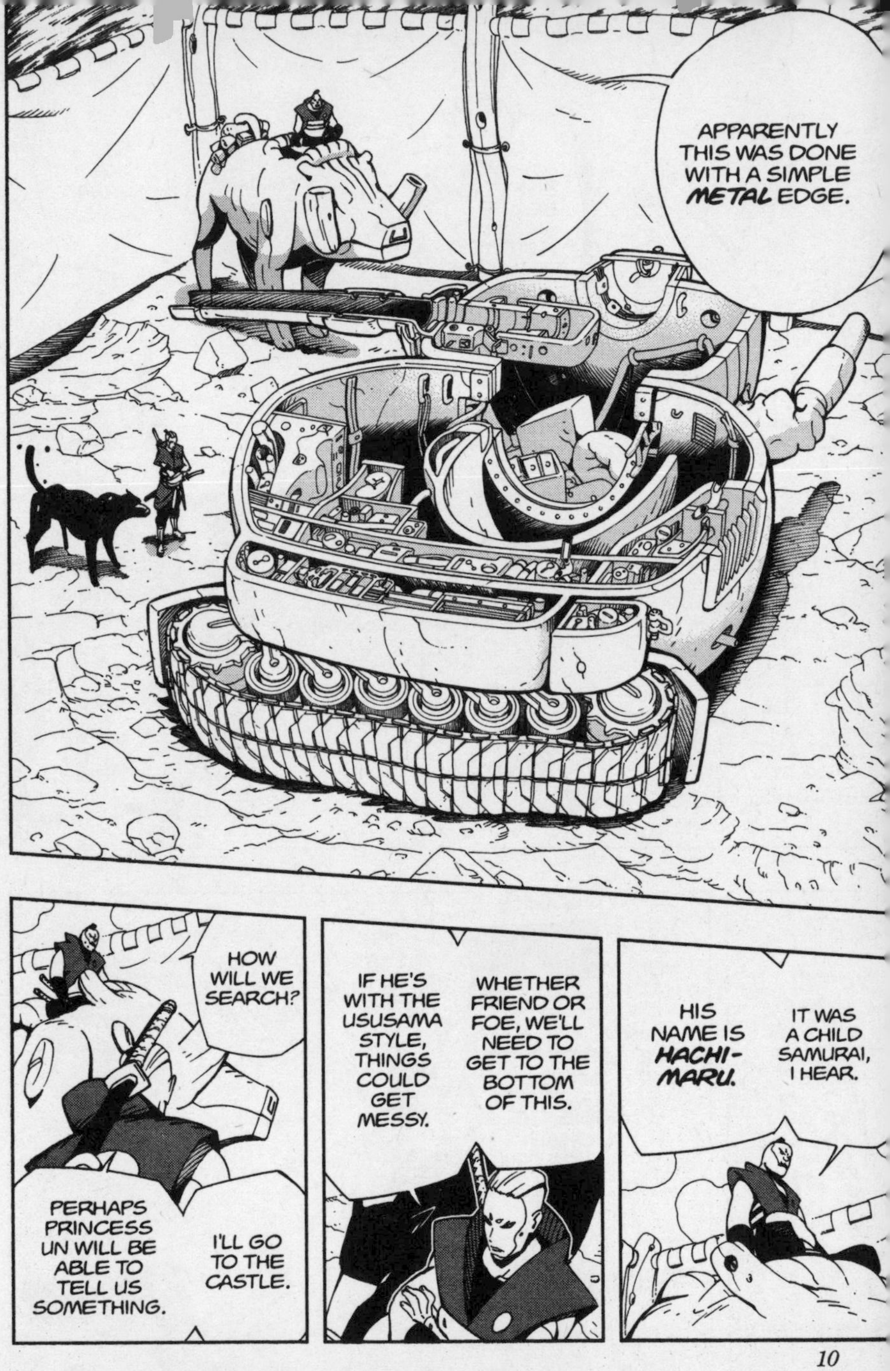
APPARENTLY THIS WAS DONE WITH A SIMPLE METAL EDGE.
IT WAS A CHILD SAMURAI, I HEAR.
HIS NAME IS HACHI-MARU.
WHETHER FRIEND OR FOE, WE'LL NEED TO GET TO THE BOTTOM OF THIS.
IF HE'S WITH THE USUSAMA STYLE, THINGS COULD GET MESSY.
HOW WILL WE SEARCH?
I'LL GO TO THE CASTLE.
PERHAPS PRINCESS UN WILL BE ABLE TO TELL US SOMETHING.

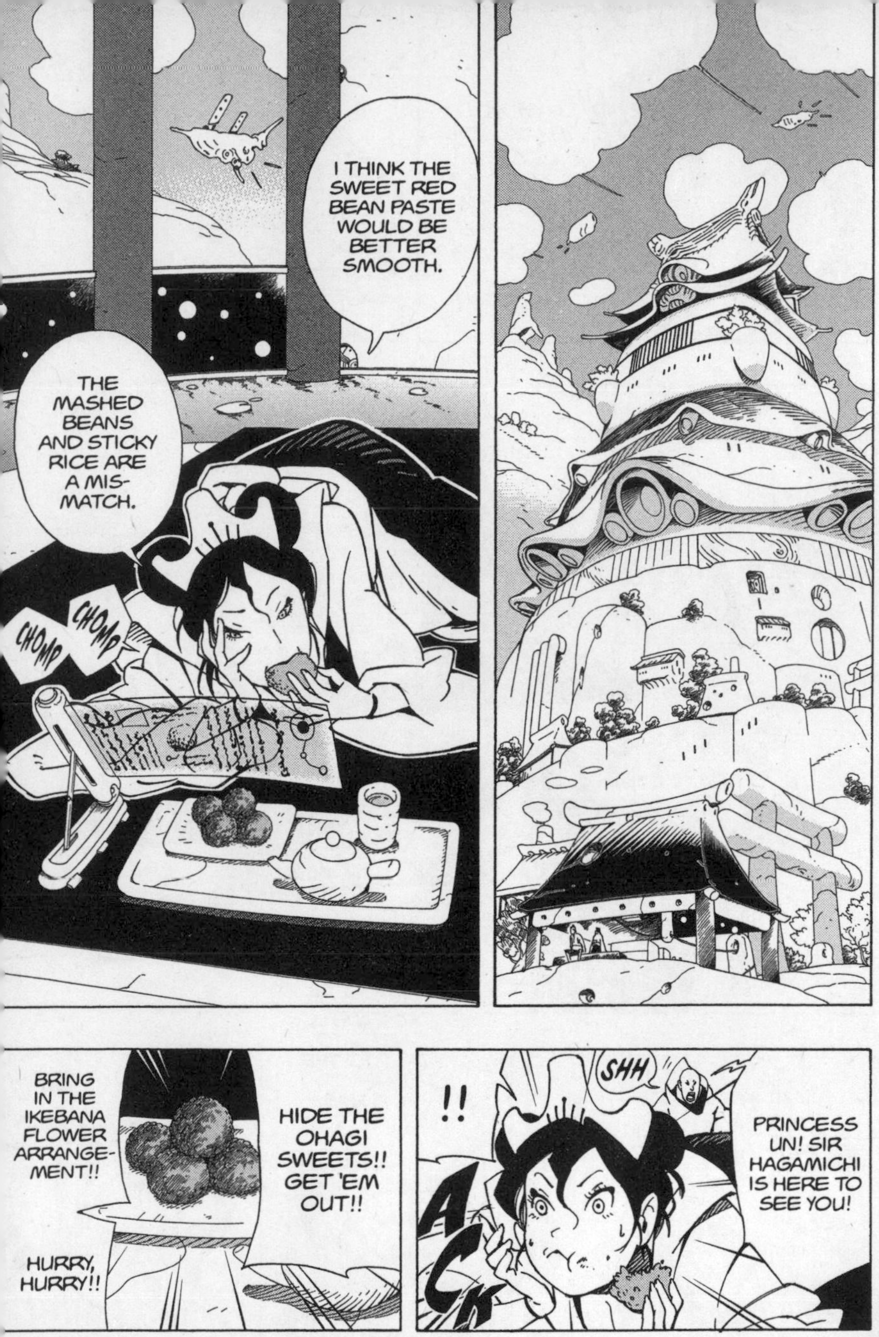

I THINK THE SWEET RED BEAN PASTE WOULD BE BETTER SMOOTH.
THE MASHED BEANS AND STICKY RICE ARE A MIS-MATCH.
CHOMP
CHOMP
SHH
PRINCESS UN! SIR HAGAMICHI IS HERE TO SEE YOU!
!!
ACK
HIDE THE OHAGI SWEETS!! GET 'EM OUT!!
BRING IN THE IKEBANA FLOWER ARRANGE-MENT!!
HURRY, HURRY!!

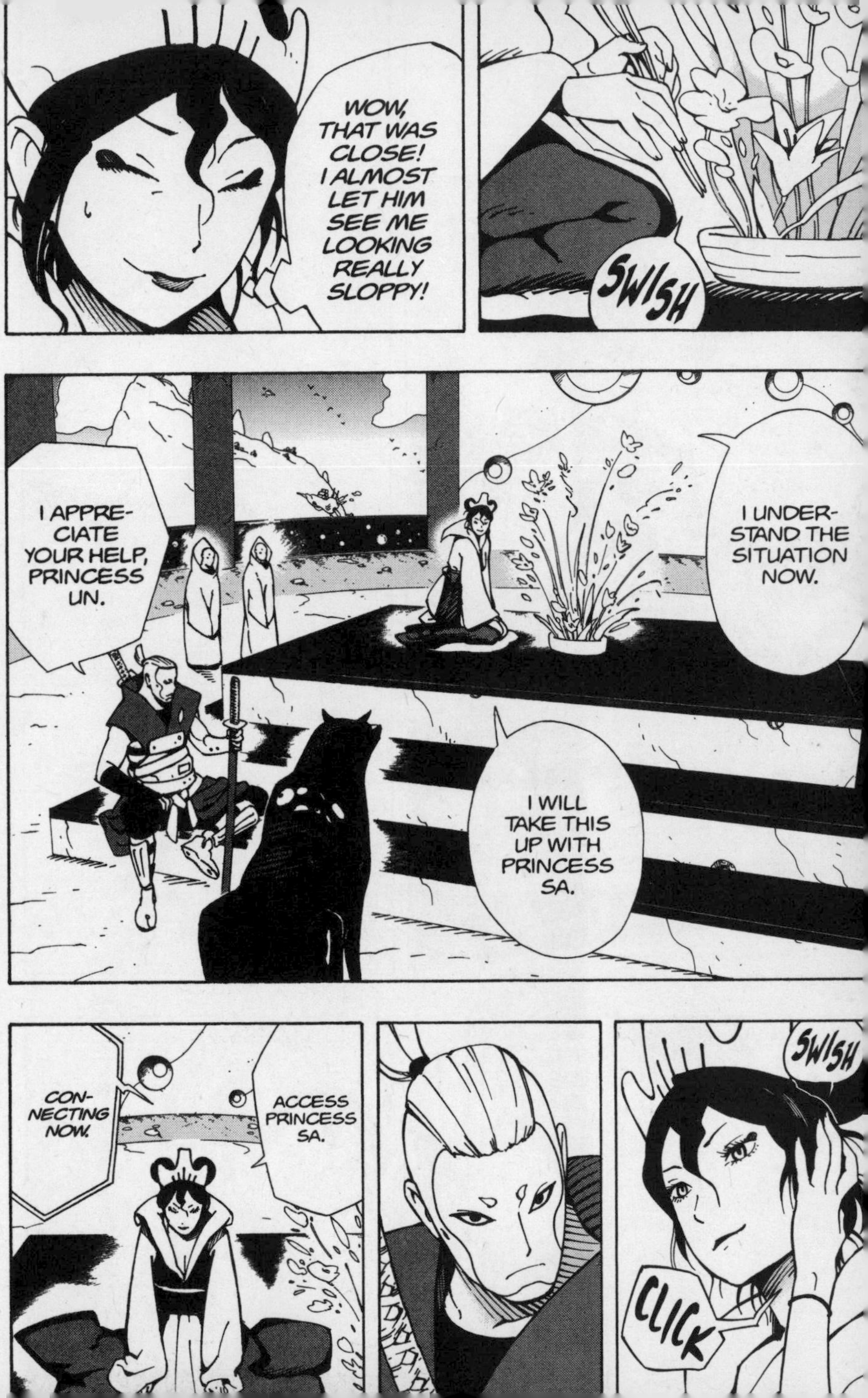
SWISH
WOW, THAT WAS CLOSE! I ALMOST LET HIM SEE ME LOOKING REALLY SLOPPY!
I UNDER-STAND THE SITUATION NOW.
I WILL TAKE THIS UP WITH PRINCESS SA.
I APPRE-CIATE YOUR HELP, PRINCESS UN.
SWISH
CLICK
ACCESS PRINCESS SA.
CON-NECTING NOW.

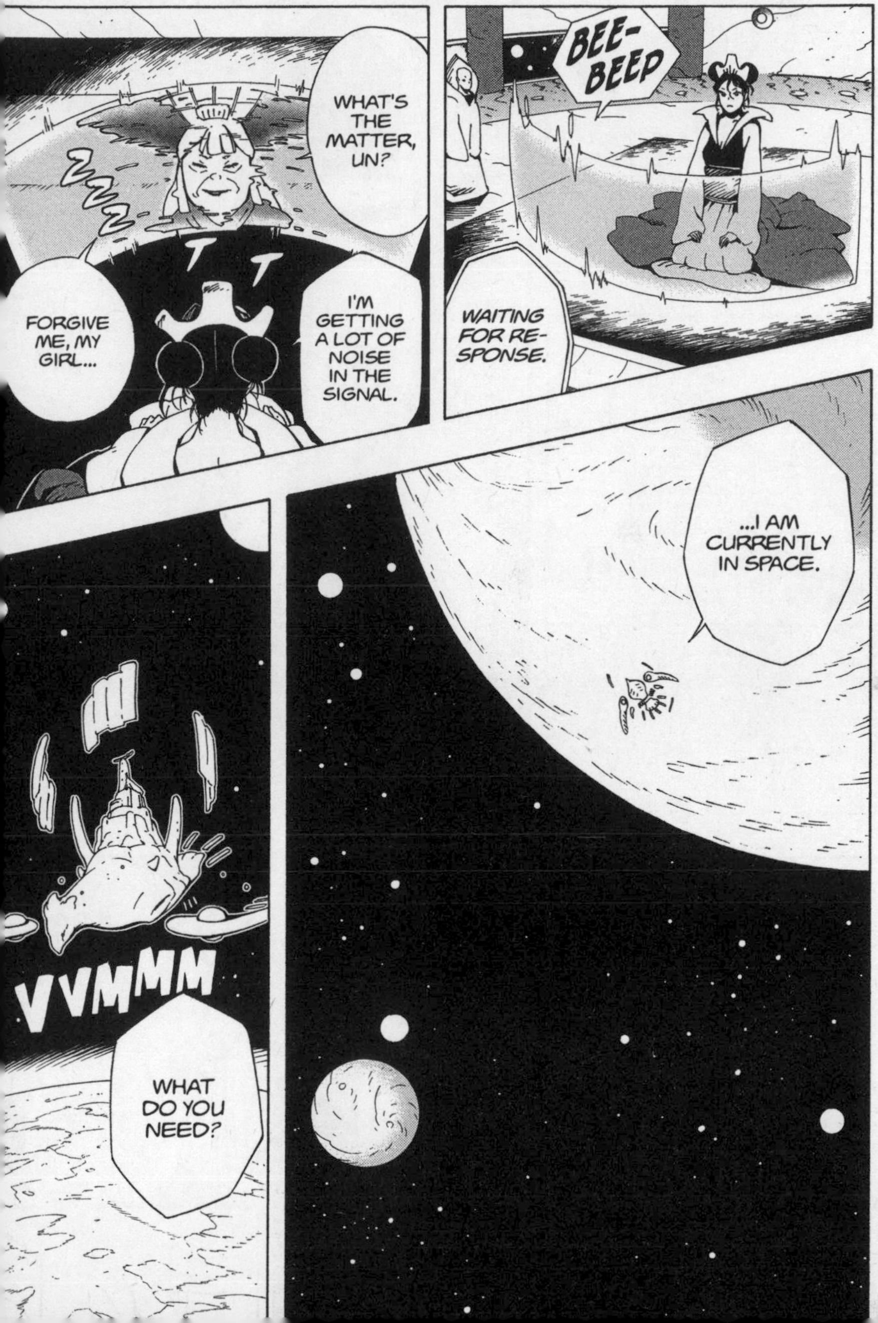
BEE-BEEP
WAITING FOR RE-SPONSE.
WHAT'S THE MATTER, UN?
I'M GETTING A LOT OF NOISE IN THE SIGNAL.
FORGIVE ME, MY GIRL...
...I AM CURRENTLY IN SPACE.
VVMMM
WHAT DO YOU NEED?

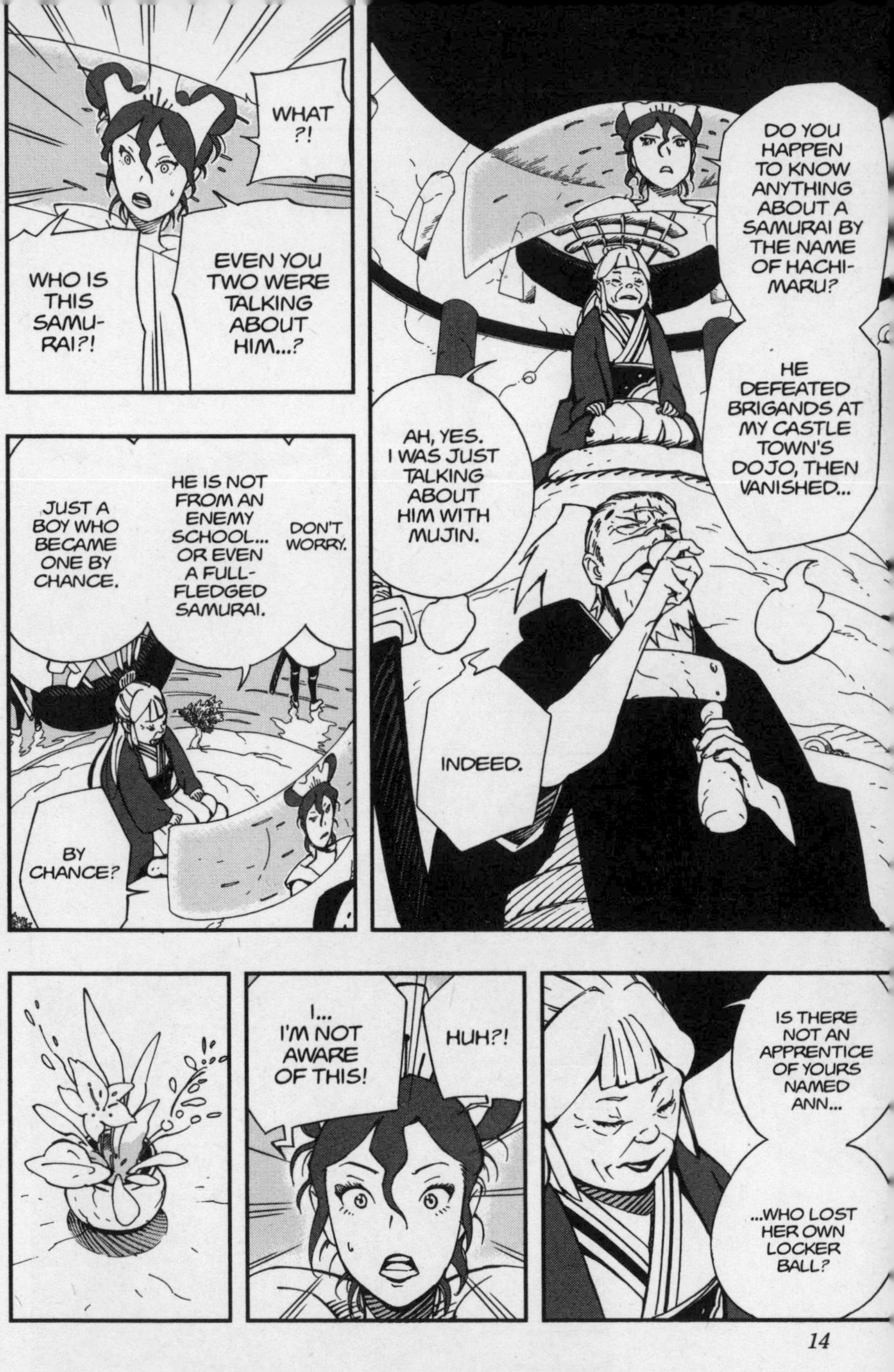
DO YOU HAPPEN TO KNOW ANYTHING ABOUT A SAMURAI BY THE NAME OF HACHI-MARU?
HE DEFEATED BRIGANDS AT MY CASTLE TOWN'S DOJO, THEN VANISHED...
AH, YES. I WAS JUST TALKING ABOUT HIM WITH MUJIN.
INDEED.
WHAT?!
EVEN YOU TWO WERE TALKING ABOUT HIM...?
WHO IS THIS SAMU-RAI?!
DON'T WORRY.
HE IS NOT FROM AN ENEMY SCHOOL... OR EVEN A FULL-FLEDGED SAMURAI.
JUST A BOY WHO BECAME ONE BY CHANCE.
BY CHANCE?
IS THERE NOT AN APPRENTICE OF YOURS NAMED ANN...
...WHO LOST HER OWN LOCKER BALL?
HUH?!
I... I'M NOT AWARE OF THIS!

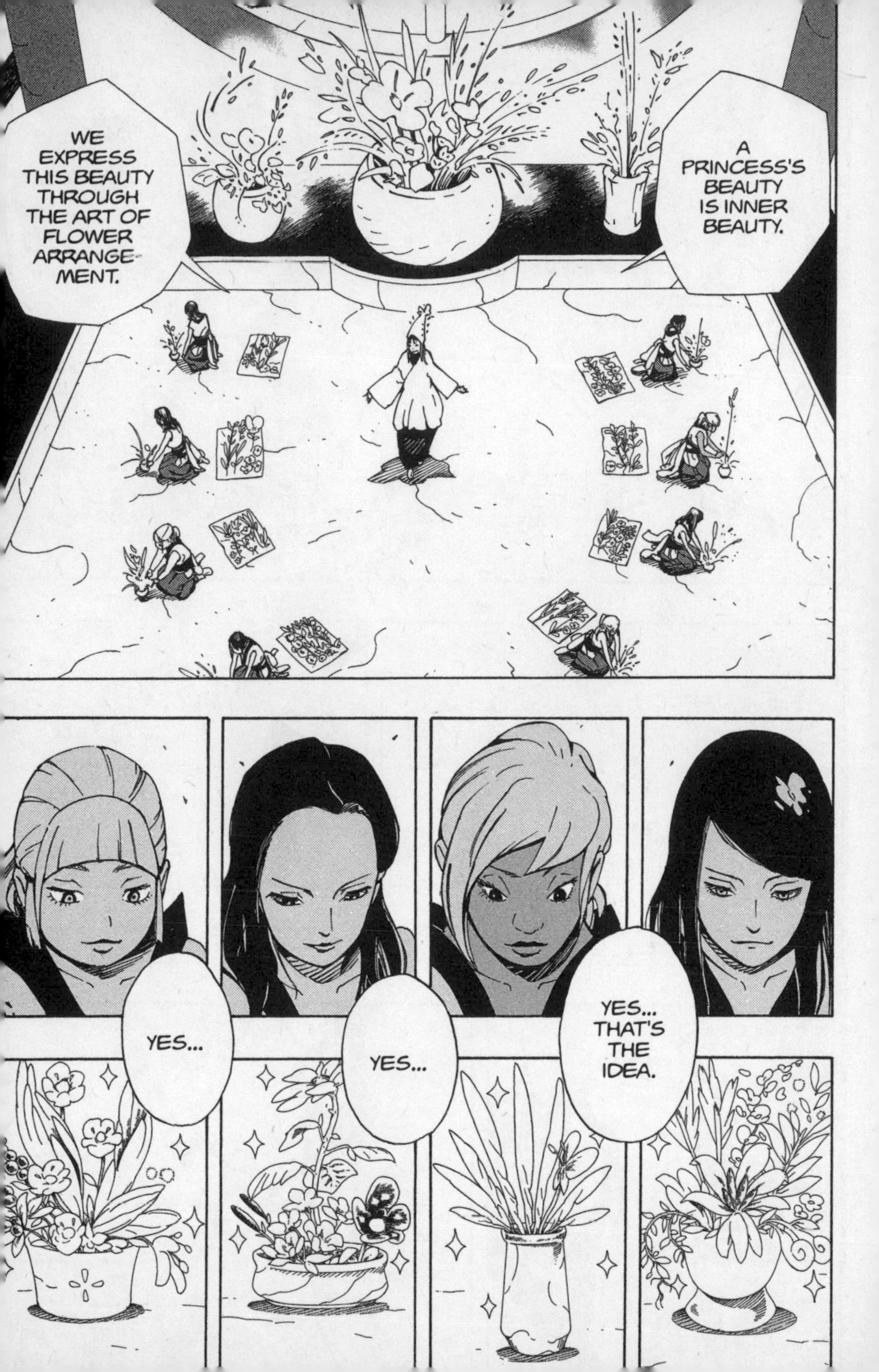
A PRINCESS'S BEAUTY IS INNER BEAUTY.
WE EXPRESS THIS BEAUTY THROUGH THE ART OF FLOWER ARRANGE-MENT.
YES... THAT'S THE IDEA.
YES...
YES...

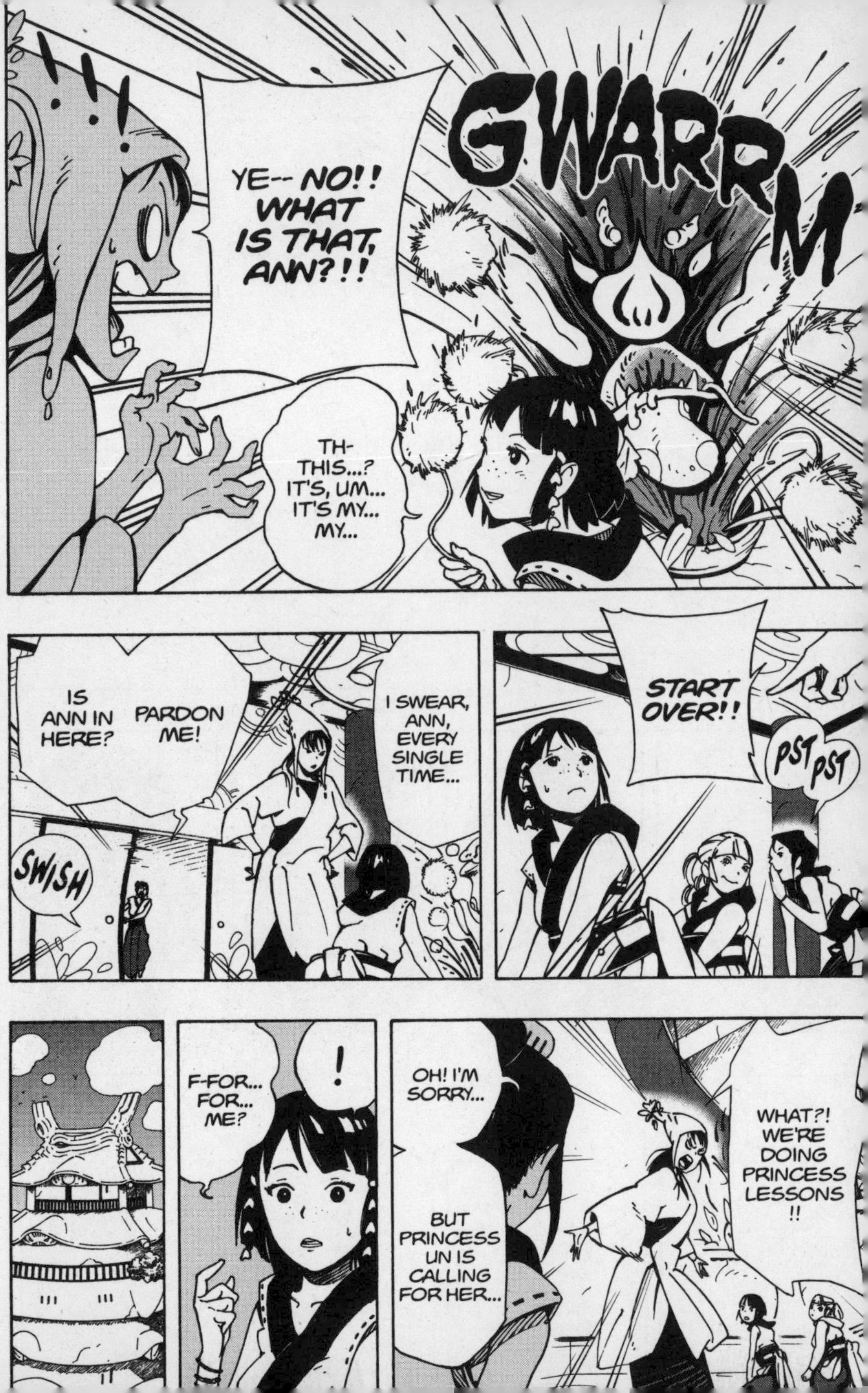
GWARRM
YE-- NO!! WHAT IS THAT, ANN?!!
TH- THIS...? IT'S, UM... IT'S MY... MY...
START OVER!!
PST PST
I SWEAR, ANN, EVERY SINGLE TIME...
PARDON ME!
IS ANN IN HERE?
SWISH
WHAT?! WE'RE DOING PRINCESS LESSONS!!
OH! I'M SORRY...
BUT PRINCESS UN IS CALLING FOR HER...
!
F-FOR... FOR... ME?

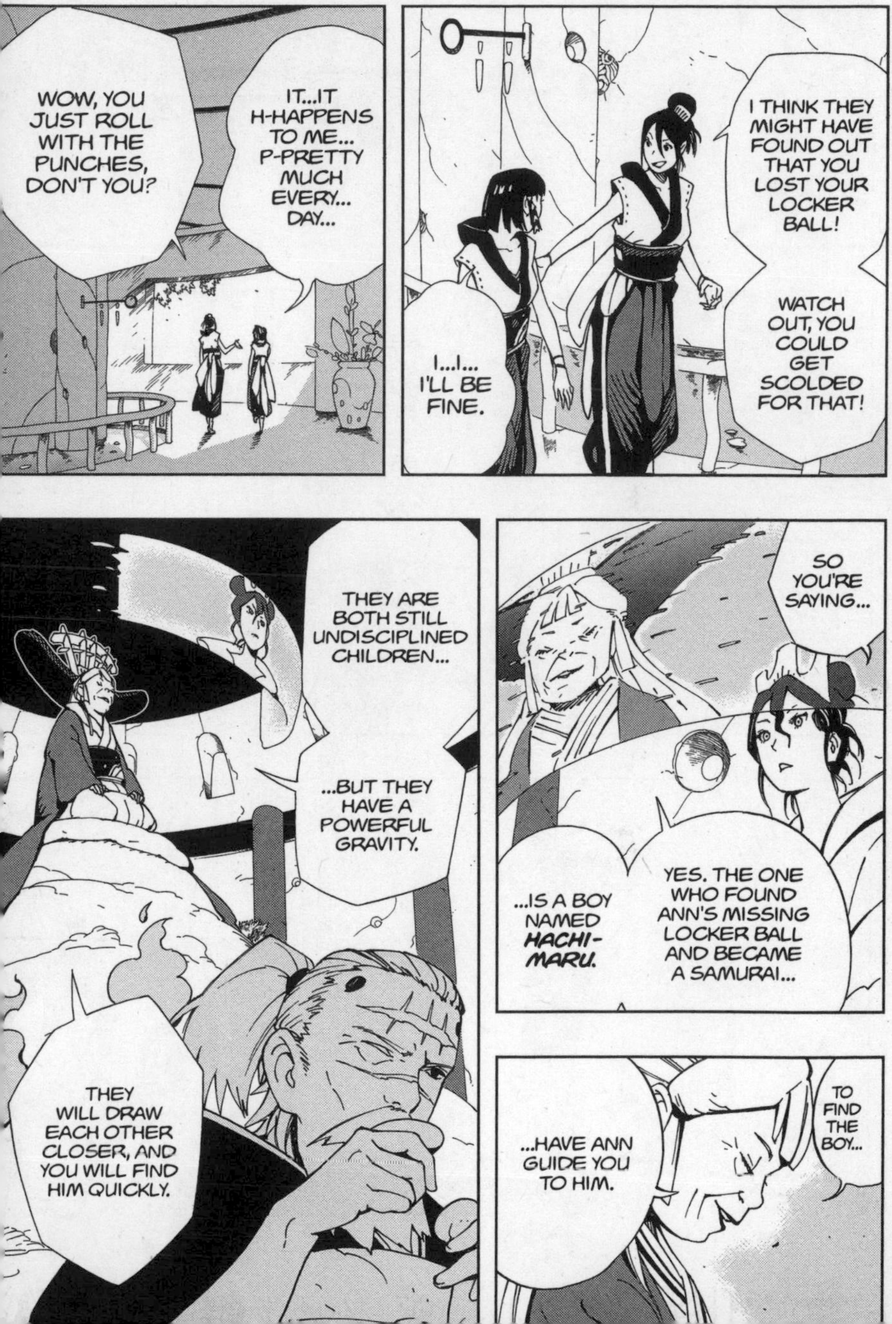

I THINK THEY MIGHT HAVE FOUND OUT THAT YOU LOST YOUR LOCKER BALL!
WATCH OUT, YOU COULD GET SCOLDED FOR THAT!
I...I... I'LL BE FINE.
IT...IT H-HAPPENS TO ME... P-PRETTY MUCH EVERY... DAY...
WOW, YOU JUST ROLL WITH THE PUNCHES, DON'T YOU?
SO YOU'RE SAYING...
YES. THE ONE WHO FOUND ANN'S MISSING LOCKER BALL AND BECAME A SAMURAI...
...IS A BOY NAMED ***HACHIMARU.***
TO FIND THE BOY...
...HAVE ANN GUIDE YOU TO HIM.
THEY ARE BOTH STILL UNDISCIPLINED CHILDREN...
...BUT THEY HAVE A POWERFUL GRAVITY.
THEY WILL DRAW EACH OTHER CLOSER, AND YOU WILL FIND HIM QUICKLY.

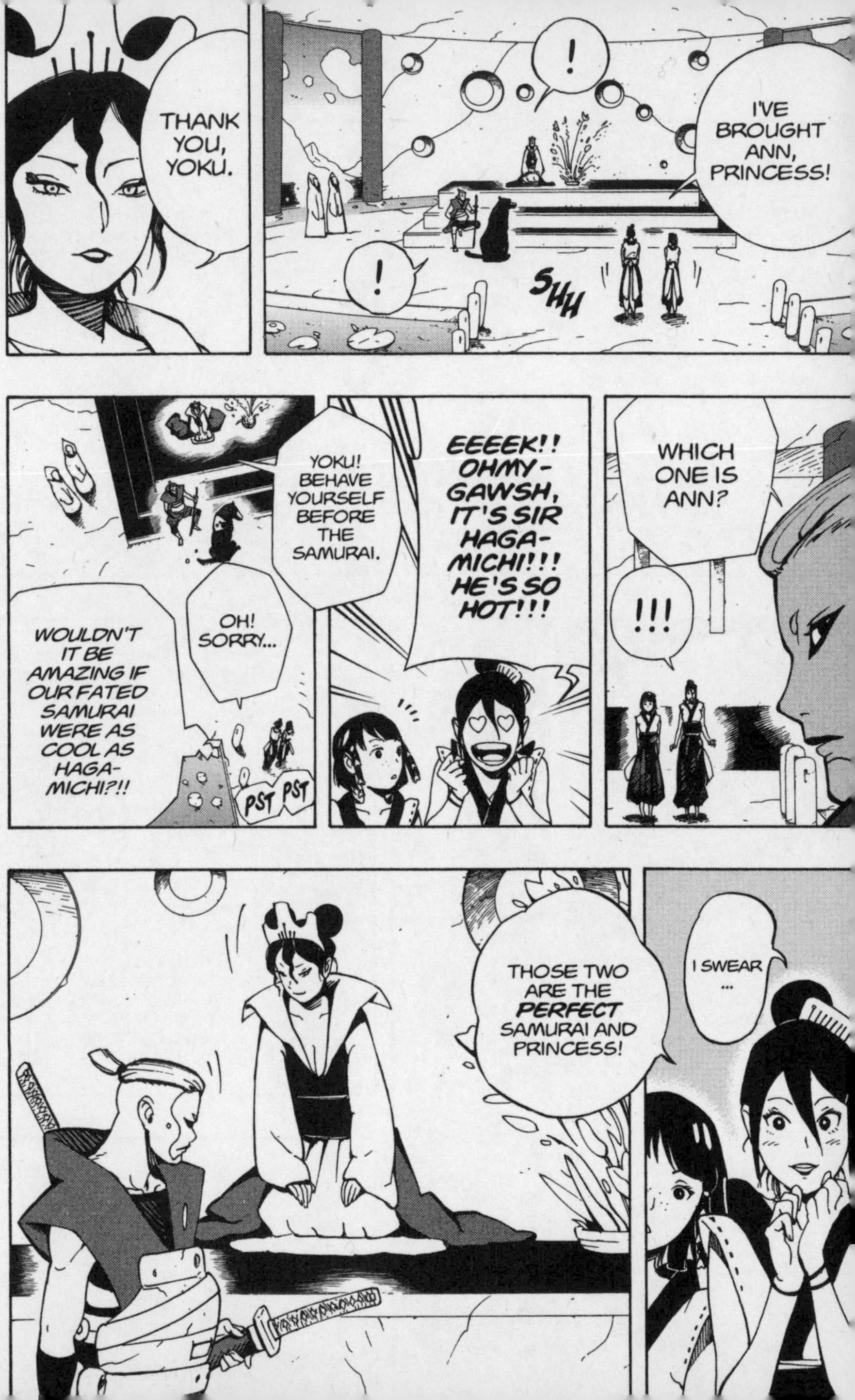
I'VE BROUGHT ANN, PRINCESS!
!
!
SHH
THANK YOU, YOKU.
WHICH ONE IS ANN?
!!!
EEEEK!! OHMY-GAWSH, IT'S SIR HAGA-MICHI!!! HE'S SO HOT!!!
YOKU! BEHAVE YOURSELF BEFORE THE SAMURAI.
OH! SORRY...
WOULDN'T IT BE AMAZING IF OUR FATED SAMURAI WERE AS COOL AS HAGA-MICHI?!!
PST PST
I SWEAR ...
THOSE TWO ARE THE PERFECT SAMURAI AND PRINCESS!

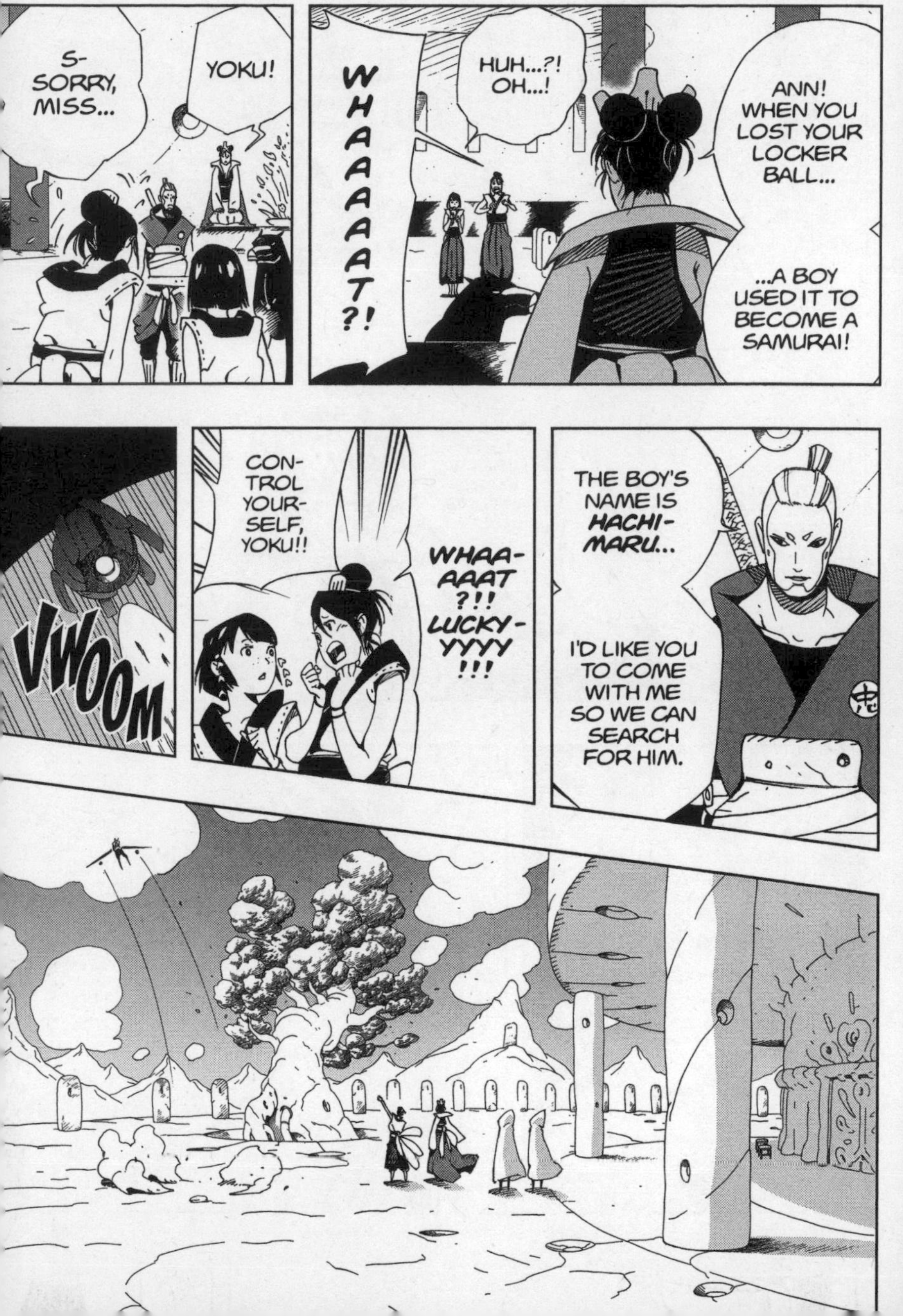
ANN! WHEN YOU LOST YOUR LOCKER BALL...
...A BOY USED IT TO BECOME A SAMURAI!
HUH...?! OH...!
WHAAAAAAAT?!
YOKU!
S-SORRY, MISS...
THE BOY'S NAME IS *HACHIMARU*...
I'D LIKE YOU TO COME WITH ME SO WE CAN SEARCH FOR HIM.
WHAAAAAT?!! LUCKY-YYYY!!!
CONTROL YOURSELF, YOKU!!
VWOOM

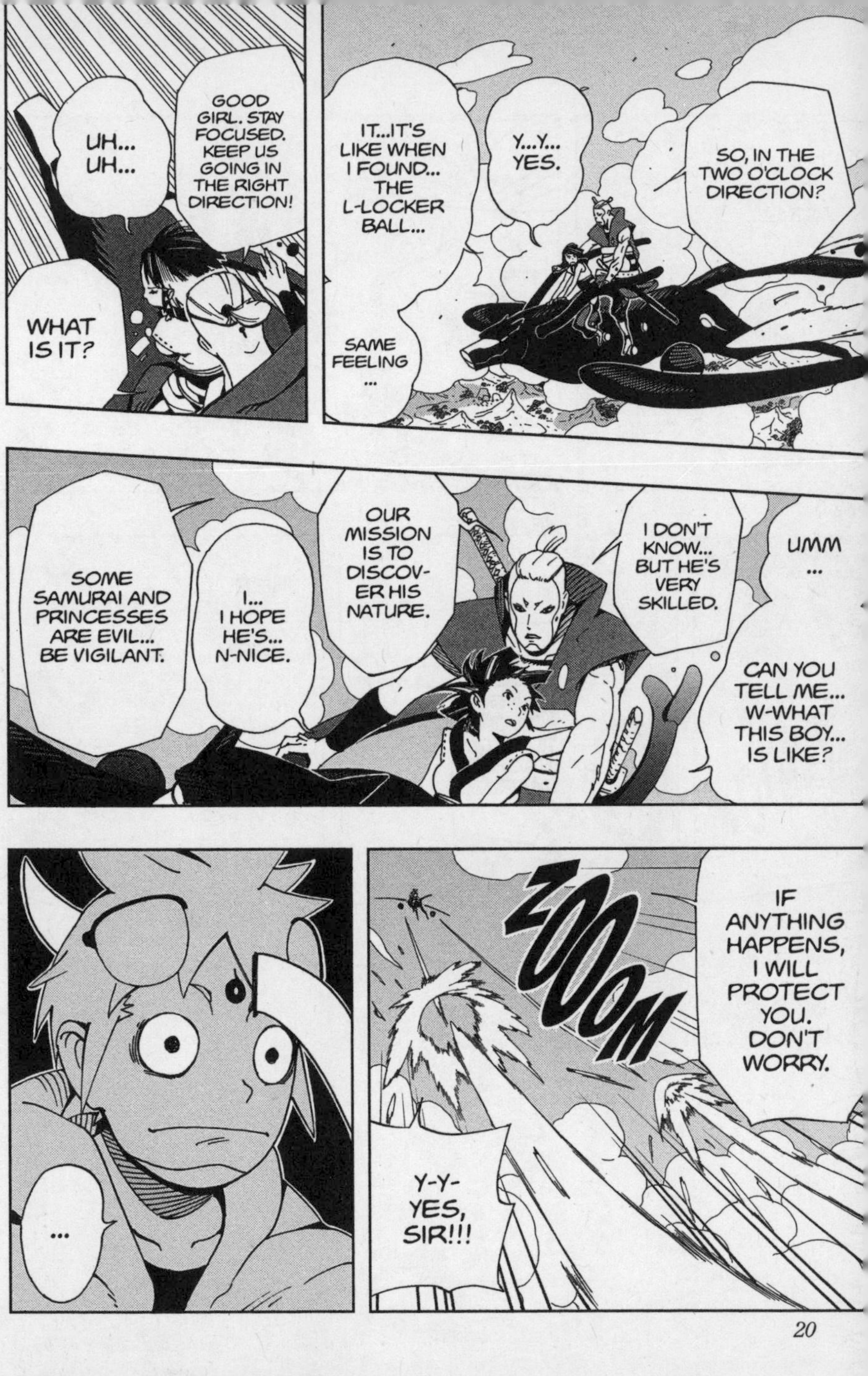
SO, IN THE TWO O'CLOCK DIRECTION?
Y...Y... YES.
IT...IT'S LIKE WHEN I FOUND... THE L-LOCKER BALL...
SAME FEELING ...
GOOD GIRL. STAY FOCUSED. KEEP US GOING IN THE RIGHT DIRECTION!
UH... UH...
WHAT IS IT?
UMM ...
CAN YOU TELL ME... W-WHAT THIS BOY... IS LIKE?
I DON'T KNOW... BUT HE'S VERY SKILLED.
OUR MISSION IS TO DISCOVER HIS NATURE.
I... I HOPE HE'S... N-NICE.
SOME SAMURAI AND PRINCESSES ARE EVIL... BE VIGILANT.
IF ANYTHING HAPPENS, I WILL PROTECT YOU. DON'T WORRY.
ZOOM
Y-Y-YES, SIR!!!
...

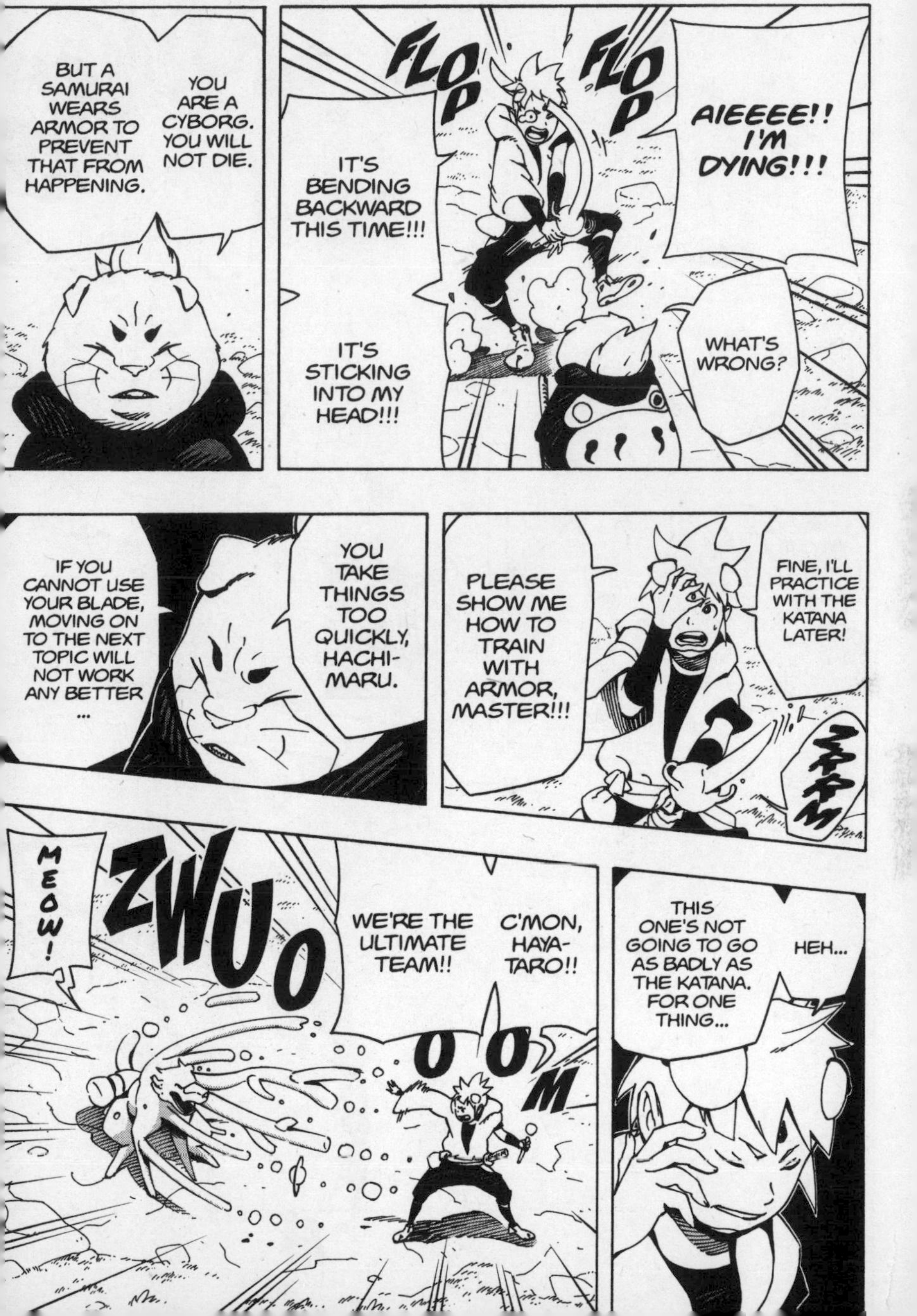
FLOP
FLOP
AIEEEE!! I'M DYING!!!
WHAT'S WRONG?
IT'S BENDING BACKWARD THIS TIME!!!
IT'S STICKING INTO MY HEAD!!!
YOU ARE A CYBORG. YOU WILL NOT DIE.
BUT A SAMURAI WEARS ARMOR TO PREVENT THAT FROM HAPPENING.
FINE, I'LL PRACTICE WITH THE KATANA LATER!
ZRRRM
PLEASE SHOW ME HOW TO TRAIN WITH ARMOR, MASTER!!!
YOU TAKE THINGS TOO QUICKLY, HACHI-MARU.
IF YOU CANNOT USE YOUR BLADE, MOVING ON TO THE NEXT TOPIC WILL NOT WORK ANY BETTER ...
HEH...
THIS ONE'S NOT GOING TO GO AS BADLY AS THE KATANA. FOR ONE THING...
C'MON, HAYA-TARO!!
WE'RE THE ULTIMATE TEAM!!
ZWUOOOOM
MEOW!

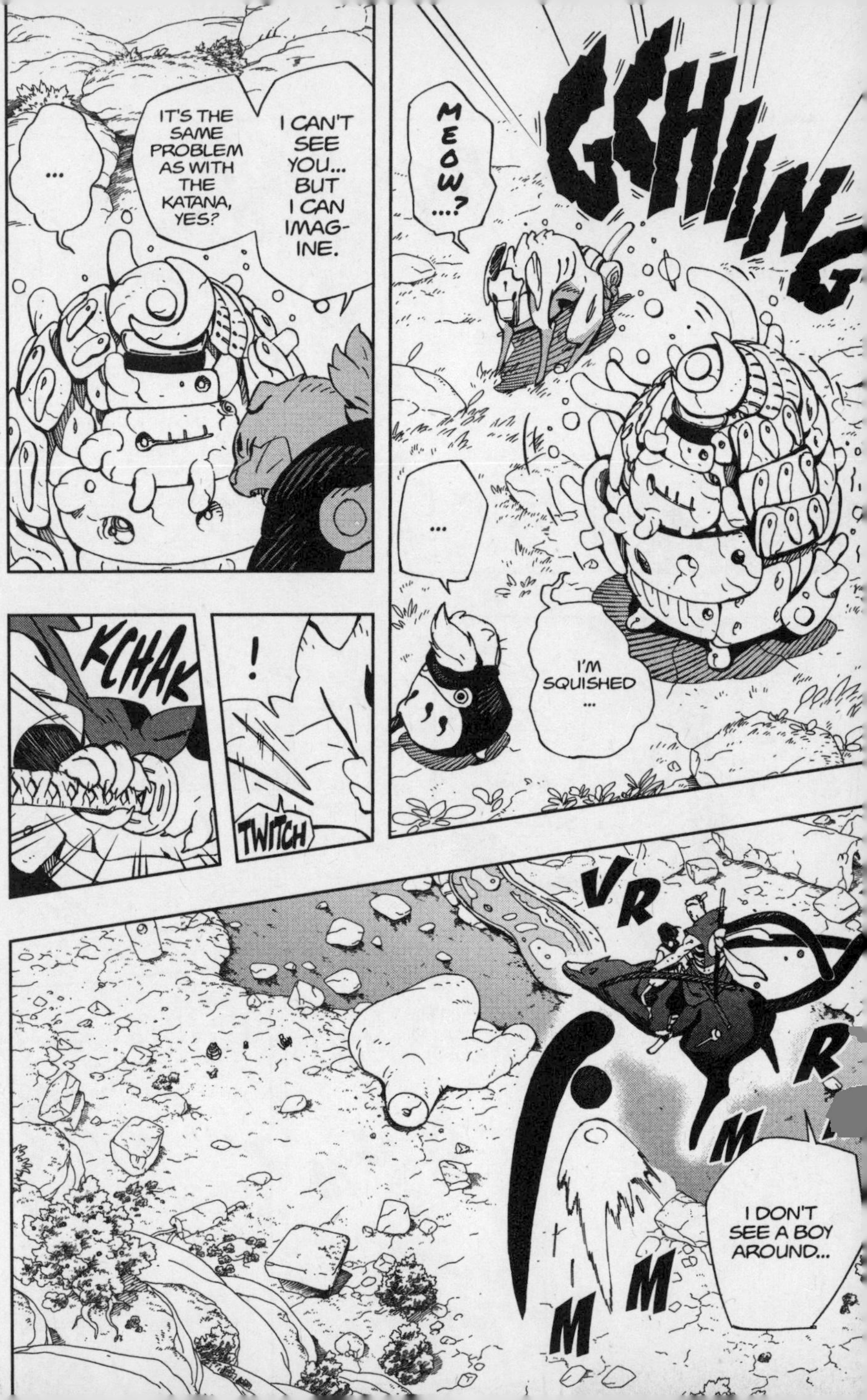
GCHING
MEOW...?
...
I'M SQUISHED...
I CAN'T SEE YOU... BUT I CAN IMAGINE.
IT'S THE SAME PROBLEM AS WITH THE KATANA, YES?
...
!
TWITCH
KCHAK
VRRMMMM
I DON'T SEE A BOY AROUND...

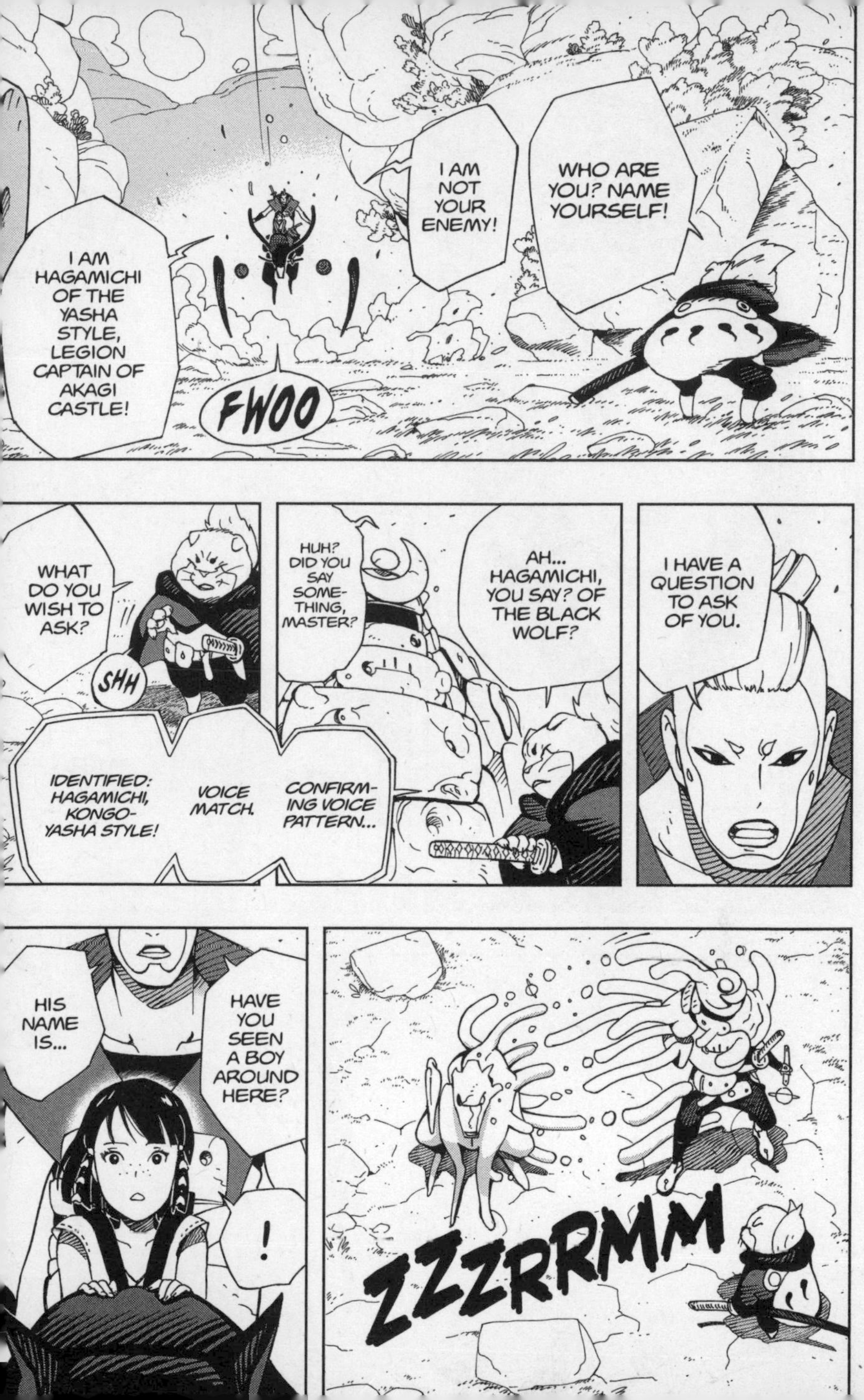
WHO ARE YOU? NAME YOURSELF!
I AM NOT YOUR ENEMY!
I AM HAGAMICHI OF THE YASHA STYLE, LEGION CAPTAIN OF AKAGI CASTLE!
FWOO
I HAVE A QUESTION TO ASK OF YOU.
AH... HAGAMICHI, YOU SAY? OF THE BLACK WOLF?
HUH? DID YOU SAY SOME-THING, MASTER?
CONFIRM-ING VOICE PATTERN...
VOICE MATCH.
IDENTIFIED: HAGAMICHI, KONGO-YASHA STYLE!
WHAT DO YOU WISH TO ASK?
SHH
ZZZRRMM
HAVE YOU SEEN A BOY AROUND HERE?
HIS NAME IS...
!

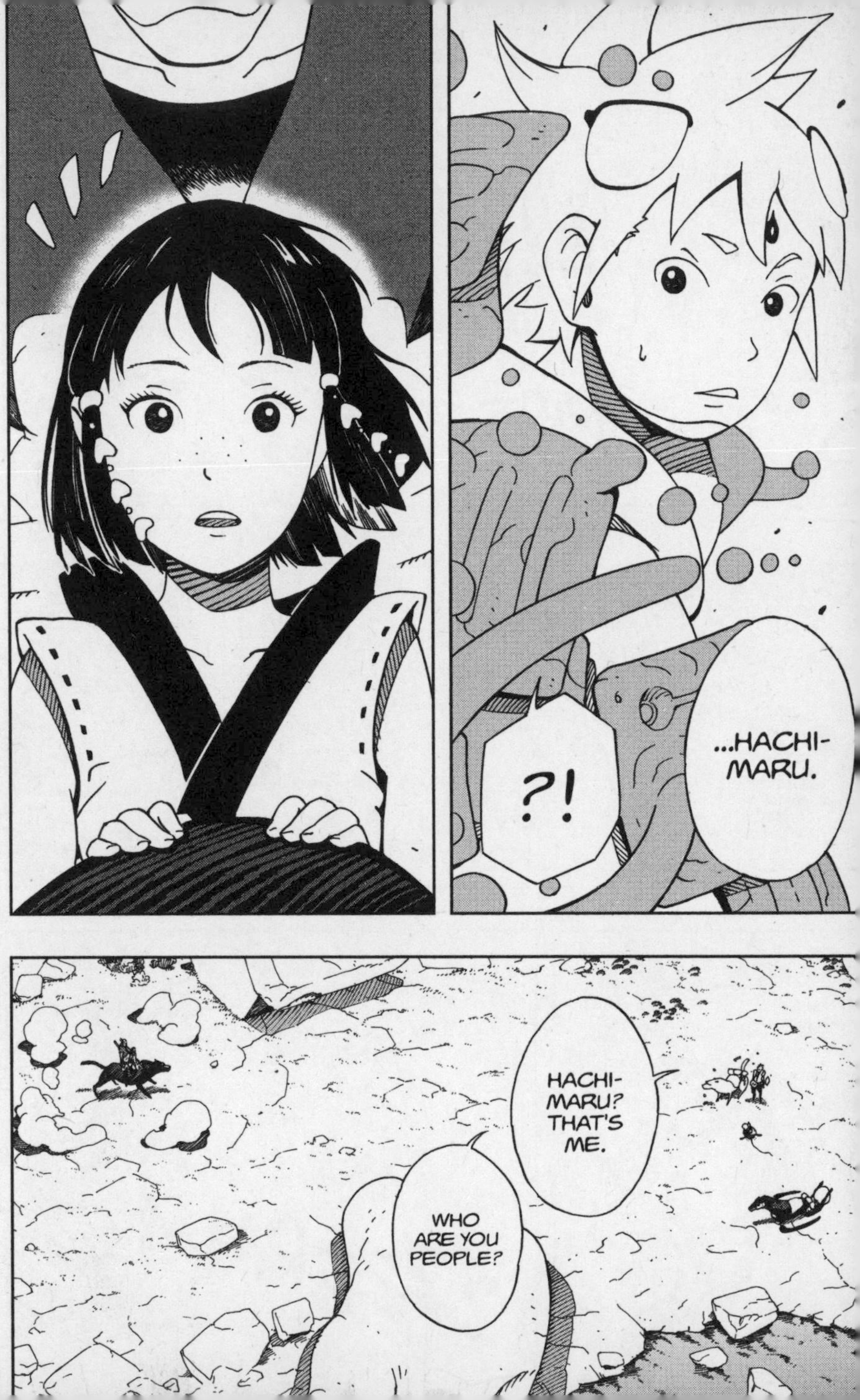
...HACHI-
MARU.
?!
HACHI-
MARU? THAT'S ME.
WHO ARE YOU PEOPLE?

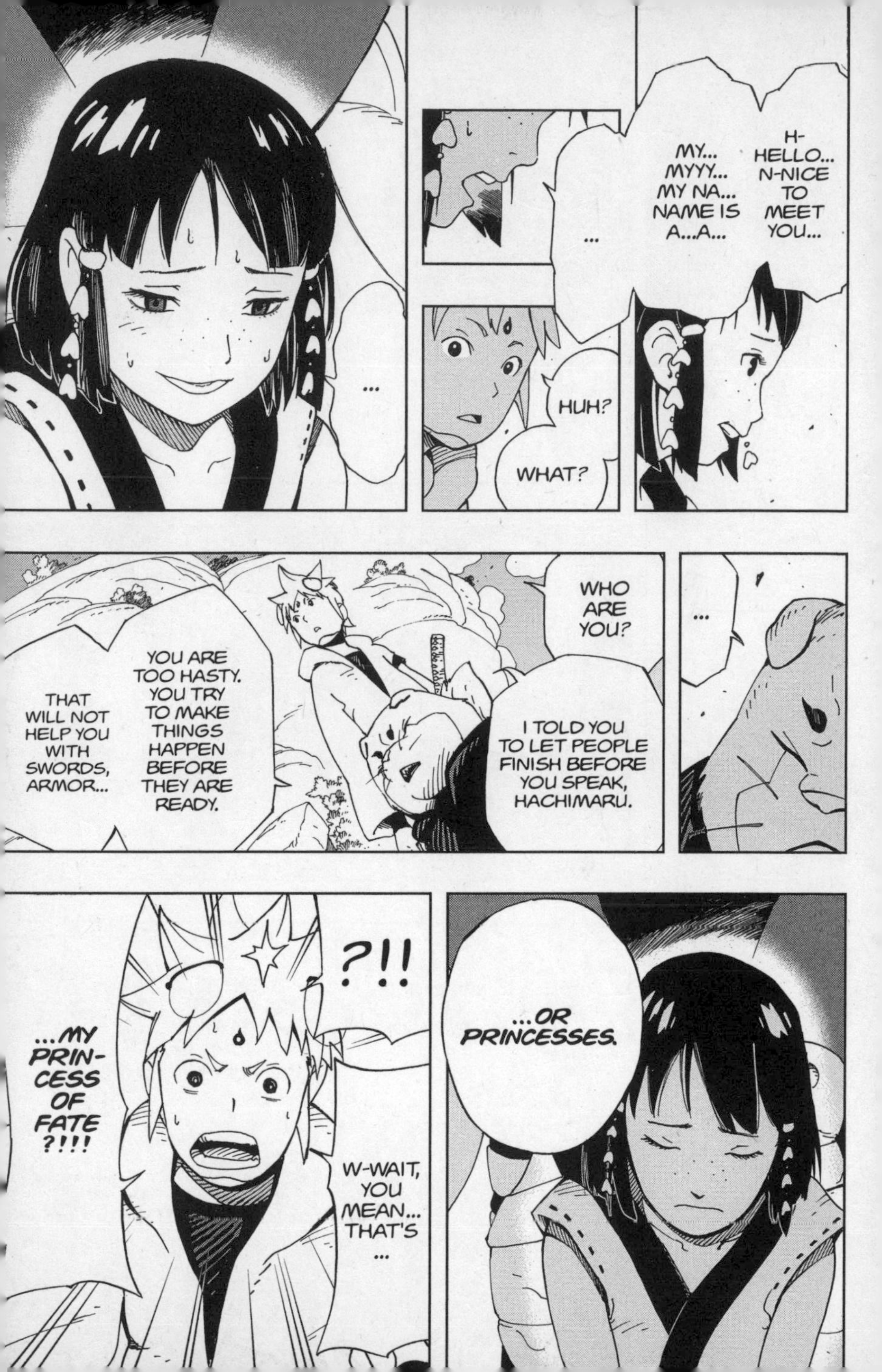
H- HELLO... N-NICE TO MEET YOU...
MY... MYYY... MY NA... NAME IS A...A...
...
HUH?
WHAT?
...
...
WHO ARE YOU?
I TOLD YOU TO LET PEOPLE FINISH BEFORE YOU SPEAK, HACHIMARU.
YOU ARE TOO HASTY. YOU TRY TO MAKE THINGS HAPPEN BEFORE THEY ARE READY.
THAT WILL NOT HELP YOU WITH SWORDS, ARMOR...
...OR PRINCESSES.
?!!
...MY PRINCESS OF FATE?!!!
W-WAIT, YOU MEAN... THAT'S ...

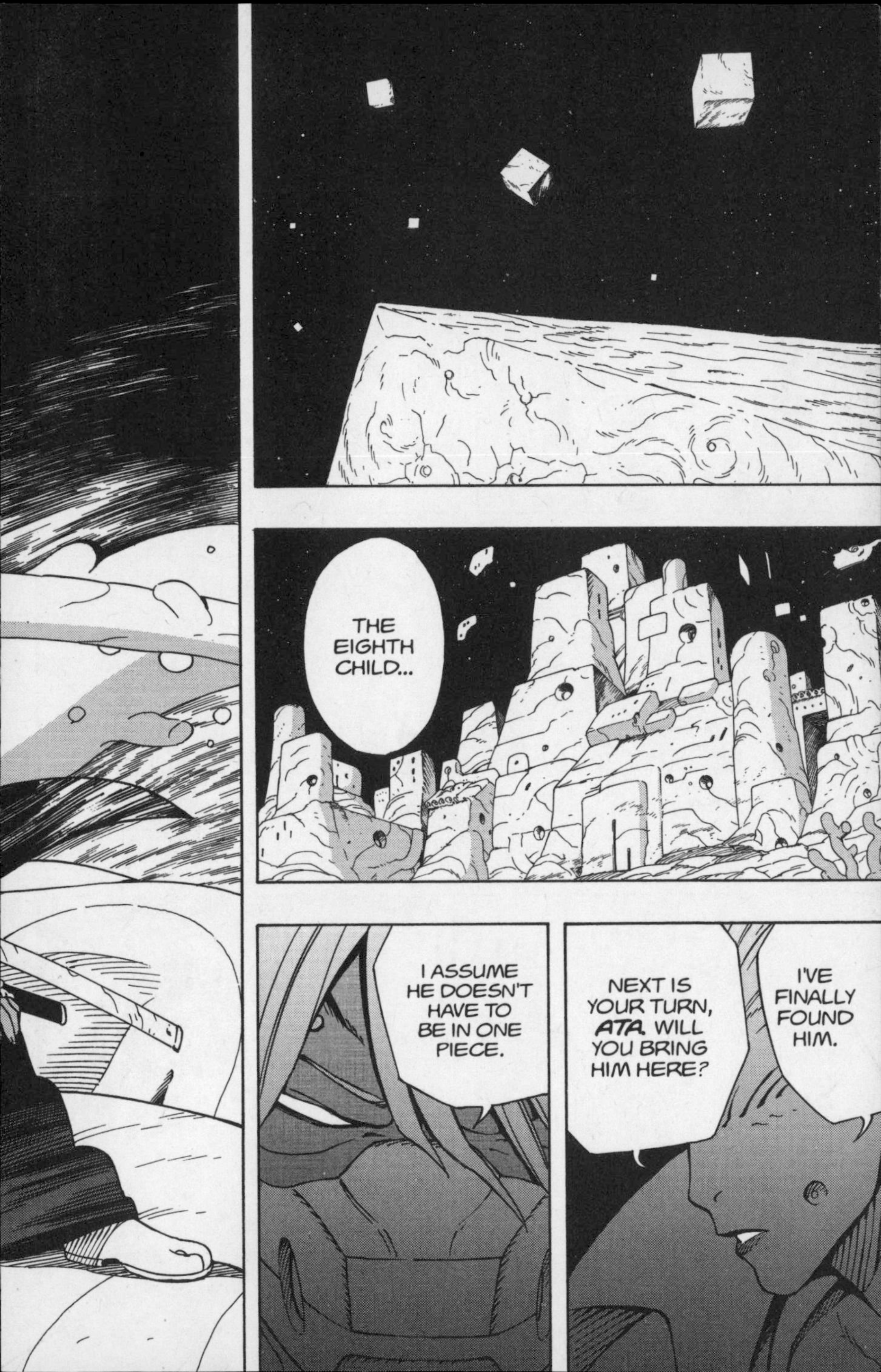
THE EIGHTH CHILD...
I'VE FINALLY FOUND HIM.
NEXT IS YOUR TURN, ATA. WILL YOU BRING HIM HERE?
I ASSUME HE DOESN'T HAVE TO BE IN ONE PIECE.

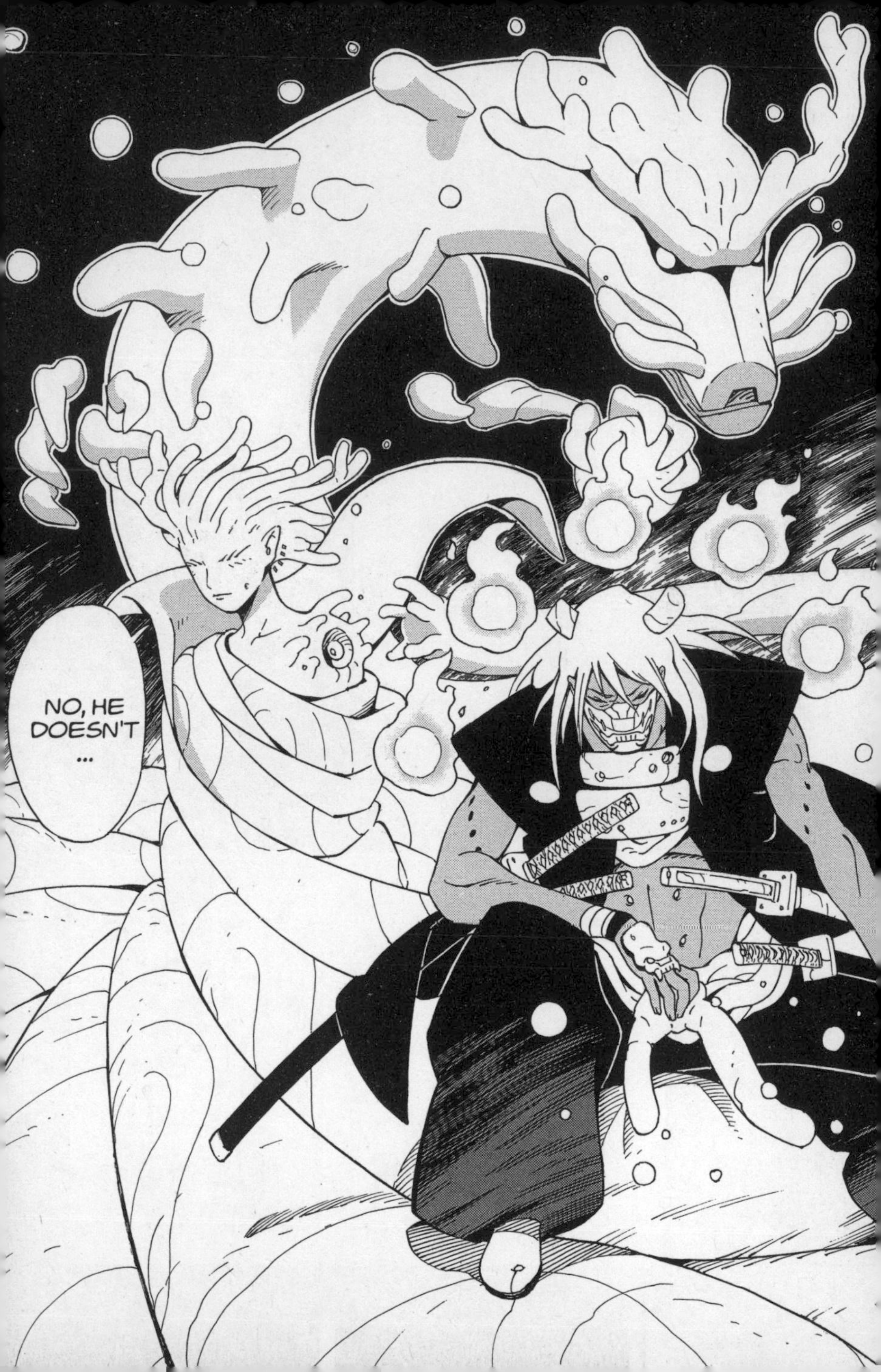
NO, HE DOESN'T ...

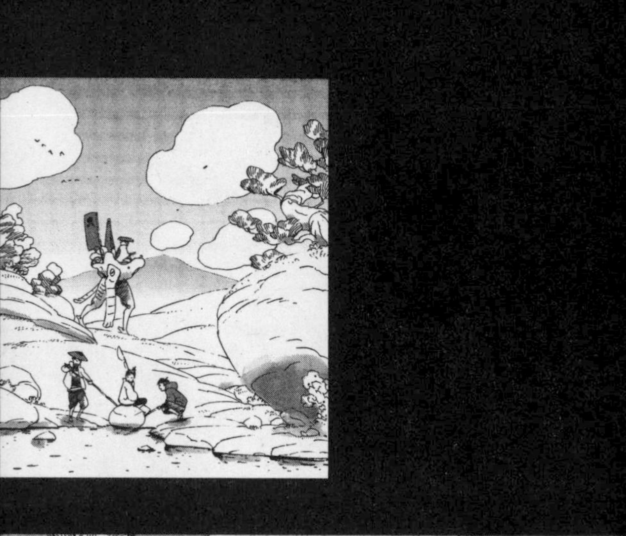
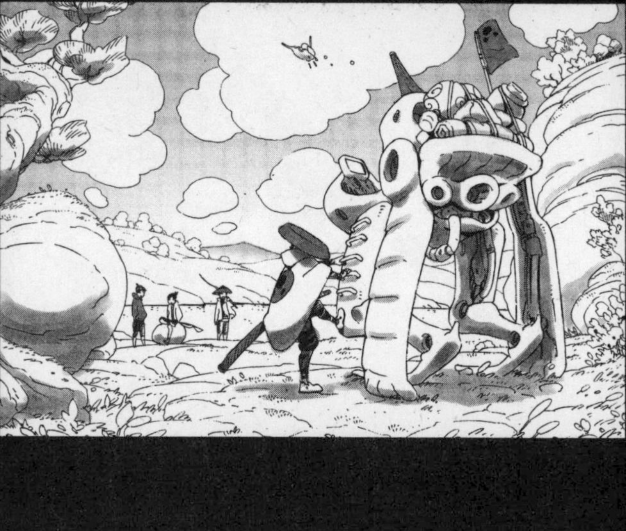

CHAPTER 8: TAKE IT SLOWLY

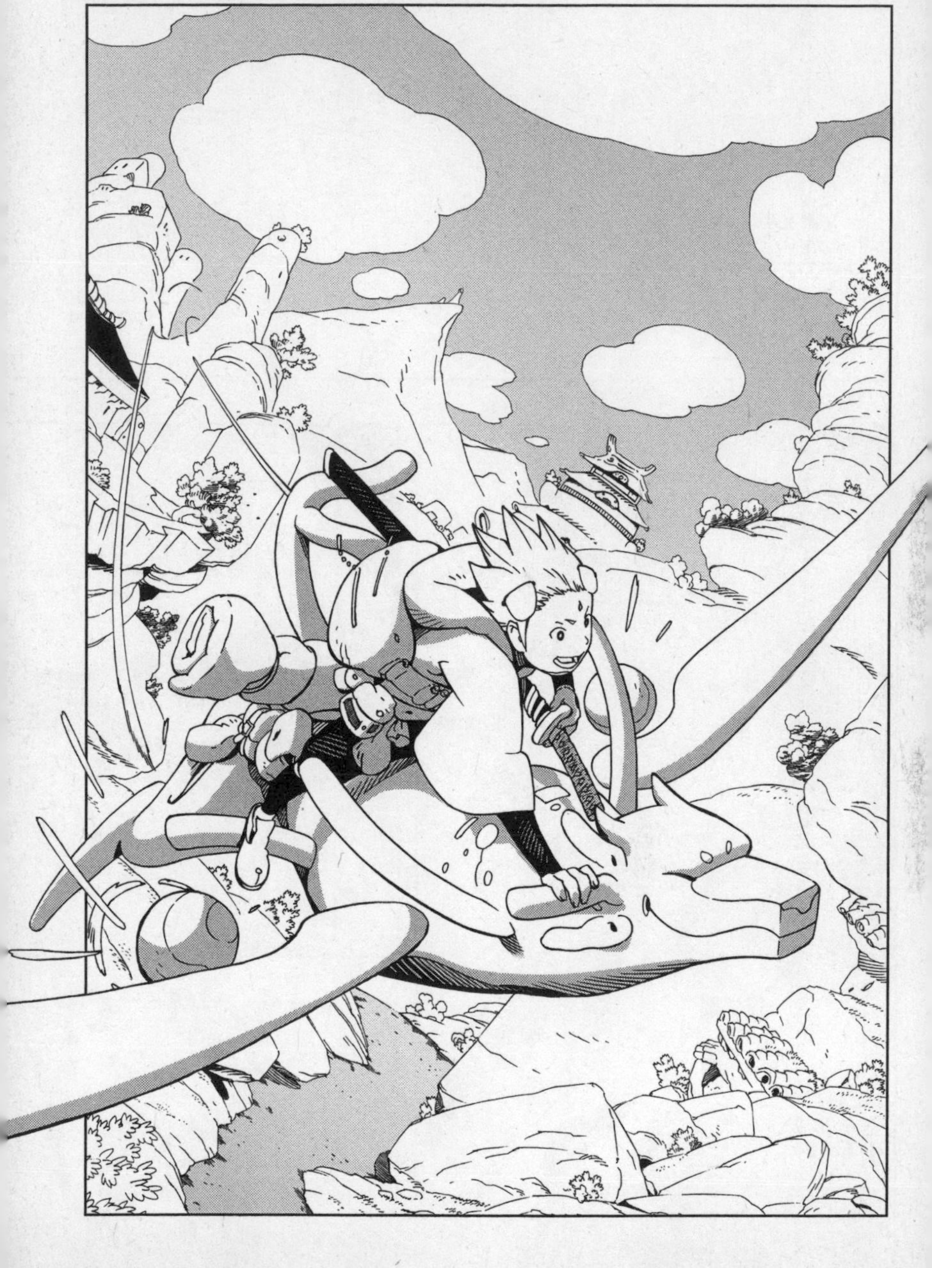

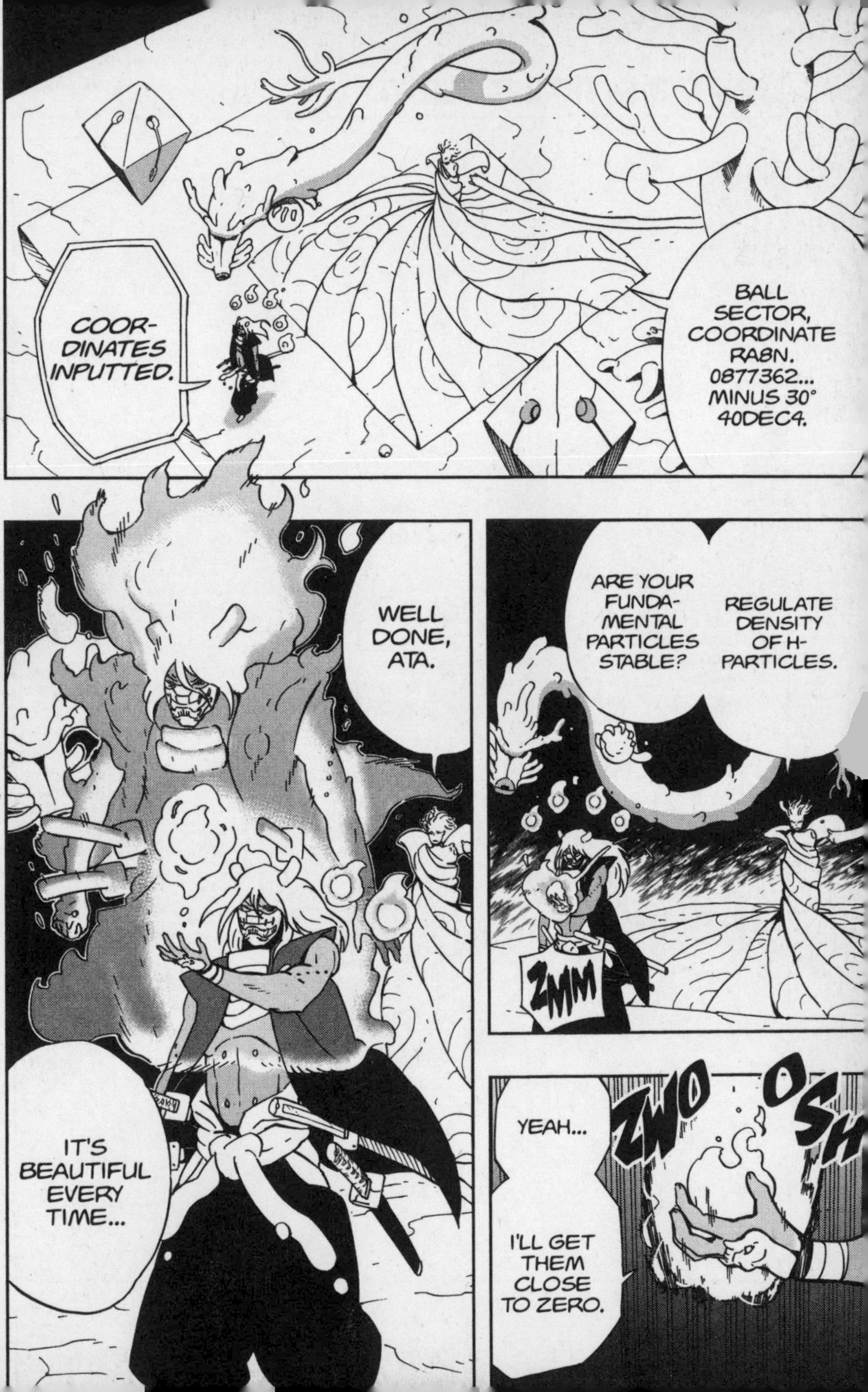
BALL SECTOR, COORDINATE RA8N. 0877362... MINUS 30° 40DEC4.
COOR-DINATES INPUTTED.
REGULATE DENSITY OF H-PARTICLES.
ARE YOUR FUNDA-MENTAL PARTICLES STABLE?
ZMM
ZWOOSH
YEAH...
I'LL GET THEM CLOSE TO ZERO.
WELL DONE, ATA.
IT'S BEAUTIFUL EVERY TIME...

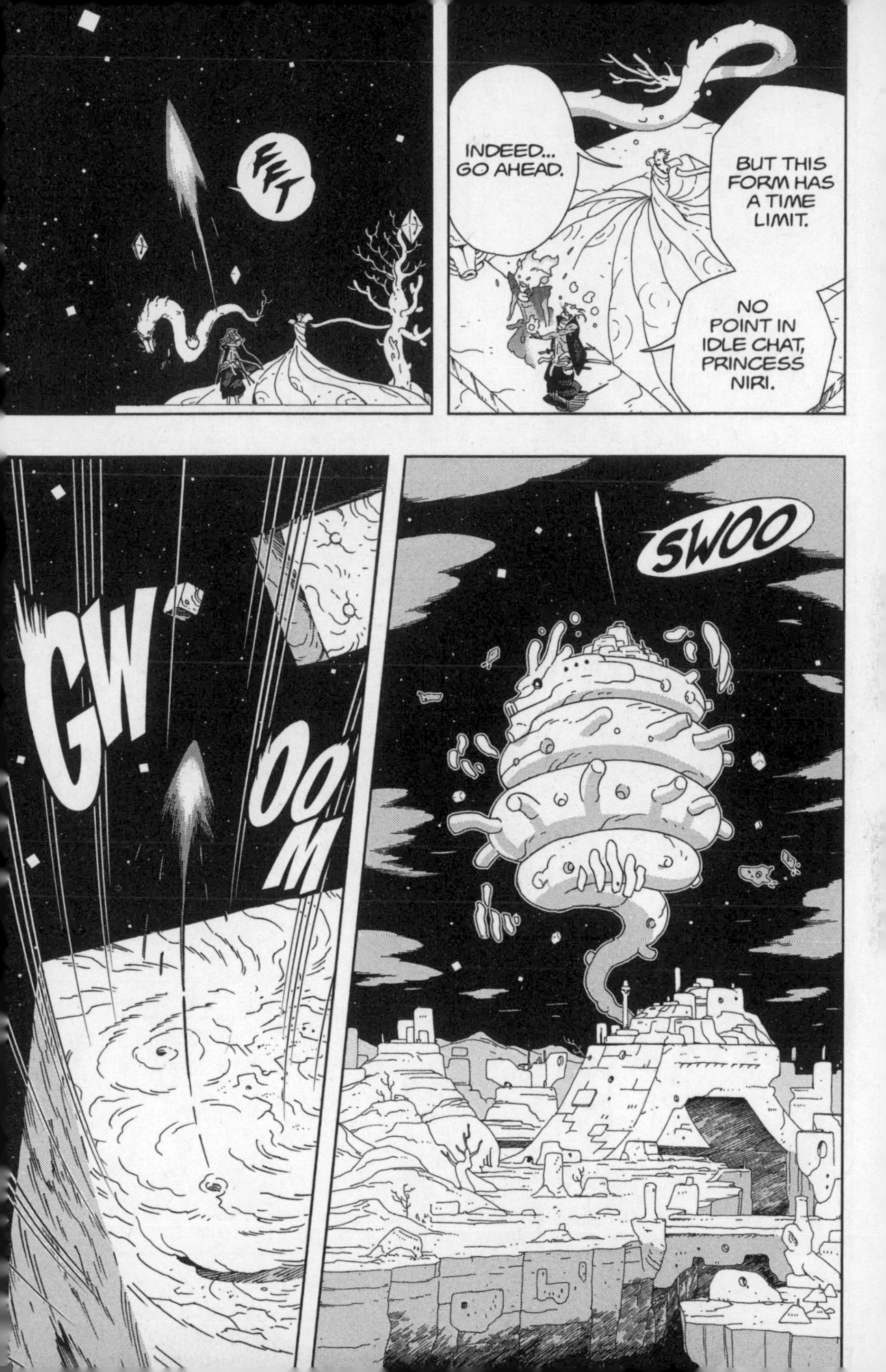
BUT THIS FORM HAS A TIME LIMIT.
NO POINT IN IDLE CHAT, PRINCESS NIRI.
INDEED... GO AHEAD.
FFT
SWOO
GWOOOM

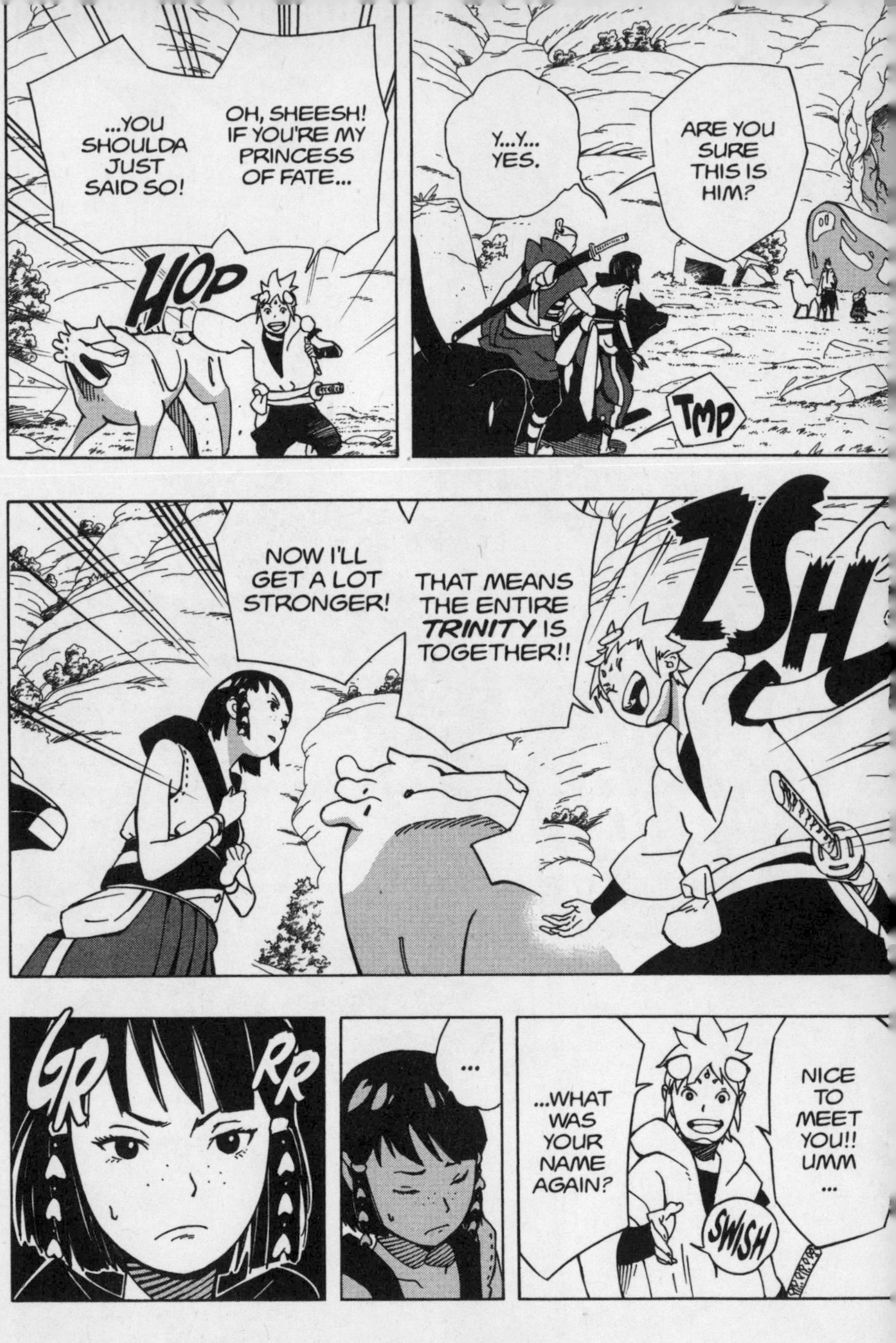
ARE YOU SURE THIS IS HIM?
Y...Y... YES.
TMP
OH, SHEESH! IF YOU'RE MY PRINCESS OF FATE...
...YOU SHOULDA JUST SAID SO!
HOP
ZSH
THAT MEANS THE ENTIRE *TRINITY* IS TOGETHER!!
NOW I'LL GET A LOT STRONGER!
NICE TO MEET YOU!! UMM ...
...WHAT WAS YOUR NAME AGAIN?
SWISH
...
GR RR

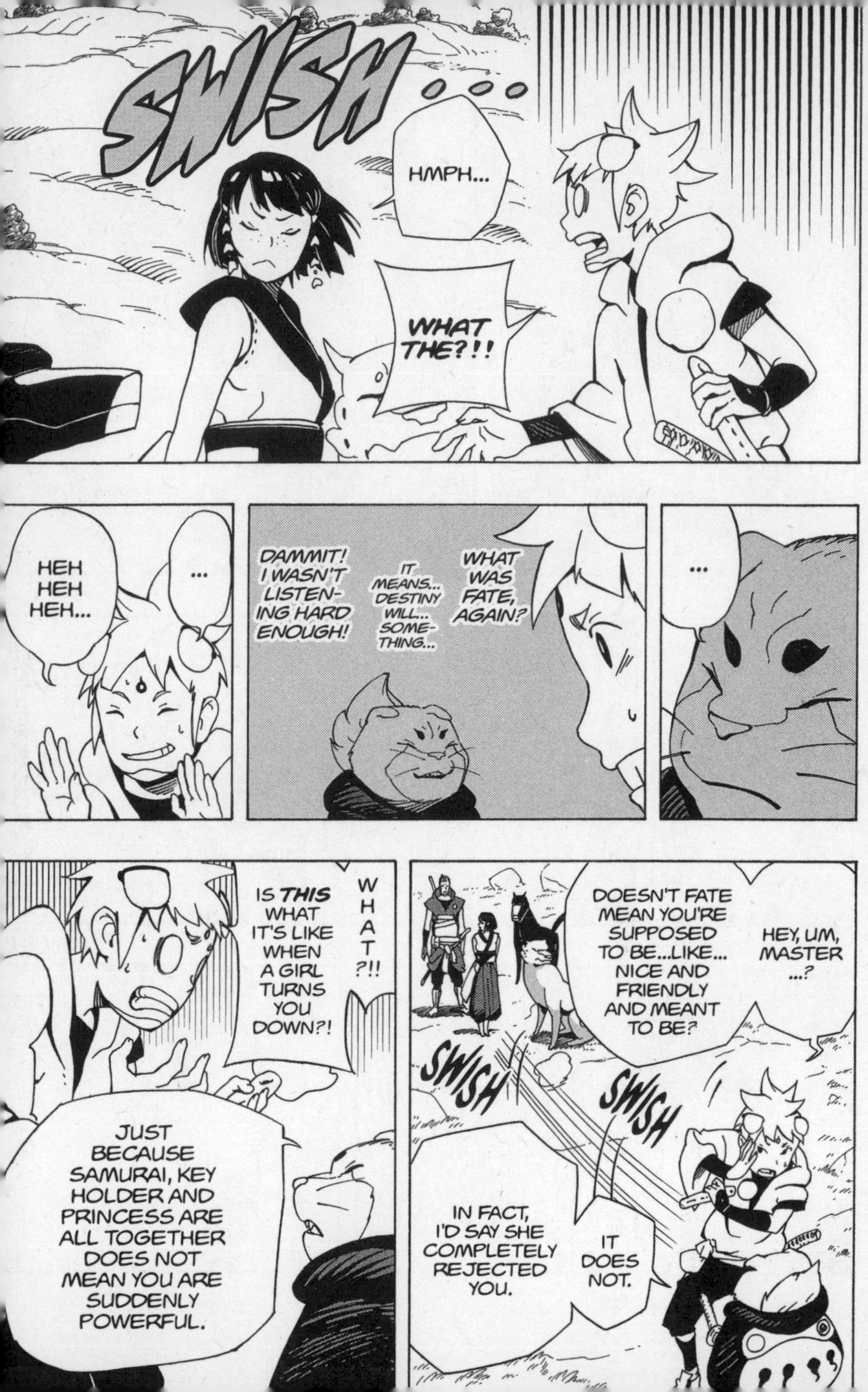
...
HMPH...
WHAT THE?!!
SWISH
...
WHAT WAS FATE, AGAIN?
IT MEANS... DESTINY WILL... SOMETHING...
DAMMIT! I WASN'T LISTENING HARD ENOUGH!
...
HEH HEH HEH...
HEY, UM, MASTER ...?
DOESN'T FATE MEAN YOU'RE SUPPOSED TO BE...LIKE... NICE AND FRIENDLY AND MEANT TO BE?
SWISH
SWISH
IT DOES NOT.
IN FACT, I'D SAY SHE COMPLETELY REJECTED YOU.
WHAT?!!
IS THIS WHAT IT'S LIKE WHEN A GIRL TURNS YOU DOWN?!
JUST BECAUSE SAMURAI, KEY HOLDER AND PRINCESS ARE ALL TOGETHER DOES NOT MEAN YOU ARE SUDDENLY POWERFUL.

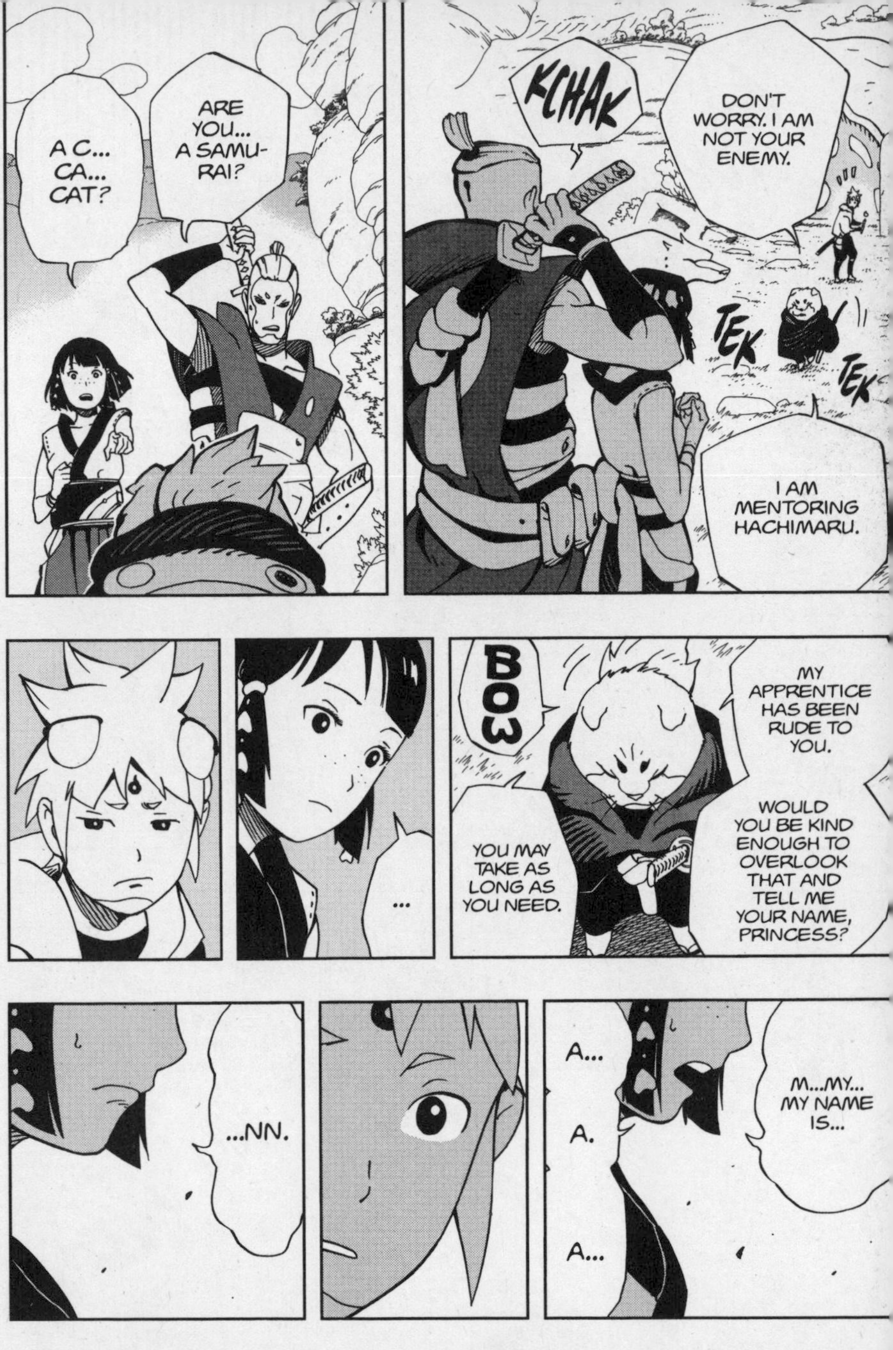
KCHAK
DON'T WORRY. I AM NOT YOUR ENEMY.
TEK
TEK
I AM MENTORING HACHIMARU.
ARE YOU... A SAMU-RAI?
A C... CA... CAT?
MY APPRENTICE HAS BEEN RUDE TO YOU.
BOW
WOULD YOU BE KIND ENOUGH TO OVERLOOK THAT AND TELL ME YOUR NAME, PRINCESS?
YOU MAY TAKE AS LONG AS YOU NEED.
...
M...MY... MY NAME IS...
A...
A.
A...
...NN.

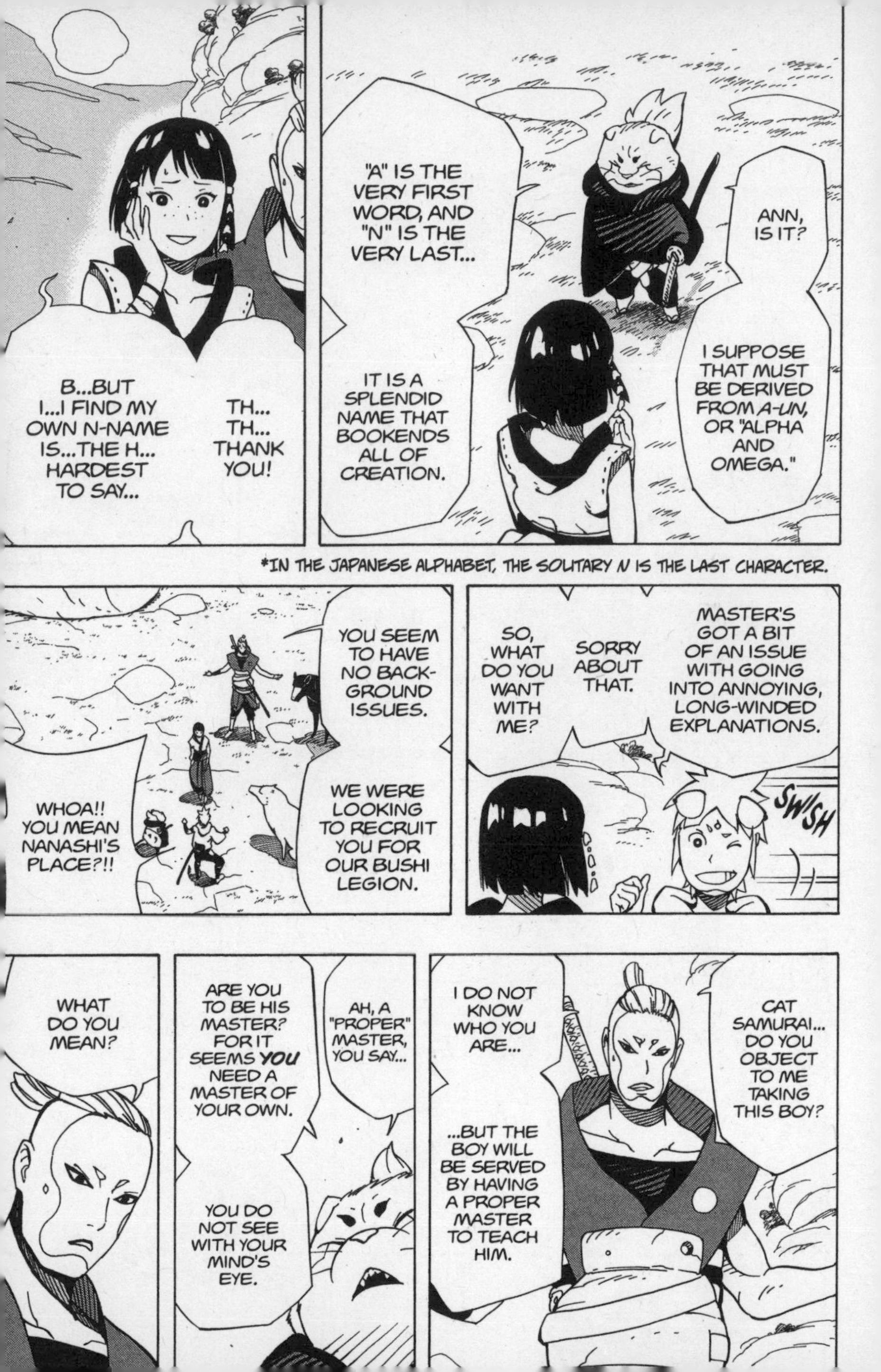
ANN, IS IT?
I SUPPOSE THAT MUST BE DERIVED FROM A-UN, OR "ALPHA AND OMEGA."
"A" IS THE VERY FIRST WORD, AND "N" IS THE VERY LAST...
IT IS A SPLENDID NAME THAT BOOKENDS ALL OF CREATION.
TH... TH... THANK YOU!
B...BUT I...I FIND MY OWN N-NAME IS...THE H... HARDEST TO SAY...
*IN THE JAPANESE ALPHABET, THE SOLITARY N IS THE LAST CHARACTER.
MASTER'S GOT A BIT OF AN ISSUE WITH GOING INTO ANNOYING, LONG-WINDED EXPLANATIONS.
SORRY ABOUT THAT.
SO, WHAT DO YOU WANT WITH ME?
SWISH
YOU SEEM TO HAVE NO BACK-GROUND ISSUES.
WE WERE LOOKING TO RECRUIT YOU FOR OUR BUSHI LEGION.
WHOA!! YOU MEAN NANASHI'S PLACE?!!
CAT SAMURAI... DO YOU OBJECT TO ME TAKING THIS BOY?
I DO NOT KNOW WHO YOU ARE...
...BUT THE BOY WILL BE SERVED BY HAVING A PROPER MASTER TO TEACH HIM.
AH, A "PROPER" MASTER, YOU SAY...
ARE YOU TO BE HIS MASTER? FOR IT SEEMS YOU NEED A MASTER OF YOUR OWN.
YOU DO NOT SEE WITH YOUR MIND'S EYE.
WHAT DO YOU MEAN?

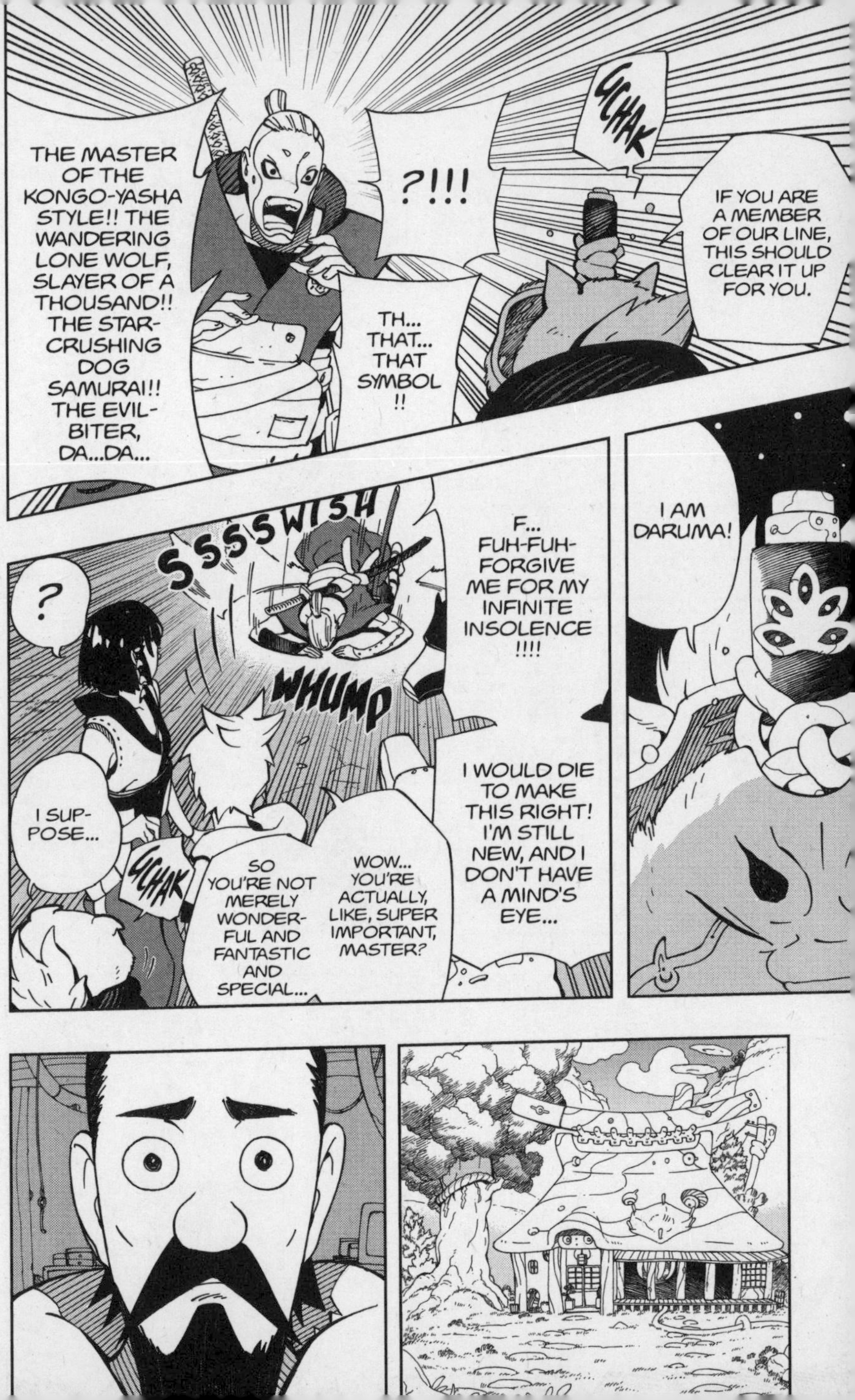
UCHAK
IF YOU ARE A MEMBER OF OUR LINE, THIS SHOULD CLEAR IT UP FOR YOU.
?!!!
TH... THAT... THAT SYMBOL !!
THE MASTER OF THE KONGO-YASHA STYLE!! THE WANDERING LONE WOLF, SLAYER OF A THOUSAND!! THE STAR-CRUSHING DOG SAMURAI!! THE EVIL-BITER, DA...DA...
I AM DARUMA!
F... FUH-FUH-FORGIVE ME FOR MY INFINITE INSOLENCE !!!!
SSSSWISH
?
WHUMP
I WOULD DIE TO MAKE THIS RIGHT! I'M STILL NEW, AND I DON'T HAVE A MIND'S EYE...
WOW... YOU'RE ACTUALLY, LIKE, SUPER IMPORTANT, MASTER?
SO YOU'RE NOT MERELY WONDERFUL AND FANTASTIC AND SPECIAL...
UCHAK
I SUP-POSE...

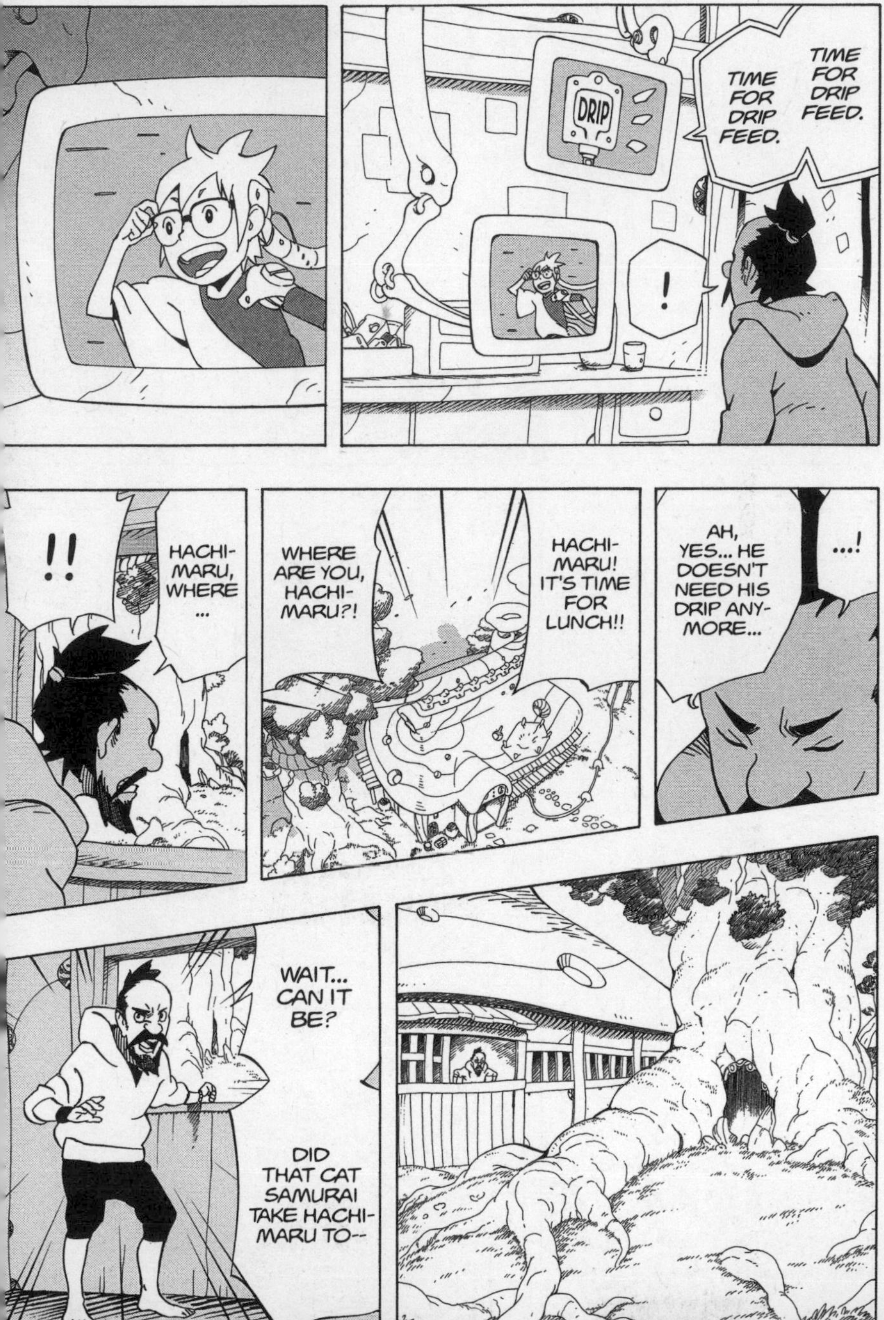
TIME FOR DRIP FEED.
TIME FOR DRIP FEED.
!
...!
AH, YES... HE DOESN'T NEED HIS DRIP ANYMORE...
HACHI-MARU! IT'S TIME FOR LUNCH!!
WHERE ARE YOU, HACHI-MARU?!
HACHI-MARU, WHERE ...
!!
WAIT... CAN IT BE?
DID THAT CAT SAMURAI TAKE HACHI-MARU TO--

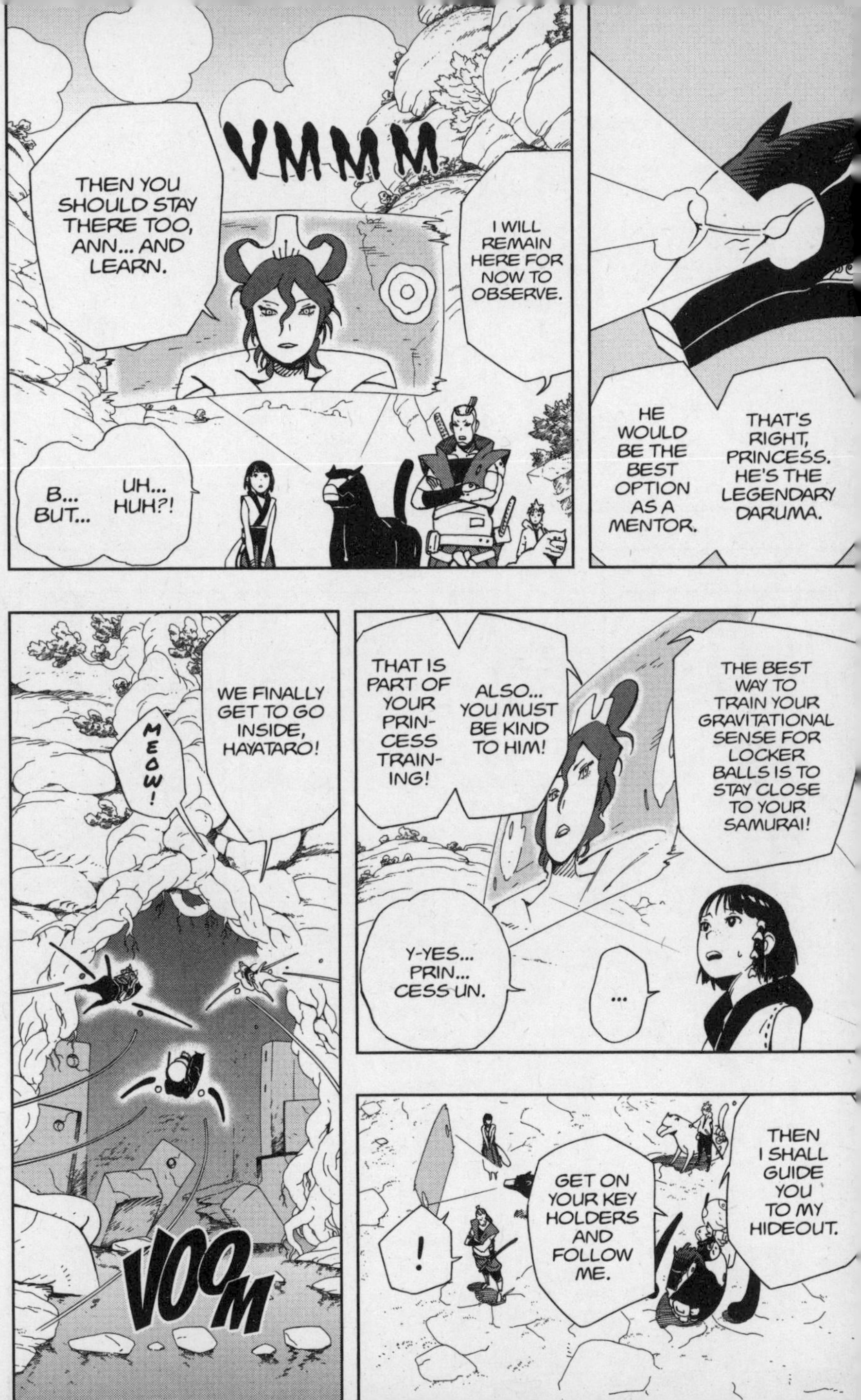
THAT'S RIGHT, PRINCESS. HE'S THE LEGENDARY DARUMA.
HE WOULD BE THE BEST OPTION AS A MENTOR.
I WILL REMAIN HERE FOR NOW TO OBSERVE.
VMMM
THEN YOU SHOULD STAY THERE TOO, ANN... AND LEARN.
UH... HUH?!
B... BUT...
THE BEST WAY TO TRAIN YOUR GRAVITATIONAL SENSE FOR LOCKER BALLS IS TO STAY CLOSE TO YOUR SAMURAI!
ALSO... YOU MUST BE KIND TO HIM!
THAT IS PART OF YOUR PRIN-CESS TRAIN-ING!
...
Y-YES... PRIN... CESS UN.
THEN I SHALL GUIDE YOU TO MY HIDEOUT.
GET ON YOUR KEY HOLDERS AND FOLLOW ME.
!
WE FINALLY GET TO GO INSIDE, HAYATARO!
MEOW!
VOOM

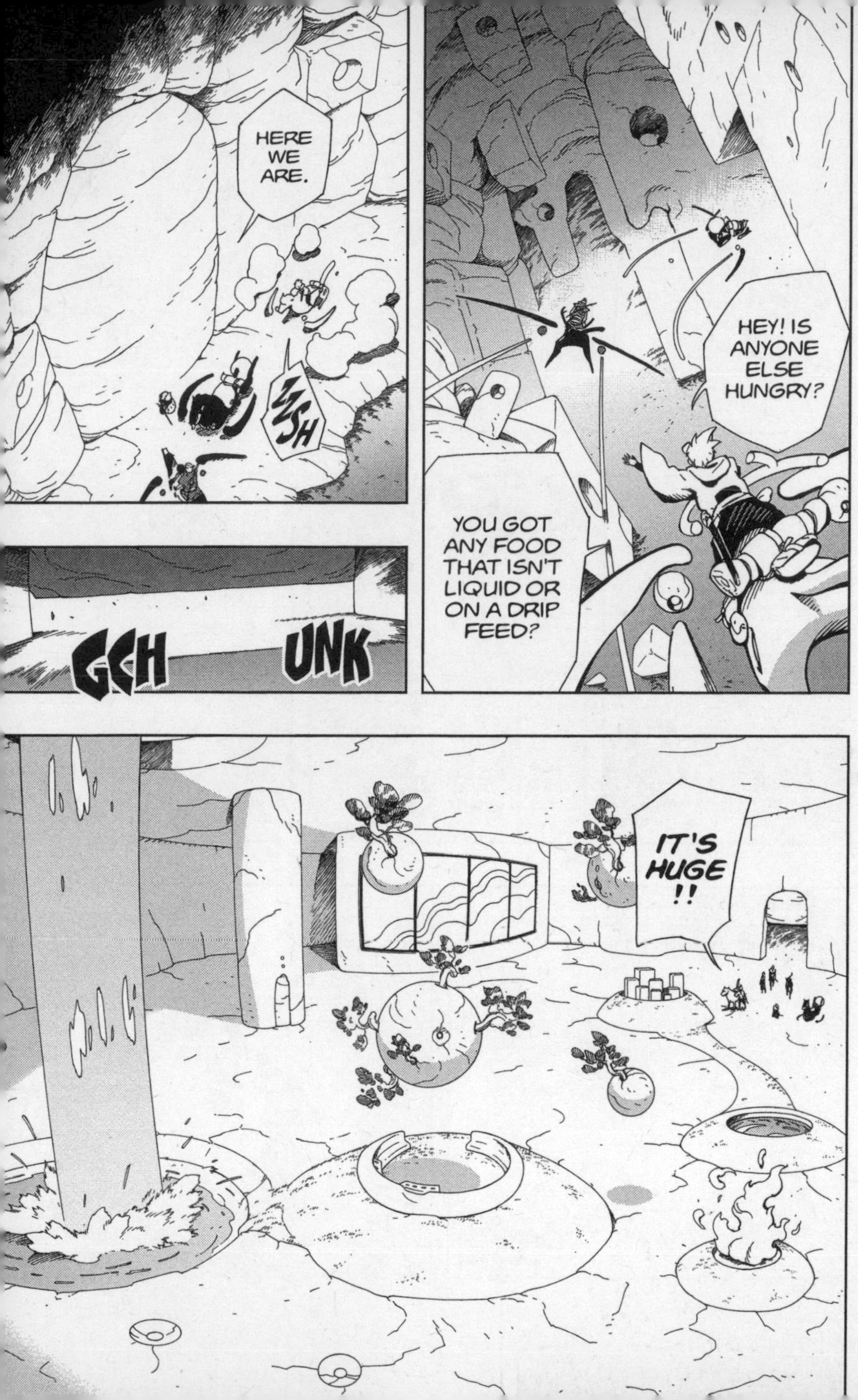
HEY! IS ANYONE ELSE HUNGRY?
YOU GOT ANY FOOD THAT ISN'T LIQUID OR ON A DRIP FEED?
HERE WE ARE.
GCH
UNK
IT'S HUGE!!

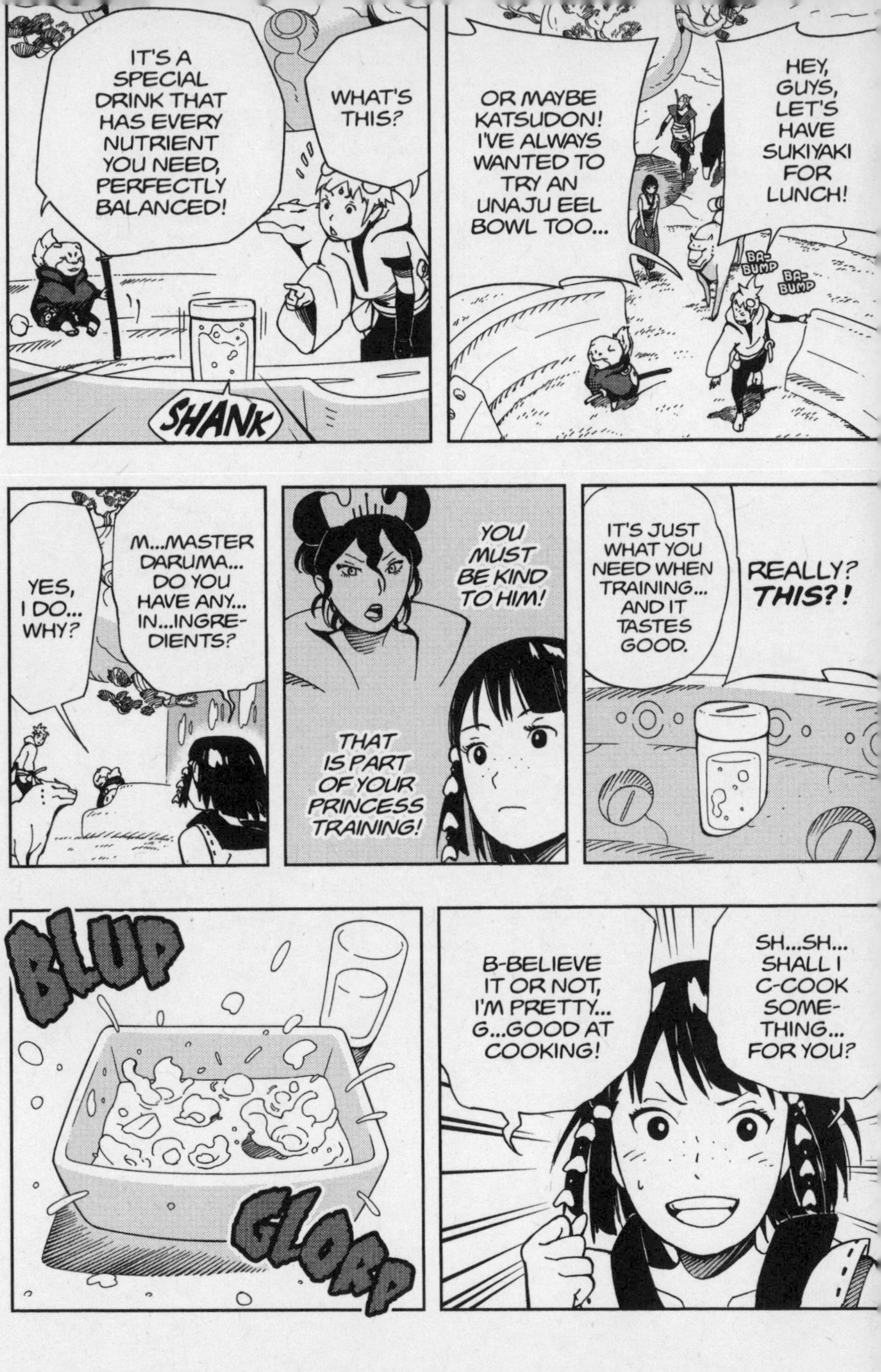
HEY, GUYS, LET'S HAVE SUKIYAKI FOR LUNCH!
OR MAYBE KATSUDON! I'VE ALWAYS WANTED TO TRY AN UNAJU EEL BOWL TOO...
BA-BUMP
BA-BUMP
WHAT'S THIS?
IT'S A SPECIAL DRINK THAT HAS EVERY NUTRIENT YOU NEED, PERFECTLY BALANCED!
SHANK
REALLY? THIS?!
IT'S JUST WHAT YOU NEED WHEN TRAINING... AND IT TASTES GOOD.
YOU MUST BE KIND TO HIM!
THAT IS PART OF YOUR PRINCESS TRAINING!
M...MASTER DARUMA... DO YOU HAVE ANY... IN...INGREDIENTS?
YES, I DO... WHY?
SH...SH... SHALL I C-COOK SOMETHING... FOR YOU?
B-BELIEVE IT OR NOT, I'M PRETTY... G...GOOD AT COOKING!
BLUP
GLORP

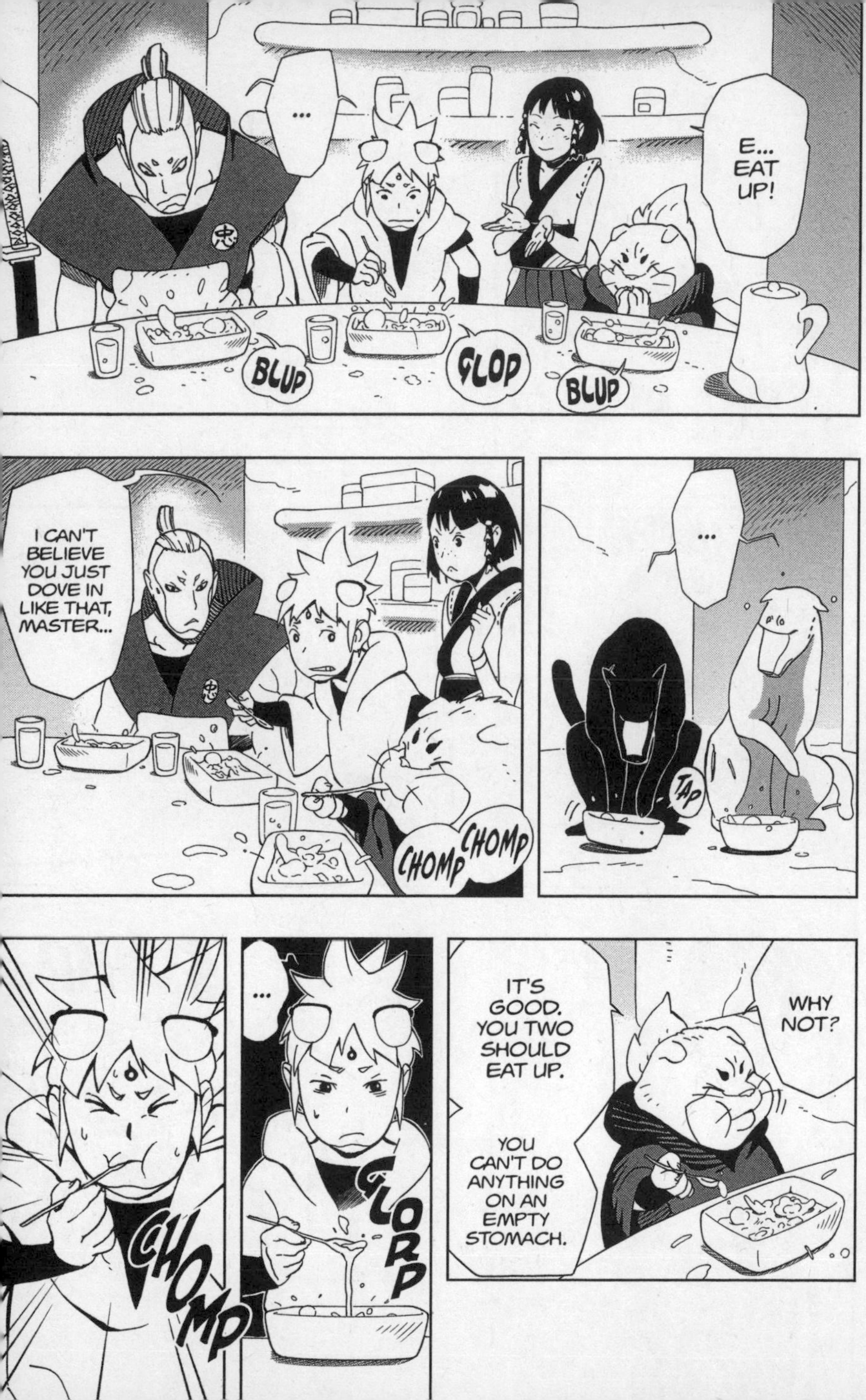
E... EAT UP!
...
BLUP
GLOP
BLUP
...
TAP
I CAN'T BELIEVE YOU JUST DOVE IN LIKE THAT, MASTER...
CHOMP
CHOMP
WHY NOT?
IT'S GOOD. YOU TWO SHOULD EAT UP.
YOU CAN'T DO ANYTHING ON AN EMPTY STOMACH.
...
GLORP
CHOMP

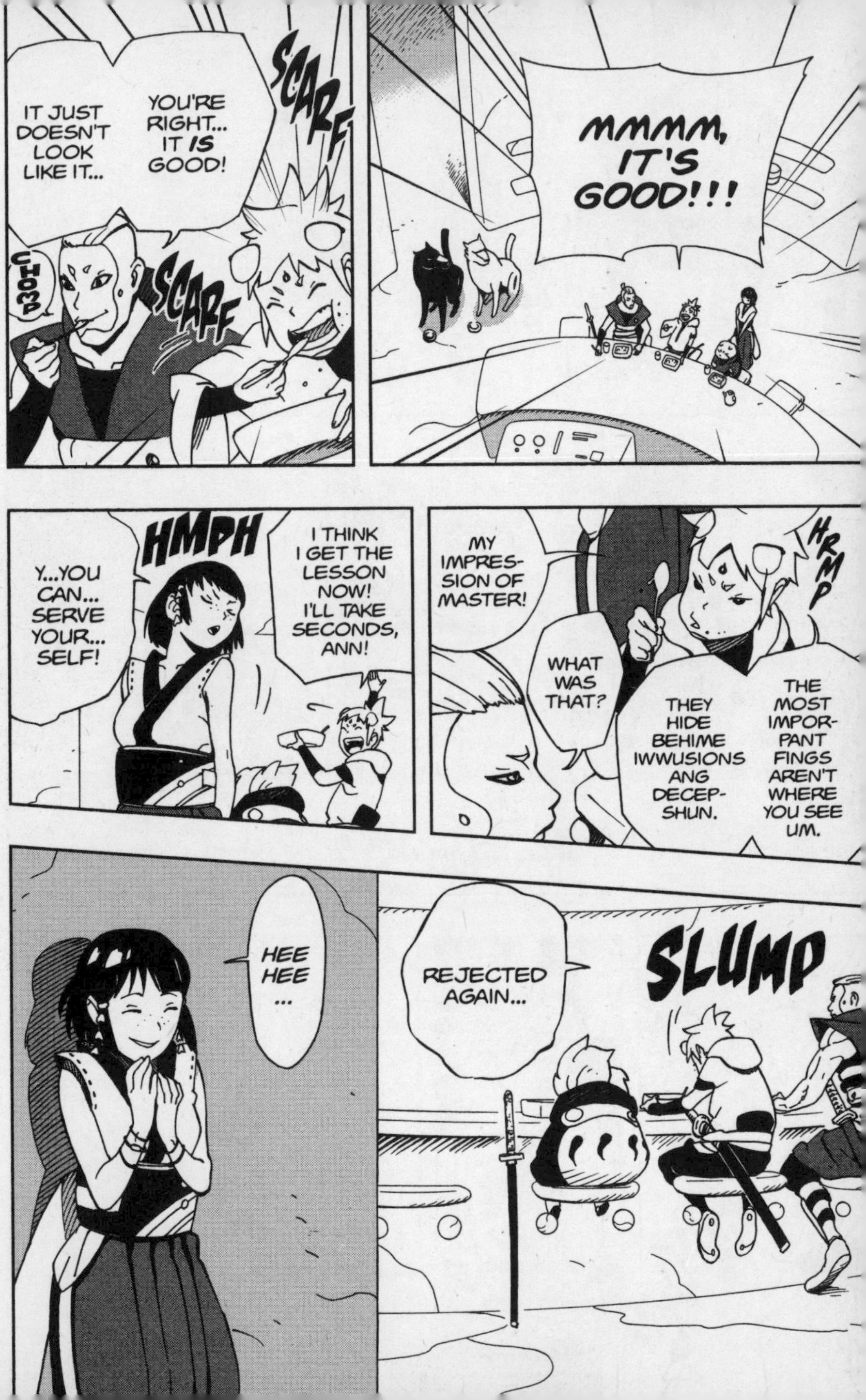
MMMM, IT'S GOOD!!!
SCARF
YOU'RE RIGHT... IT IS GOOD!
IT JUST DOESN'T LOOK LIKE IT...
CHOMP
SCARF
HRMP
MY IMPRES-SION OF MASTER!
THE MOST IMPOR-PANT FINGS AREN'T WHERE YOU SEE UM.
THEY HIDE BEHIME IWWUSIONS ANG DECEP-SHUN.
WHAT WAS THAT?
I THINK I GET THE LESSON NOW! I'LL TAKE SECONDS, ANN!
HMPH
Y...YOU CAN... SERVE YOUR... SELF!
SLUMP
REJECTED AGAIN...
HEE HEE ...

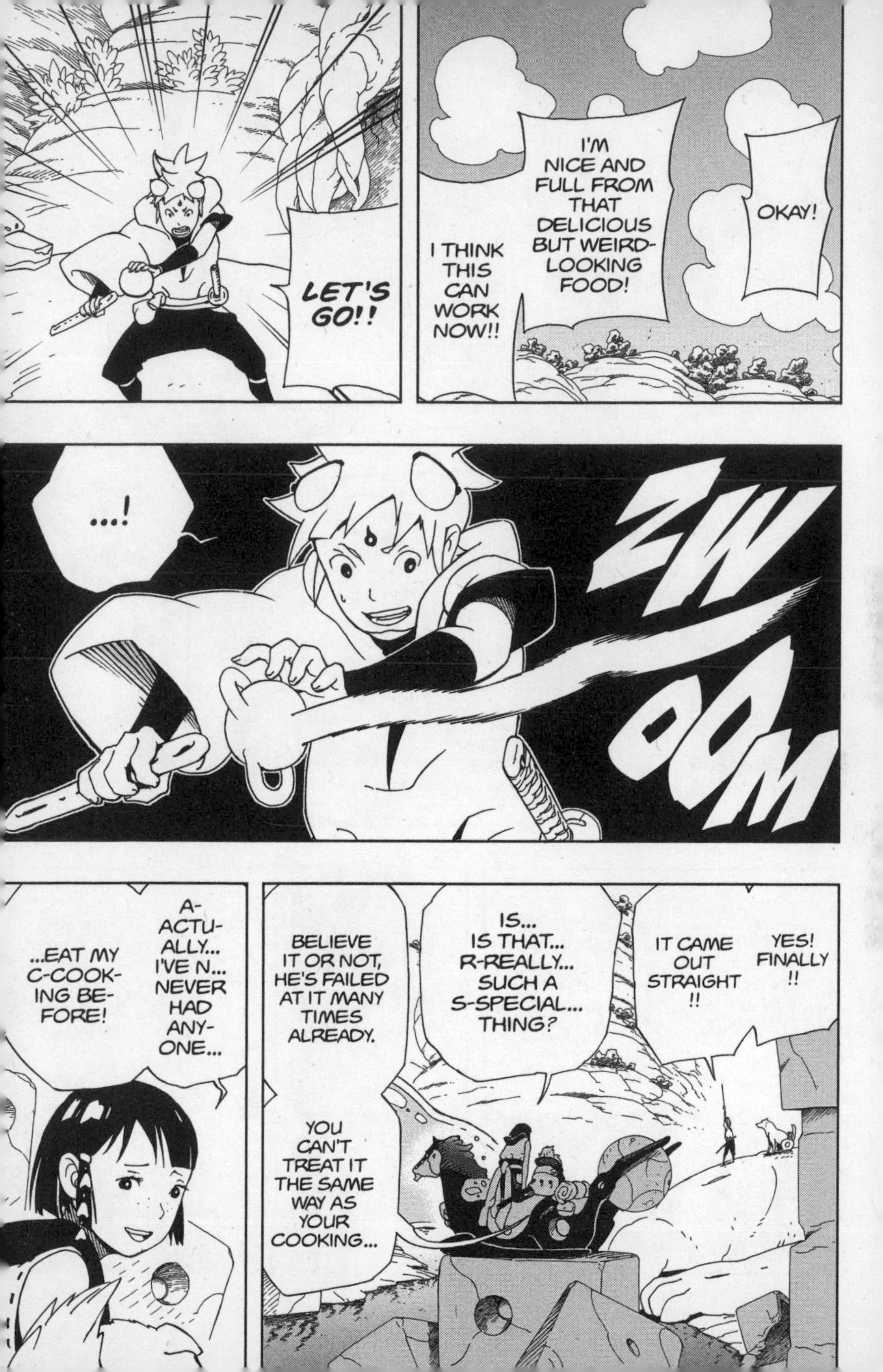
OKAY!
I'M NICE AND FULL FROM THAT DELICIOUS BUT WEIRD-LOOKING FOOD!
I THINK THIS CAN WORK NOW!!
LET'S GO!!
ZWOOM
...!
YES! FINALLY!!
IT CAME OUT STRAIGHT!!
IS... IS THAT... R-REALLY... SUCH A S-SPECIAL... THING?
BELIEVE IT OR NOT, HE'S FAILED AT IT MANY TIMES ALREADY.
YOU CAN'T TREAT IT THE SAME WAY AS YOUR COOKING...
A-ACTUALLY... I'VE N... NEVER HAD ANYONE...
...EAT MY C-COOKING BEFORE!

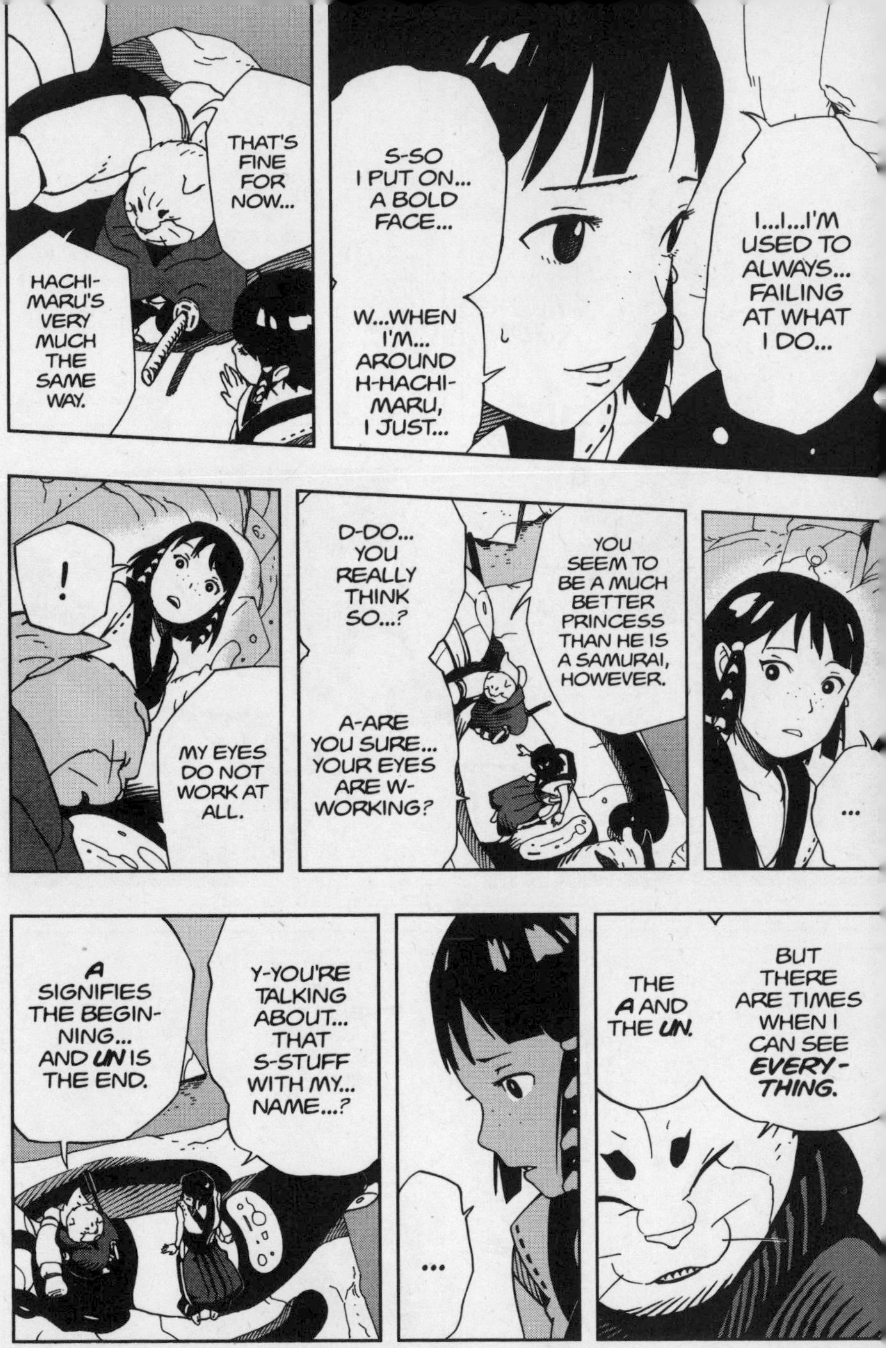
I...I...I'M USED TO ALWAYS... FAILING AT WHAT I DO...
S-SO I PUT ON... A BOLD FACE...
W...WHEN I'M... AROUND H-HACHI-MARU, I JUST...
THAT'S FINE FOR NOW...
HACHI-MARU'S VERY MUCH THE SAME WAY.
...
YOU SEEM TO BE A MUCH BETTER PRINCESS THAN HE IS A SAMURAI, HOWEVER.
D-DO... YOU REALLY THINK SO...?
A-ARE YOU SURE... YOUR EYES ARE W-WORKING?
!
MY EYES DO NOT WORK AT ALL.
BUT THERE ARE TIMES WHEN I CAN SEE *EVERYTHING.*
THE *A* AND THE *UN.*
...
Y-YOU'RE TALKING ABOUT... THAT S-STUFF WITH MY... NAME...?
A SIGNIFIES THE BEGINNING... AND *UN* IS THE END.

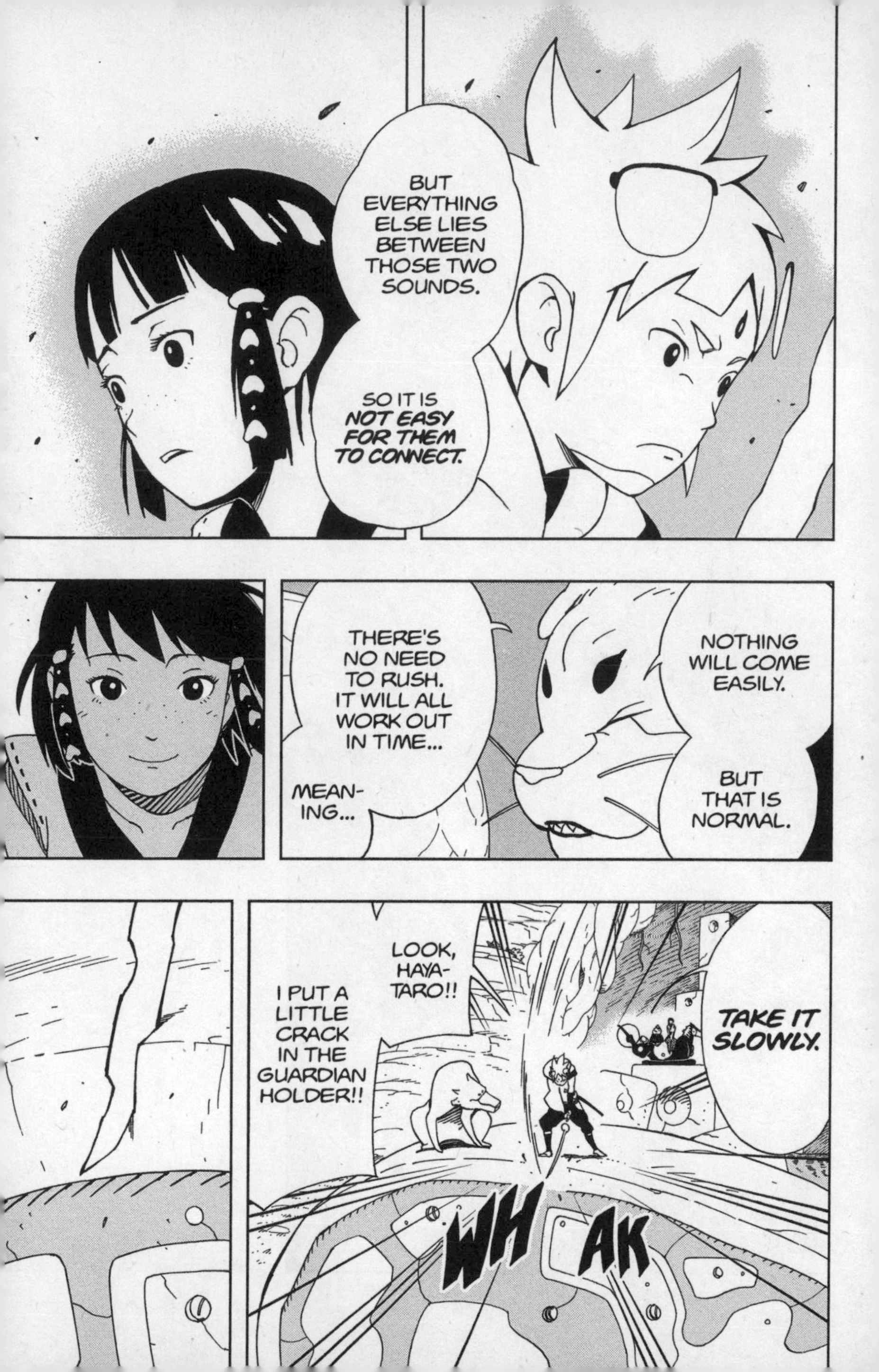
BUT EVERYTHING ELSE LIES BETWEEN THOSE TWO SOUNDS.
SO IT IS *NOT EASY FOR THEM TO CONNECT.*
NOTHING WILL COME EASILY.
BUT THAT IS NORMAL.
THERE'S NO NEED TO RUSH. IT WILL ALL WORK OUT IN TIME...
MEAN-ING...
TAKE IT SLOWLY.
LOOK, HAYA-TARO!!
I PUT A LITTLE CRACK IN THE GUARDIAN HOLDER!!
WHAK

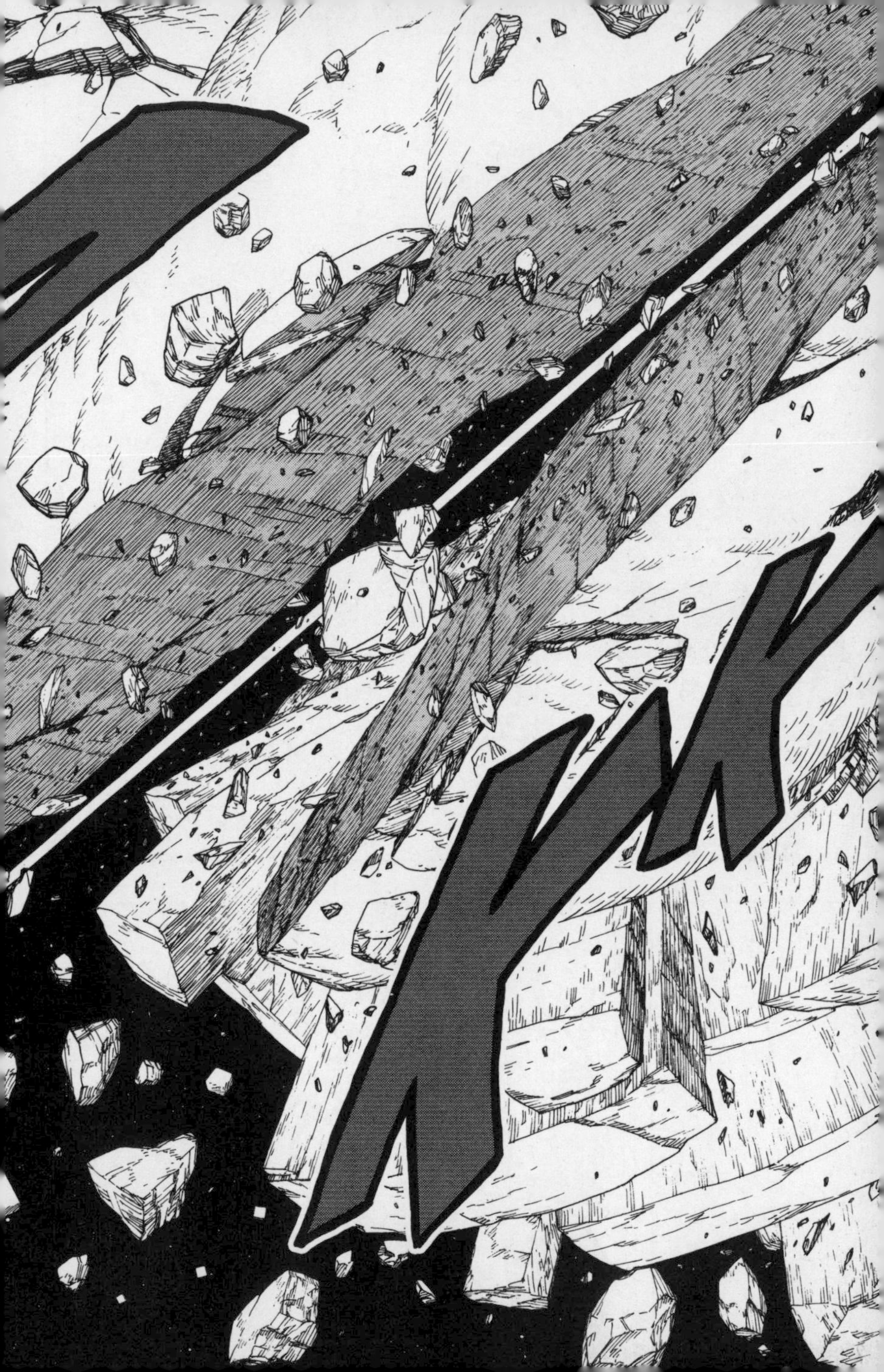

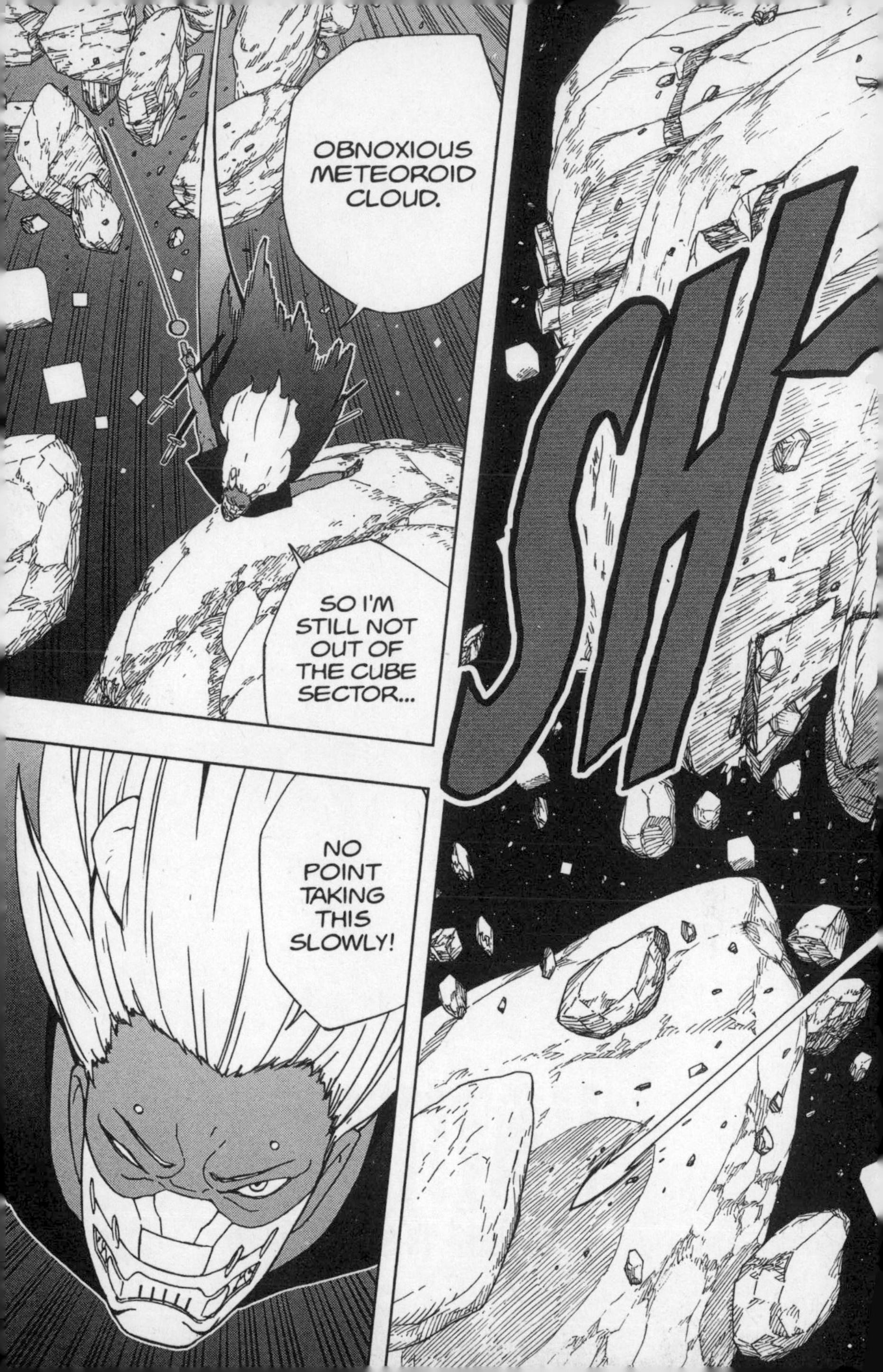
OBNOXIOUS METEOROID CLOUD.
SO I'M STILL NOT OUT OF THE CUBE SECTOR...
NO POINT TAKING THIS SLOWLY!

SAMURAI 8

THE TALE OF HACHIMARU

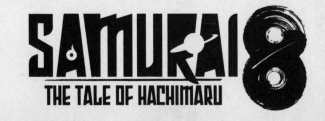

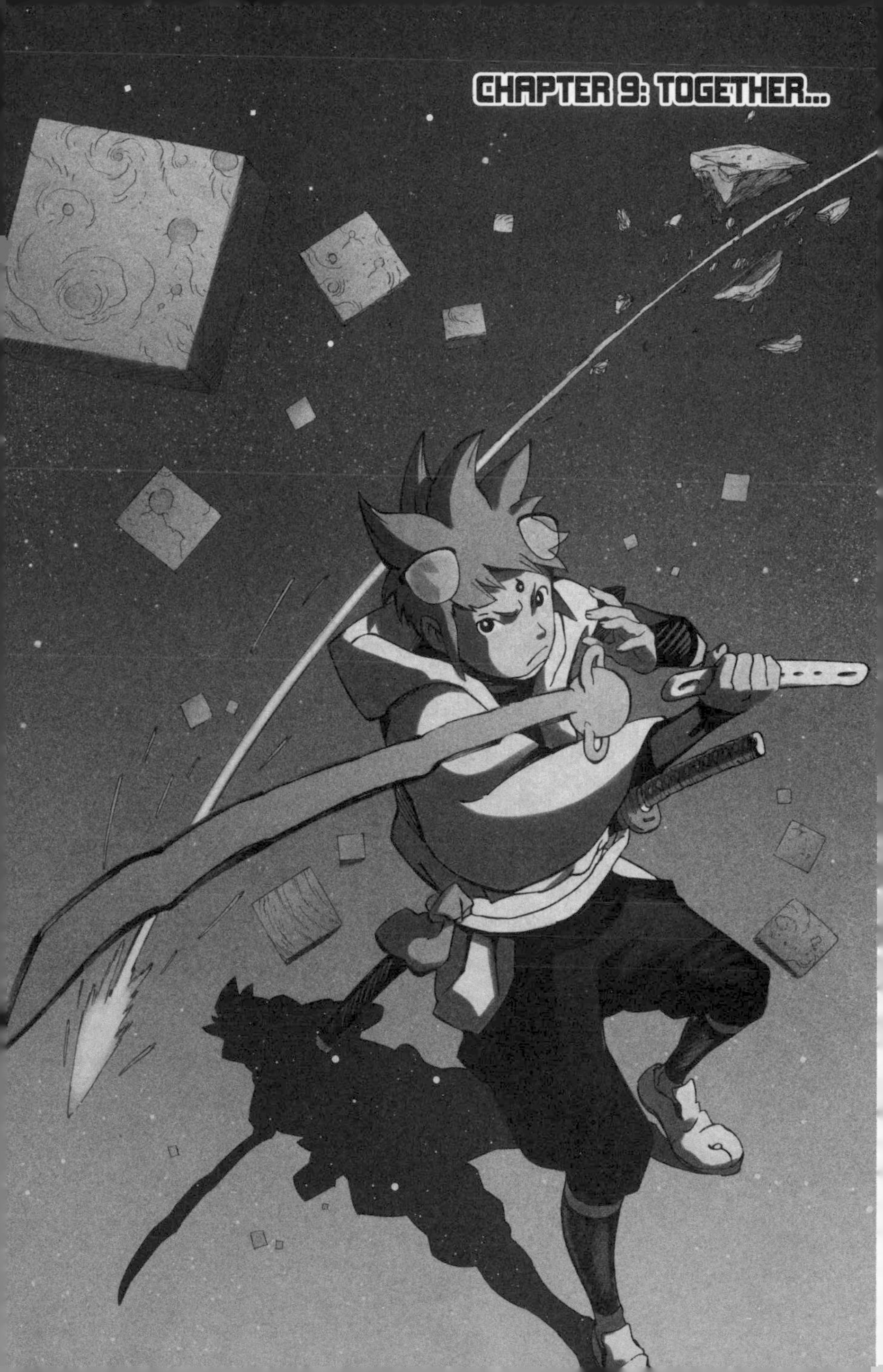
CHAPTER 9: TOGETHER...

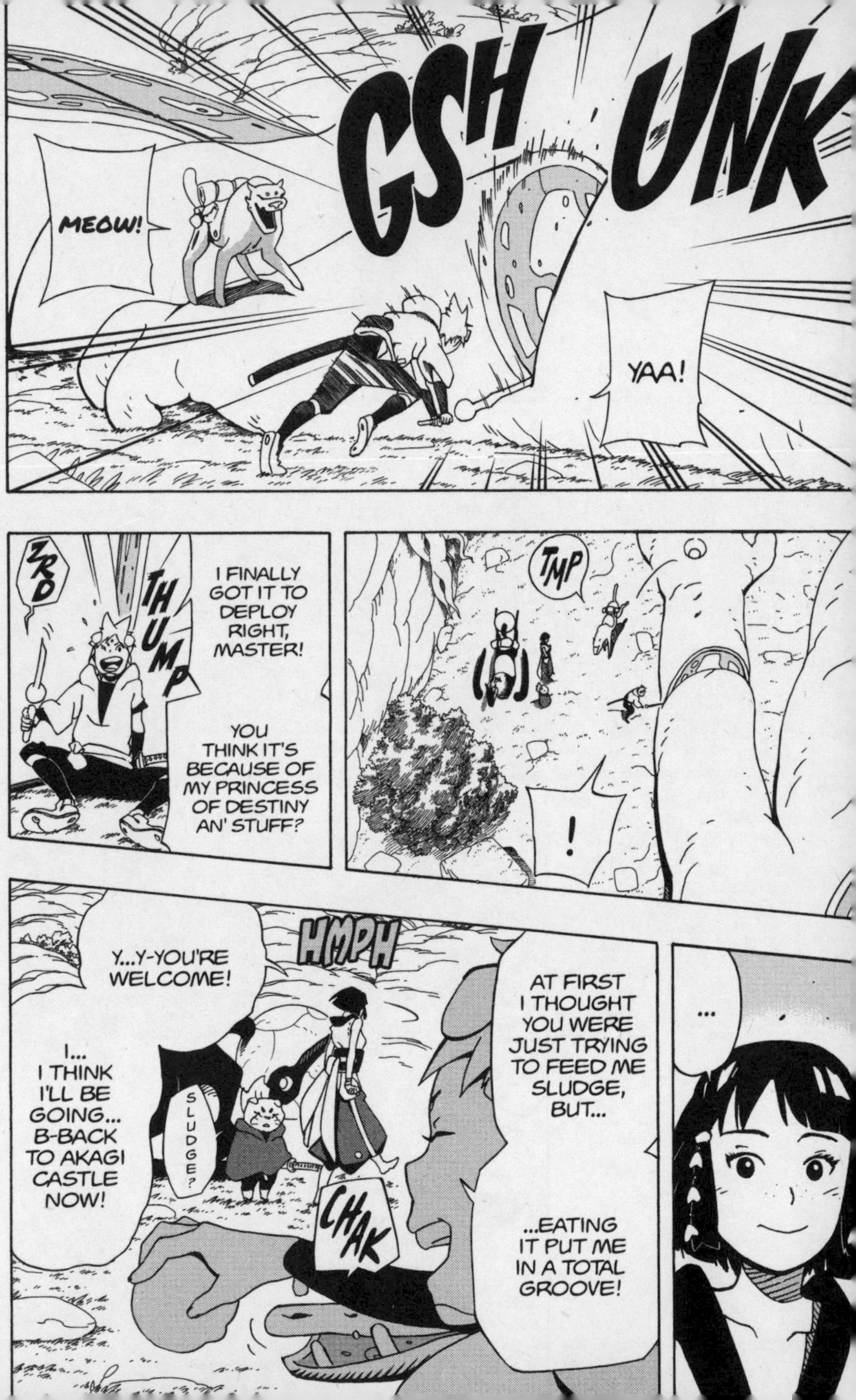
GSHUNK
YAA!
MEOW!
TMP
!
I FINALLY GOT IT TO DEPLOY RIGHT, MASTER!
YOU THINK IT'S BECAUSE OF MY PRINCESS OF DESTINY AN' STUFF?
THUMP
ZRD
...
AT FIRST I THOUGHT YOU WERE JUST TRYING TO FEED ME SLUDGE, BUT...
...EATING IT PUT ME IN A TOTAL GROOVE!
HMPH
Y...Y-YOU'RE WELCOME!
SLUDGE?
I... I THINK I'LL BE GOING... B-BACK TO AKAGI CASTLE NOW!
CHAK

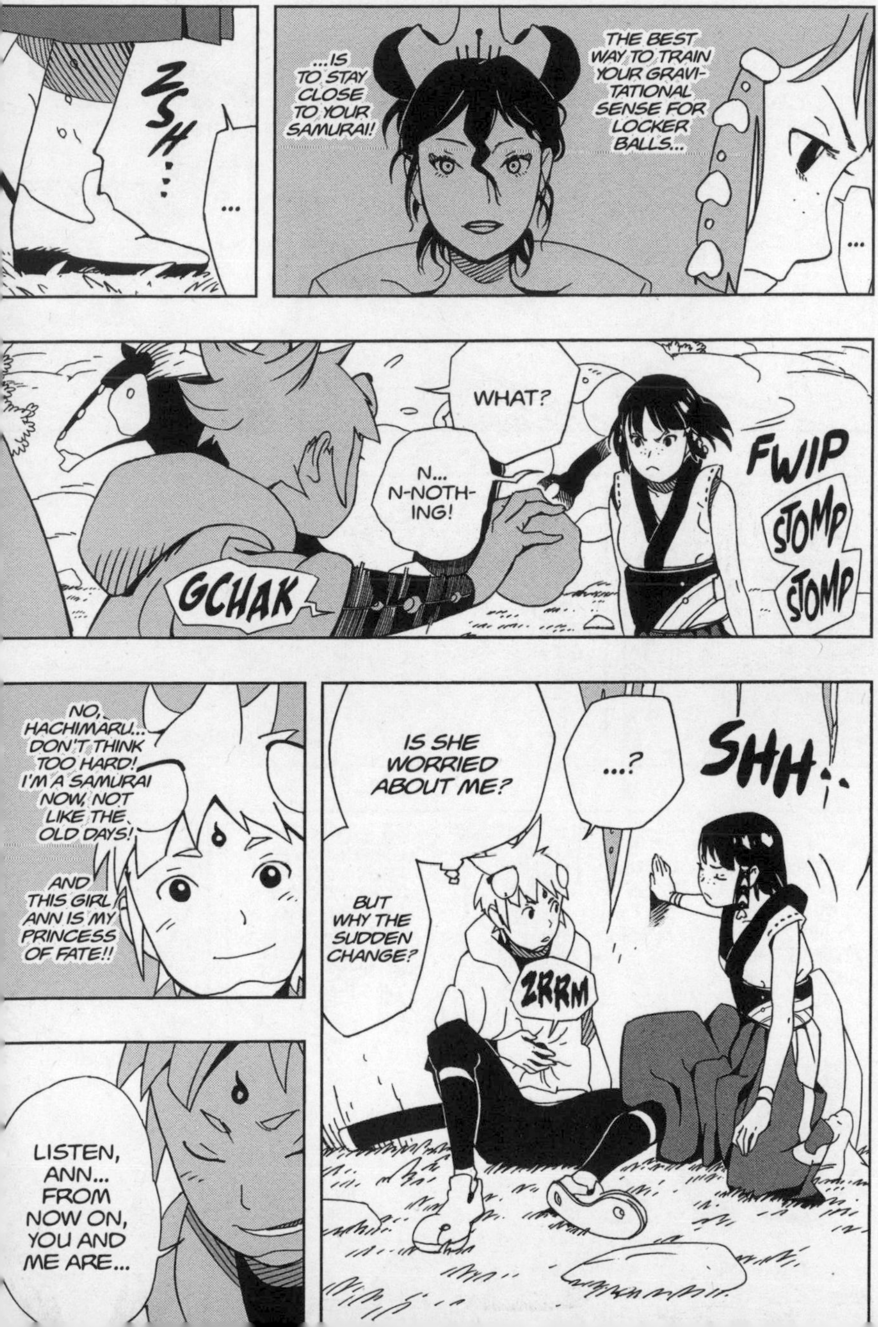

THE BEST WAY TO TRAIN YOUR GRAVI-TATIONAL SENSE FOR LOCKER BALLS...
...IS TO STAY CLOSE TO YOUR SAMURAI!
...
ZSH...
...
FWIP
STOMP
STOMP
WHAT?
N... N-NOTH-ING!
GCHAK
SHH...
...?
IS SHE WORRIED ABOUT ME?
BUT WHY THE SUDDEN CHANGE?
ZRRM
NO, HACHIMARU... DON'T THINK TOO HARD! I'M A SAMURAI NOW, NOT LIKE THE OLD DAYS!
AND THIS GIRL ANN IS MY PRINCESS OF FATE!!
LISTEN, ANN... FROM NOW ON, YOU AND ME ARE...

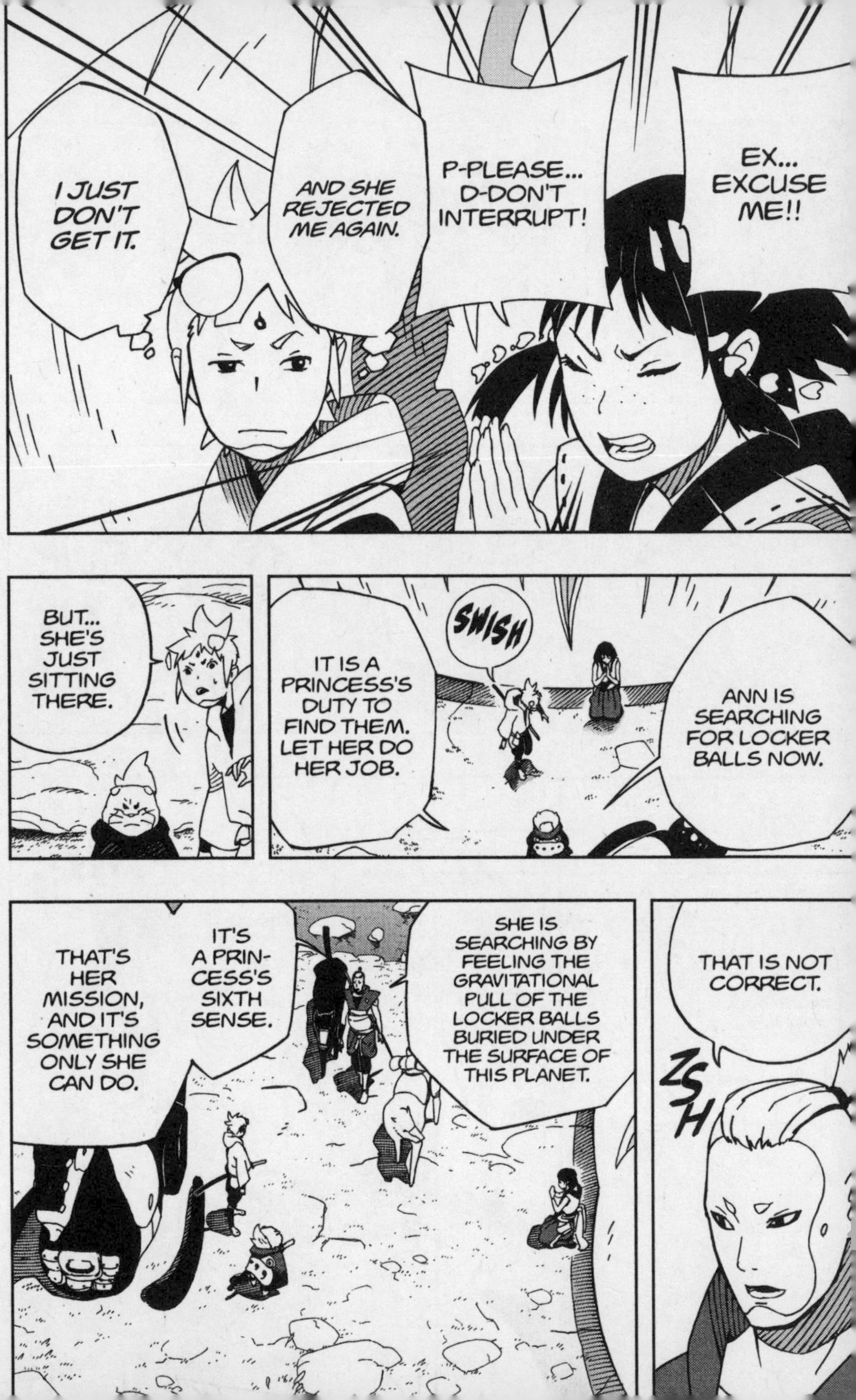
EX... EXCUSE ME!!
P-PLEASE... D-DON'T INTERRUPT!
AND SHE REJECTED ME AGAIN.
I JUST DON'T GET IT.
ANN IS SEARCHING FOR LOCKER BALLS NOW.
SWISH
IT IS A PRINCESS'S DUTY TO FIND THEM. LET HER DO HER JOB.
BUT... SHE'S JUST SITTING THERE.
THAT IS NOT CORRECT.
ZSH
SHE IS SEARCHING BY FEELING THE GRAVITATIONAL PULL OF THE LOCKER BALLS BURIED UNDER THE SURFACE OF THIS PLANET.
IT'S A PRIN-CESS'S SIXTH SENSE.
THAT'S HER MISSION, AND IT'S SOMETHING ONLY SHE CAN DO.

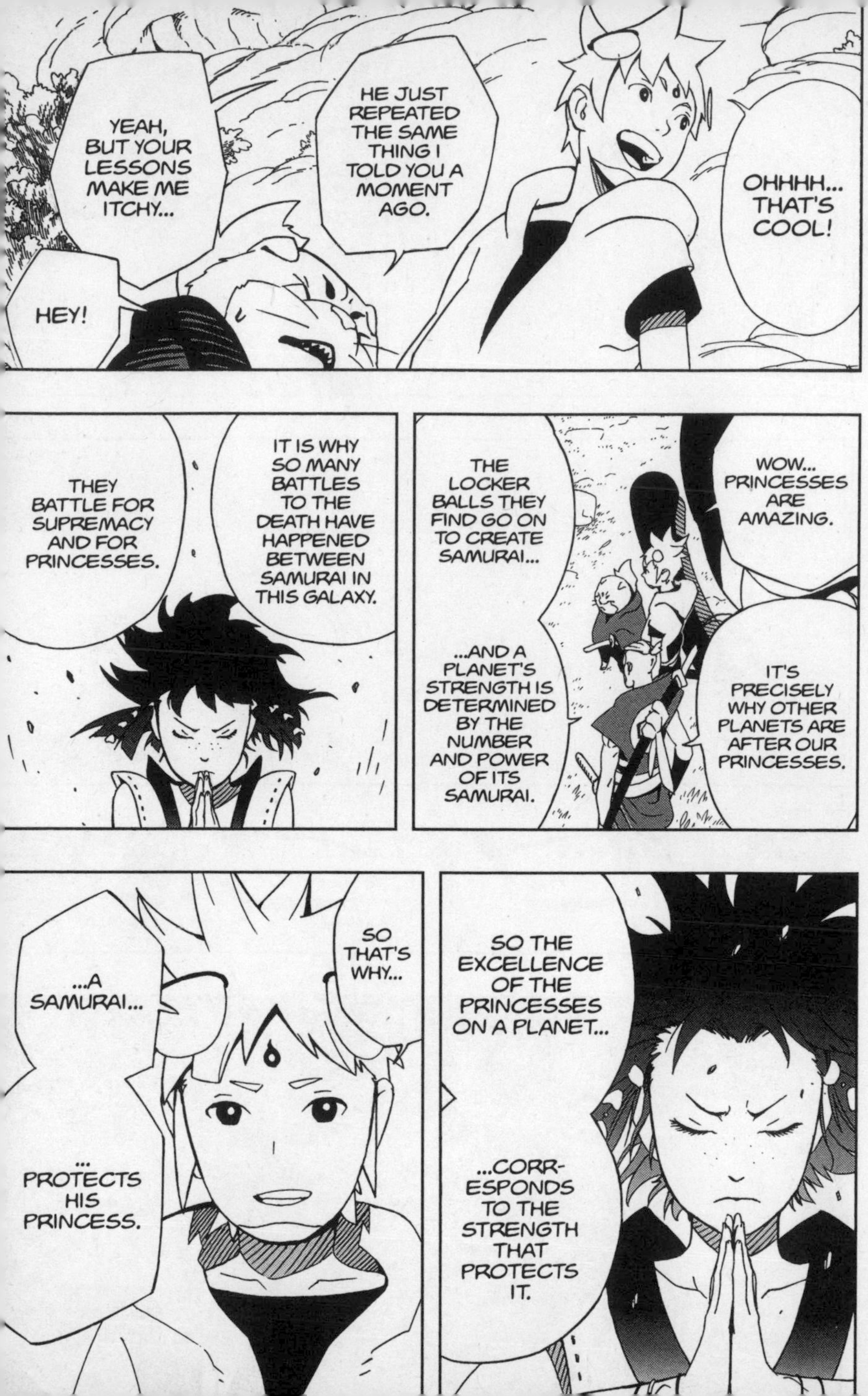
OHHHH... THAT'S COOL!
HE JUST REPEATED THE SAME THING I TOLD YOU A MOMENT AGO.
YEAH, BUT YOUR LESSONS MAKE ME ITCHY...
HEY!
WOW... PRINCESSES ARE AMAZING.
IT'S PRECISELY WHY OTHER PLANETS ARE AFTER OUR PRINCESSES.
THE LOCKER BALLS THEY FIND GO ON TO CREATE SAMURAI...
...AND A PLANET'S STRENGTH IS DETERMINED BY THE NUMBER AND POWER OF ITS SAMURAI.
IT IS WHY SO MANY BATTLES TO THE DEATH HAVE HAPPENED BETWEEN SAMURAI IN THIS GALAXY.
THEY BATTLE FOR SUPREMACY AND FOR PRINCESSES.
SO THE EXCELLENCE OF THE PRINCESSES ON A PLANET...
...CORR-ESPONDS TO THE STRENGTH THAT PROTECTS IT.
SO THAT'S WHY...
...A SAMURAI...
...PROTECTS HIS PRINCESS.

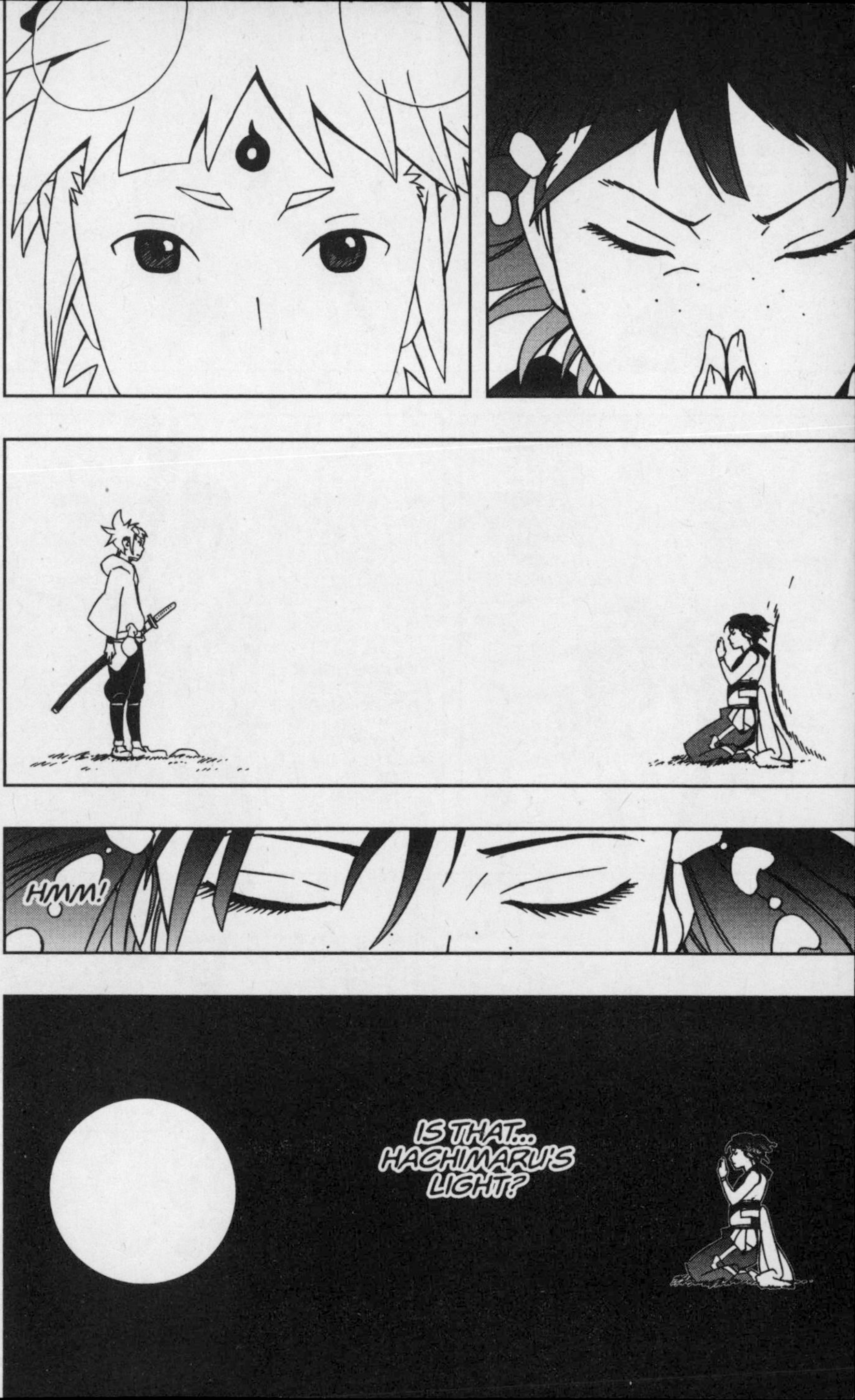
HMM!
IS THAT... HACHIMARU'S LIGHT?

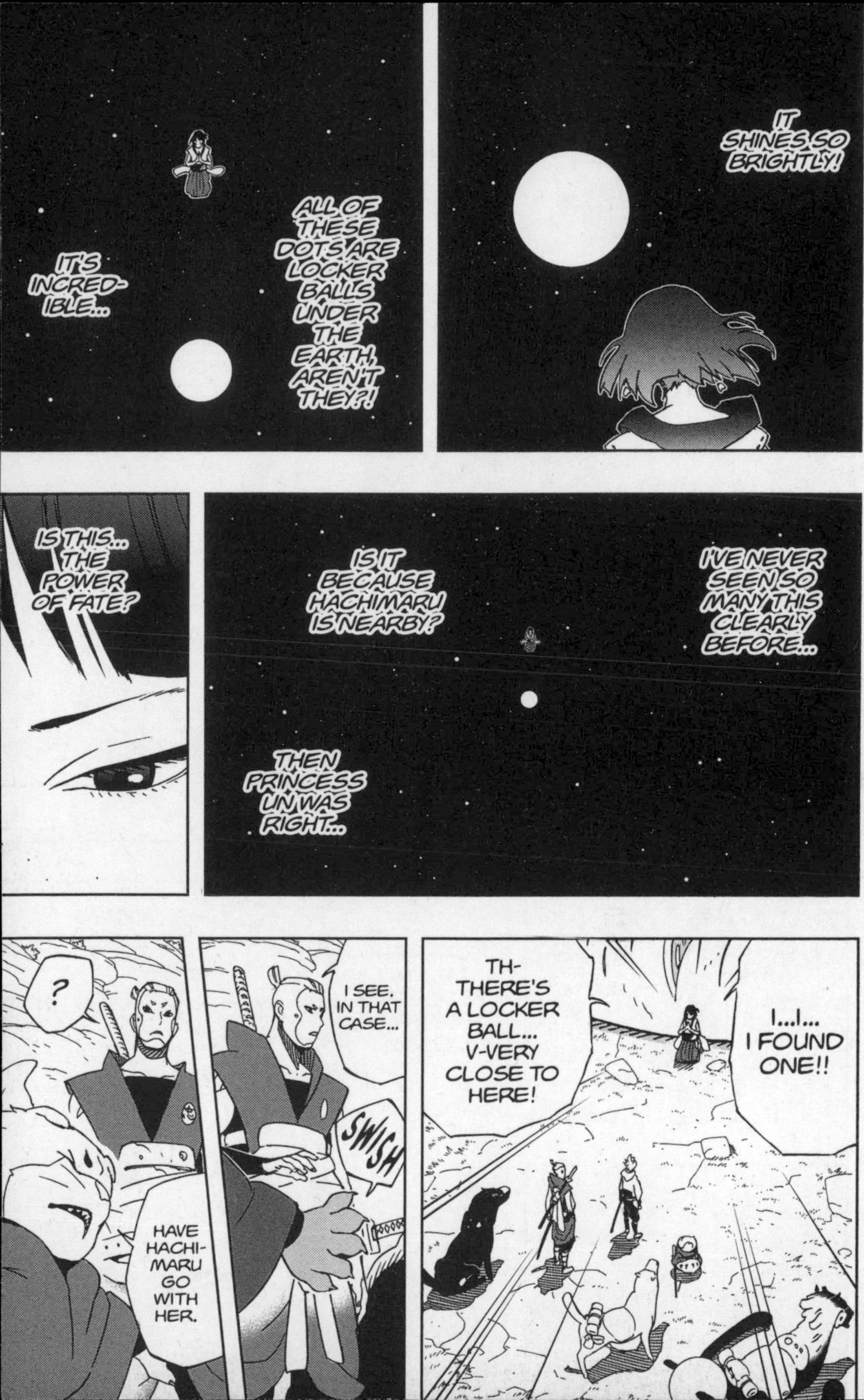
IT SHINES SO BRIGHTLY!
ALL OF THESE DOTS ARE LOCKER BALLS UNDER THE EARTH, AREN'T THEY?!
IT'S INCREDIBLE...
I'VE NEVER SEEN SO MANY THIS CLEARLY BEFORE...
IS IT BECAUSE HACHIMARU IS NEARBY?
THEN PRINCESS UN WAS RIGHT...
IS THIS... THE POWER OF FATE?
I...I... I FOUND ONE!!
TH-THERE'S A LOCKER BALL... V-VERY CLOSE TO HERE!
I SEE. IN THAT CASE...
SWISH
HAVE HACHIMARU GO WITH HER.
?

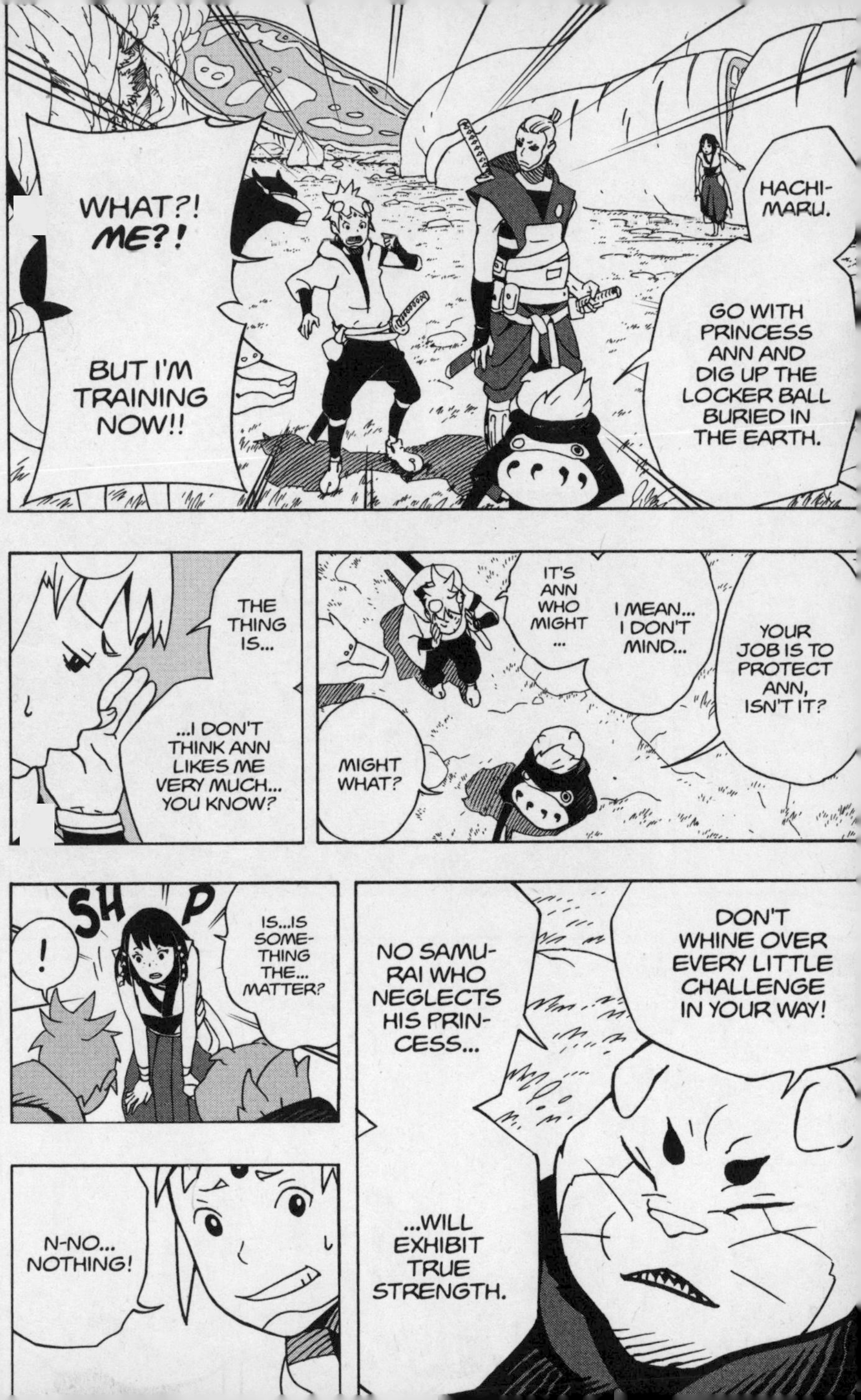
HACHI-MARU.
GO WITH PRINCESS ANN AND DIG UP THE LOCKER BALL BURIED IN THE EARTH.
WHAT?! ME?!
BUT I'M TRAINING NOW!!
YOUR JOB IS TO PROTECT ANN, ISN'T IT?
I MEAN... I DON'T MIND...
IT'S ANN WHO MIGHT ...
MIGHT WHAT?
THE THING IS...
...I DON'T THINK ANN LIKES ME VERY MUCH... YOU KNOW?
DON'T WHINE OVER EVERY LITTLE CHALLENGE IN YOUR WAY!
NO SAMURAI WHO NEGLECTS HIS PRINCESS...
...WILL EXHIBIT TRUE STRENGTH.
SH P
!
IS...IS SOMETHING THE... MATTER?
N-NO... NOTHING!

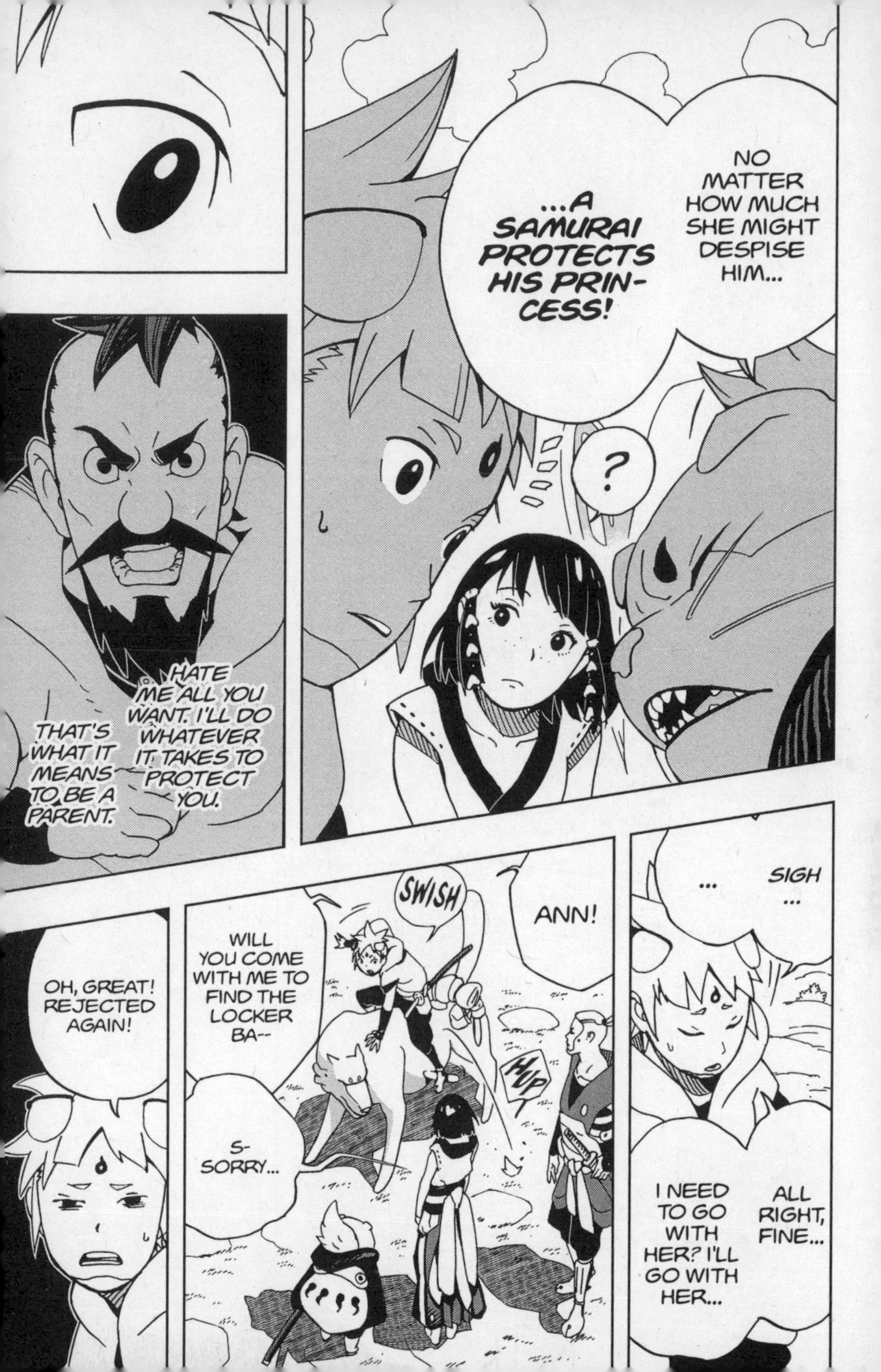
NO MATTER HOW MUCH SHE MIGHT DESPISE HIM...
...A SAMURAI PROTECTS HIS PRIN-CESS!
?
HATE ME ALL YOU WANT. I'LL DO WHATEVER IT TAKES TO PROTECT YOU.
THAT'S WHAT IT MEANS TO BE A PARENT.
SIGH...
...
ALL RIGHT, FINE...
I NEED TO GO WITH HER? I'LL GO WITH HER...
ANN!
SWISH
WILL YOU COME WITH ME TO FIND THE LOCKER BA--
HUP
S-SORRY...
OH, GREAT! REJECTED AGAIN!

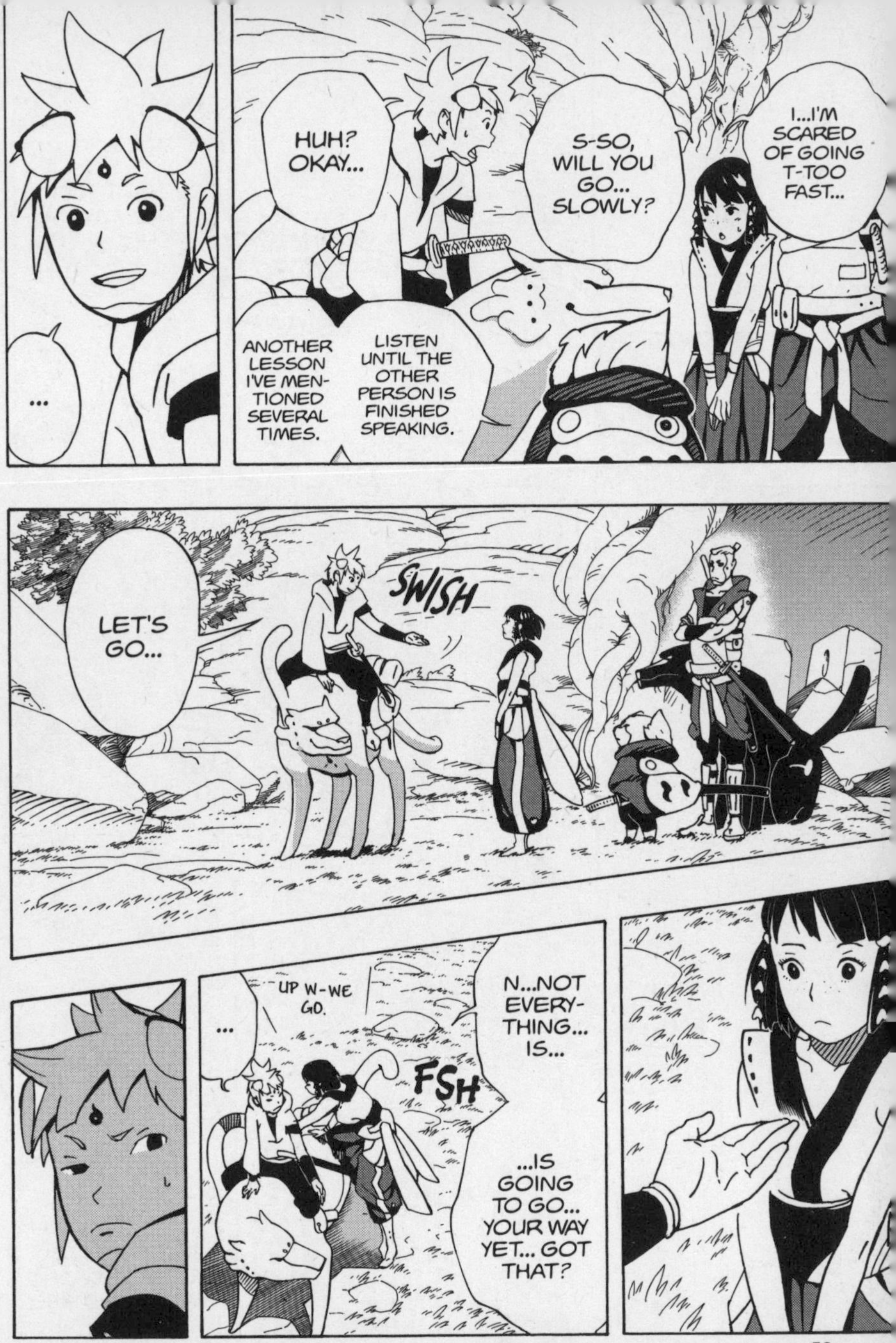
I...I'M SCARED OF GOING T-TOO FAST...
S-SO, WILL YOU GO... SLOWLY?
HUH? OKAY...
LISTEN UNTIL THE OTHER PERSON IS FINISHED SPEAKING.
ANOTHER LESSON I'VE MENTIONED SEVERAL TIMES.
...
SWISH
LET'S GO...
N...NOT EVERYTHING... IS...
...IS GOING TO GO... YOUR WAY YET... GOT THAT?
FSH
UP W-WE GO.
...

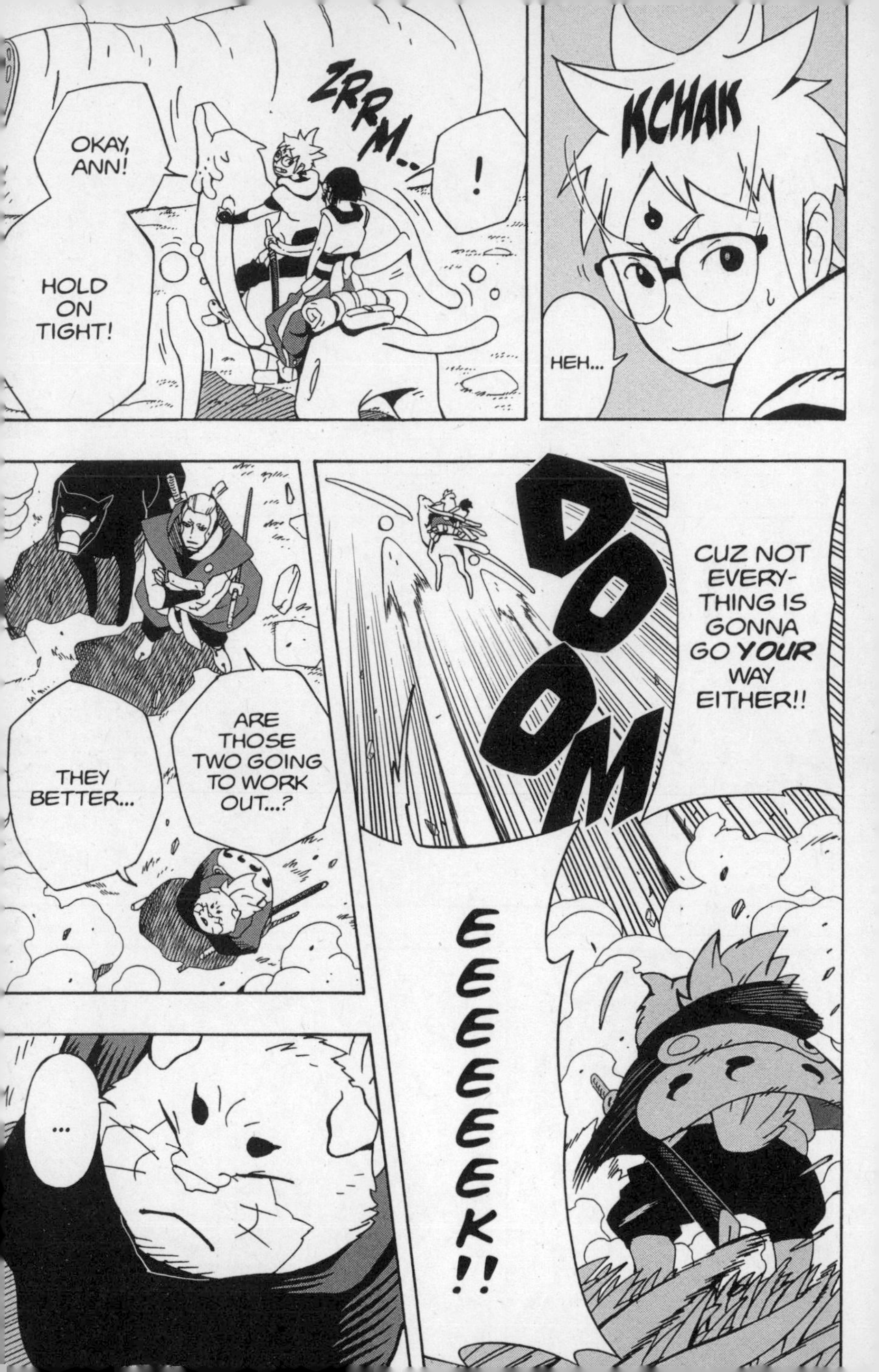
KCHAK
HEH...
!
ZRRM...
OKAY, ANN!
HOLD ON TIGHT!
DOOOM
CUZ NOT EVERYTHING IS GONNA GO **YOUR** WAY EITHER!!
EEEEEEEK!!
ARE THOSE TWO GOING TO WORK OUT...?
THEY BETTER...
...

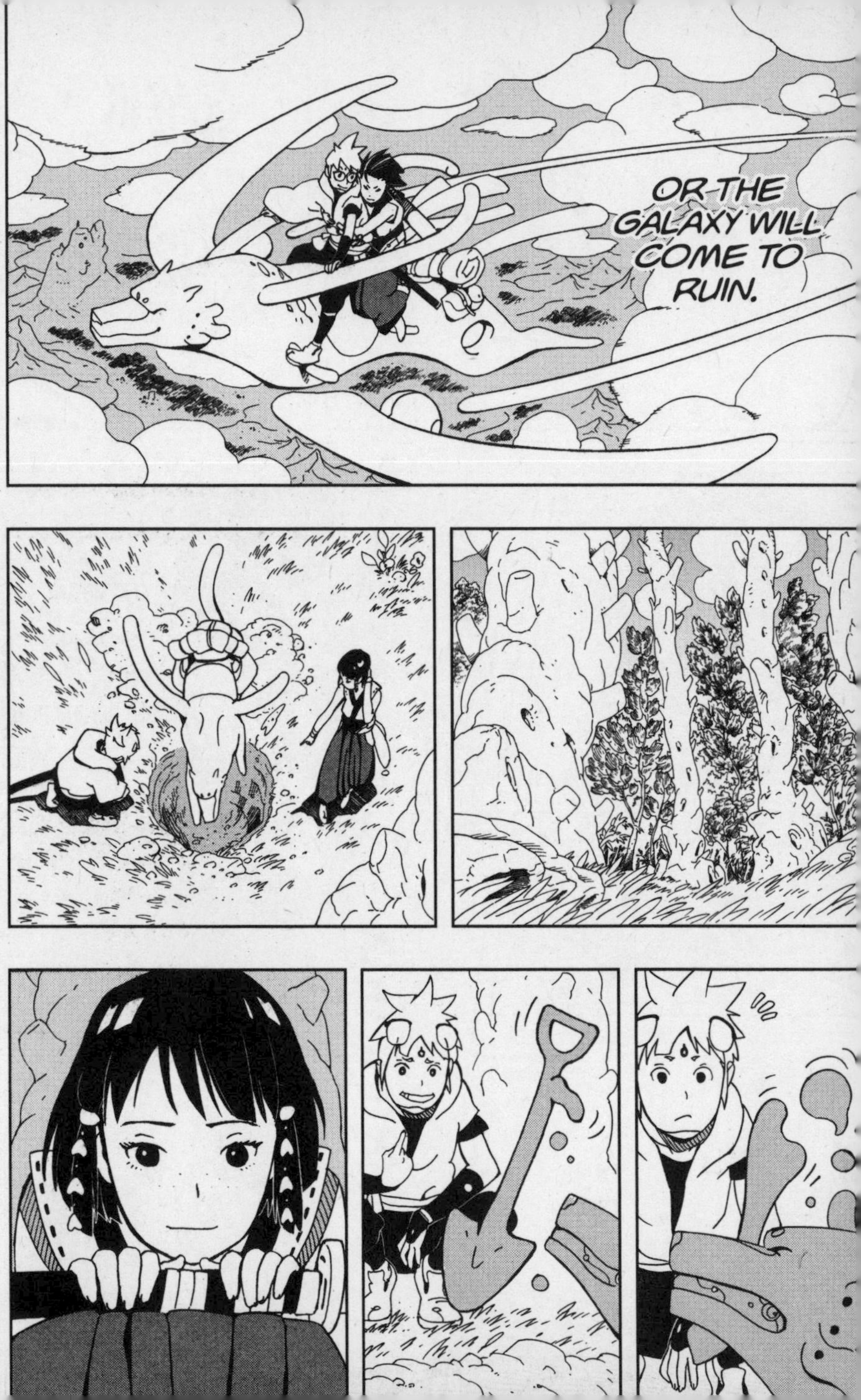
OR THE GALAXY WILL COME TO RUIN.

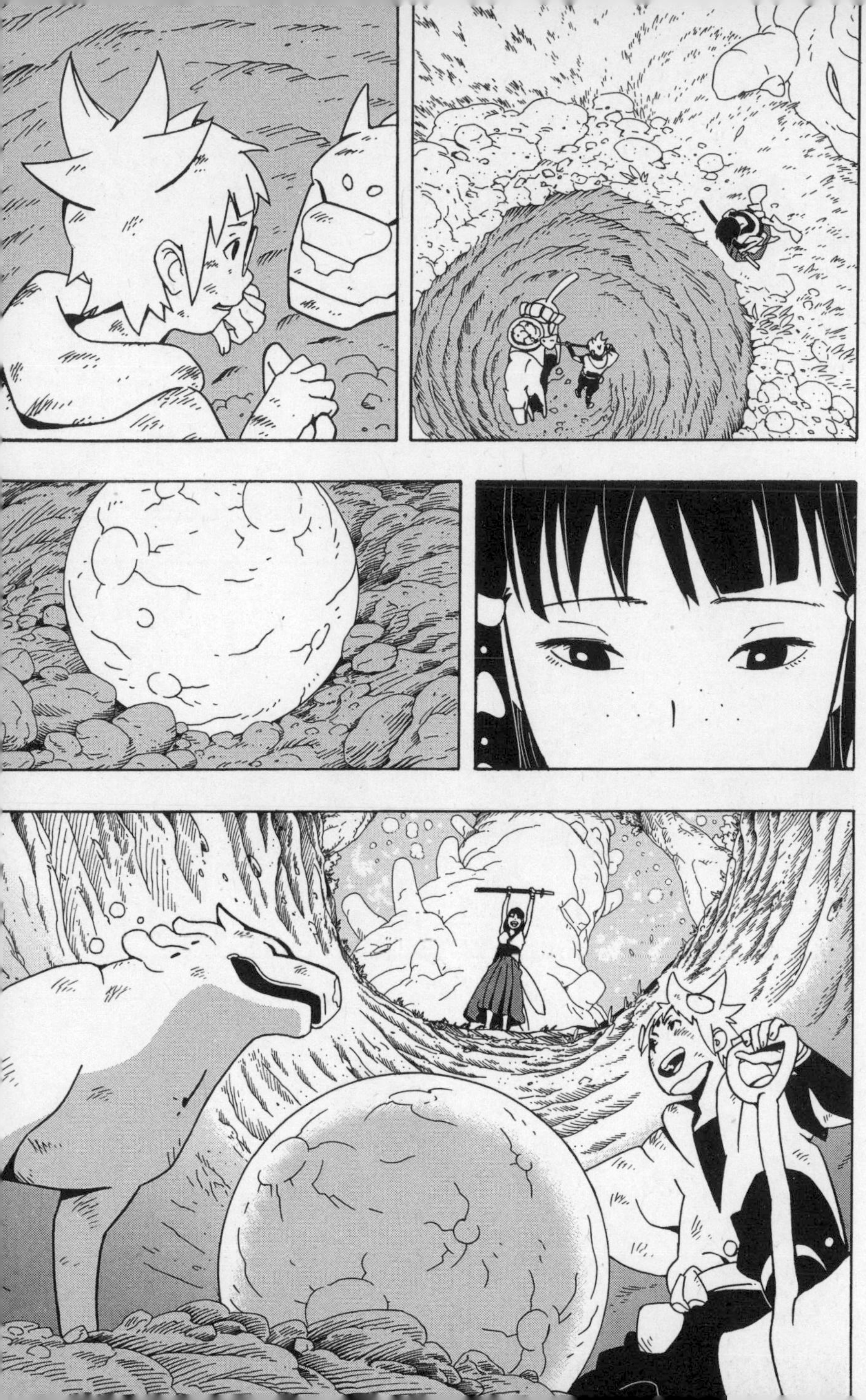

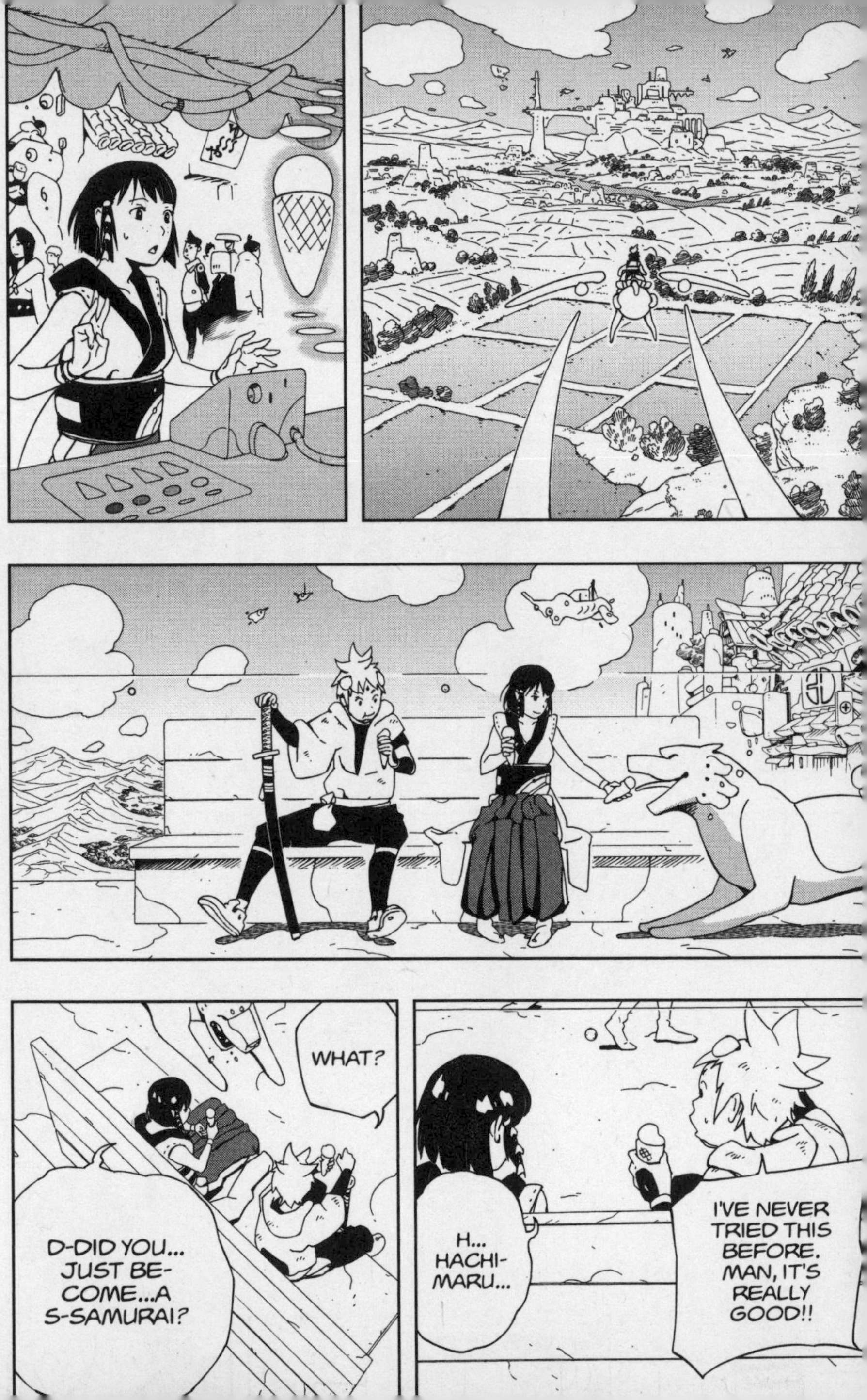
I'VE NEVER TRIED THIS BEFORE. MAN, IT'S REALLY GOOD!!
H... HACHI-MARU...
WHAT?
D-DID YOU... JUST BE-COME...A S-SAMURAI?

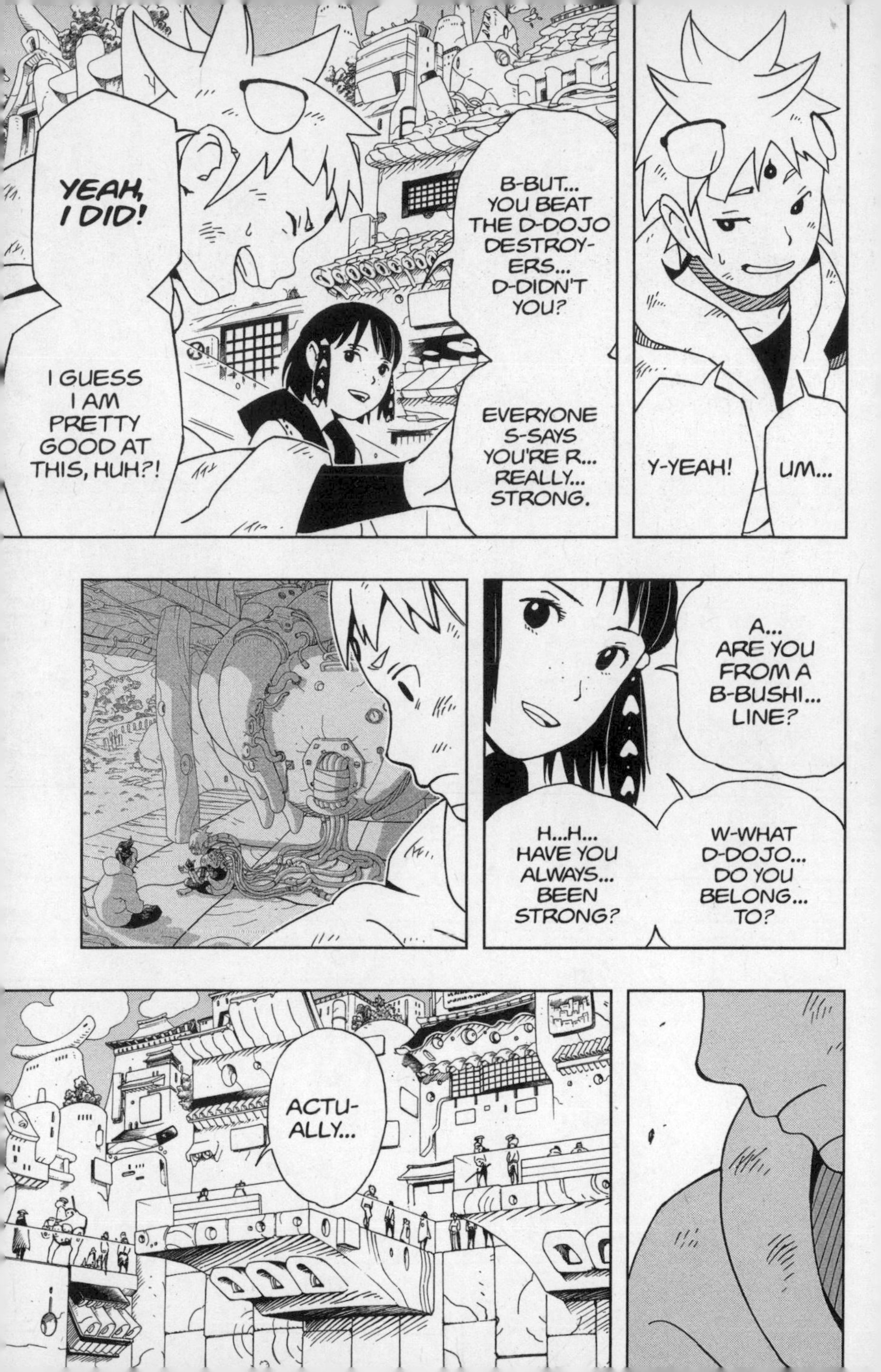
UM...
Y-YEAH!
B-BUT... YOU BEAT THE D-DOJO DESTROY-ERS... D-DIDN'T YOU?
EVERYONE S-SAYS YOU'RE R... REALLY... STRONG.
YEAH, I DID!
I GUESS I AM PRETTY GOOD AT THIS, HUH?!
A... ARE YOU FROM A B-BUSHI... LINE?
W-WHAT D-DOJO... DO YOU BELONG... TO?
H...H... HAVE YOU ALWAYS... BEEN STRONG?
ACTU-ALLY...

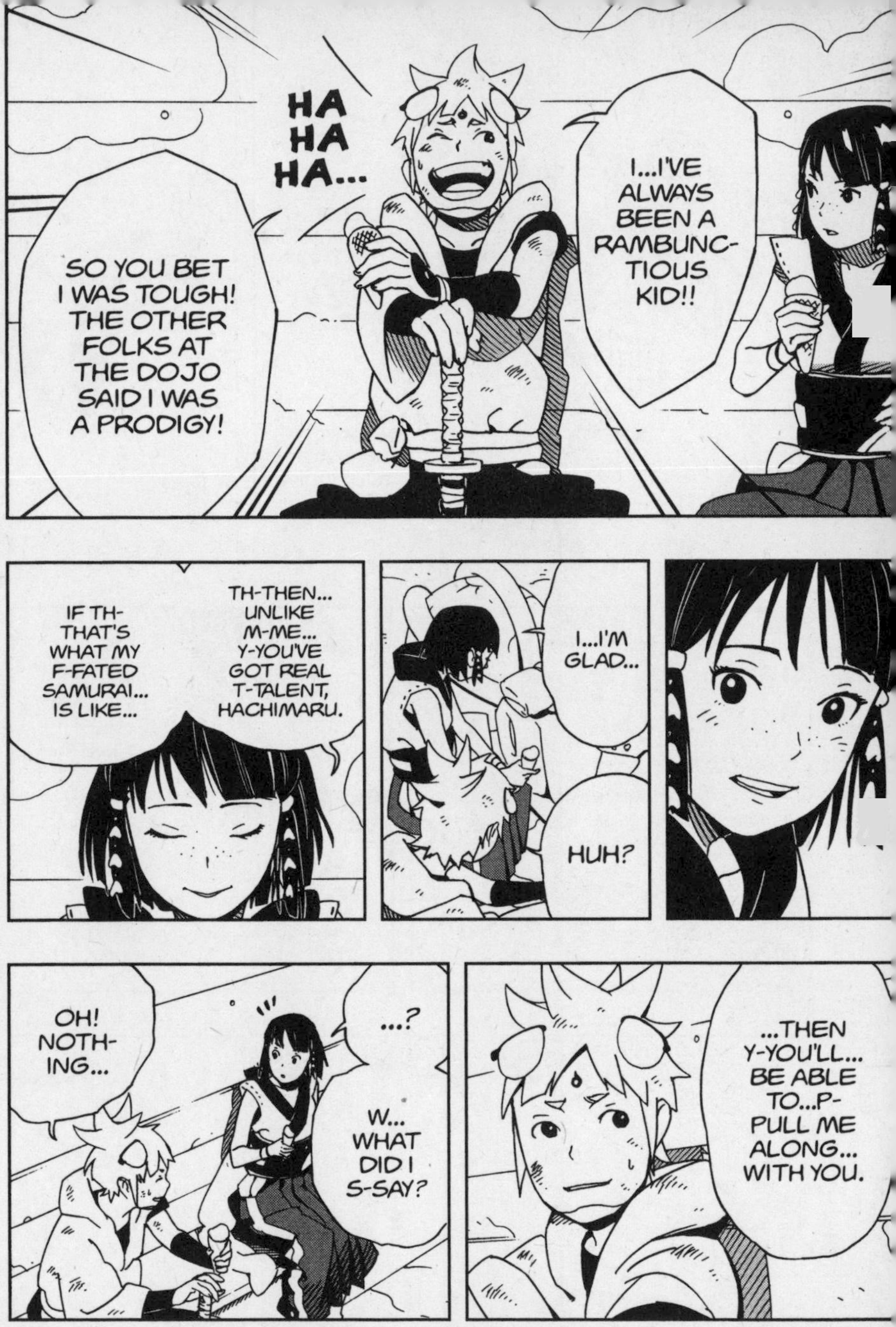
I...I'VE ALWAYS BEEN A RAMBUNC-TIOUS KID!!
HA HA HA...
SO YOU BET I WAS TOUGH! THE OTHER FOLKS AT THE DOJO SAID I WAS A PRODIGY!
I...I'M GLAD...
HUH?
TH-THEN... UNLIKE M-ME... Y-YOU'VE GOT REAL T-TALENT, HACHIMARU.
IF TH-THAT'S WHAT MY F-FATED SAMURAI... IS LIKE...
...THEN Y-YOU'LL... BE ABLE TO...P-PULL ME ALONG... WITH YOU.
...?
W... WHAT DID I S-SAY?
OH! NOTH-ING...

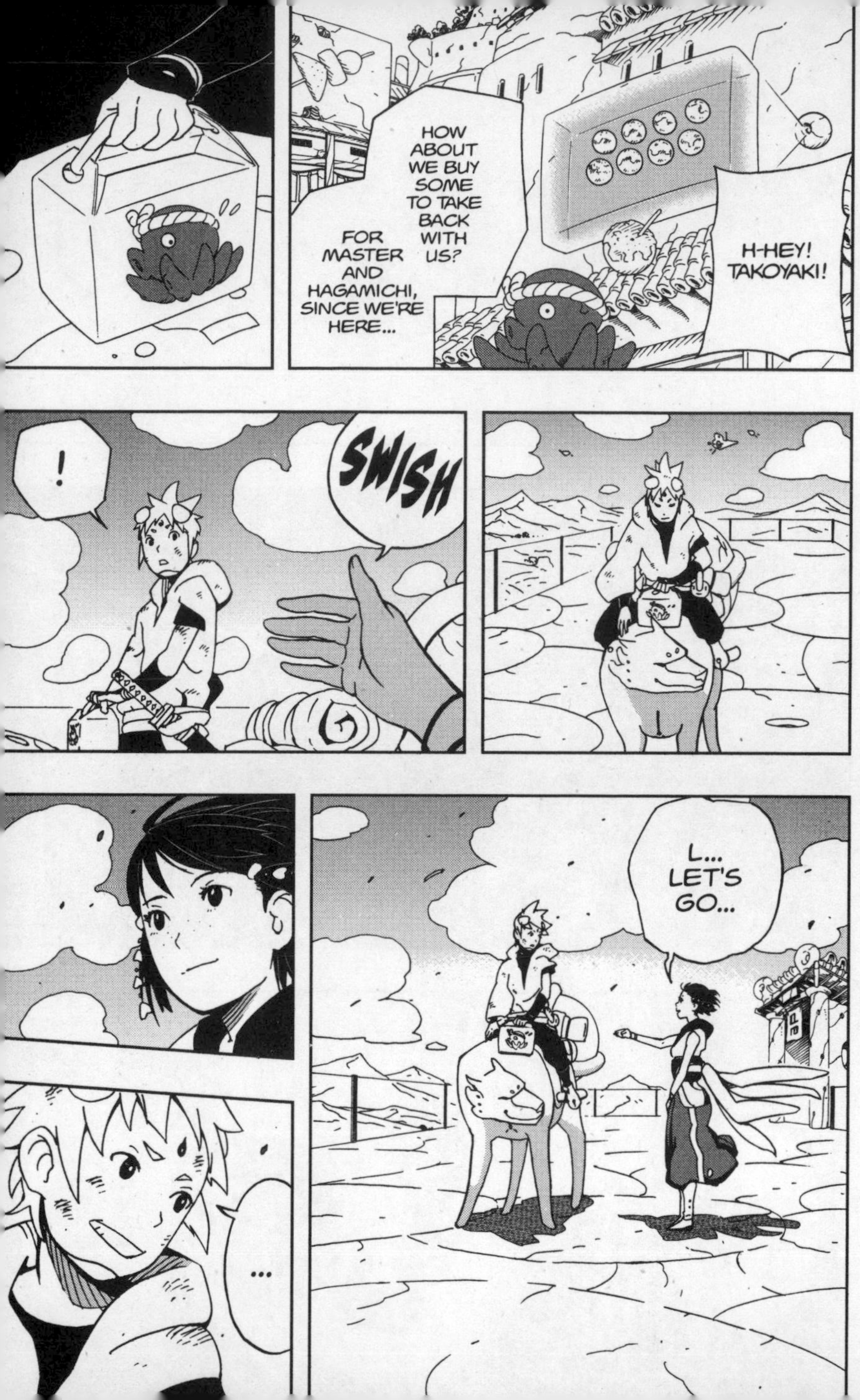
H-HEY! TAKOYAKI!
HOW ABOUT WE BUY SOME TO TAKE BACK WITH US?
FOR MASTER AND HAGAMICHI, SINCE WE'RE HERE...
SWISH
!
L... LET'S GO...
...

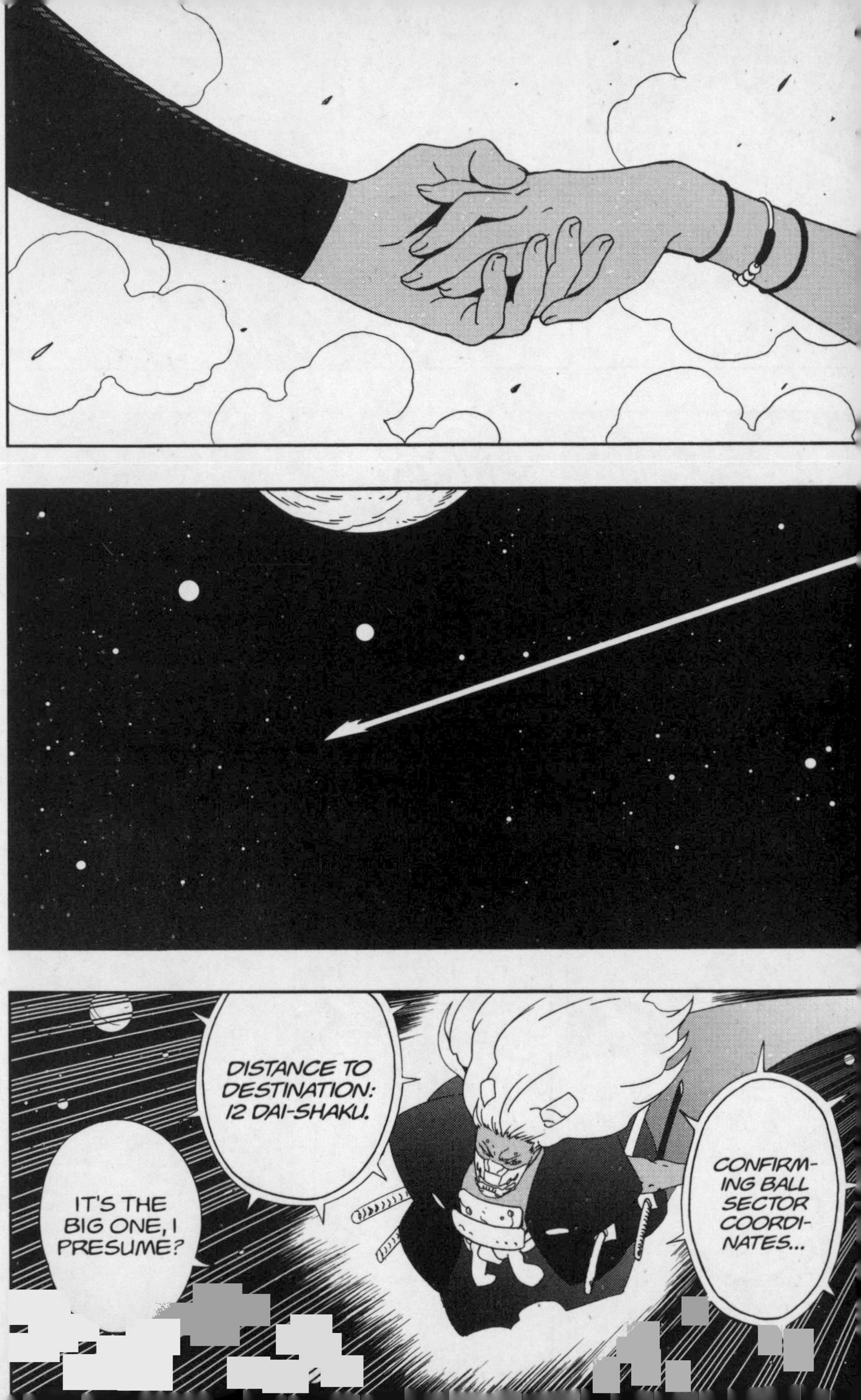
CONFIRMING BALL SECTOR COORDINATES...
DISTANCE TO DESTINATION: 12 DAI-SHAKU.
IT'S THE BIG ONE, I PRESUME?

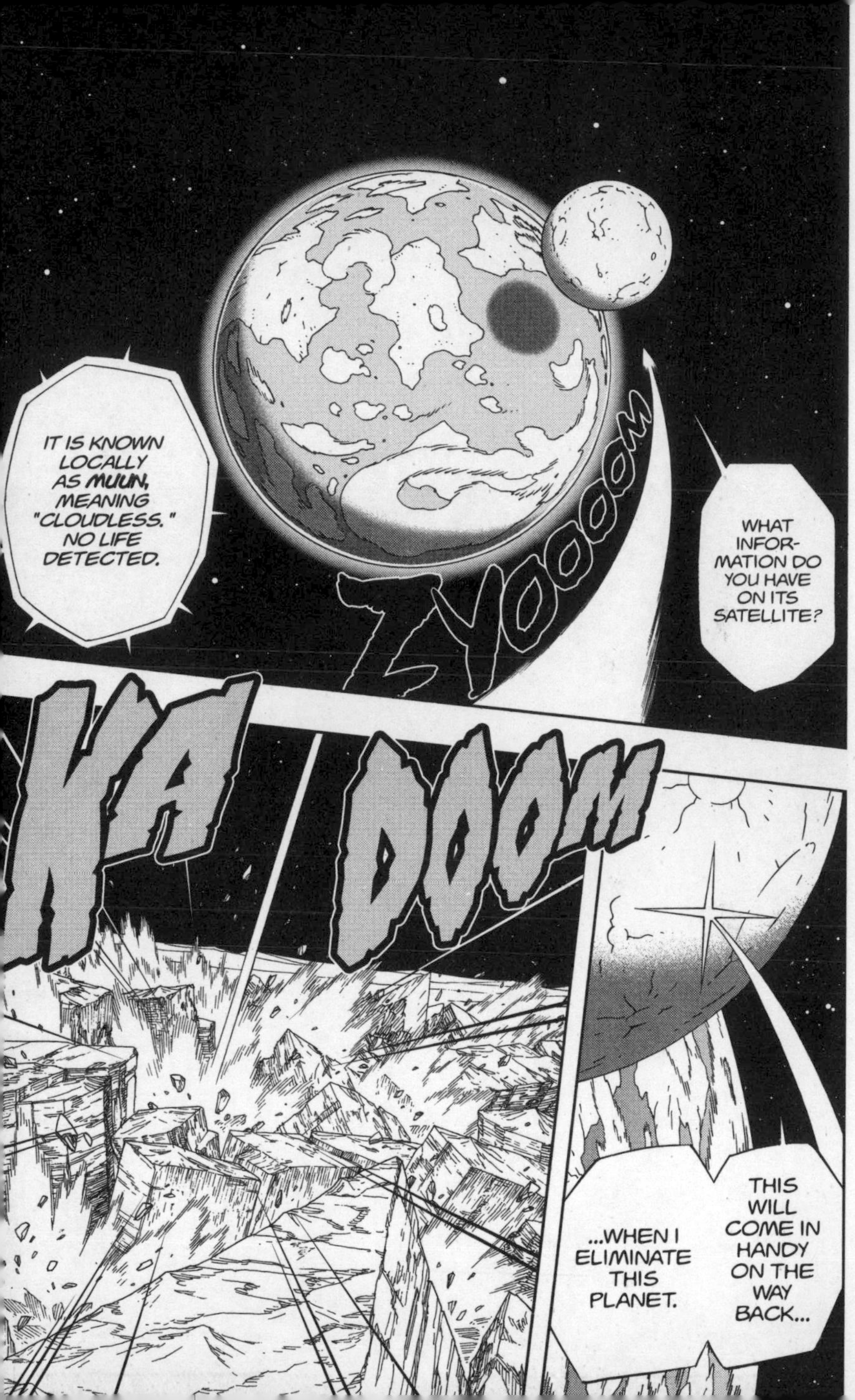
IT IS KNOWN LOCALLY AS **MUUN,** MEANING "CLOUDLESS." NO LIFE DETECTED.
WHAT INFOR-MATION DO YOU HAVE ON ITS SATELLITE?
ZYOOOOM
KA DOOM
THIS WILL COME IN HANDY ON THE WAY BACK...
...WHEN I ELIMINATE THIS PLANET.

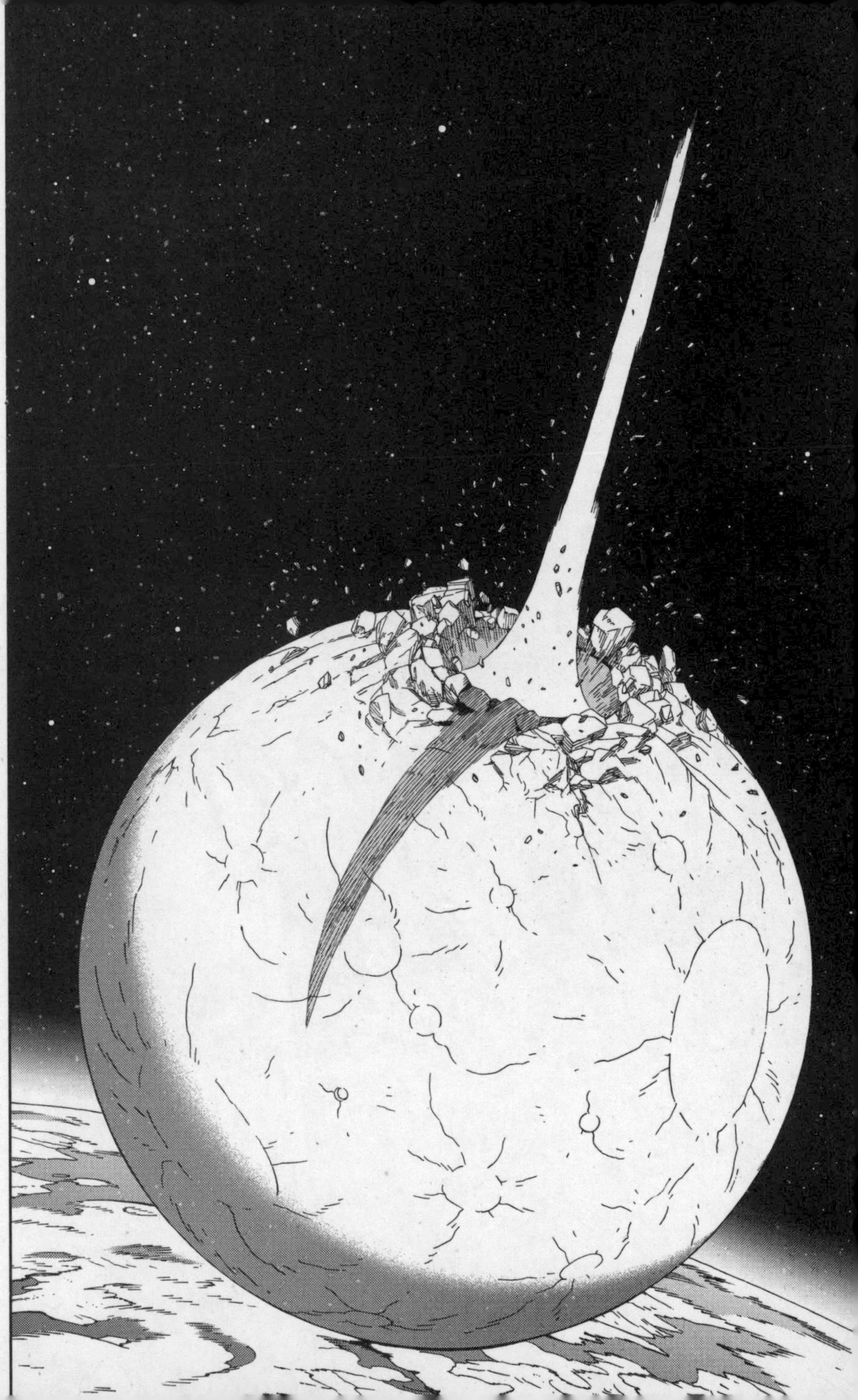

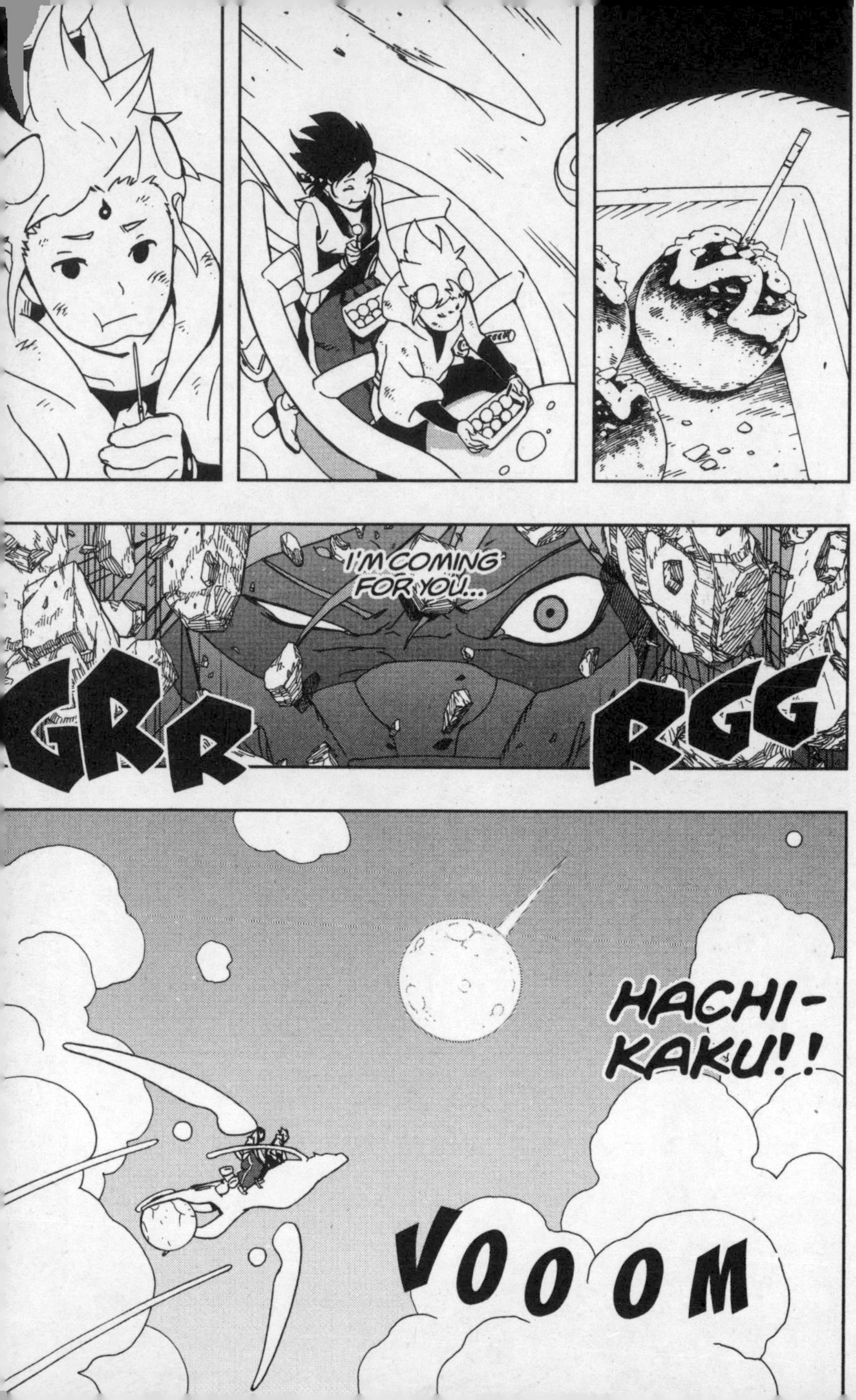
I'M COMING FOR YOU...
GRR
RGG
HACHI-KAKU!!
VOOOM

CHAPTER 10: TARGET ACQUIRED

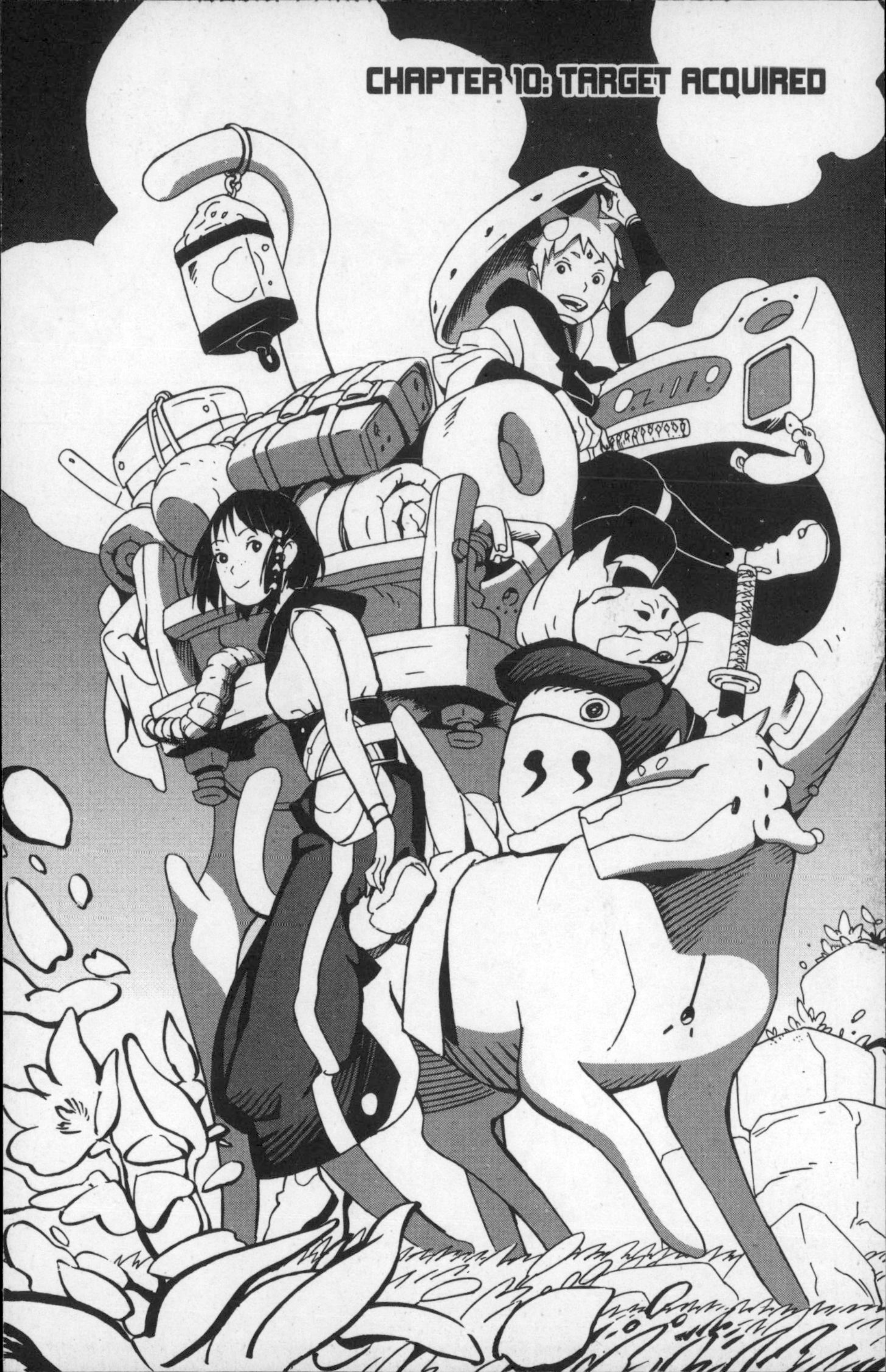

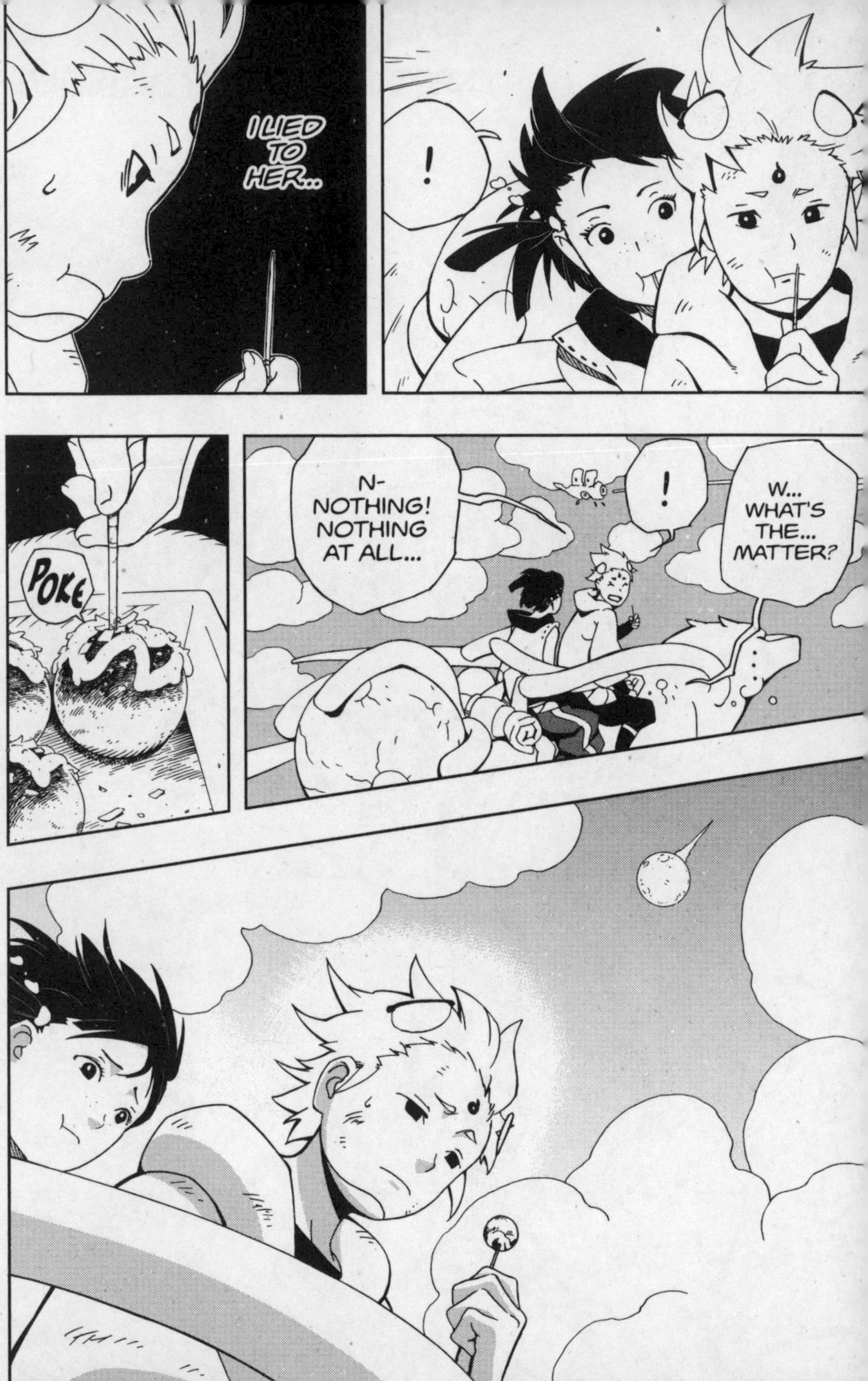
!
I LIED TO HER...
W... WHAT'S THE... MATTER?
!
N- NOTHING! NOTHING AT ALL...
POKE

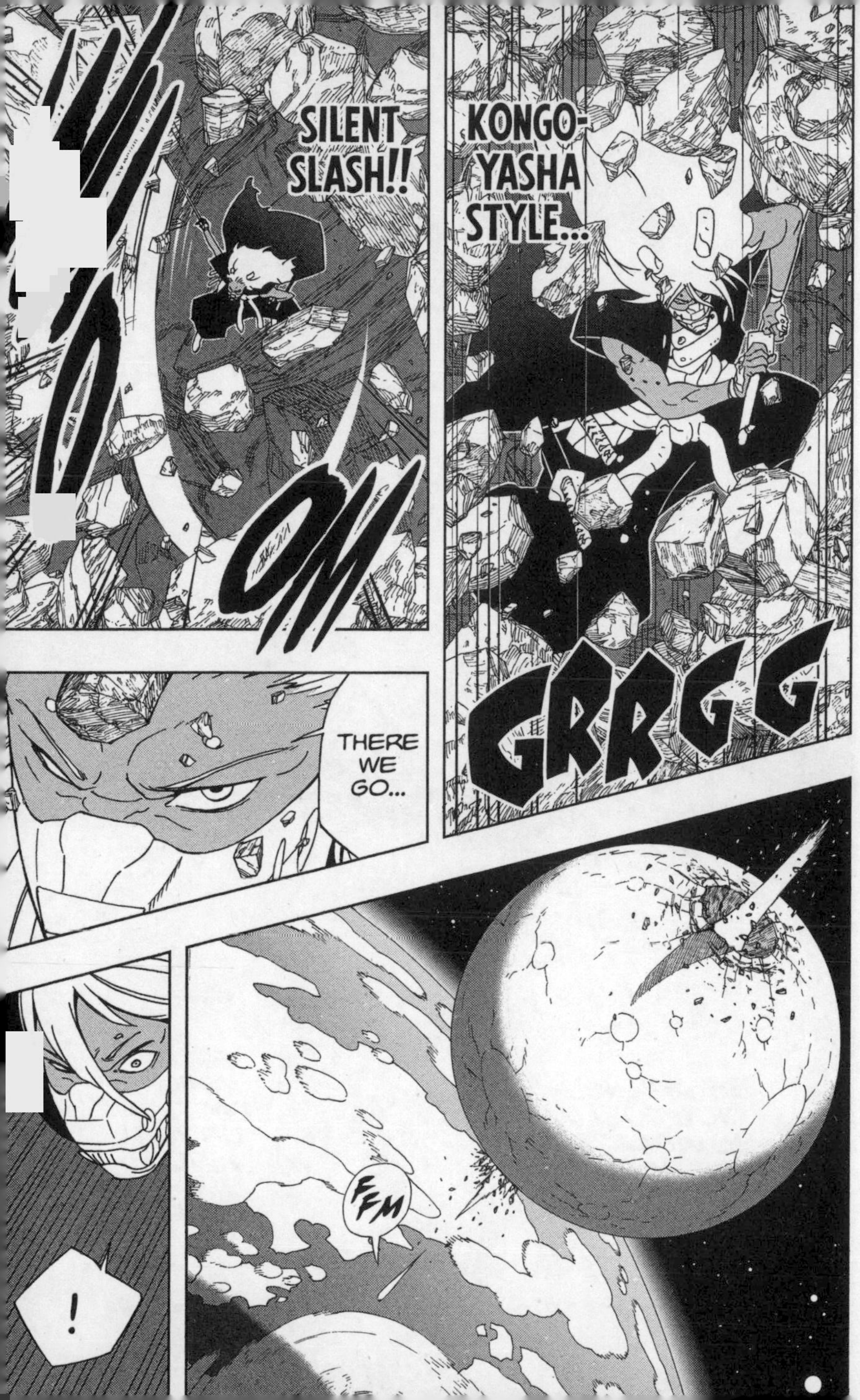
KONGO-YASHA STYLE...
GRRGG
SILENT SLASH!!
OM
THERE WE GO...
FFM
!

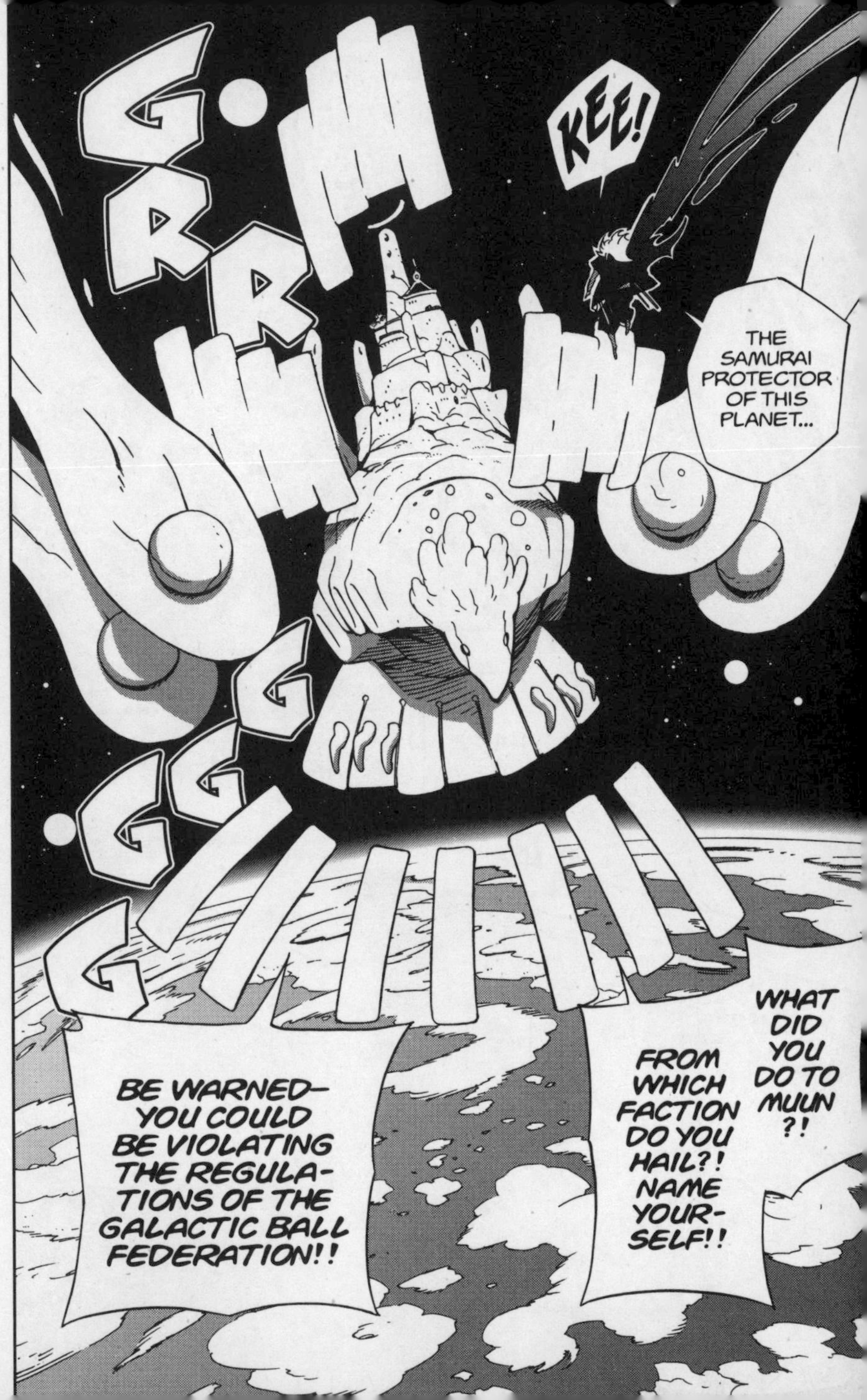
KEE!
THE SAMURAI PROTECTOR OF THIS PLANET...
WHAT DID YOU DO TO MUUN?!
FROM WHICH FACTION DO YOU HAIL?! NAME YOURSELF!!
BE WARNED- YOU COULD BE VIOLATING THE REGULATIONS OF THE GALACTIC BALL FEDERATION!!

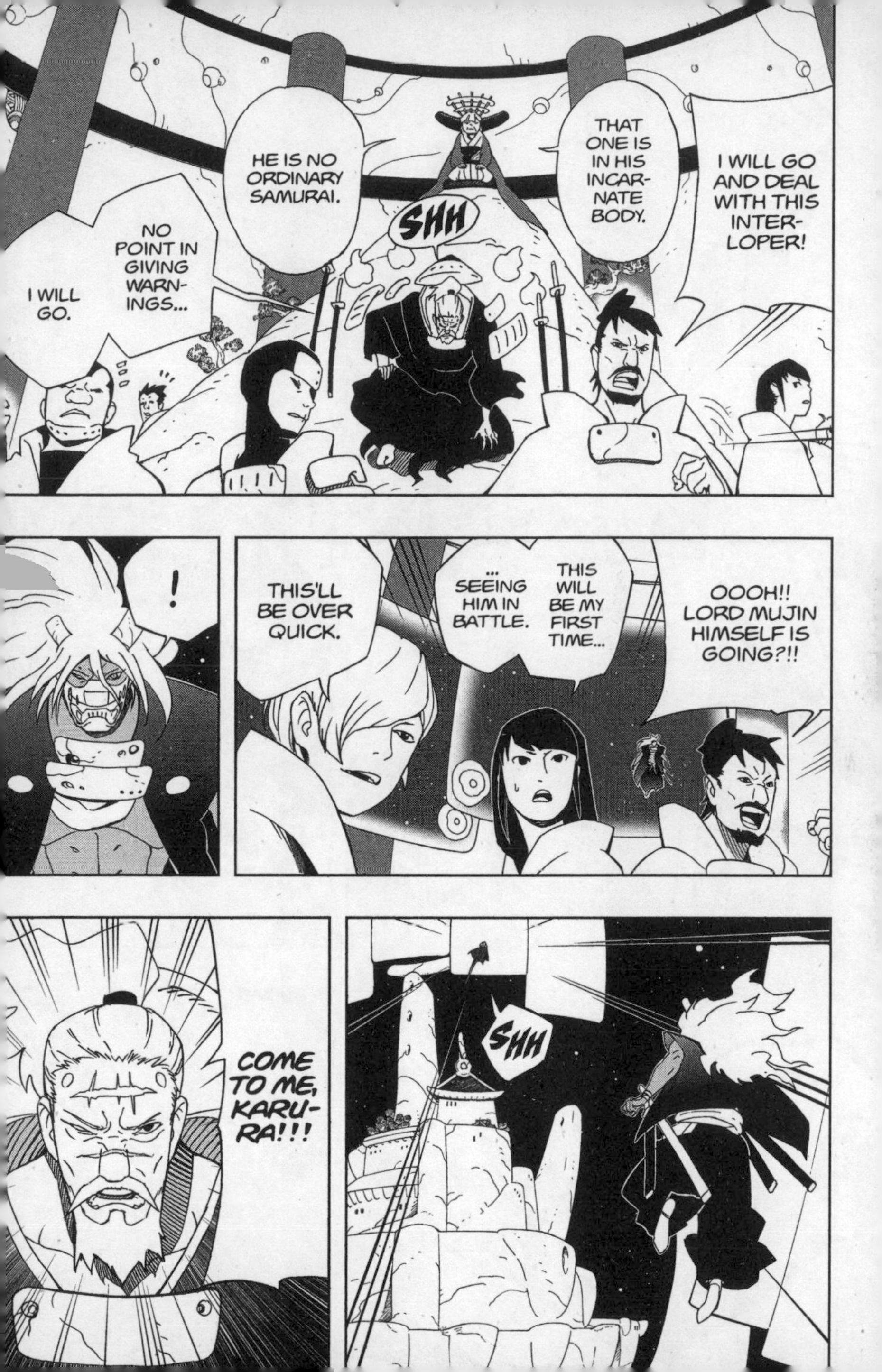
I WILL GO AND DEAL WITH THIS INTERLOPER!
THAT ONE IS IN HIS INCARNATE BODY.
SHH
HE IS NO ORDINARY SAMURAI.
NO POINT IN GIVING WARNINGS...
I WILL GO.
OOOH!! LORD MUJIN HIMSELF IS GOING?!!
THIS WILL BE MY FIRST TIME...
... SEEING HIM IN BATTLE.
THIS'LL BE OVER QUICK.
!
SHH
COME TO ME, KARURA!!!

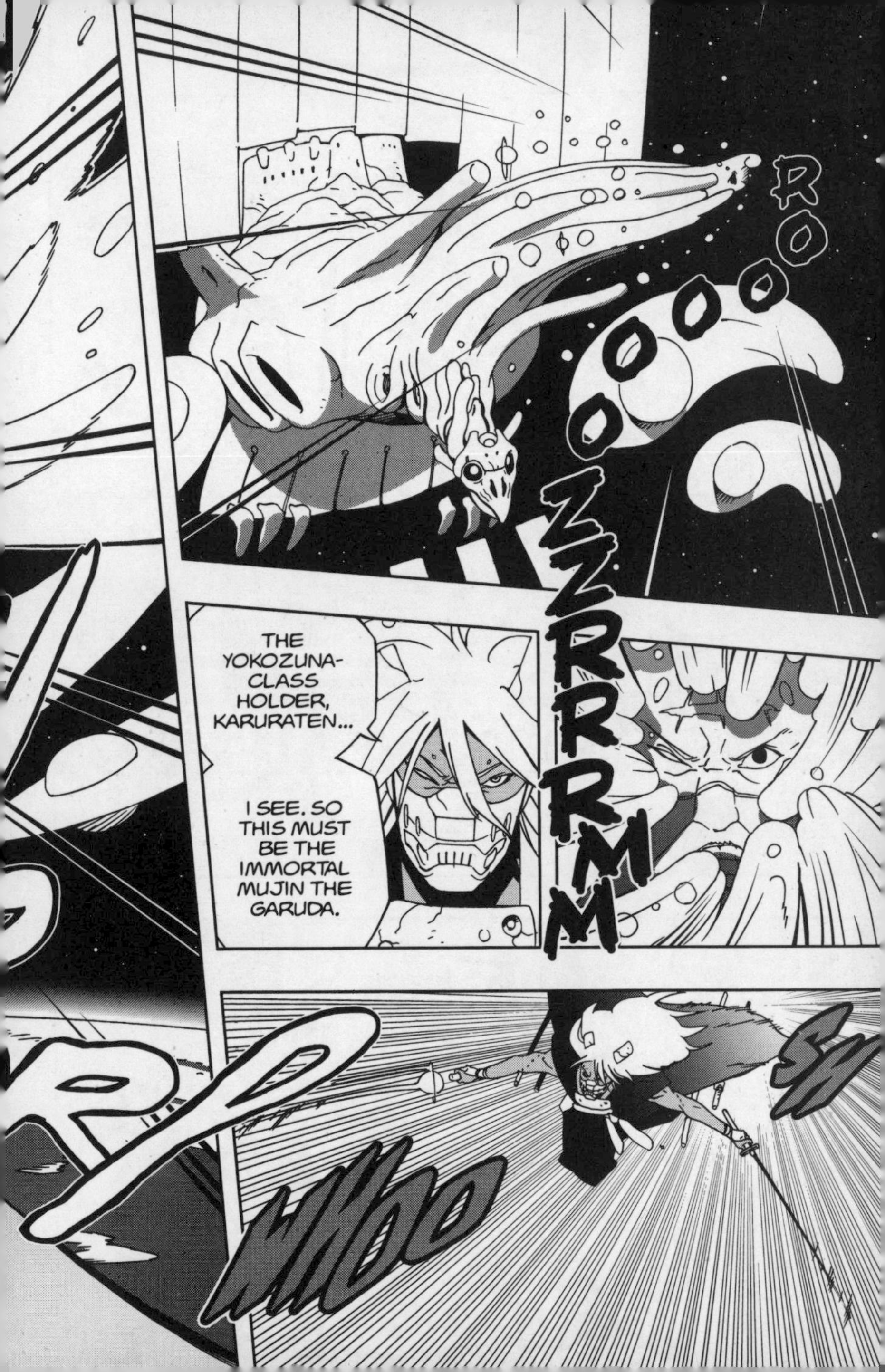
ROOOOOOZZRRRMM
THE YOKOZUNA-CLASS HOLDER, KARURATEN...
I SEE. SO THIS MUST BE THE IMMORTAL MUJIN THE GARUDA.
SH
WHOO

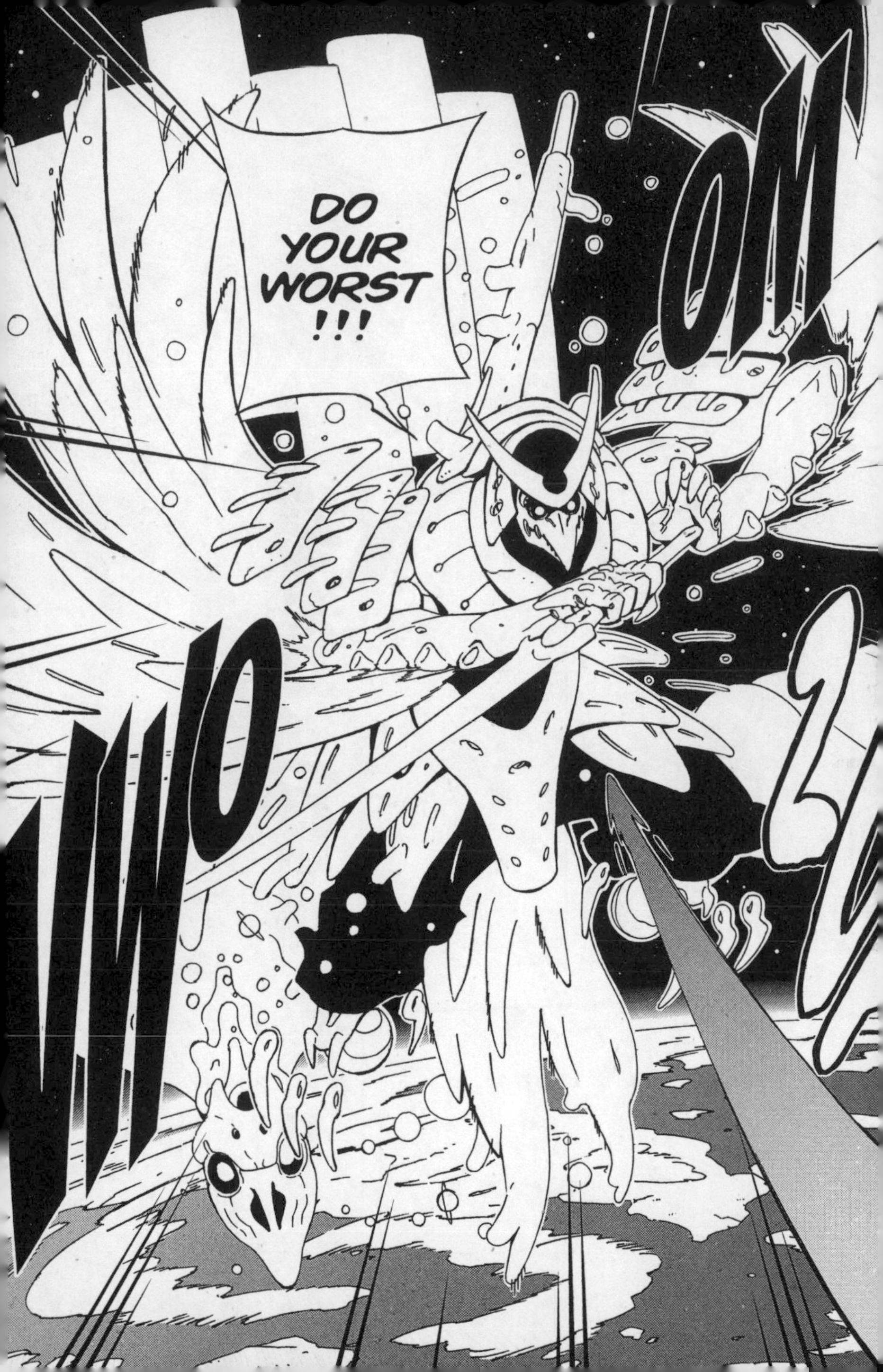
DO YOUR WORST !!!

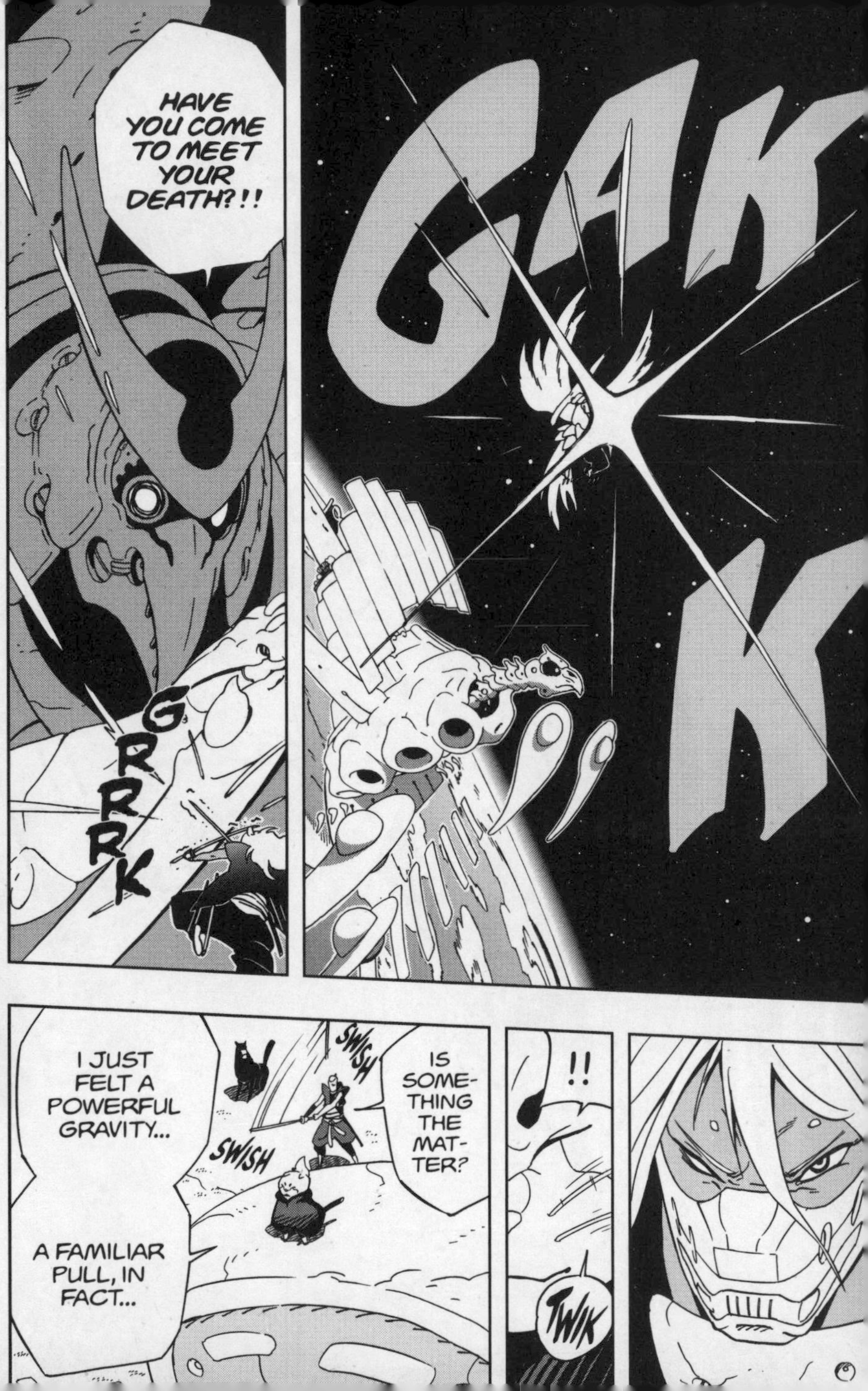
GAKK
HAVE YOU COME TO MEET YOUR DEATH?!!
GRRRK
!!
TWIK
SWISH
IS SOMETHING THE MATTER?
I JUST FELT A POWERFUL GRAVITY...
SWISH
A FAMILIAR PULL, IN FACT...

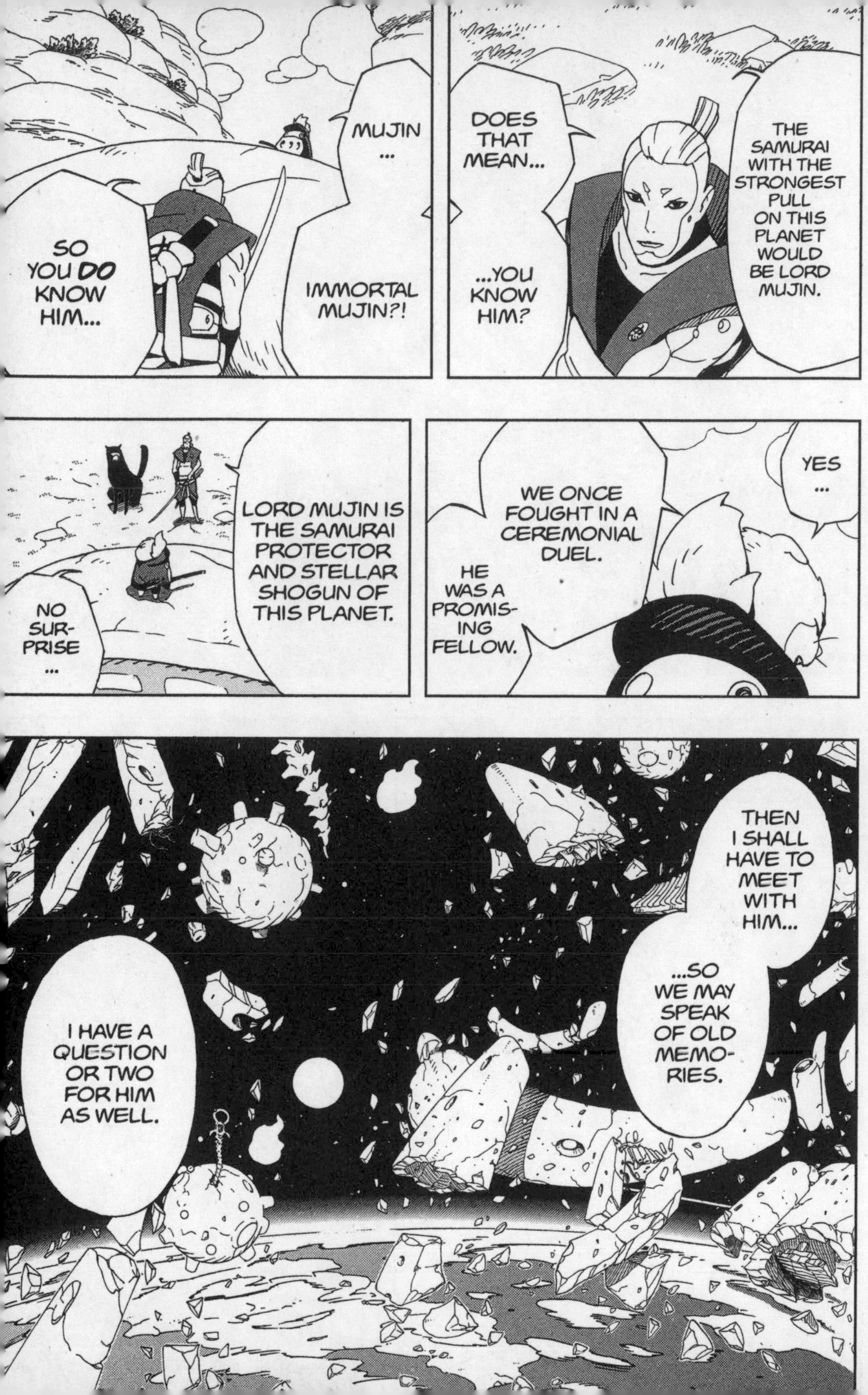
THE SAMURAI WITH THE STRONGEST PULL ON THIS PLANET WOULD BE LORD MUJIN.
DOES THAT MEAN...
...YOU KNOW HIM?
MUJIN ...
IMMORTAL MUJIN?!
SO YOU **DO** KNOW HIM...
YES ...
WE ONCE FOUGHT IN A CEREMONIAL DUEL.
HE WAS A PROMISING FELLOW.
LORD MUJIN IS THE SAMURAI PROTECTOR AND STELLAR SHOGUN OF THIS PLANET.
NO SURPRISE ...
THEN I SHALL HAVE TO MEET WITH HIM...
...SO WE MAY SPEAK OF OLD MEMORIES.
I HAVE A QUESTION OR TWO FOR HIM AS WELL.

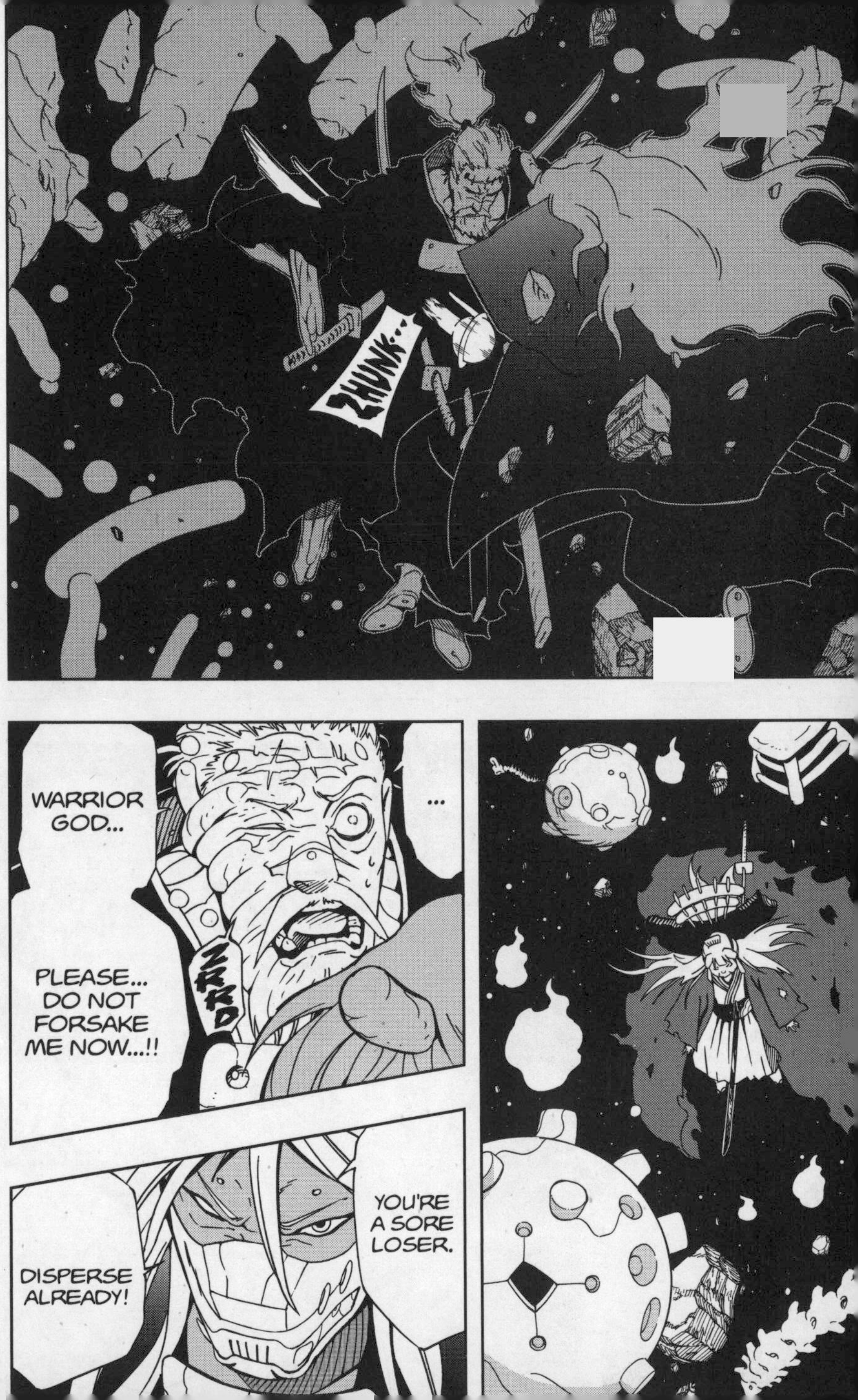
ZHUNK...
...
WARRIOR GOD...
ZRRD
PLEASE... DO NOT FORSAKE ME NOW...!!
YOU'RE A SORE LOSER.
DISPERSE ALREADY!

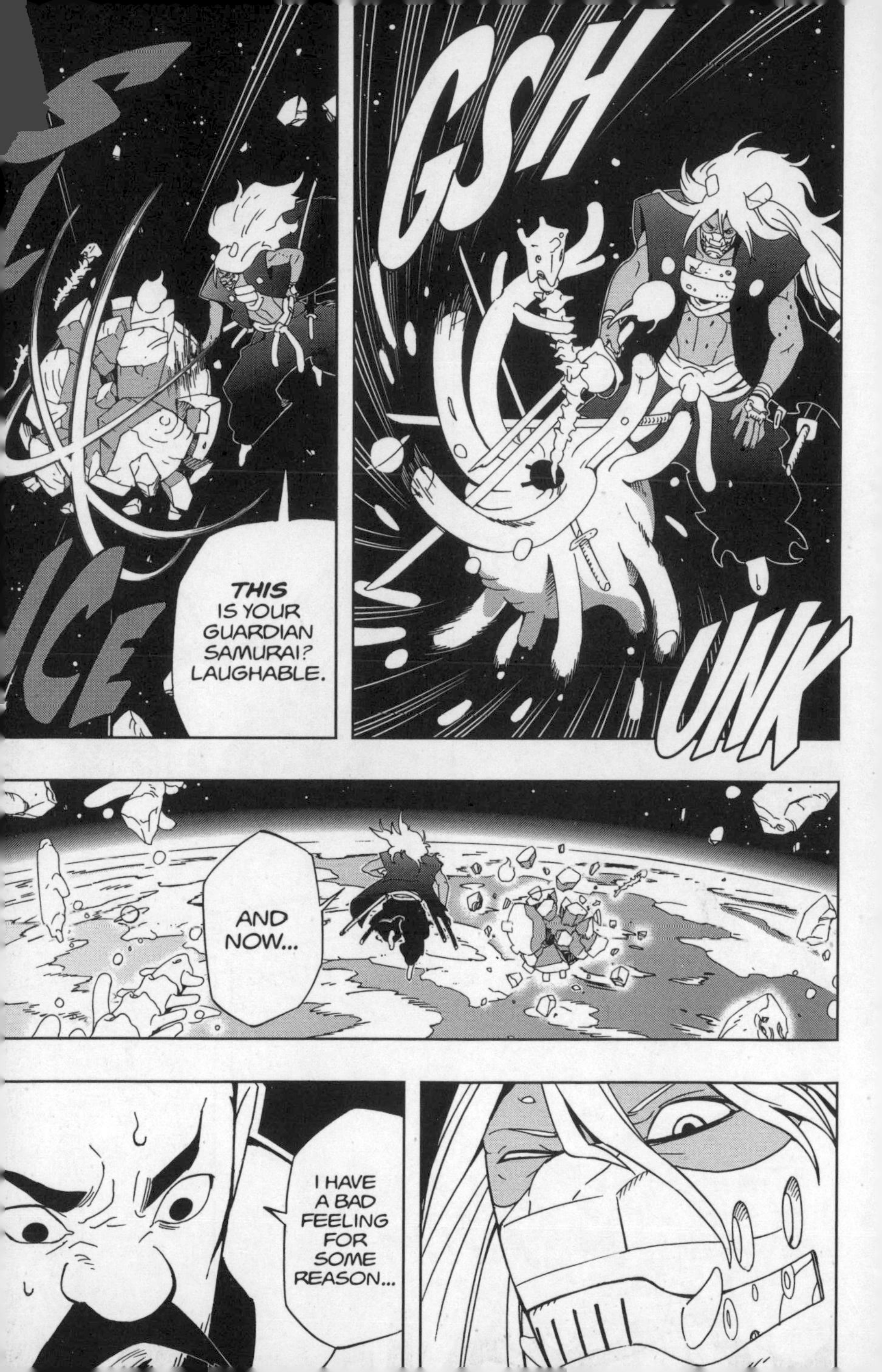
GSH
UNK
THIS IS YOUR GUARDIAN SAMURAI? LAUGHABLE.
AND NOW...
I HAVE A BAD FEELING FOR SOME REASON...

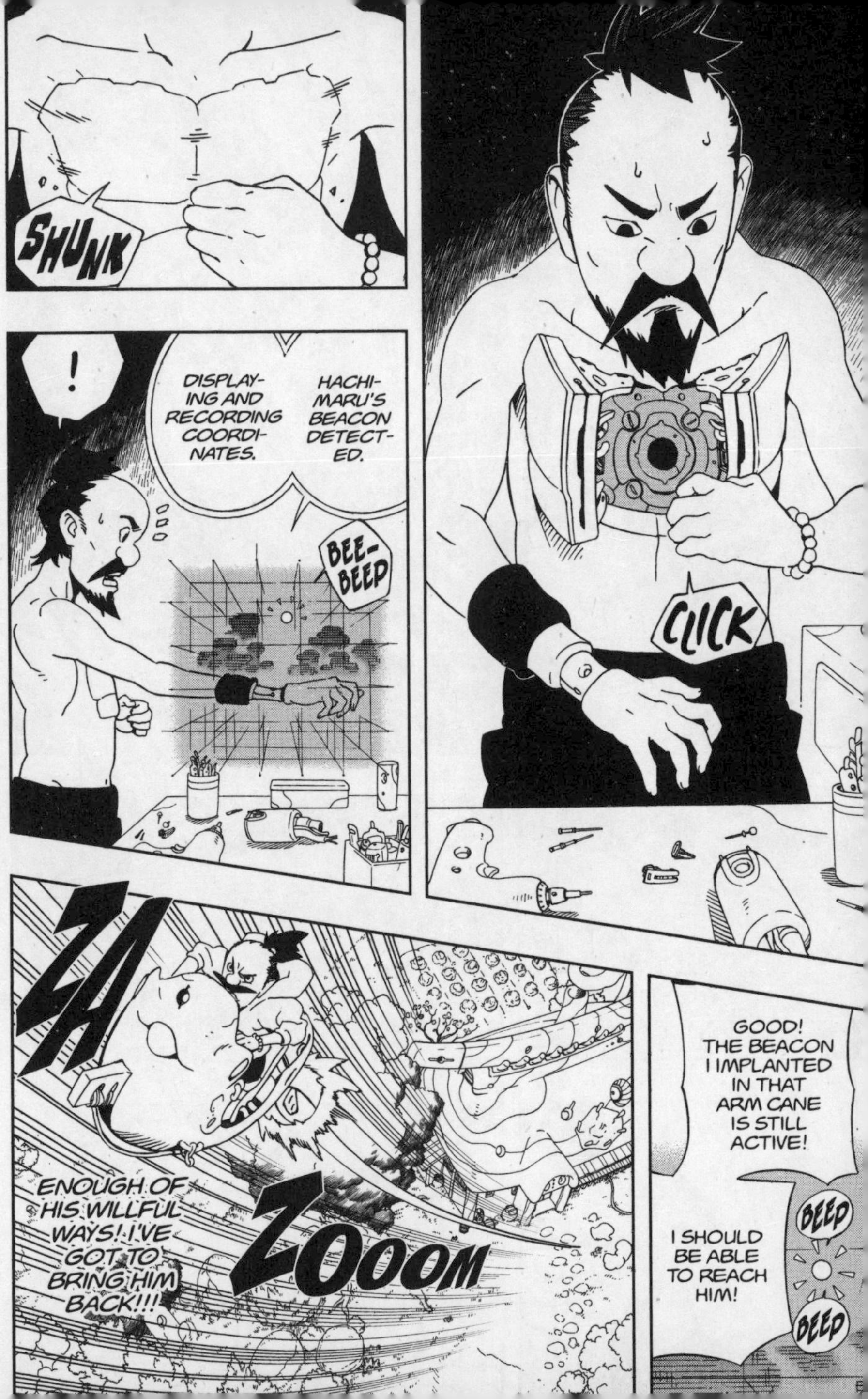
CLICK
SHUNK
!
HACHI-MARU'S BEACON DETECT-ED.
DISPLAY-ING AND RECORDING COORDI-NATES.
BEE-BEEP
GOOD! THE BEACON I IMPLANTED IN THAT ARM CANE IS STILL ACTIVE!
I SHOULD BE ABLE TO REACH HIM!
BEEP
BEEP
ZA
ENOUGH OF HIS WILLFUL WAYS! I'VE GOT TO BRING HIM BACK!!!
ZOOOM

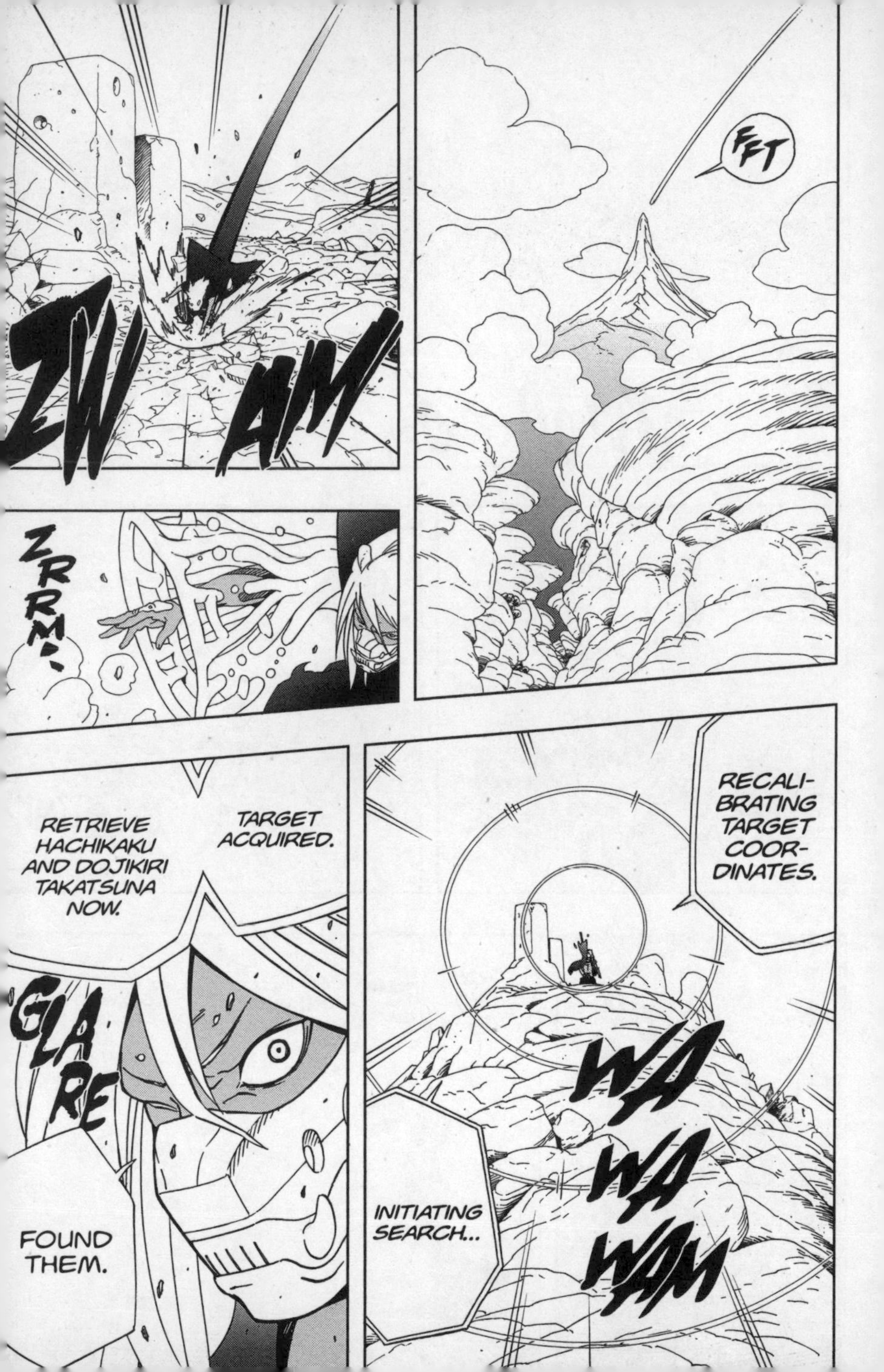
FFT
ZWAM
ZRRM
RECALI-BRATING TARGET COOR-DINATES.
WA WA WAM
INITIATING SEARCH...
TARGET ACQUIRED.
RETRIEVE HACHIKAKU AND DOJIKIRI TAKATSUNA NOW.
GLARE
FOUND THEM.

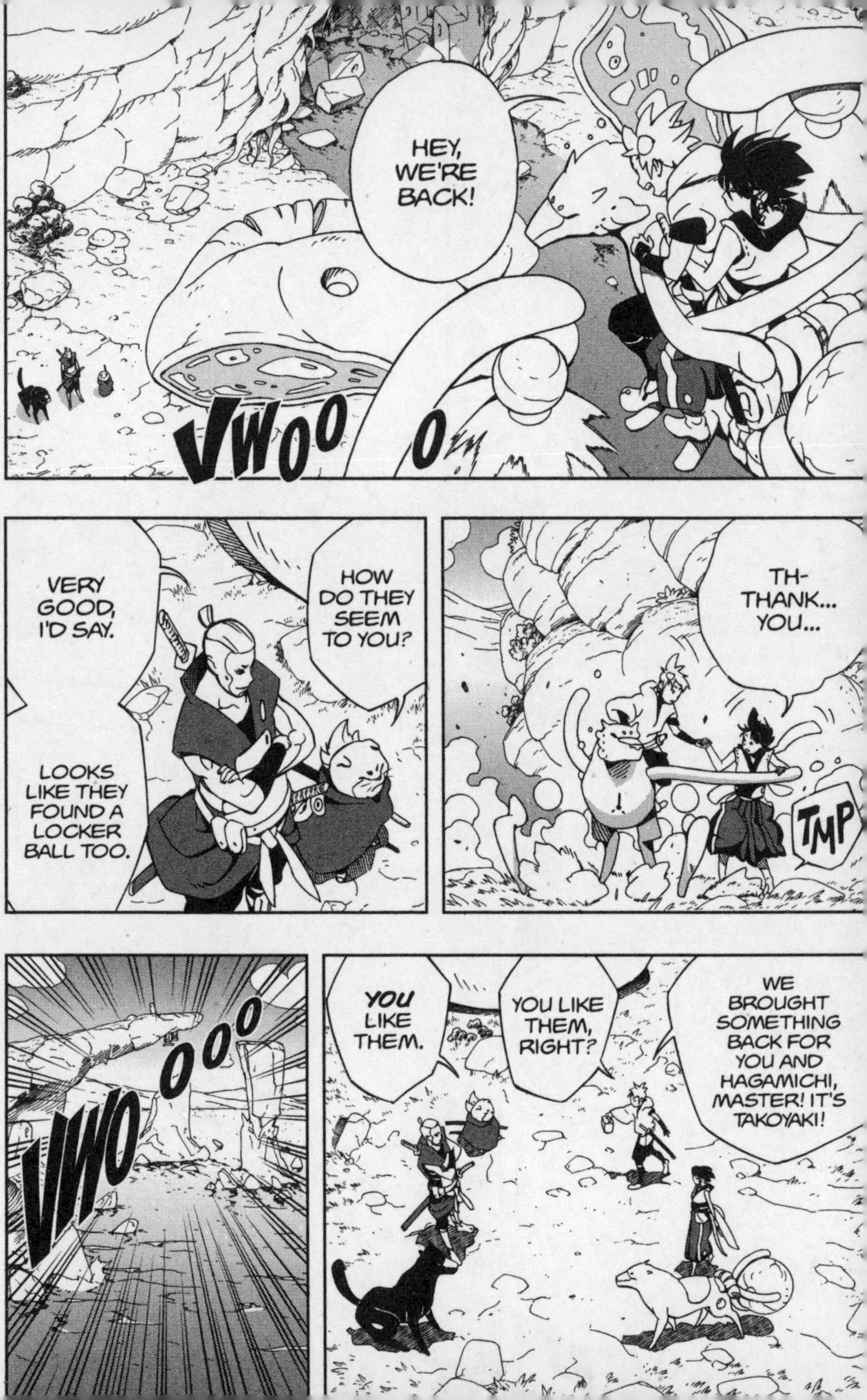
HEY, WE'RE BACK!
VWOO O
TH- THANK... YOU...
TMP
HOW DO THEY SEEM TO YOU?
VERY GOOD, I'D SAY.
LOOKS LIKE THEY FOUND A LOCKER BALL TOO.
WE BROUGHT SOMETHING BACK FOR YOU AND HAGAMICHI, MASTER! IT'S TAKOYAKI!
YOU LIKE THEM, RIGHT?
YOU LIKE THEM.
VWOOOO

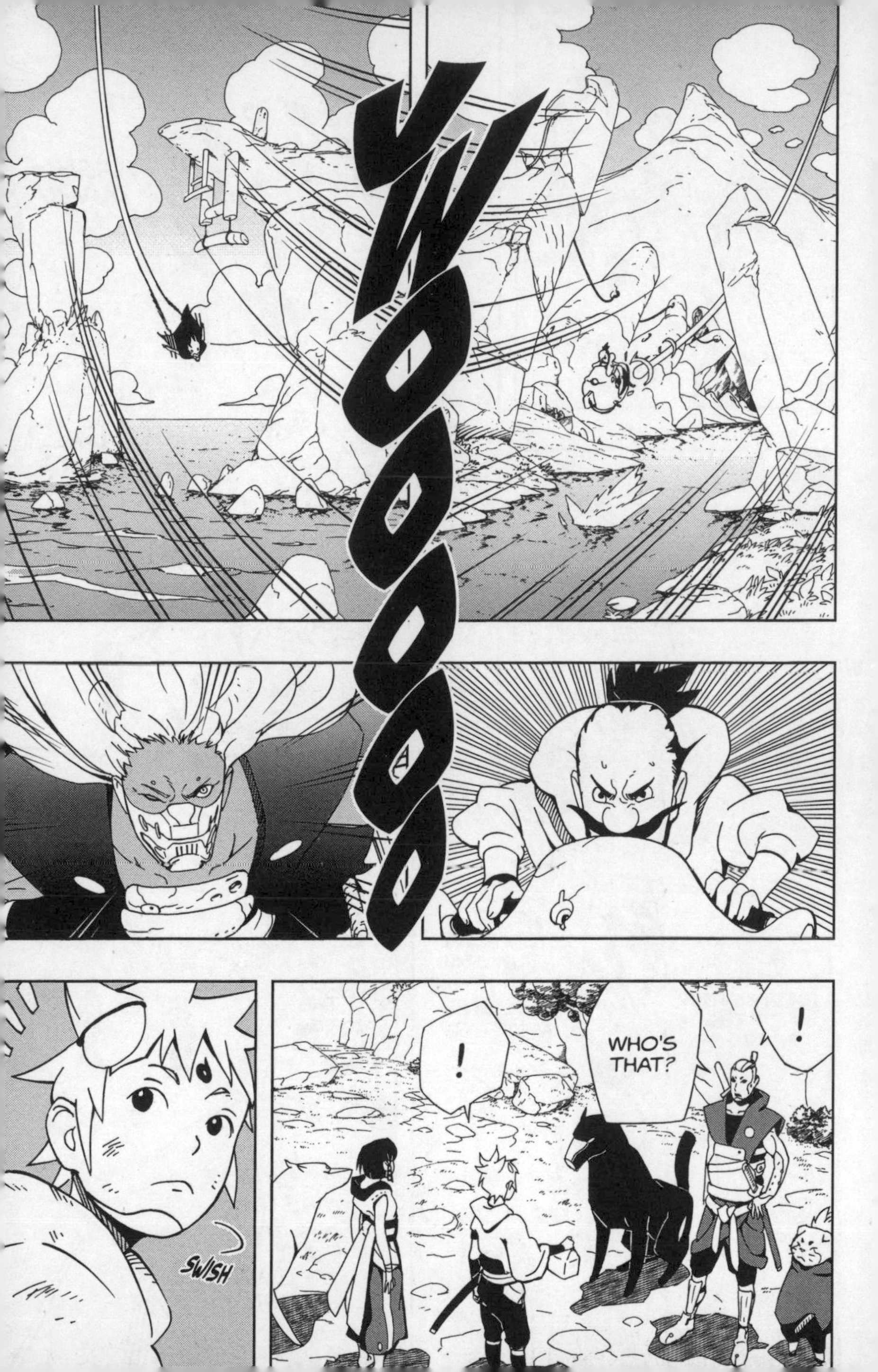
!
WHO'S THAT?
!
SWISH

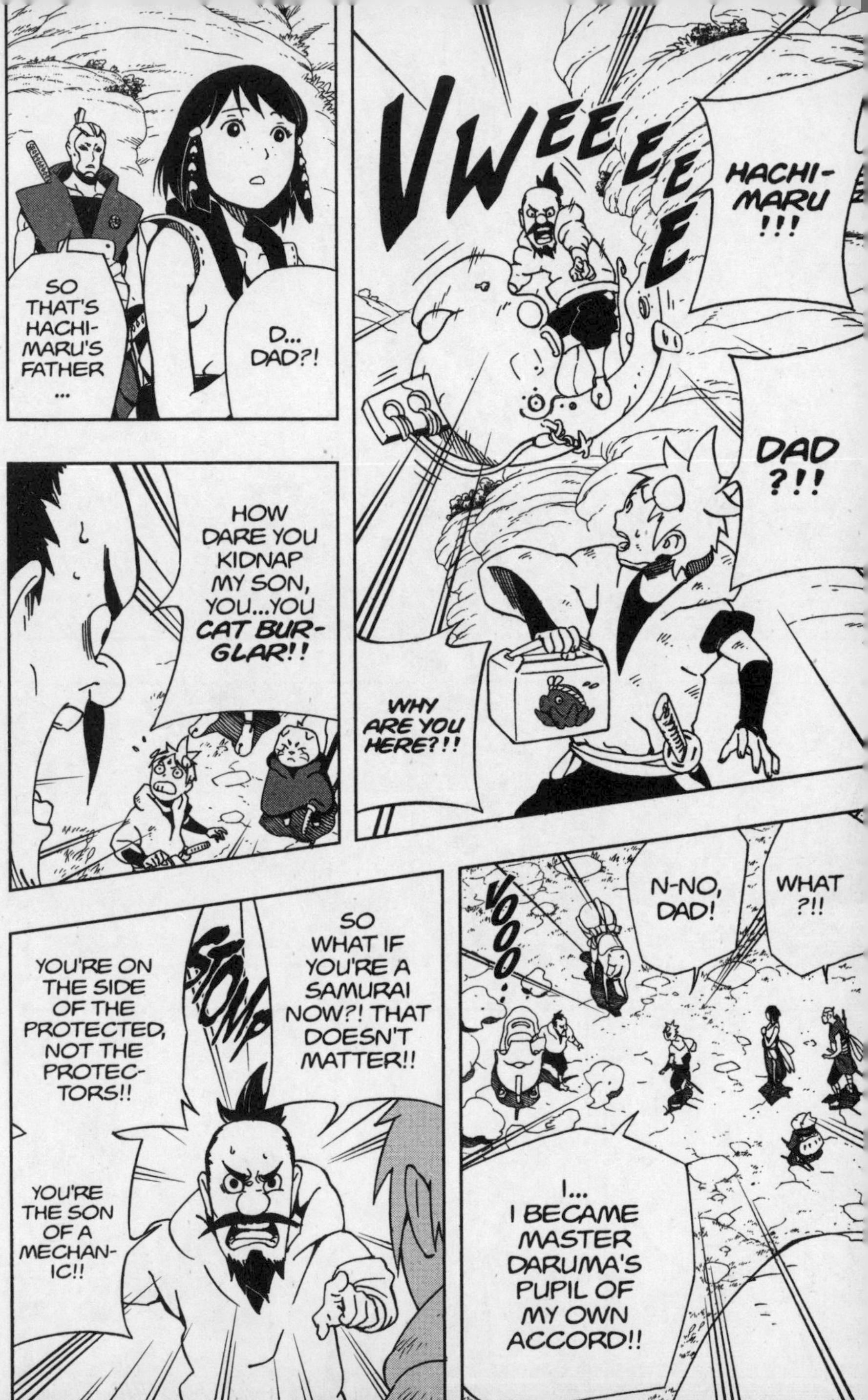
HACHI-MARU!!!
VWEEEEEE
DAD?!!
WHY ARE YOU HERE?!!
D... DAD?!
SO THAT'S HACHI-MARU'S FATHER...
HOW DARE YOU KIDNAP MY SON, YOU...YOU CAT BURGLAR!!
WHAT?!!
N-NO, DAD!
VOOO...
I... I BECAME MASTER DARUMA'S PUPIL OF MY OWN ACCORD!!
SO WHAT IF YOU'RE A SAMURAI NOW?! THAT DOESN'T MATTER!!
STOMP
YOU'RE ON THE SIDE OF THE PROTECTED, NOT THE PROTECTORS!!
YOU'RE THE SON OF A MECHANIC!!

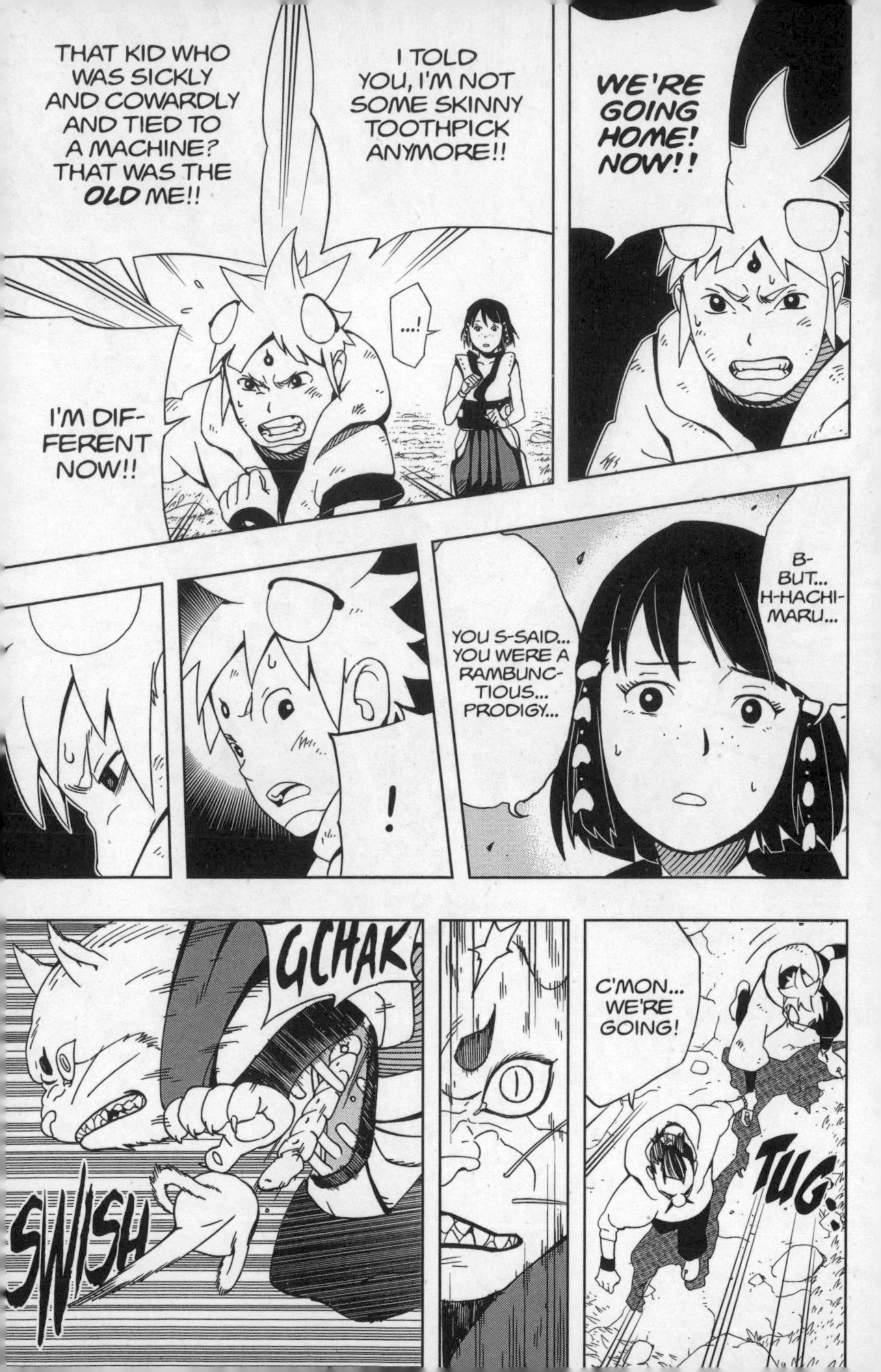

WE'RE GOING HOME! NOW!!
I TOLD YOU, I'M NOT SOME SKINNY TOOTHPICK ANYMORE!!
THAT KID WHO WAS SICKLY AND COWARDLY AND TIED TO A MACHINE? THAT WAS THE *OLD* ME!!
...!
I'M DIF-FERENT NOW!!
B-BUT... H-HACHI-MARU...
YOU S-SAID... YOU WERE A RAMBUNC-TIOUS... PRODIGY...
!
C'MON... WE'RE GOING!
TUG.
GCHAK
SWISH

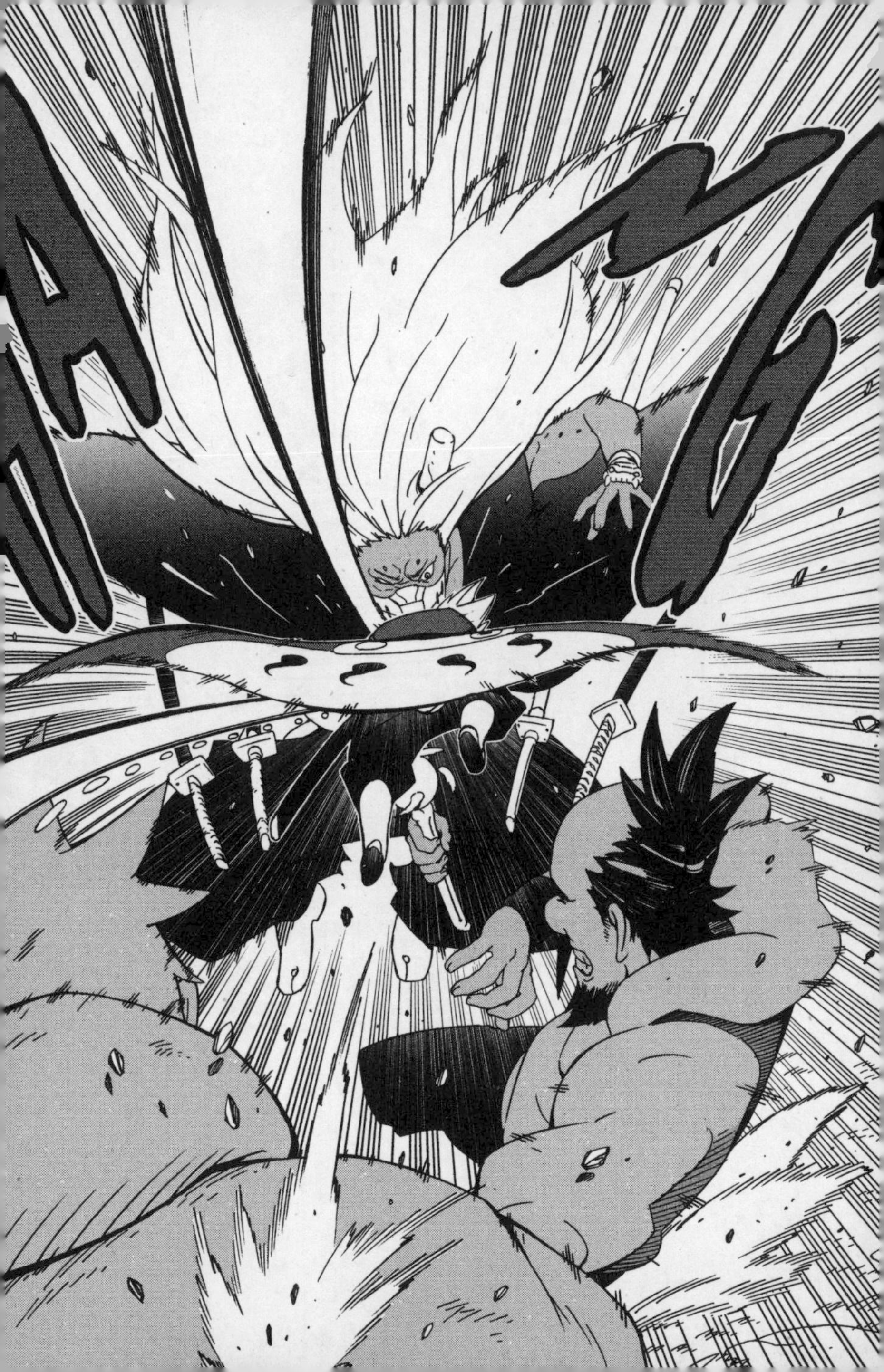

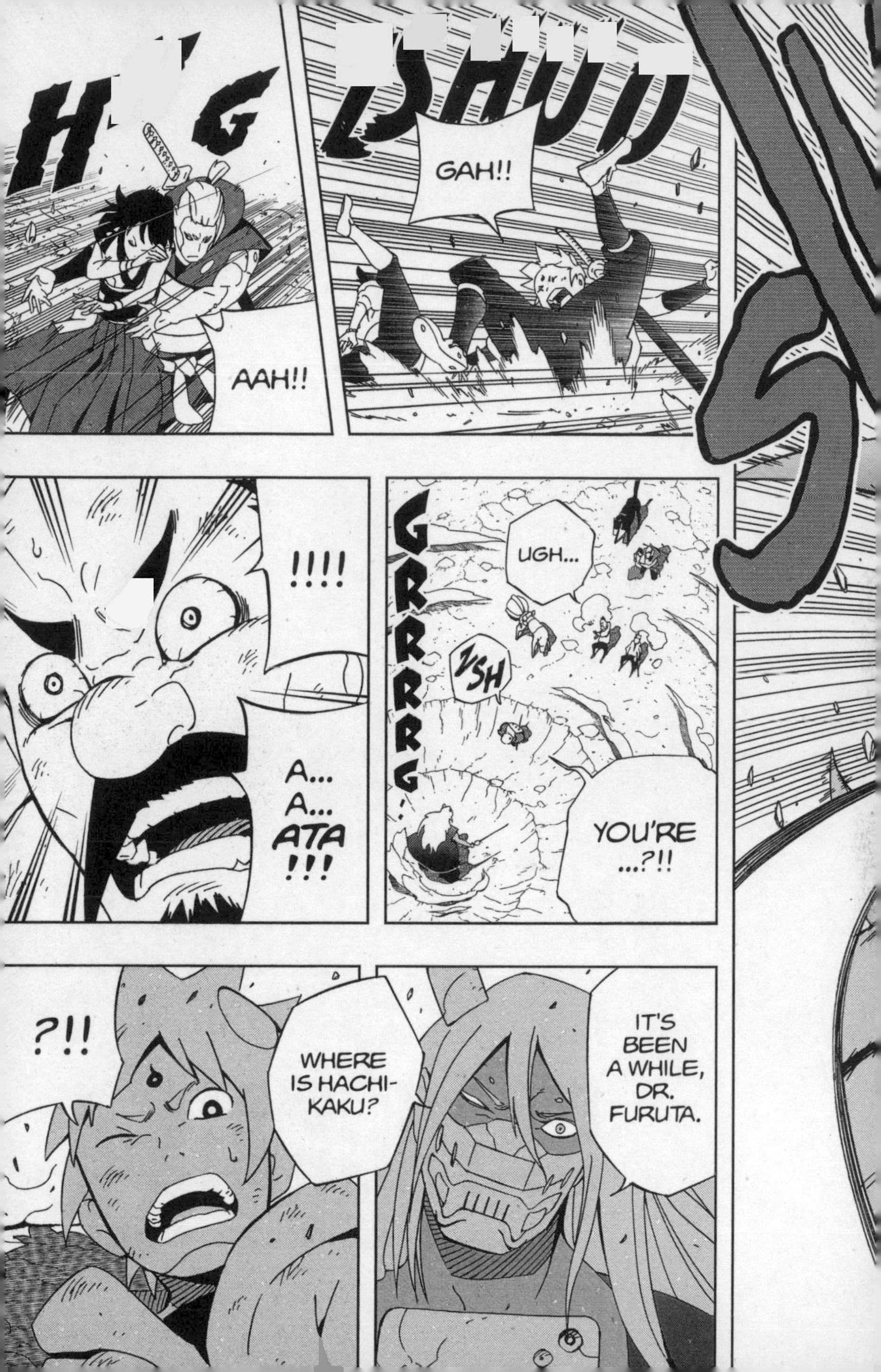
GAH!!
AAH!!
GRRRRG!
UGH...
ZSH
YOU'RE ...?!!
!!!!
A... A... ATA!!!
IT'S BEEN A WHILE, DR. FURUTA.
WHERE IS HACHI-KAKU?
?!!

SAMURAI 8
THE TALE OF HACHIMARU

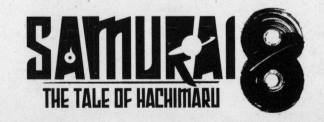

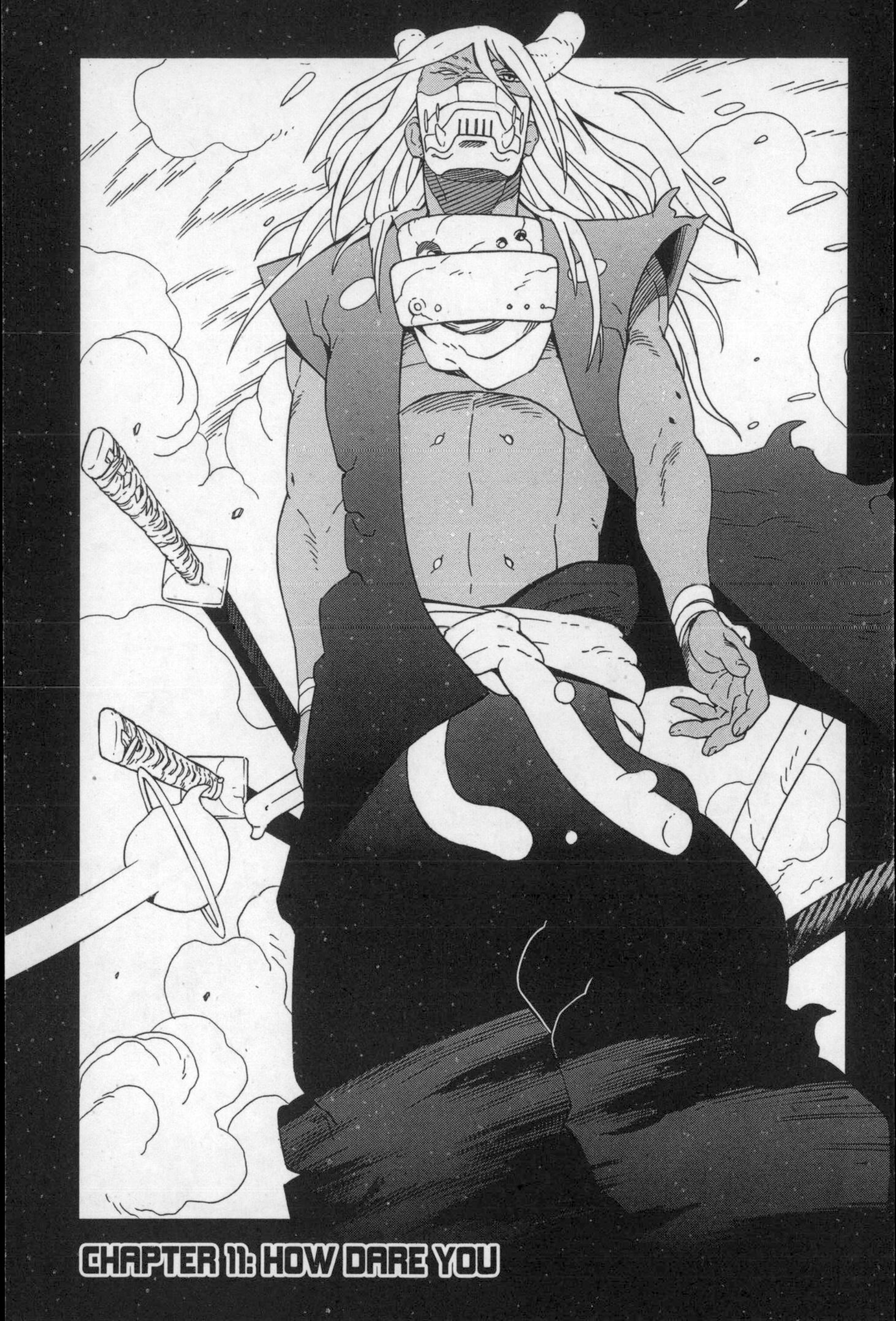

CHAPTER 11: HOW DARE YOU

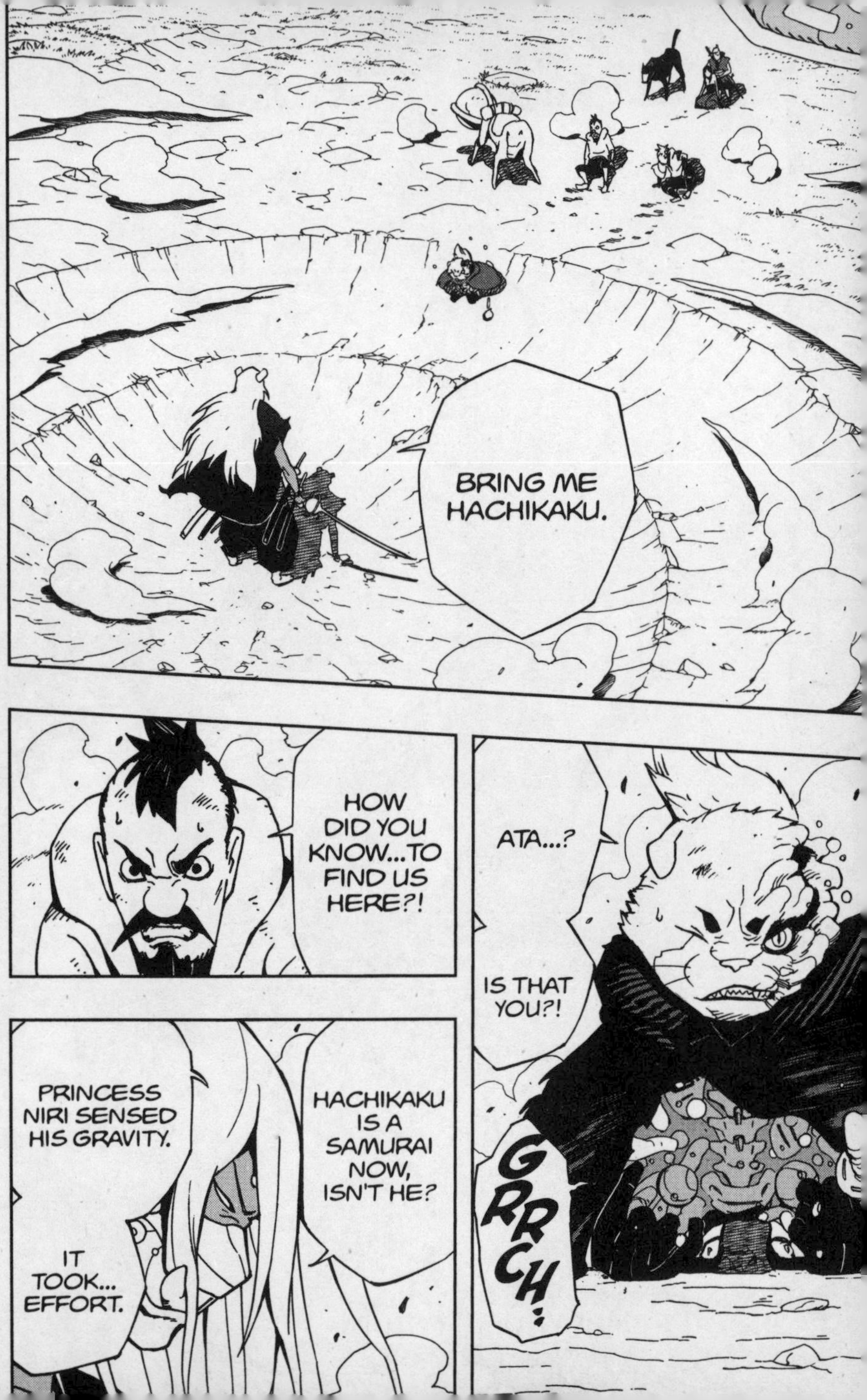
BRING ME HACHIKAKU.
ATA...?
IS THAT YOU?!
GRRCH
HOW DID YOU KNOW...TO FIND US HERE?!
HACHIKAKU IS A SAMURAI NOW, ISN'T HE?
PRINCESS NIRI SENSED HIS GRAVITY.
IT TOOK... EFFORT.

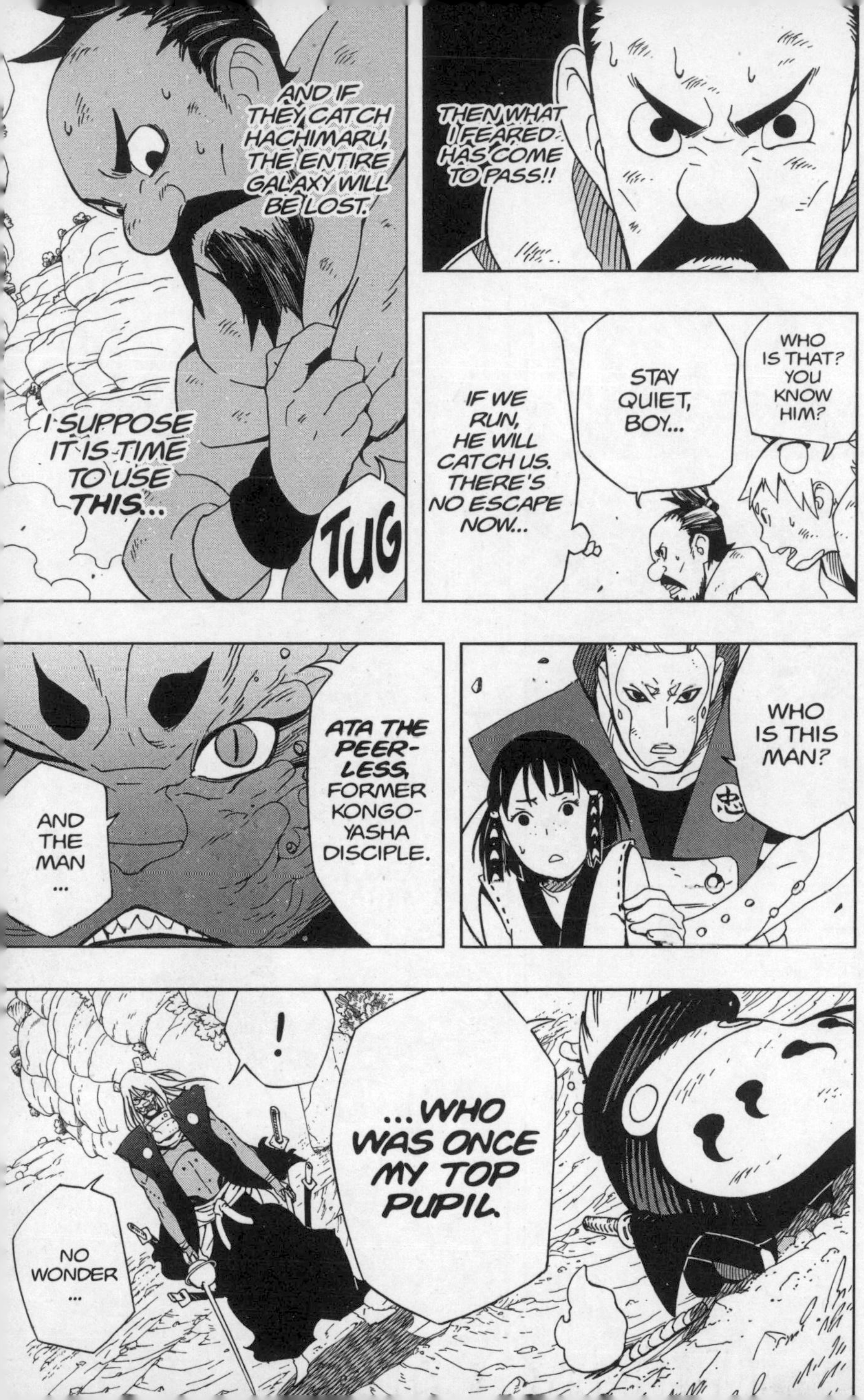
THEN WHAT I FEARED HAS COME TO PASS!!
WHO IS THAT? YOU KNOW HIM?
STAY QUIET, BOY...
IF WE RUN, HE WILL CATCH US. THERE'S NO ESCAPE NOW...
AND IF THEY CATCH HACHIMARU, THE ENTIRE GALAXY WILL BE LOST.
I SUPPOSE IT IS TIME TO USE THIS...
TUG
WHO IS THIS MAN?
ATA THE PEERLESS, FORMER KONGO-YASHA DISCIPLE.
AND THE MAN ...
!
...WHO WAS ONCE MY TOP PUPIL.
NO WONDER ...

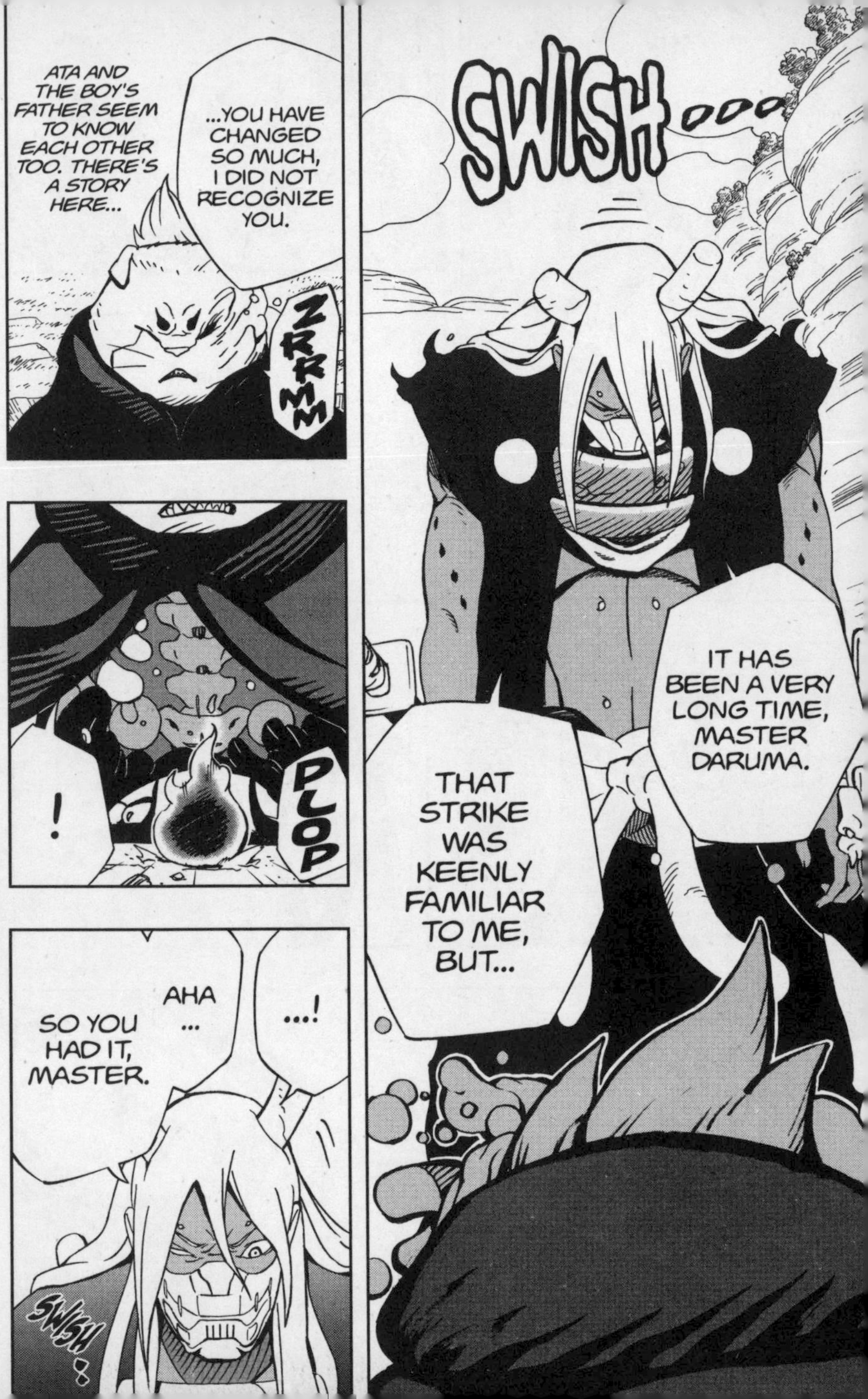
SWISH ooo
IT HAS BEEN A VERY LONG TIME, MASTER DARUMA.
THAT STRIKE WAS KEENLY FAMILIAR TO ME, BUT...
...YOU HAVE CHANGED SO MUCH, I DID NOT RECOGNIZE YOU.
ATA AND THE BOY'S FATHER SEEM TO KNOW EACH OTHER TOO. THERE'S A STORY HERE...
ZRRMM
PLOP
!
...!
AHA ...
SO YOU HAD IT, MASTER.
SWISH

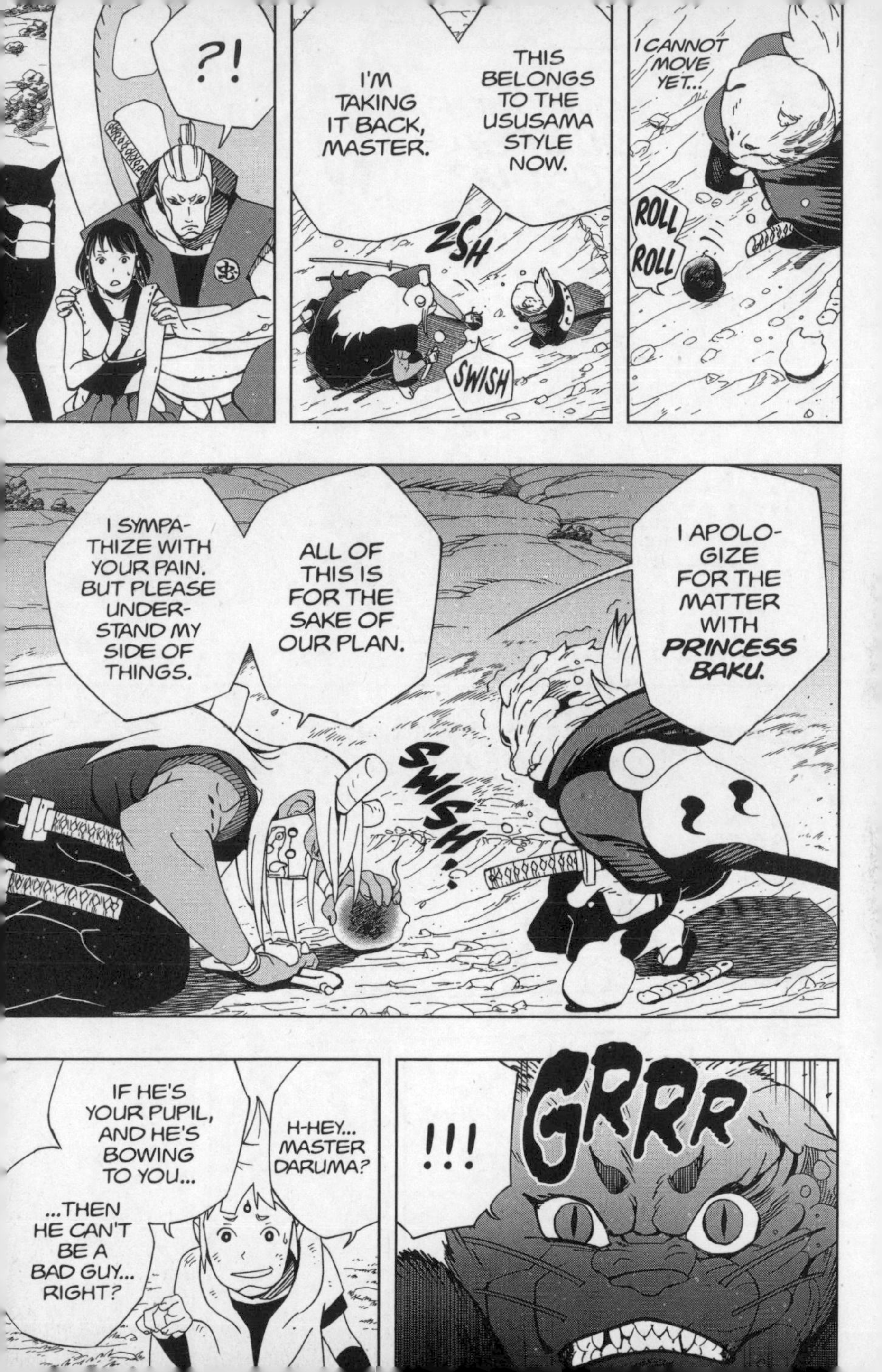
I CANNOT MOVE YET...
ROLL ROLL
THIS BELONGS TO THE USUSAMA STYLE NOW.
I'M TAKING IT BACK, MASTER.
ZSH
SWISH
?!
I APOLO-GIZE FOR THE MATTER WITH PRINCESS BAKU.
ALL OF THIS IS FOR THE SAKE OF OUR PLAN.
I SYMPA-THIZE WITH YOUR PAIN. BUT PLEASE UNDER-STAND MY SIDE OF THINGS.
SWISH!
GRRR
!!!
H-HEY... MASTER DARUMA?
IF HE'S YOUR PUPIL, AND HE'S BOWING TO YOU...
...THEN HE CAN'T BE A BAD GUY... RIGHT?

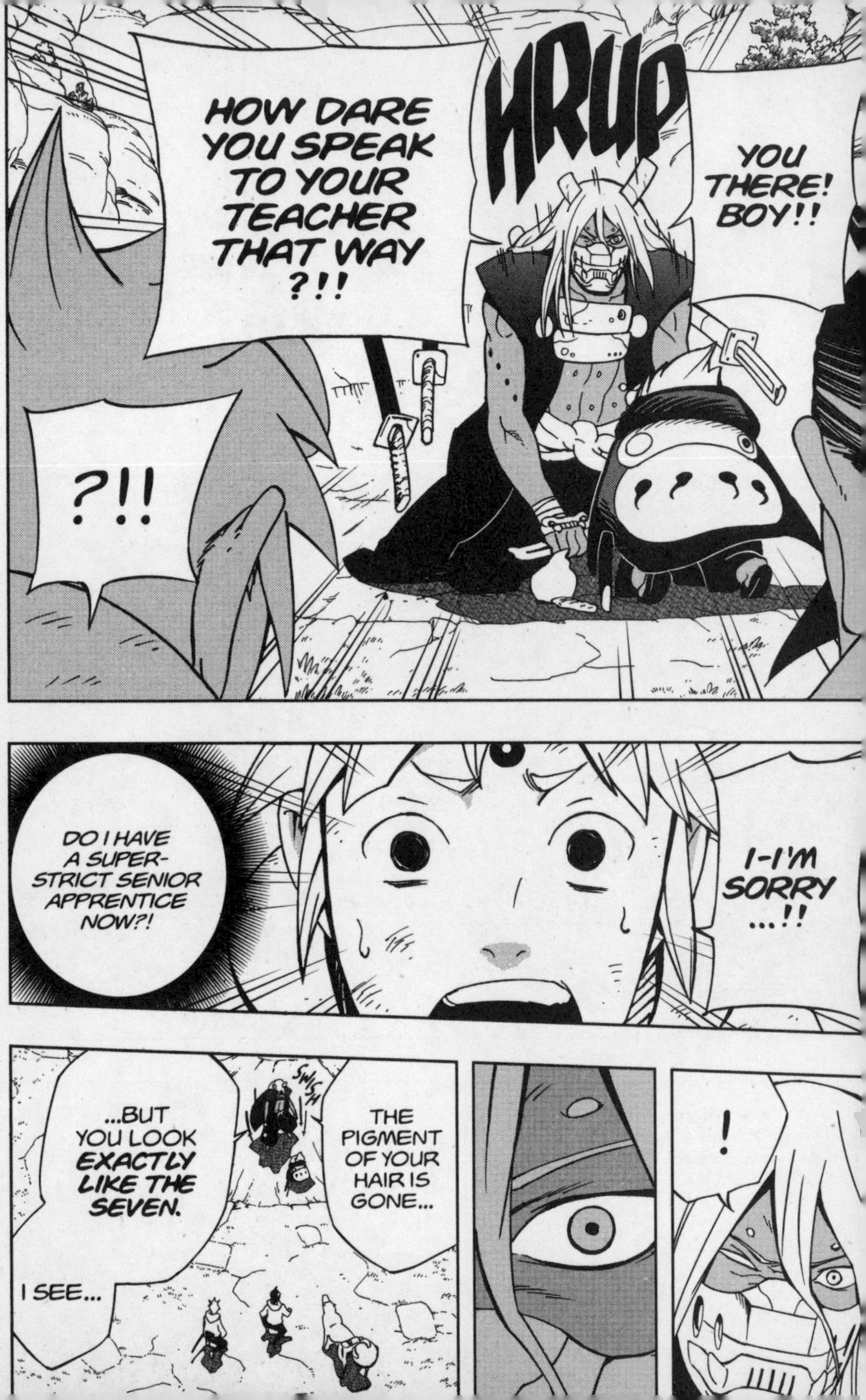
YOU THERE! BOY!!
HRUP
HOW DARE YOU SPEAK TO YOUR TEACHER THAT WAY ?!!
?!!
I-I'M SORRY ...!!
DO I HAVE A SUPER-STRICT SENIOR APPRENTICE NOW?!
!
THE PIGMENT OF YOUR HAIR IS GONE...
SWISH
...BUT YOU LOOK EXACTLY LIKE THE SEVEN.
I SEE...

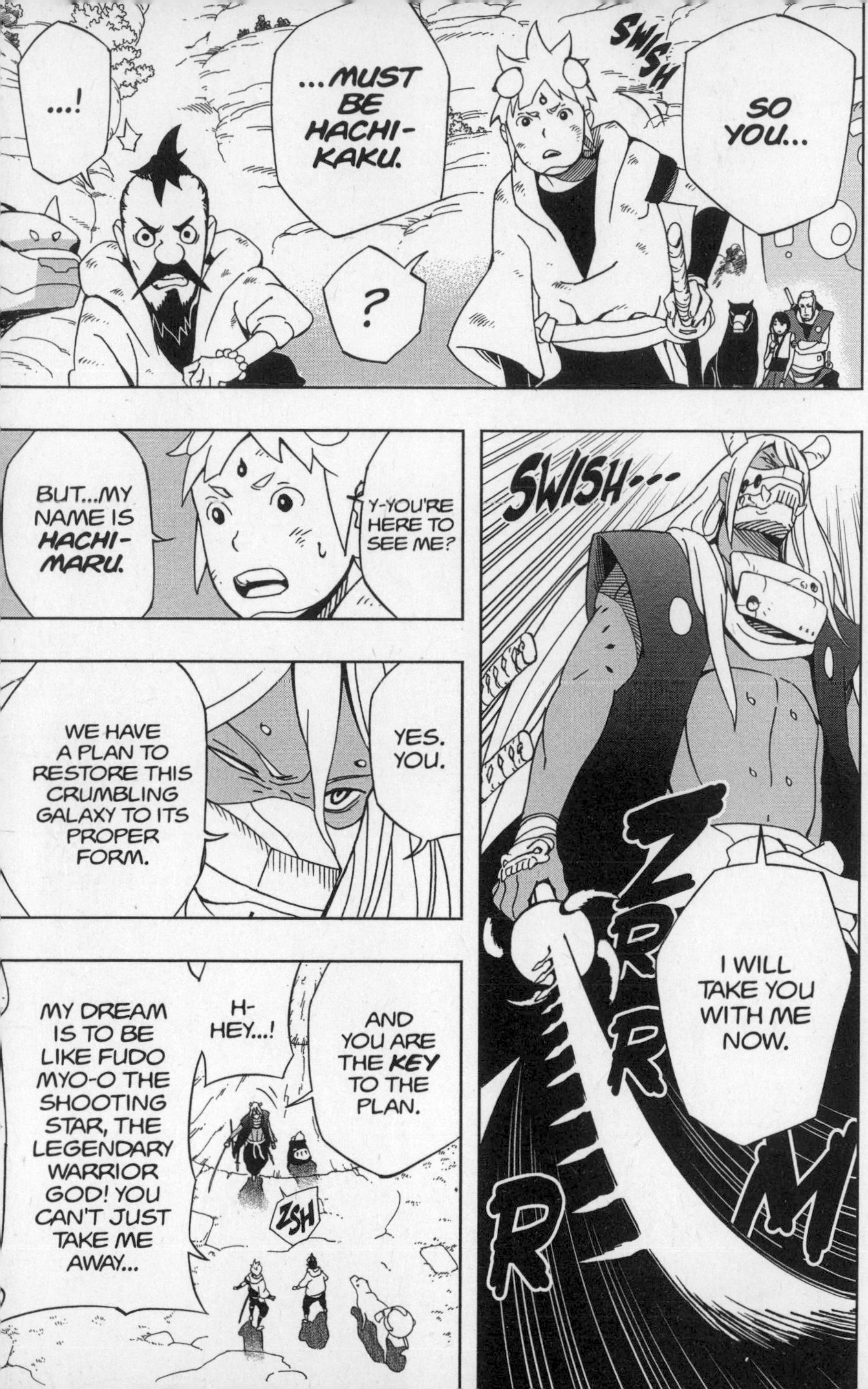
SWISH
SO YOU...
...MUST BE HACHI-KAKU.
?
...!
SWISH...
I WILL TAKE YOU WITH ME NOW.
ZRRRMM
Y-YOU'RE HERE TO SEE ME?
BUT...MY NAME IS HACHI-MARU.
YES. YOU.
WE HAVE A PLAN TO RESTORE THIS CRUMBLING GALAXY TO ITS PROPER FORM.
AND YOU ARE THE KEY TO THE PLAN.
H-HEY...!
ZSH
MY DREAM IS TO BE LIKE FUDO MYO-O THE SHOOTING STAR, THE LEGENDARY WARRIOR GOD! YOU CAN'T JUST TAKE ME AWAY...

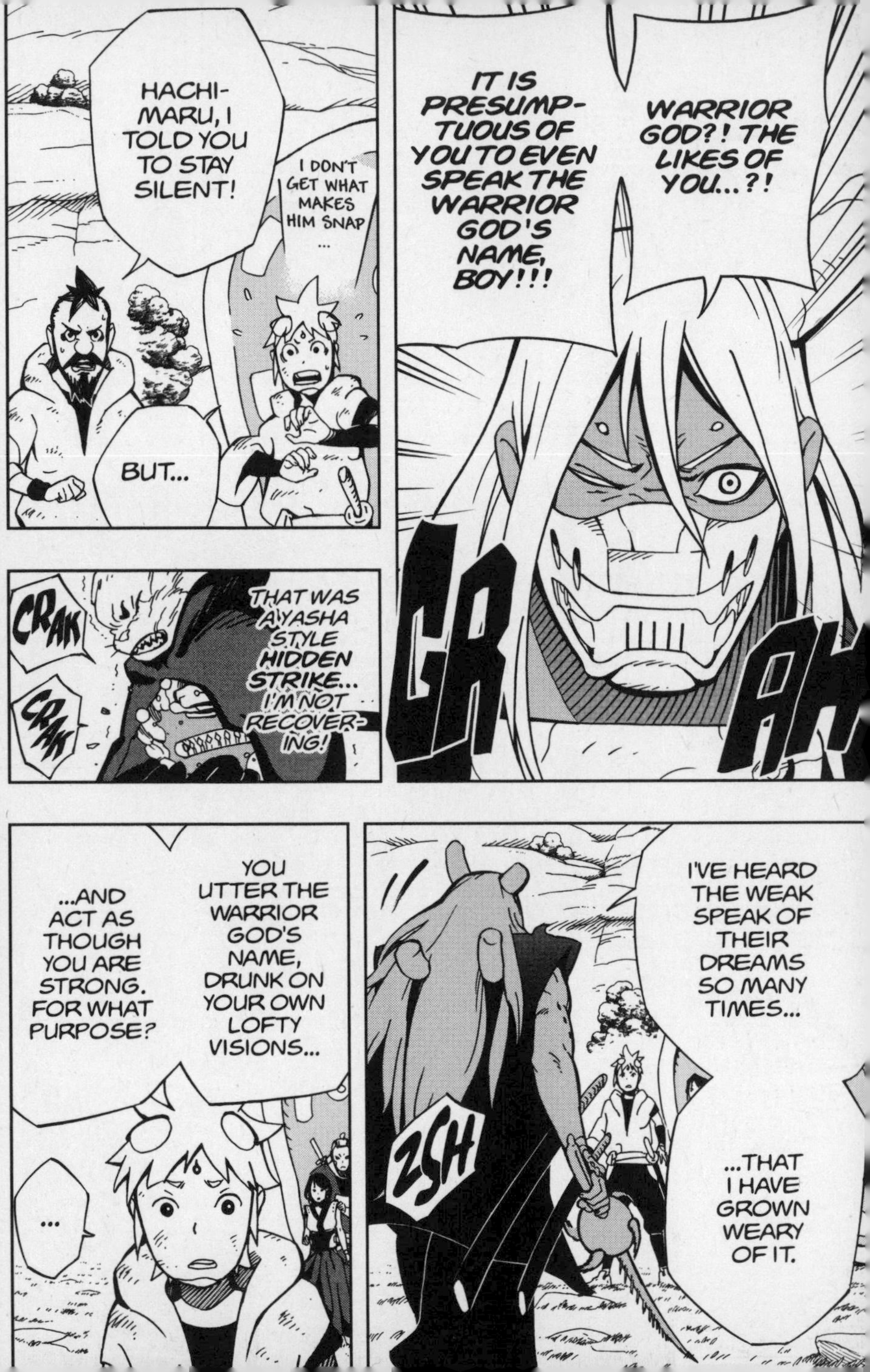
WARRIOR GOD?! THE LIKES OF YOU...?!
IT IS PRESUMPTUOUS OF YOU TO EVEN SPEAK THE WARRIOR GOD'S NAME, BOY!!!
GRAAH
I DON'T GET WHAT MAKES HIM SNAP...
HACHIMARU, I TOLD YOU TO STAY SILENT!
BUT...
CRAK
CRAK
THAT WAS A YASHA STYLE HIDDEN STRIKE... I'M NOT RECOVERING!
I'VE HEARD THE WEAK SPEAK OF THEIR DREAMS SO MANY TIMES...
...THAT I HAVE GROWN WEARY OF IT.
ZSH
YOU UTTER THE WARRIOR GOD'S NAME, DRUNK ON YOUR OWN LOFTY VISIONS...
...AND ACT AS THOUGH YOU ARE STRONG. FOR WHAT PURPOSE?
...

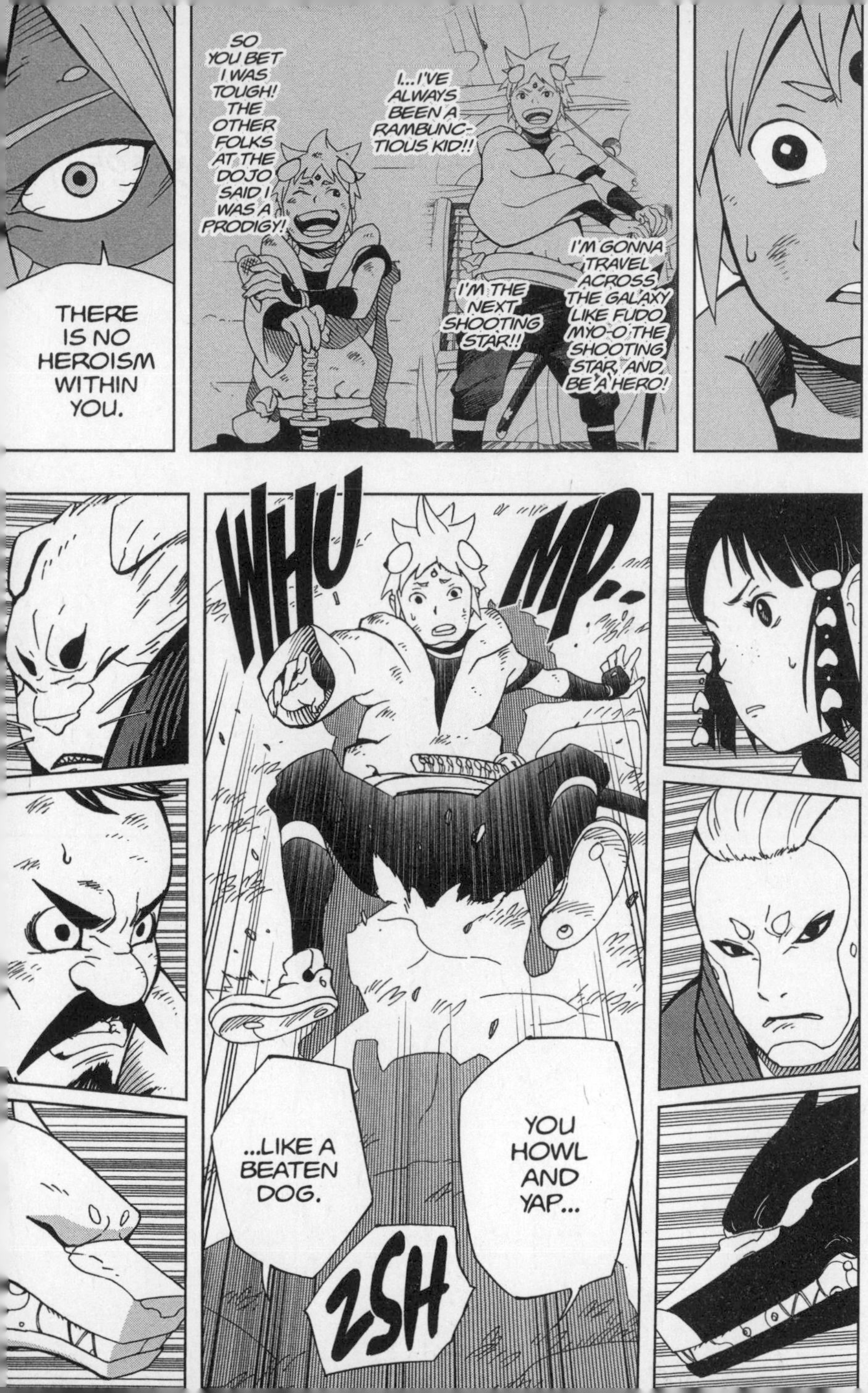
I...I'VE ALWAYS BEEN A RAMBUNCTIOUS KID!!
I'M GONNA TRAVEL ACROSS THE GALAXY LIKE FUDO MYO-O THE SHOOTING STAR, AND BE A HERO!
I'M THE NEXT SHOOTING STAR!!
SO YOU BET I WAS TOUGH! THE OTHER FOLKS AT THE DOJO SAID I WAS A PRODIGY!
THERE IS NO HEROISM WITHIN YOU.
WHUMP..
YOU HOWL AND YAP...
...LIKE A BEATEN DOG.
ZSH

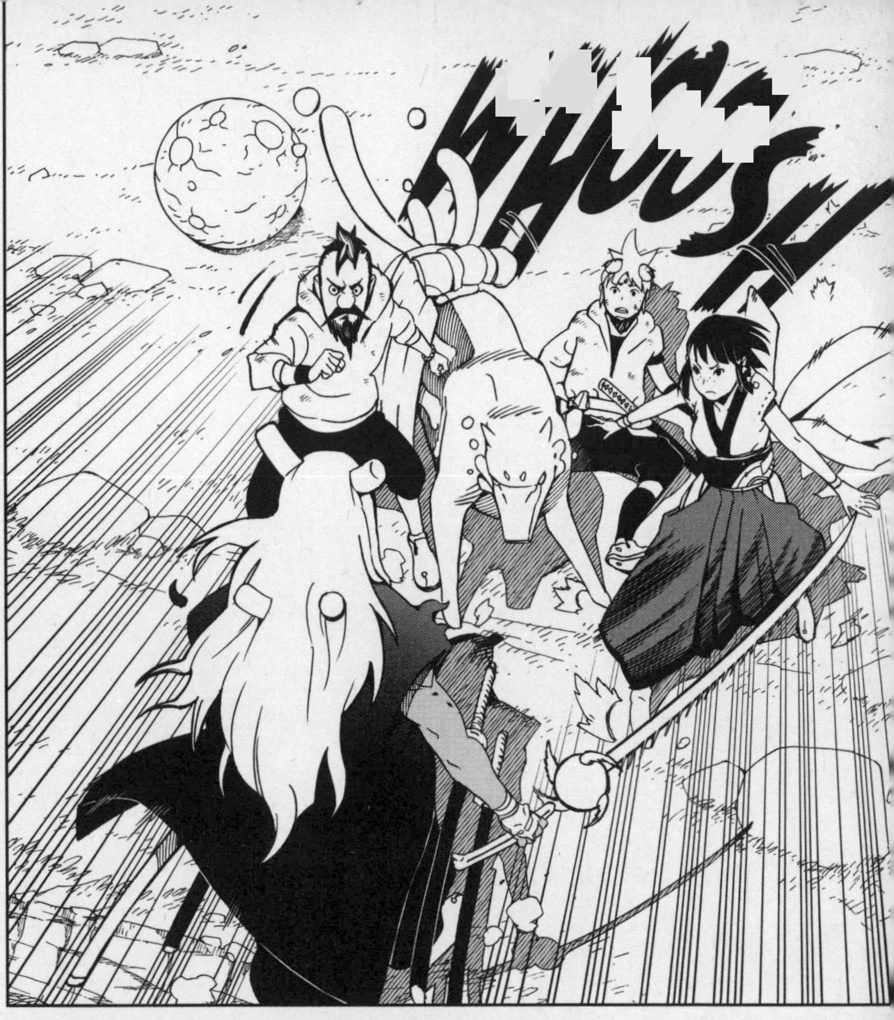
WHOOSH
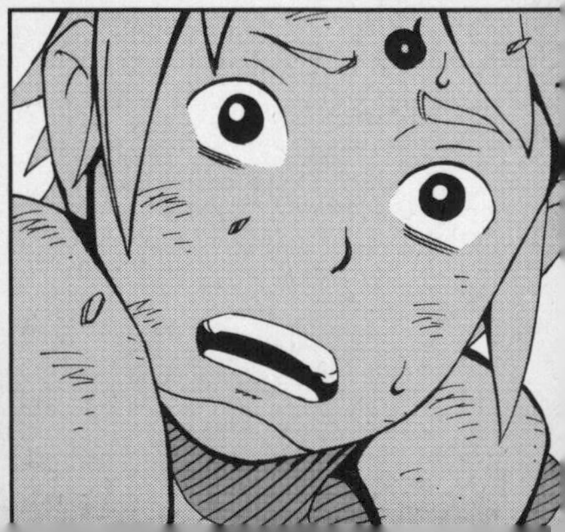
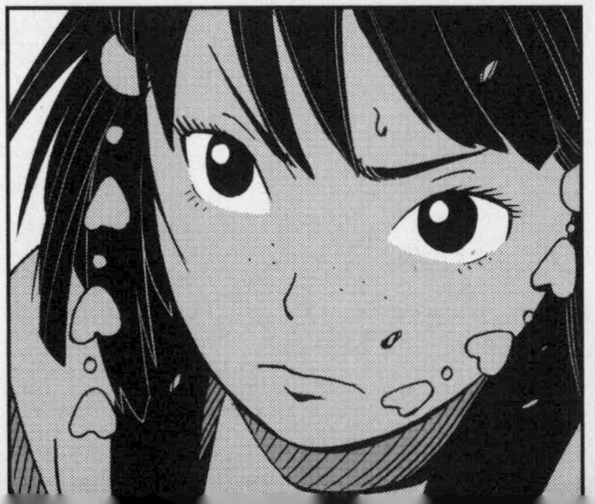

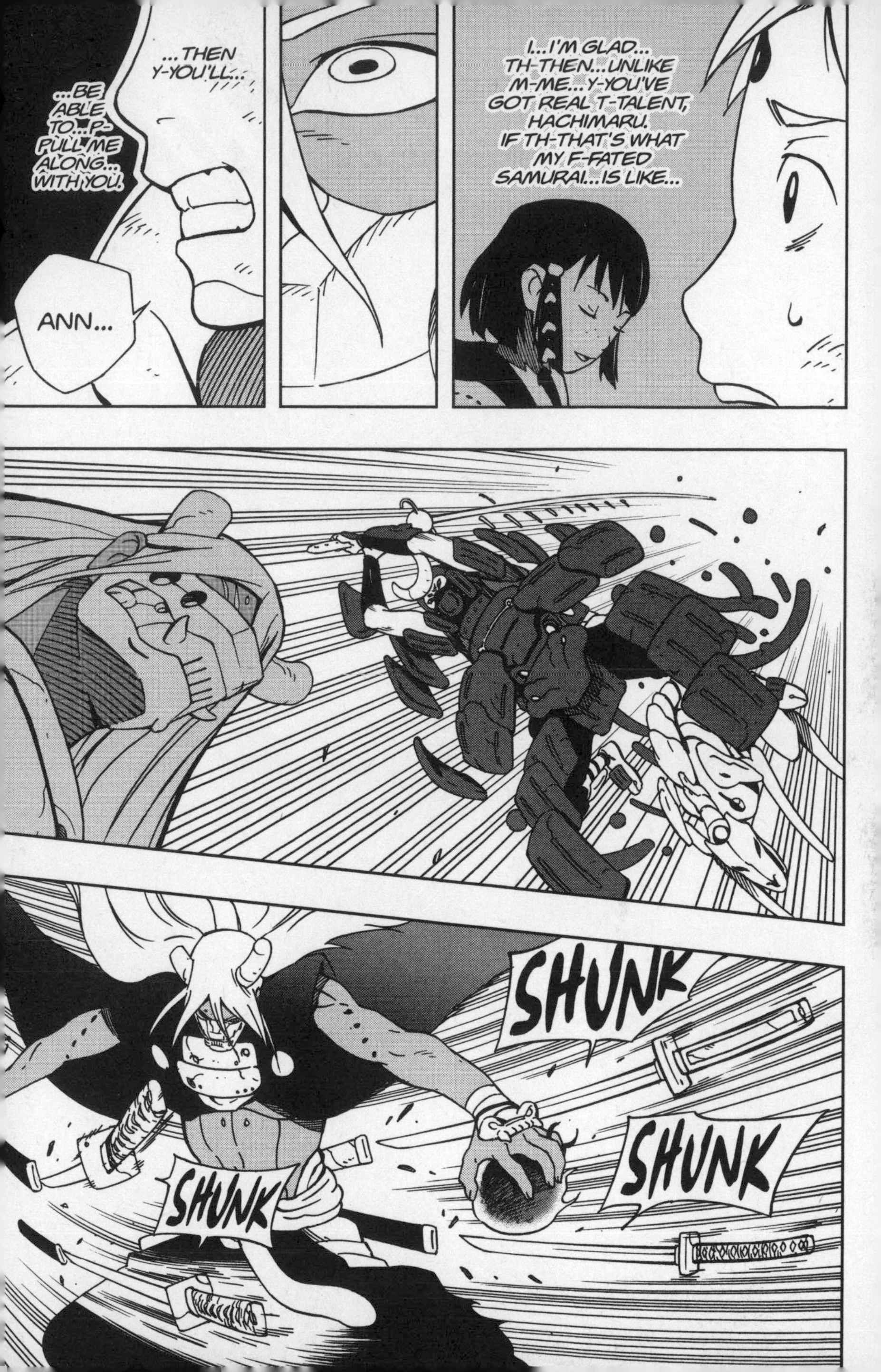
I...I'M GLAD... TH-THEN...UNLIKE M-ME...Y-YOU'VE GOT REAL T-TALENT, HACHIMARU. IF TH-THAT'S WHAT MY F-FATED SAMURAI...IS LIKE...
...THEN Y-YOU'LL...
...BE ABLE TO...P-PULL ME ALONG... WITH YOU.
ANN...
SHUNK
SHUNK
SHUNK

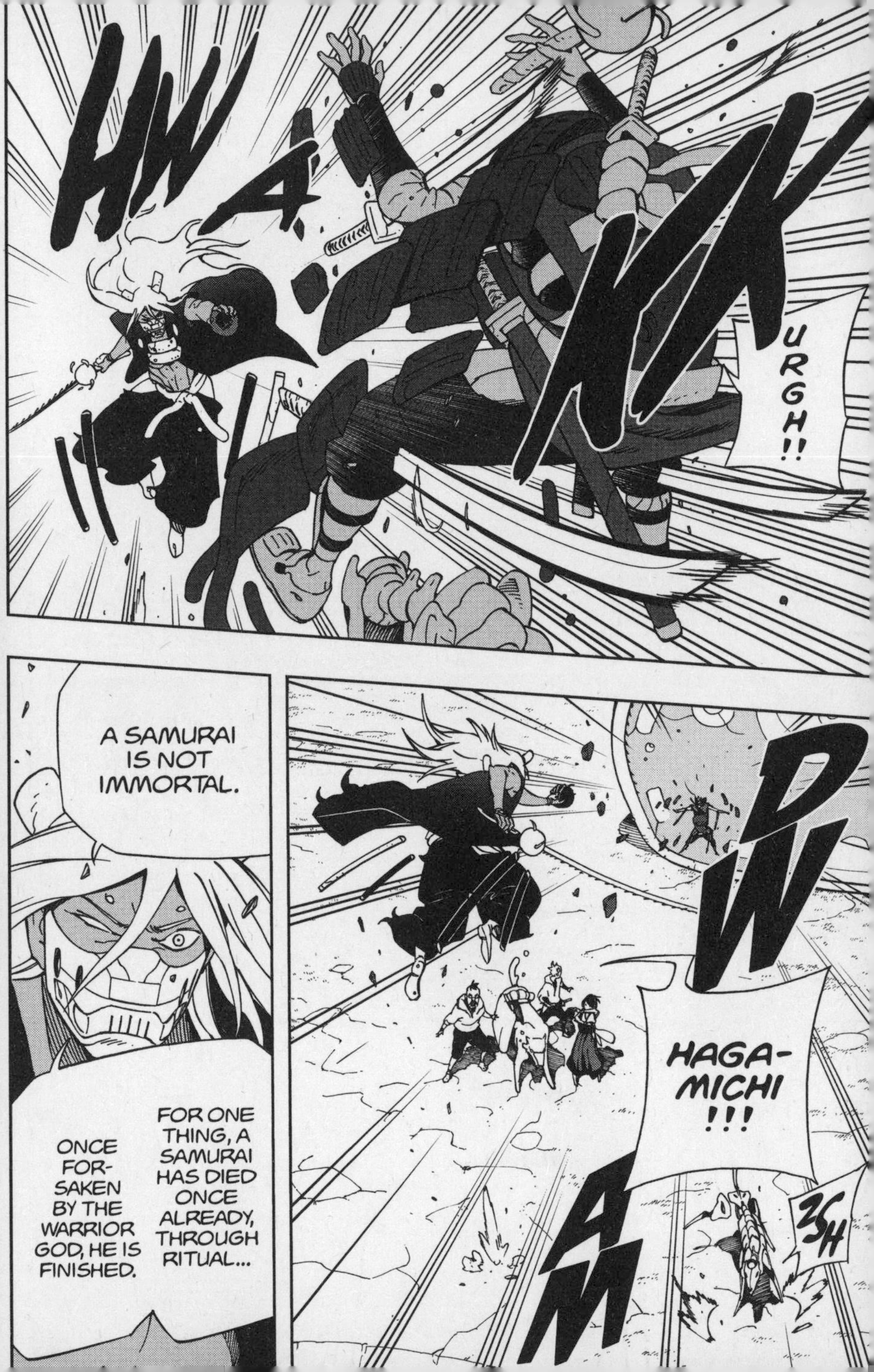
URGH!!
HAGA-MICHI!!!
ZSH
A SAMURAI IS NOT IMMORTAL.
FOR ONE THING, A SAMURAI HAS DIED ONCE ALREADY, THROUGH RITUAL...
ONCE FOR-SAKEN BY THE WARRIOR GOD, HE IS FINISHED.

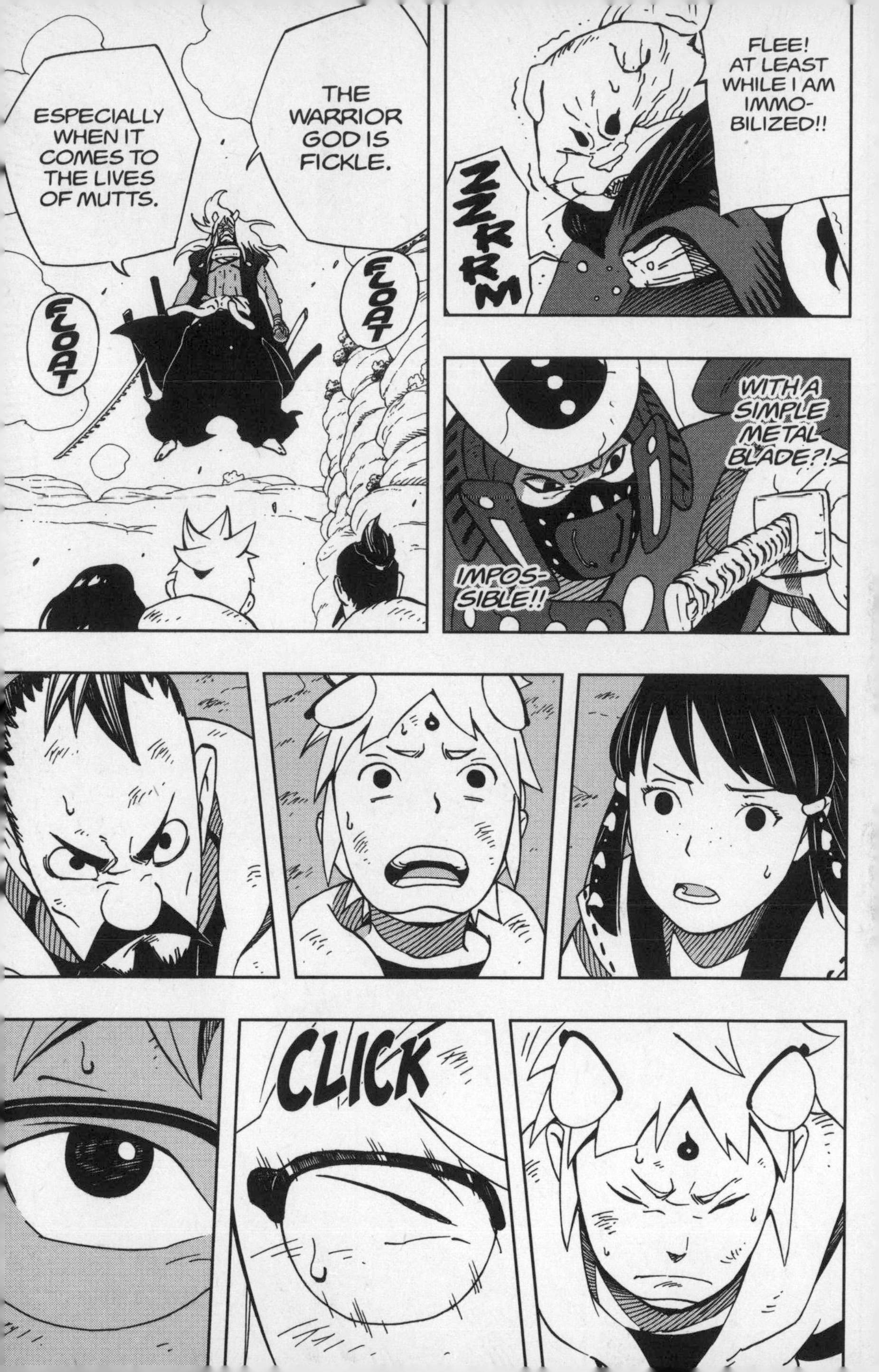
FLEE! AT LEAST WHILE I AM IMMO-BILIZED!!
ZZRRM
WITH A SIMPLE METAL BLADE?!
IMPOS-SIBLE!!
THE WARRIOR GOD IS FICKLE.
ESPECIALLY WHEN IT COMES TO THE LIVES OF MUTTS.
FLOAT
FLOAT
CLICK

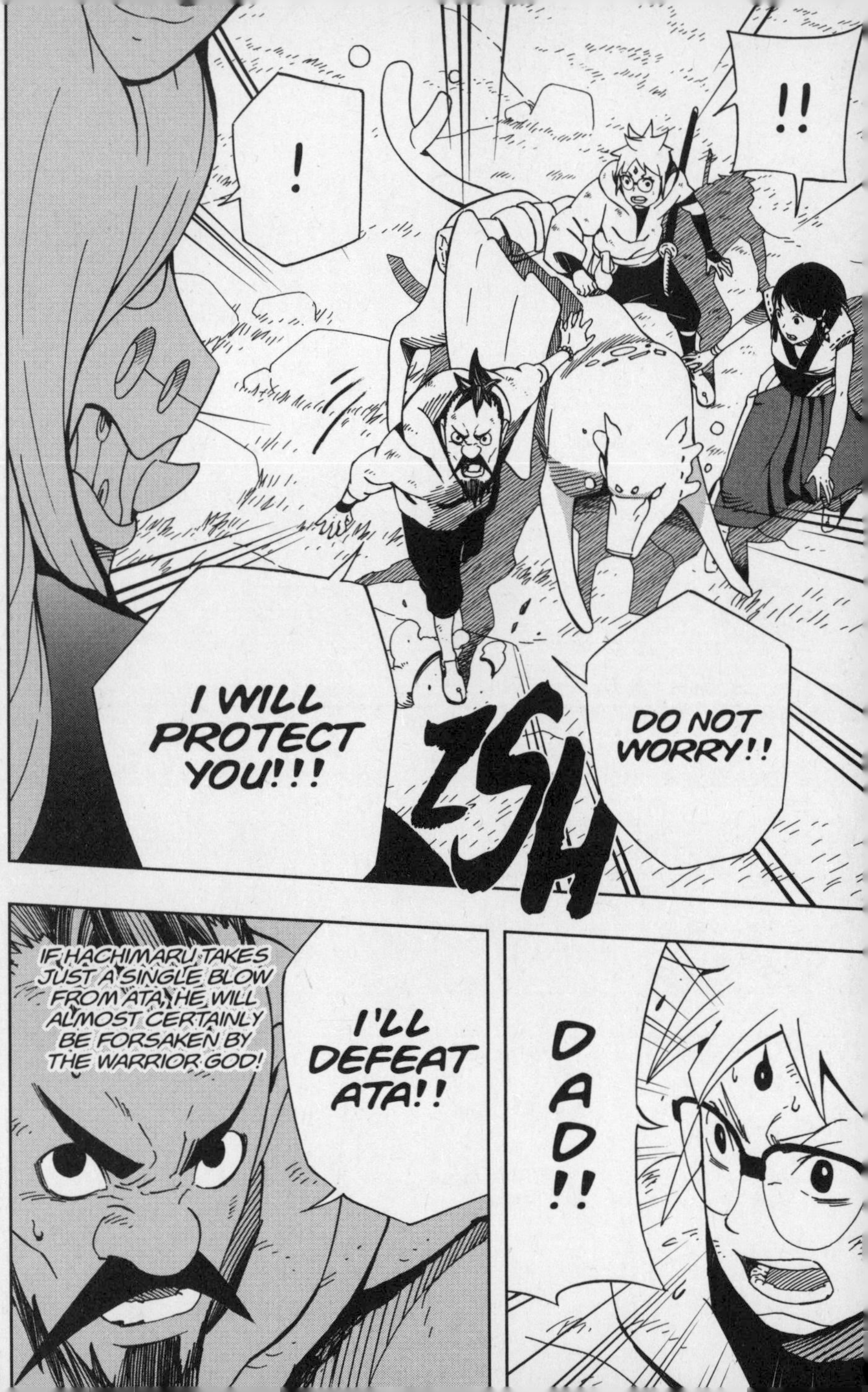
!!
!
DO NOT WORRY!!
ZSH
I WILL PROTECT YOU!!!
DAD!!
I'LL DEFEAT ATA!!
IF HACHIMARU TAKES JUST A SINGLE BLOW FROM ATA, HE WILL ALMOST CERTAINLY BE FORSAKEN BY THE WARRIOR GOD!

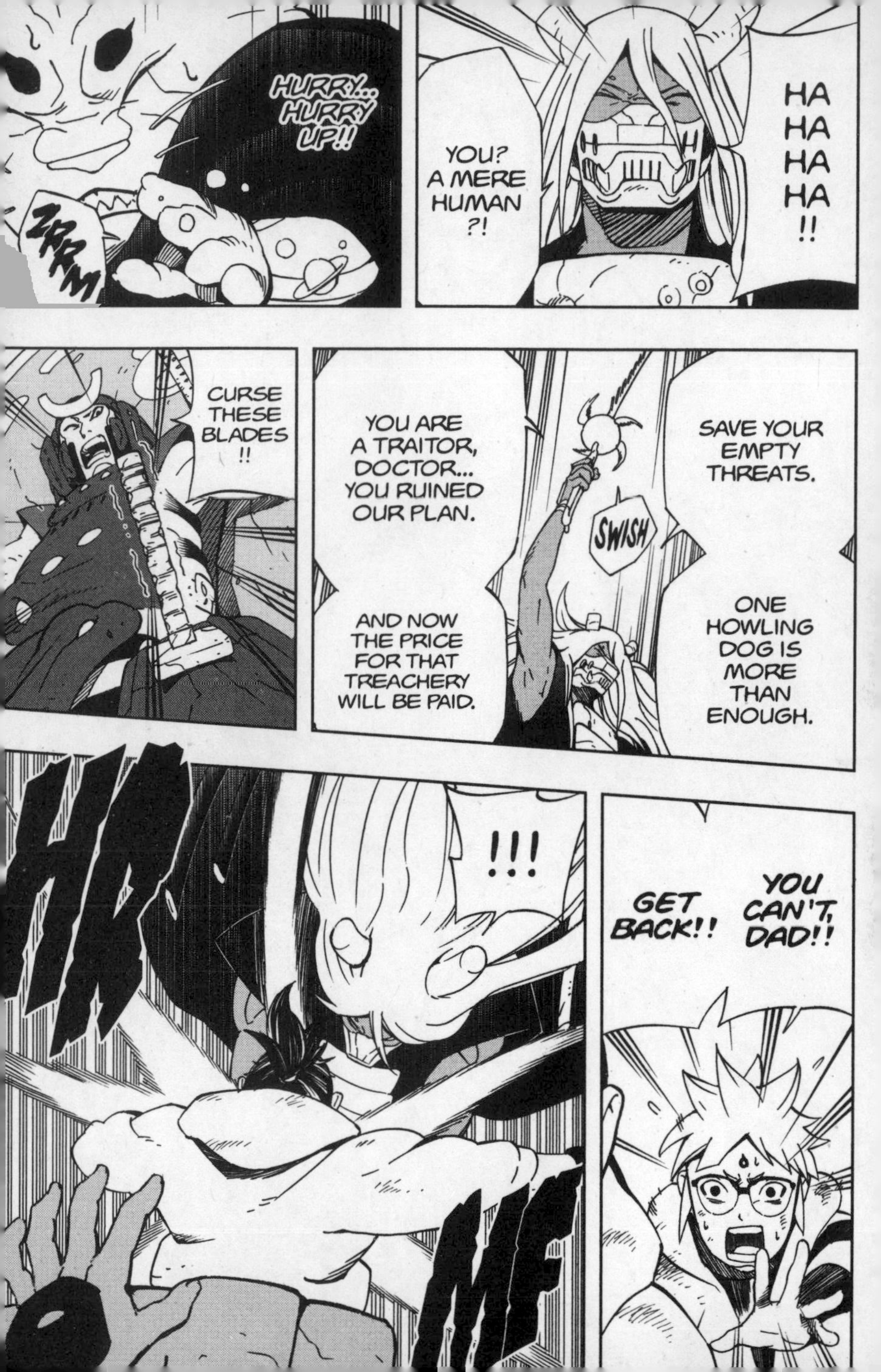
HA HA HA HA!!
YOU? A MERE HUMAN?!
HURRY... HURRY UP!!
ZRRRM
SAVE YOUR EMPTY THREATS.
YOU ARE A TRAITOR, DOCTOR... YOU RUINED OUR PLAN.
SWISH
ONE HOWLING DOG IS MORE THAN ENOUGH.
AND NOW THE PRICE FOR THAT TREACHERY WILL BE PAID.
CURSE THESE BLADES!!
YOU CAN'T, DAD!!
GET BACK!!
!!!

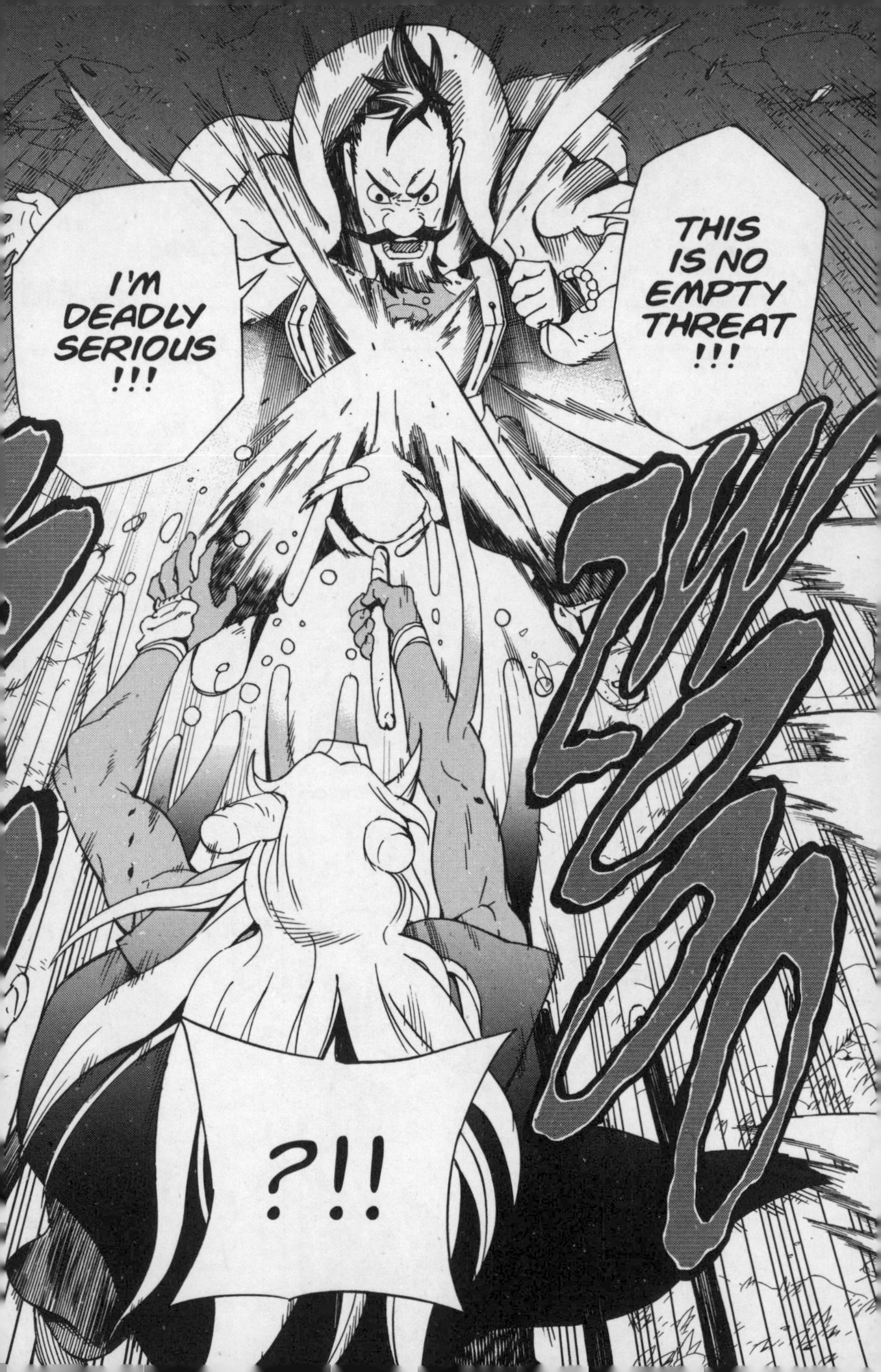
THIS IS NO EMPTY THREAT!!!
I'M DEADLY SERIOUS!!!
?!!

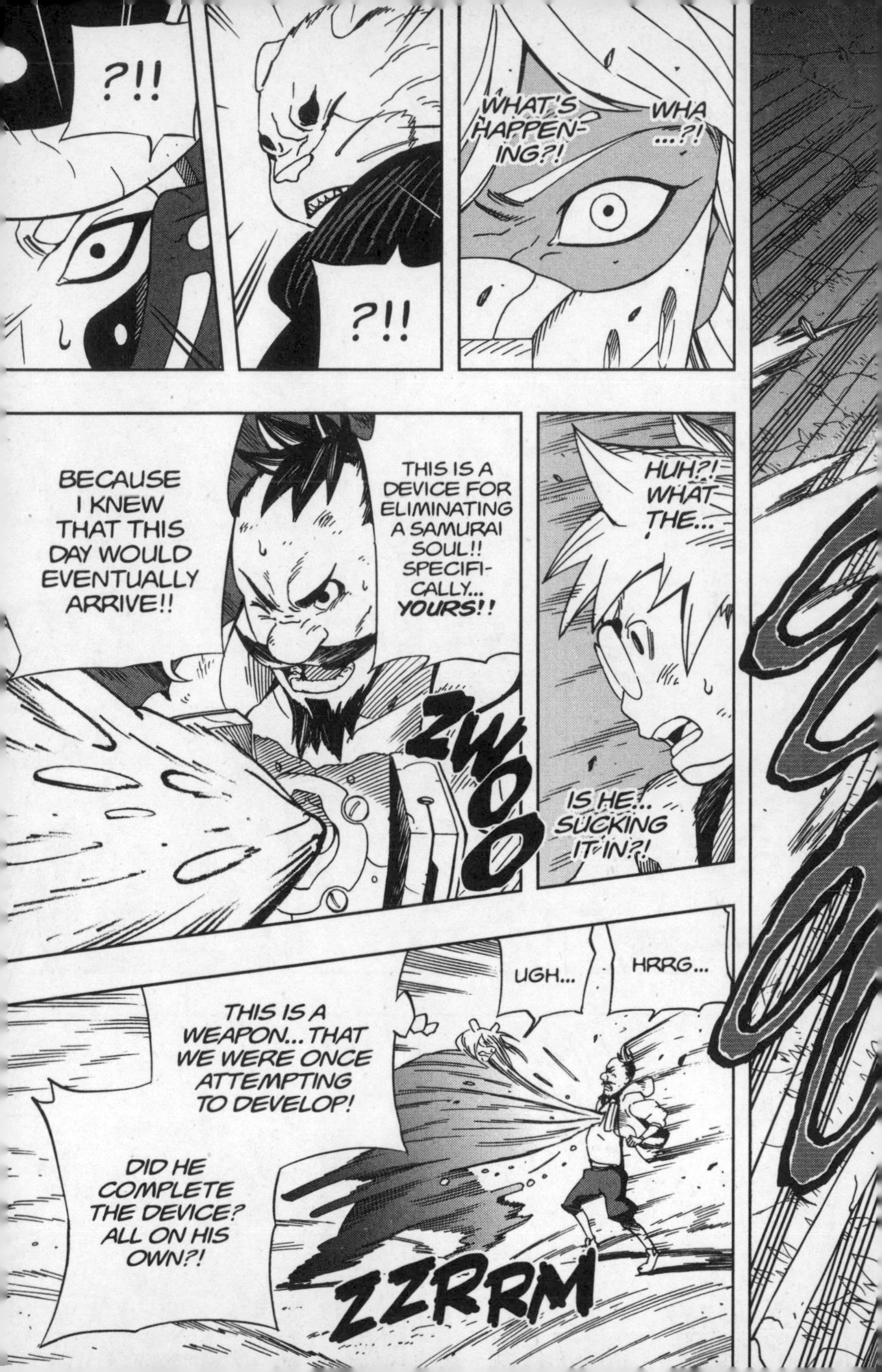
WHA ...?!
WHAT'S HAPPENING?!
?!!
?!!
HUH?! WHAT THE...
IS HE... SUCKING IT IN?!
THIS IS A DEVICE FOR ELIMINATING A SAMURAI SOUL!! SPECIFICALLY... YOURS!!
BECAUSE I KNEW THAT THIS DAY WOULD EVENTUALLY ARRIVE!!
ZWOOO
HRRG...
UGH...
THIS IS A WEAPON... THAT WE WERE ONCE ATTEMPTING TO DEVELOP!
DID HE COMPLETE THE DEVICE? ALL ON HIS OWN?!
ZZRRRM

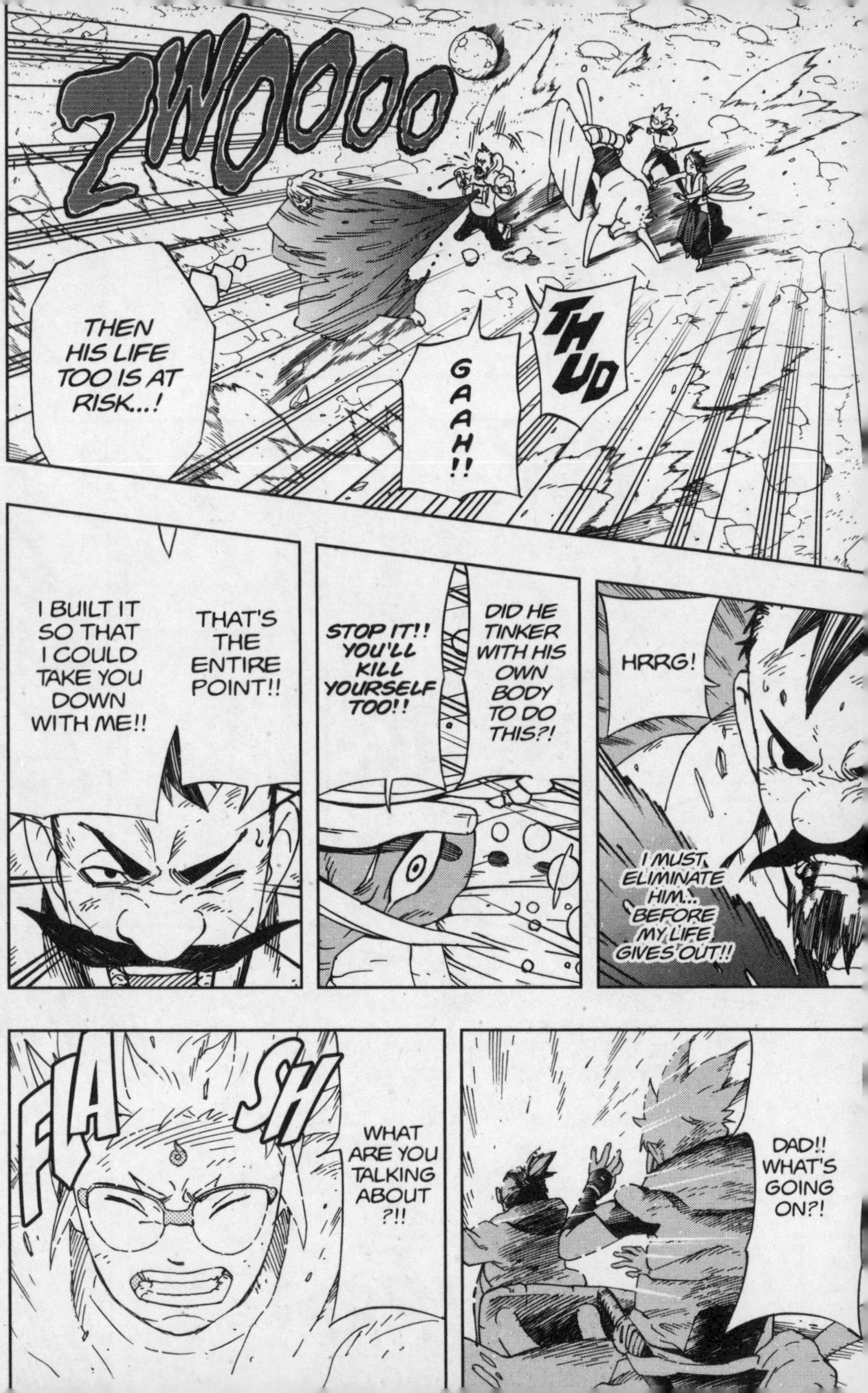
ZWOOOO
THUD
GAAH!!
THEN HIS LIFE TOO IS AT RISK...!
HRRG!
I MUST ELIMINATE HIM... BEFORE MY LIFE GIVES OUT!!
DID HE TINKER WITH HIS OWN BODY TO DO THIS?!
STOP IT!! YOU'LL KILL YOURSELF TOO!!
THAT'S THE ENTIRE POINT!!
I BUILT IT SO THAT I COULD TAKE YOU DOWN WITH ME!!
DAD!! WHAT'S GOING ON?!
WHAT ARE YOU TALKING ABOUT?!!
FLASH

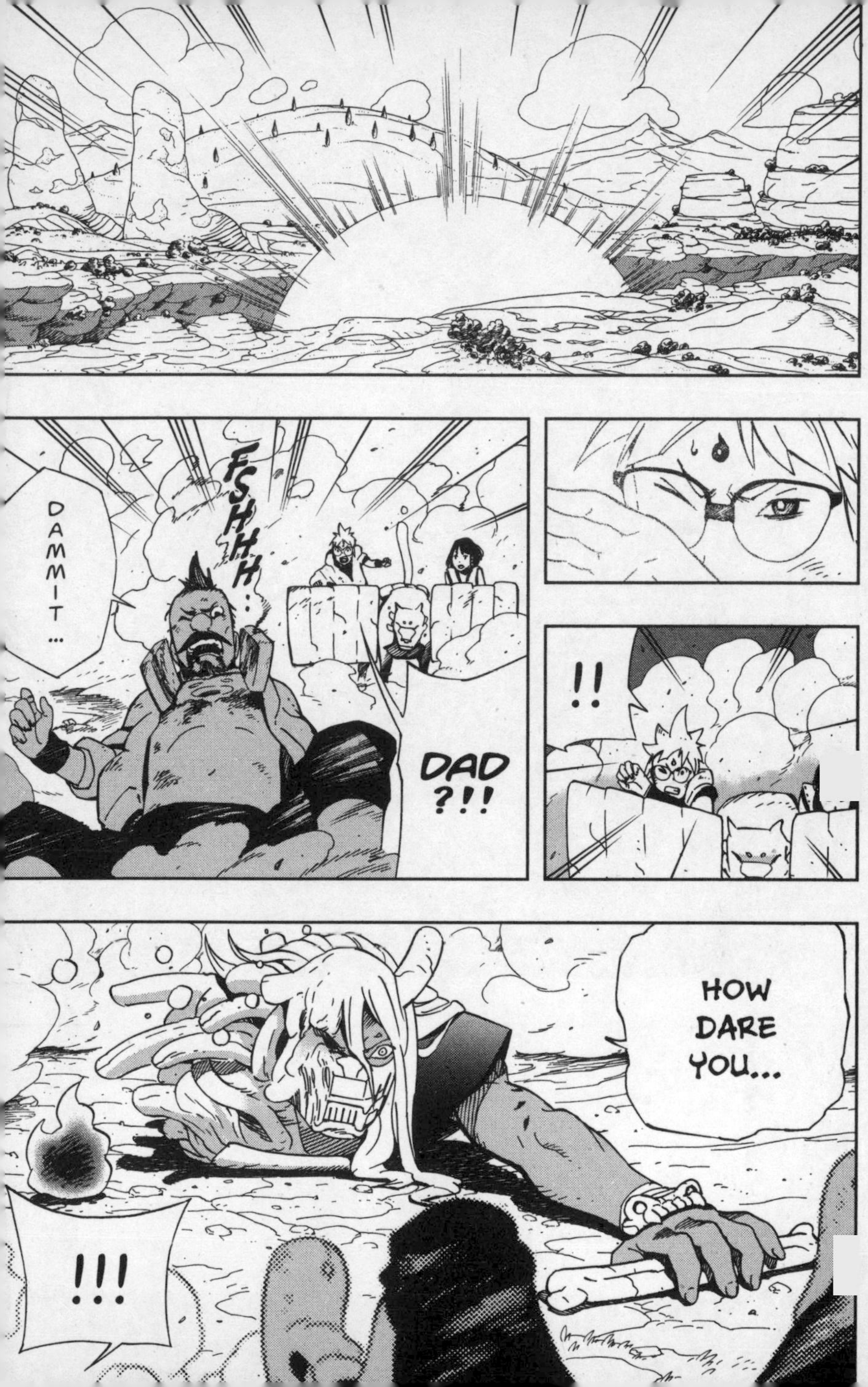
!!
FSHHH...
DAMMIT...
DAD?!!
HOW DARE YOU...
!!!

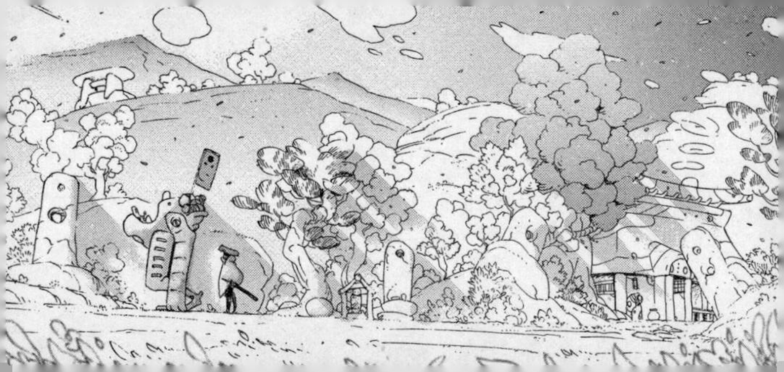

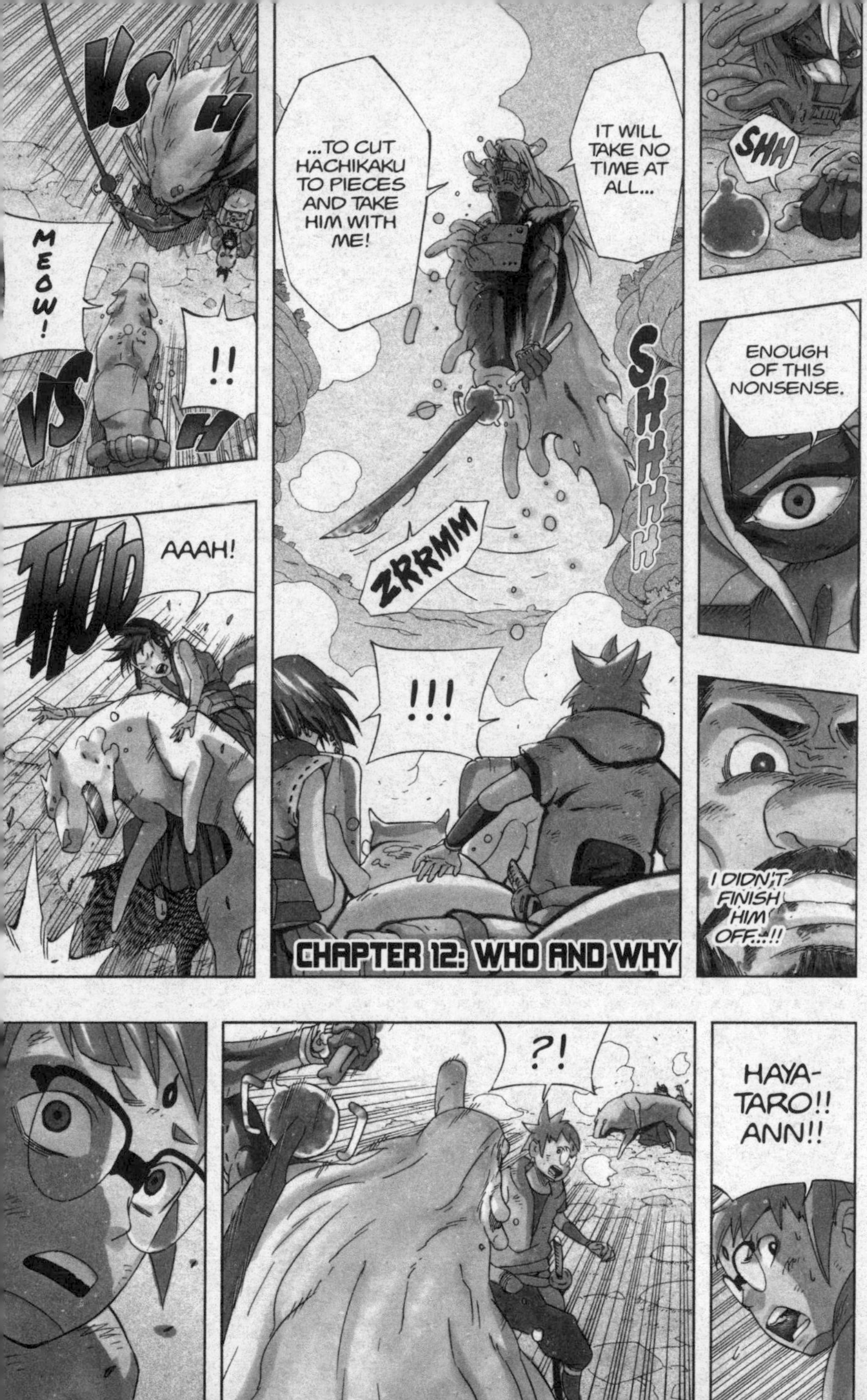
SHH
ENOUGH OF THIS NONSENSE.
I DIDN'T FINISH HIM OFF...!!
IT WILL TAKE NO TIME AT ALL...
...TO CUT HACHIKAKU TO PIECES AND TAKE HIM WITH ME!
SHHHHHH
ZRRMM
!!!
CHAPTER 12: WHO AND WHY
VSH
MEOW!
!!
VSH
THUD
AAAH!
HAYA-TARO!! ANN!!
?!

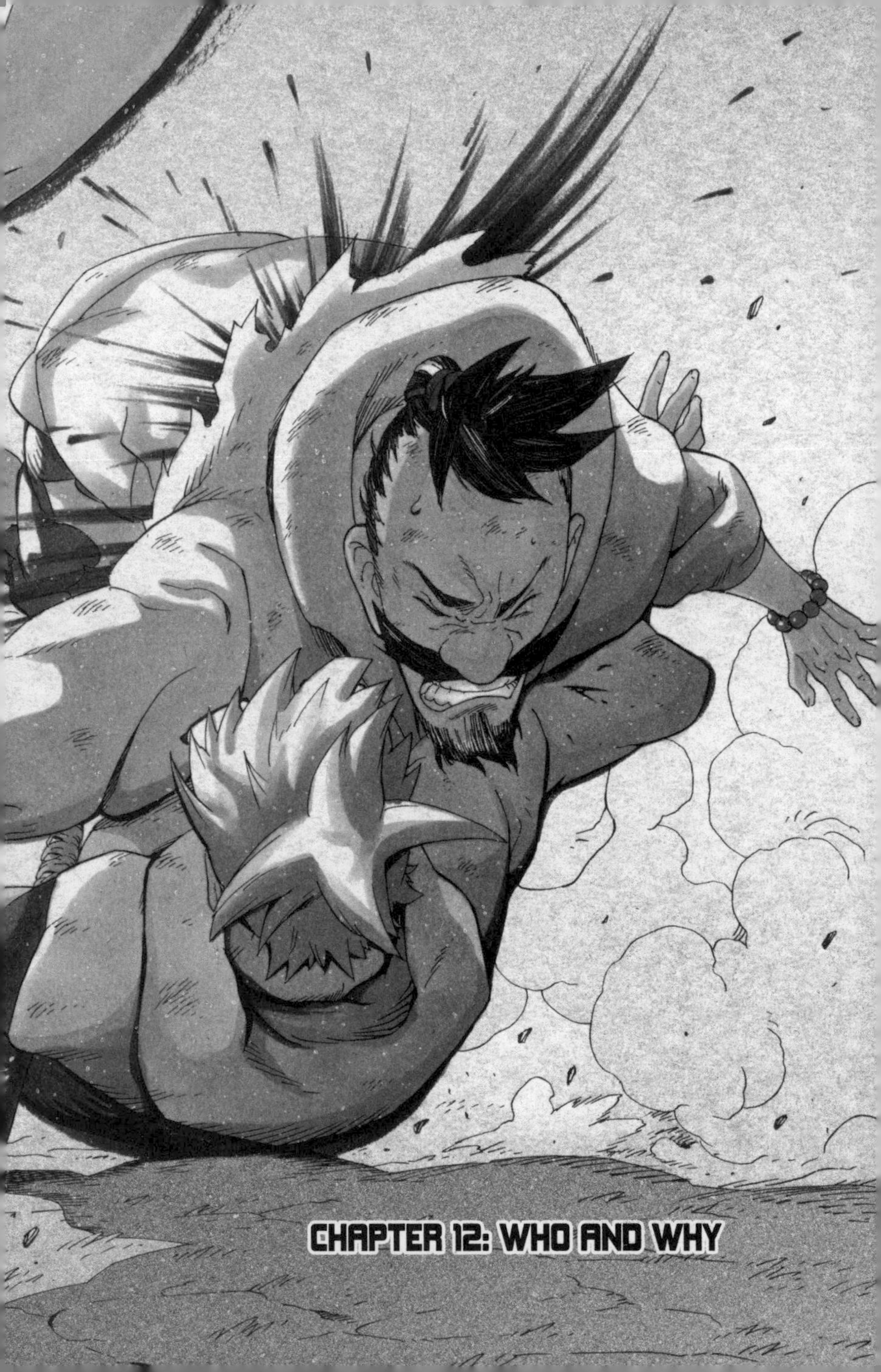
CHAPTER 12: WHO AND WHY

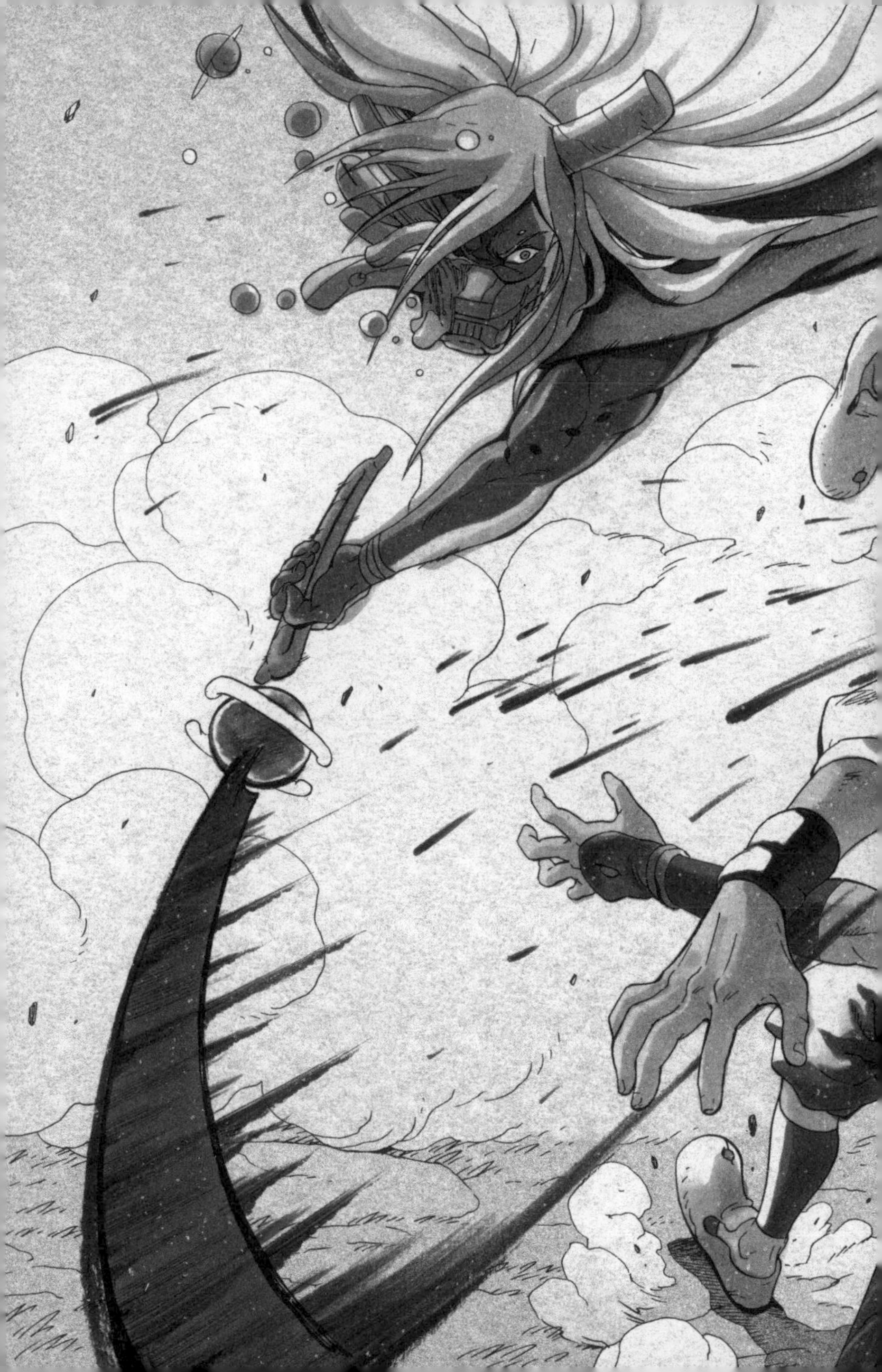

SAMURAI 8
THE TALE OF HACHIMARU

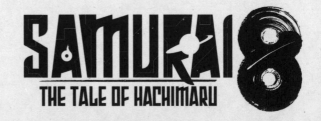

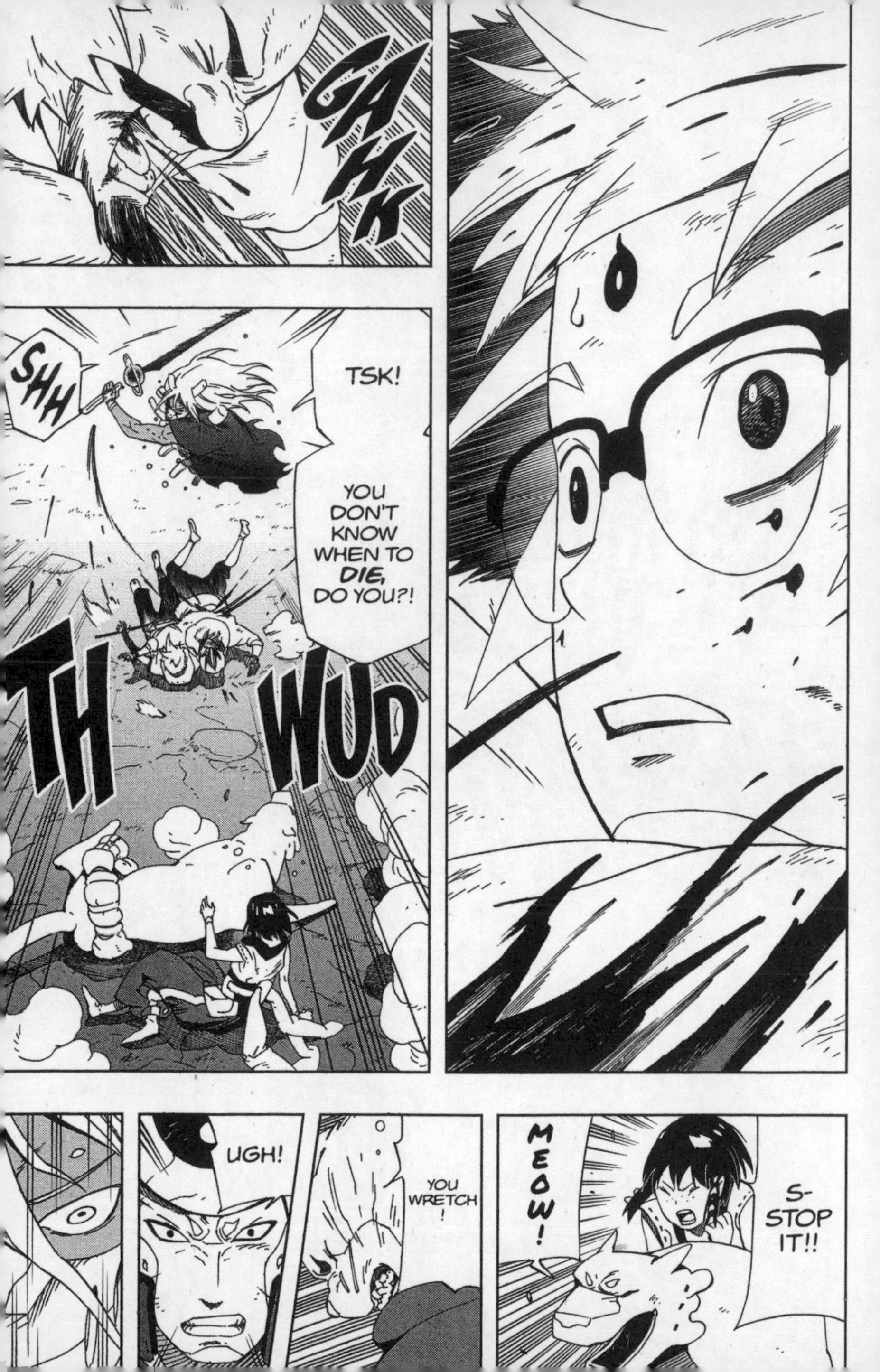
GAHNK
SHH
TSK!
YOU DON'T KNOW WHEN TO DIE, DO YOU?!
THWUD
MEOW!
S-STOP IT!!
YOU WRETCH!
UGH!

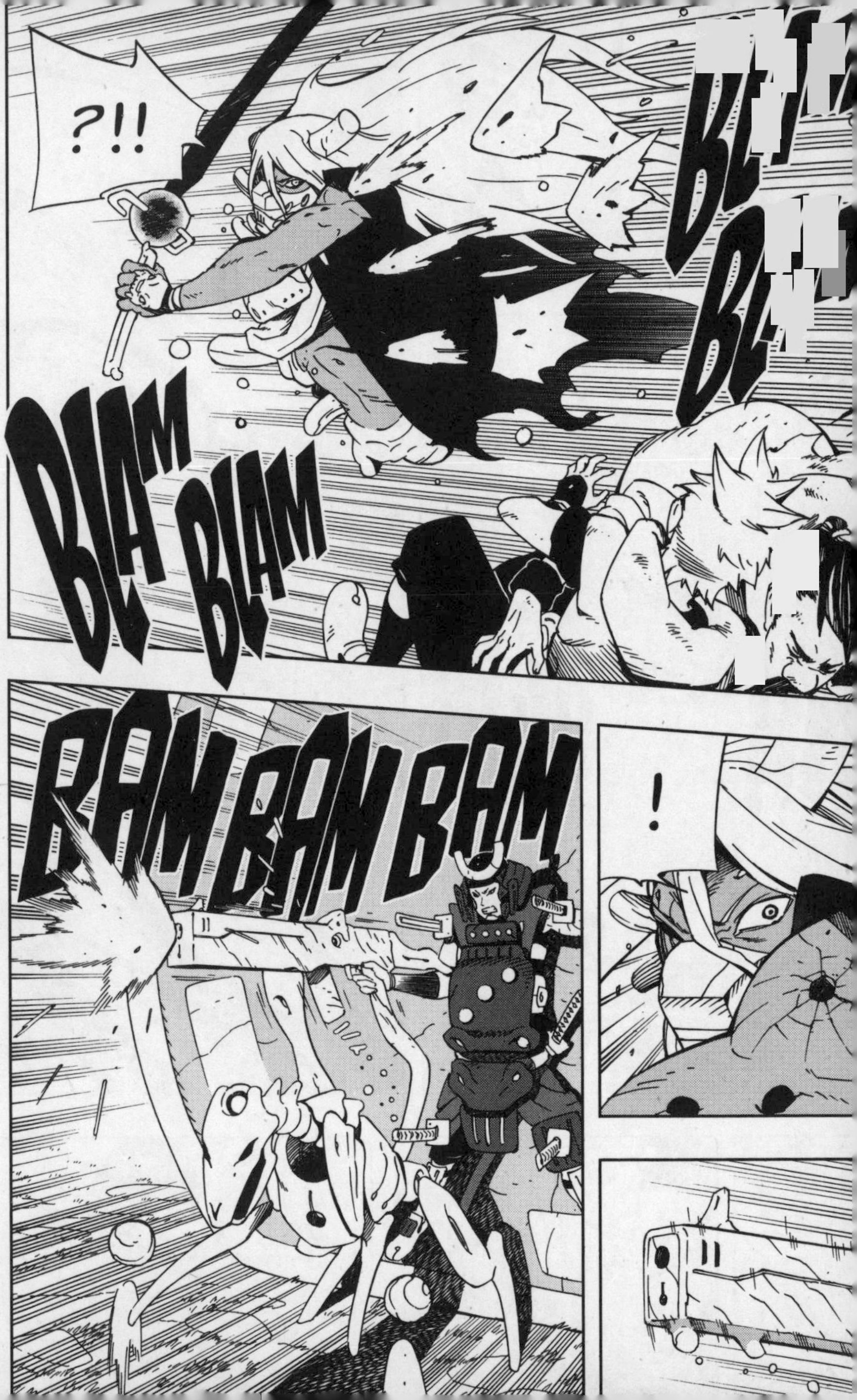
?!!
BLAM BLAM
!
BAM BAM BAM

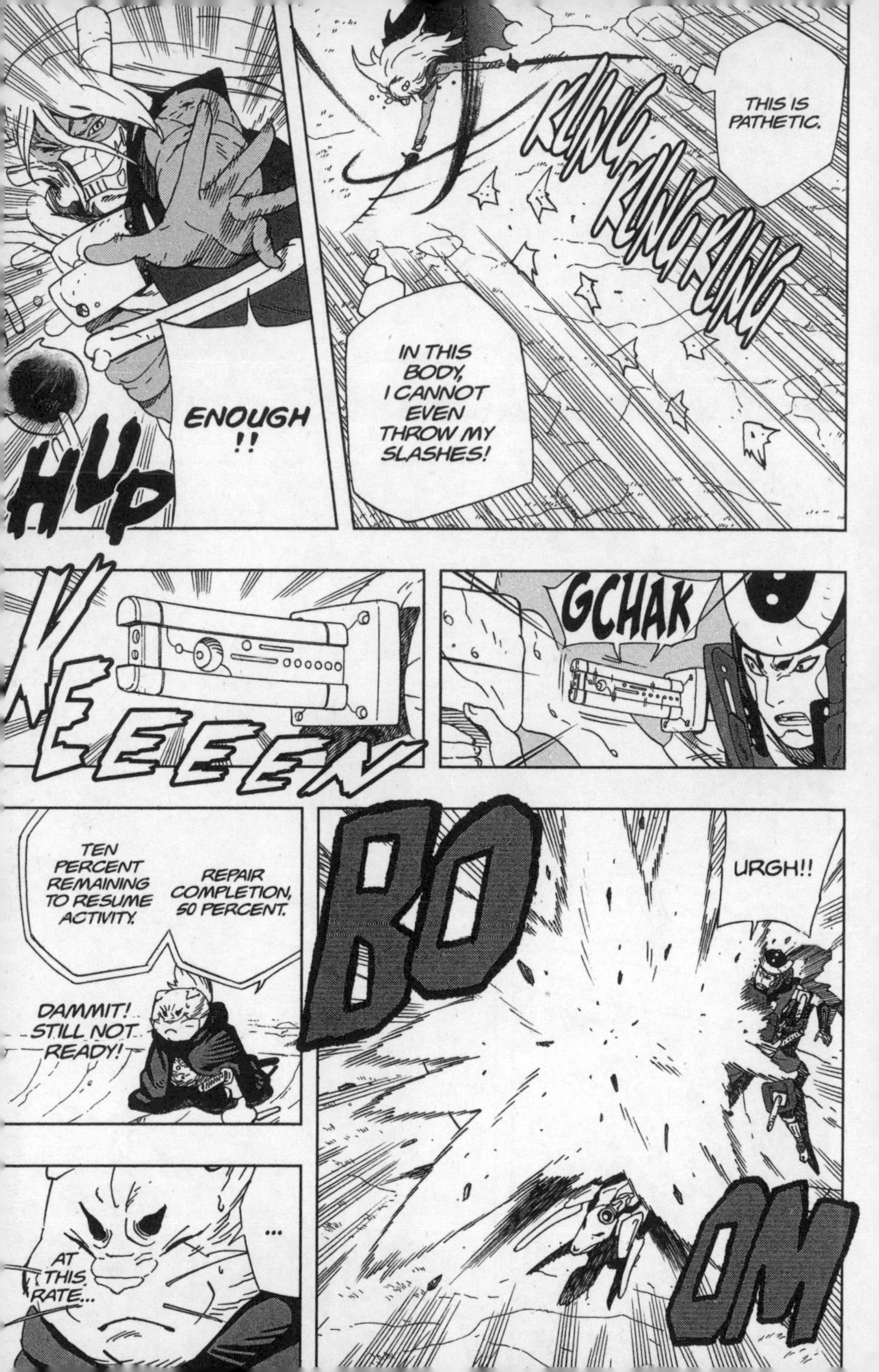
THIS IS PATHETIC.
KLNG KLNG KLNG
IN THIS BODY, I CANNOT EVEN THROW MY SLASHES!
ENOUGH!!
HUP
GCHAK
KEEEEN
BOOM
URGH!!
REPAIR COMPLETION, 50 PERCENT.
TEN PERCENT REMAINING TO RESUME ACTIVITY.
DAMMIT! STILL NOT READY!
...
AT THIS RATE...

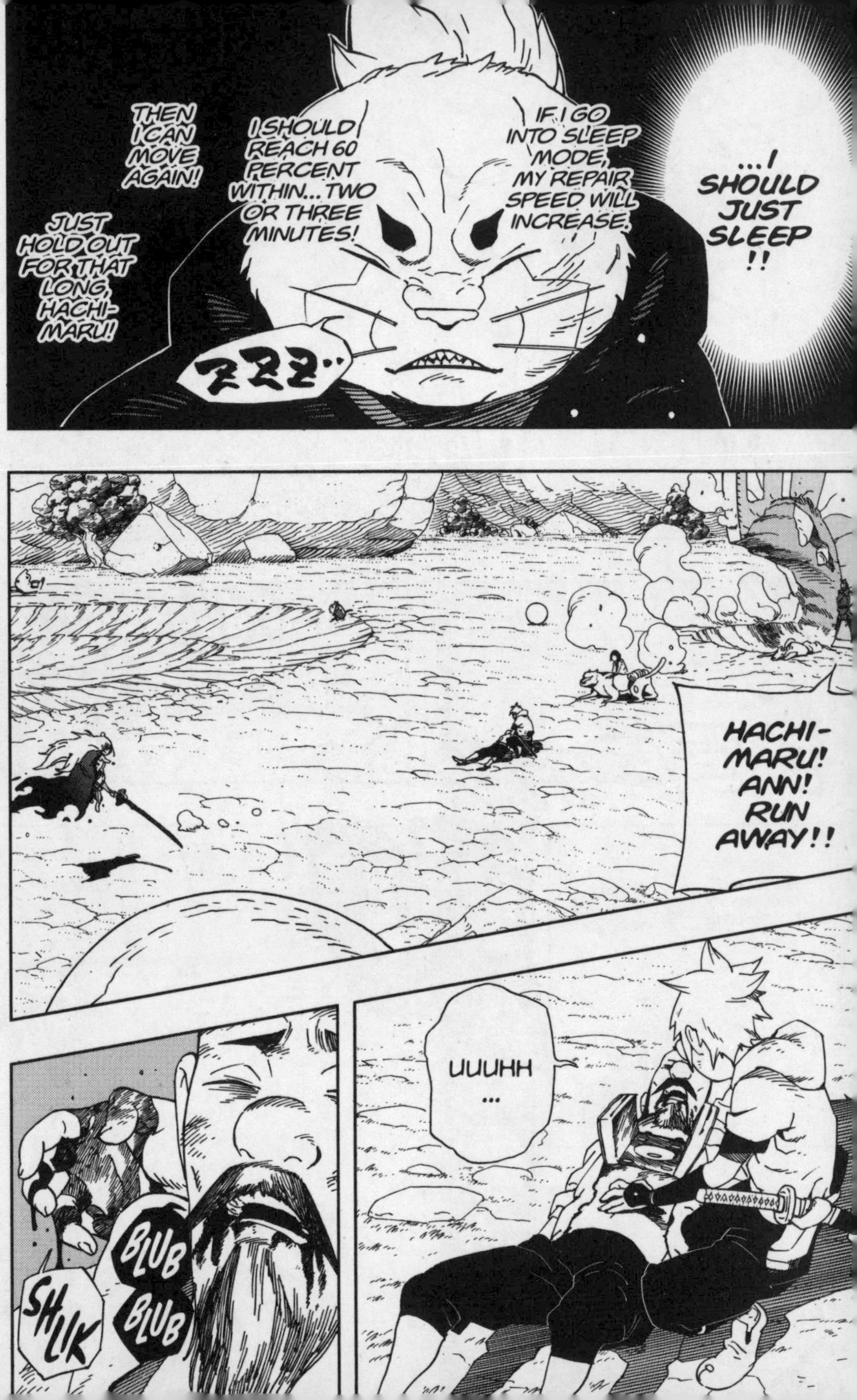
...I SHOULD JUST SLEEP!!
IF I GO INTO SLEEP MODE, MY REPAIR SPEED WILL INCREASE.
I SHOULD REACH 60 PERCENT WITHIN... TWO OR THREE MINUTES!
THEN I CAN MOVE AGAIN!
JUST HOLD OUT FOR THAT LONG, HACHI-MARU!
ZZZ...
HACHI-MARU! ANN! RUN AWAY!!
UUUHH ...
BLUB
BLUB
SHLIK

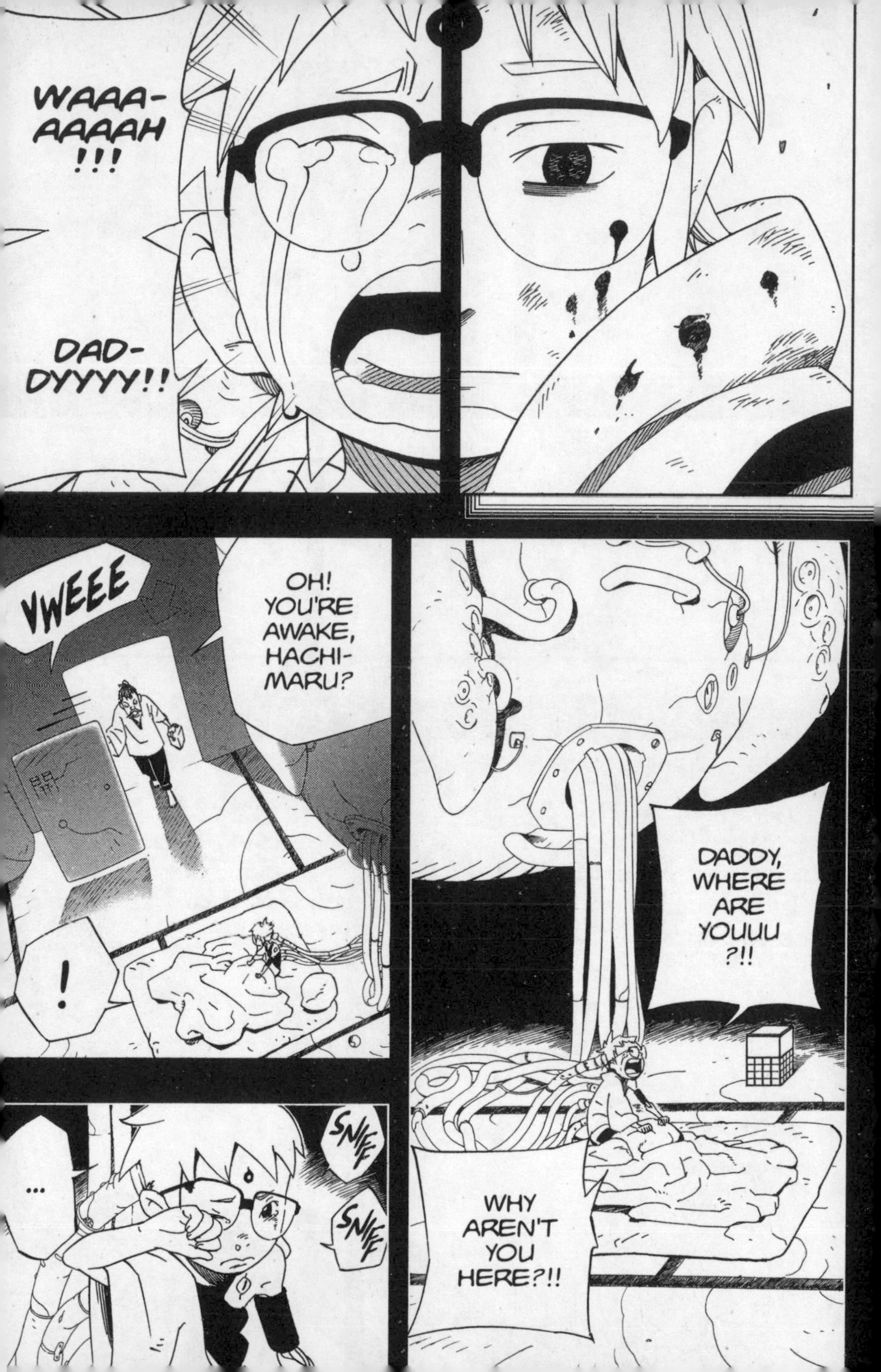
WAAAA-AAAAH!!!
DAD-DYYYY!!
DADDY, WHERE ARE YOUUU?!!
WHY AREN'T YOU HERE?!!
OH! YOU'RE AWAKE, HACHI-MARU?
VWEEE
!
SNIFF
SNIFF
...

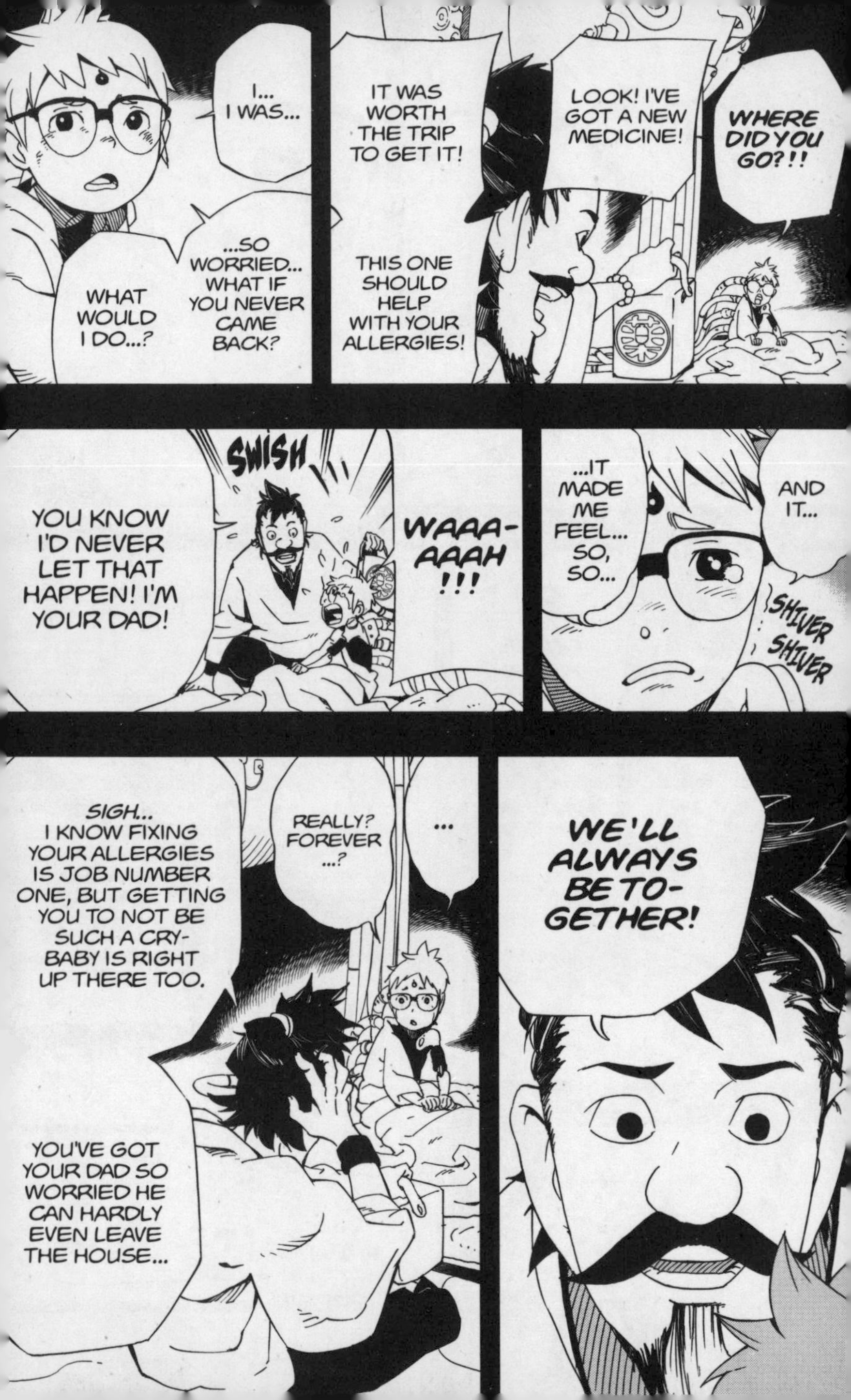
WHERE DID YOU GO?!!
LOOK! I'VE GOT A NEW MEDICINE!
IT WAS WORTH THE TRIP TO GET IT!
THIS ONE SHOULD HELP WITH YOUR ALLERGIES!
I... I WAS...
...SO WORRIED... WHAT IF YOU NEVER CAME BACK?
WHAT WOULD I DO...?
AND IT...
...IT MADE ME FEEL... SO, SO...
SHIVER SHIVER
WAAAAAAH!!!
SWISH
YOU KNOW I'D NEVER LET THAT HAPPEN! I'M YOUR DAD!
WE'LL ALWAYS BE TOGETHER!
...
REALLY? FOREVER...?
SIGH... I KNOW FIXING YOUR ALLERGIES IS JOB NUMBER ONE, BUT GETTING YOU TO NOT BE SUCH A CRY-BABY IS RIGHT UP THERE TOO.
YOU'VE GOT YOUR DAD SO WORRIED HE CAN HARDLY EVEN LEAVE THE HOUSE...

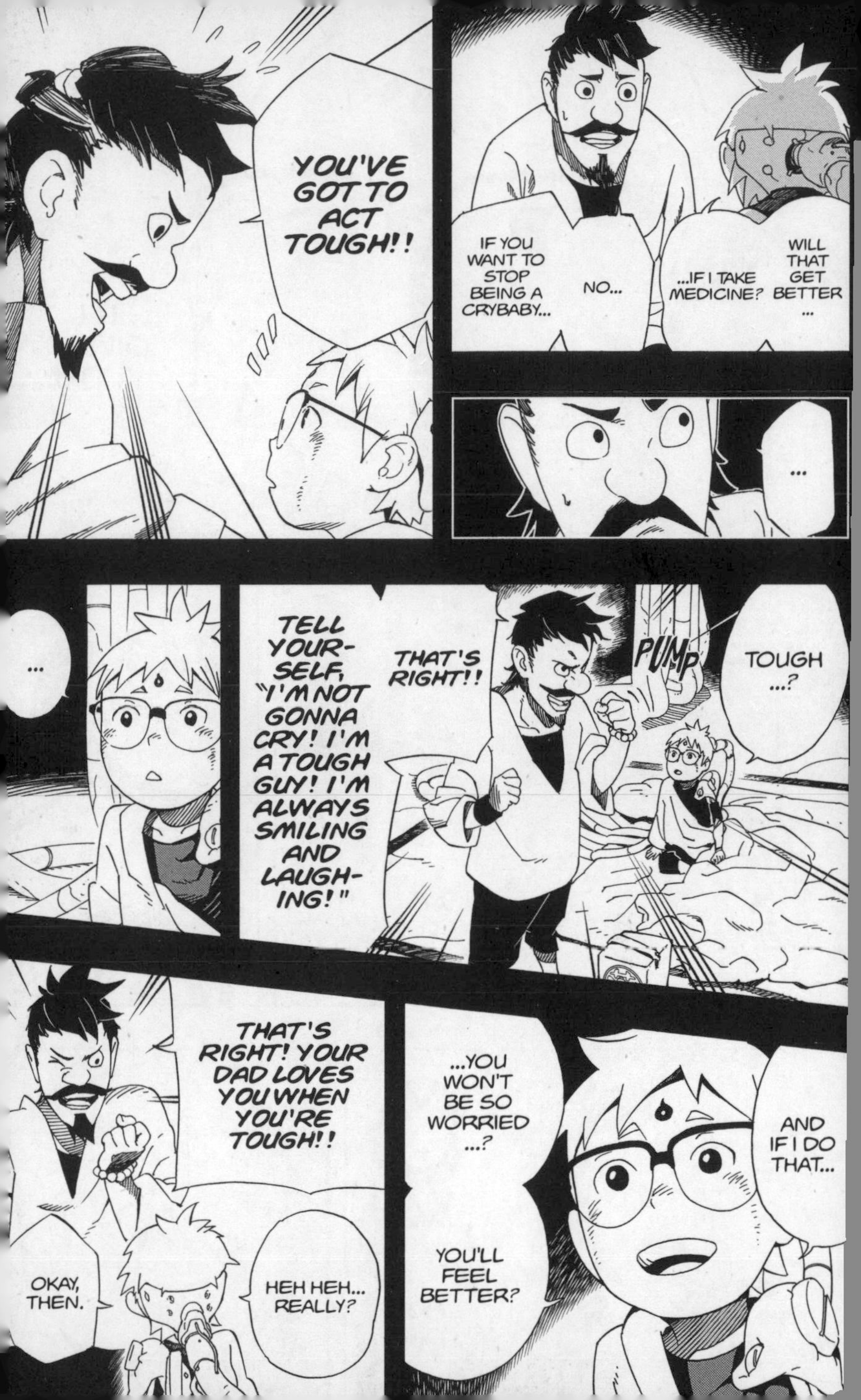
WILL THAT GET BETTER ...
...IF I TAKE MEDICINE?
NO...
IF YOU WANT TO STOP BEING A CRYBABY...
...
YOU'VE GOT TO ACT TOUGH!!
TOUGH ...?
PUMP
THAT'S RIGHT!!
TELL YOURSELF, "I'M NOT GONNA CRY! I'M A TOUGH GUY! I'M ALWAYS SMILING AND LAUGHING!"
...
AND IF I DO THAT...
...YOU WON'T BE SO WORRIED ...?
YOU'LL FEEL BETTER?
THAT'S RIGHT! YOUR DAD LOVES YOU WHEN YOU'RE TOUGH!!
HEH HEH... REALLY?
OKAY, THEN.

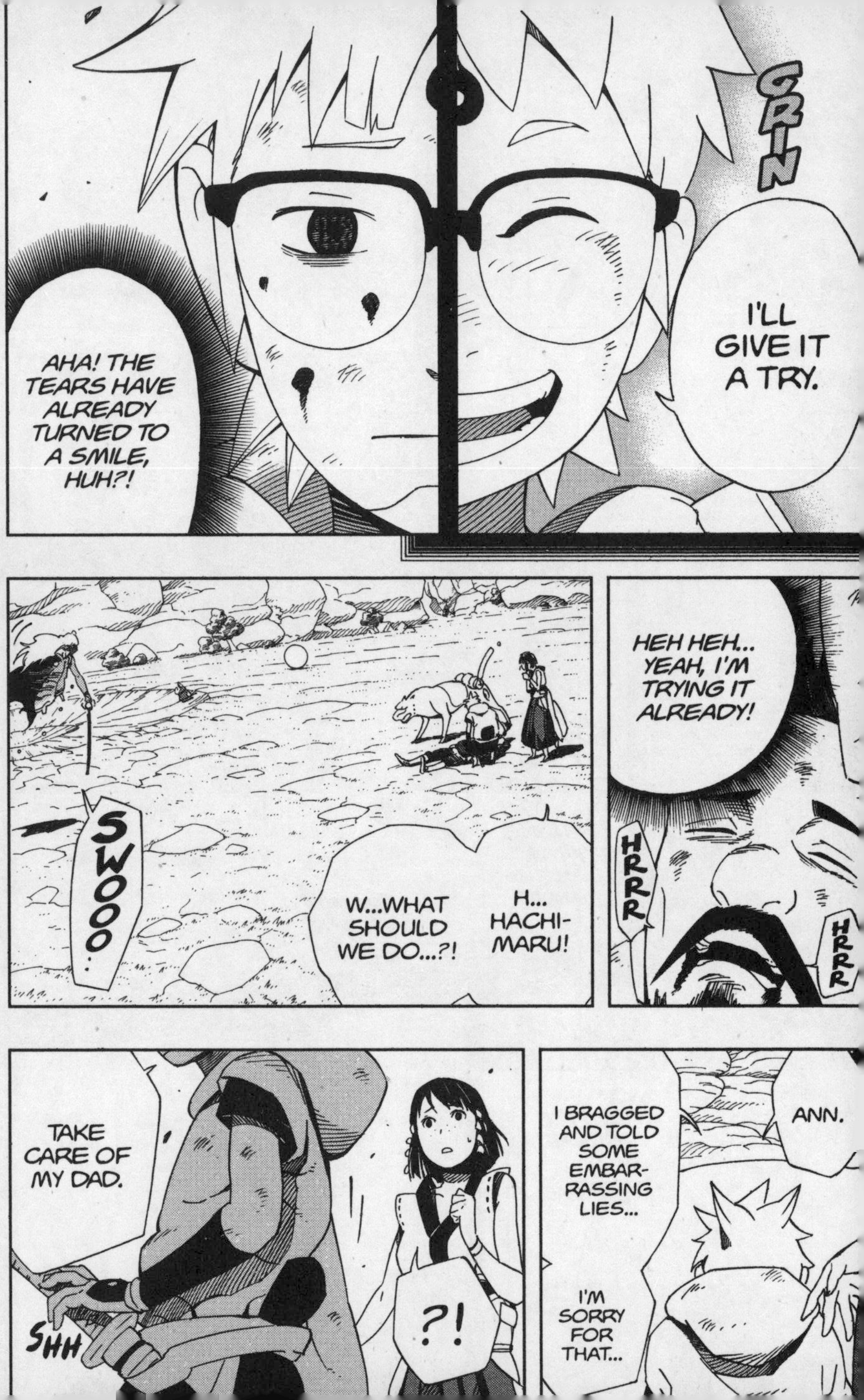
GRIN
I'LL GIVE IT A TRY.
AHA! THE TEARS HAVE ALREADY TURNED TO A SMILE, HUH?!
HEH HEH... YEAH, I'M TRYING IT ALREADY!
HRRR
HRRR
H... HACHI-MARU!
W...WHAT SHOULD WE DO...?!
SWOOO...
ANN.
I BRAGGED AND TOLD SOME EMBAR-RASSING LIES...
I'M SORRY FOR THAT...
?!
TAKE CARE OF MY DAD.
SHH

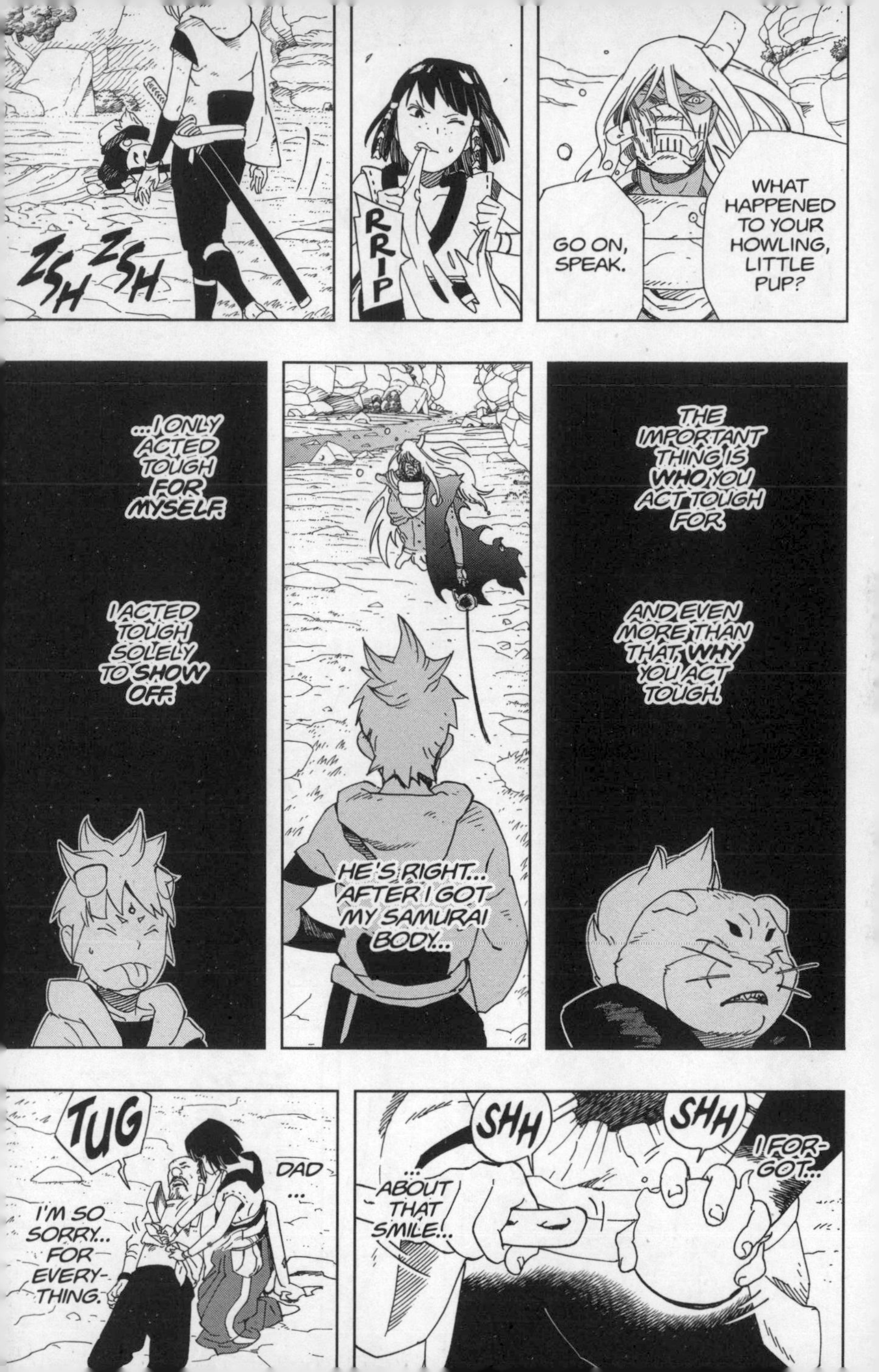
WHAT HAPPENED TO YOUR HOWLING, LITTLE PUP?
GO ON, SPEAK.
RRIP
ZSH
ZSH
THE IMPORTANT THING IS WHO YOU ACT TOUGH FOR.
AND EVEN MORE THAN THAT, WHY YOU ACT TOUGH.
HE'S RIGHT... AFTER I GOT MY SAMURAI BODY...
...I ONLY ACTED TOUGH FOR MYSELF.
I ACTED TOUGH SOLELY TO SHOW OFF.
SHH
SHH
I FOR-GOT...
...ABOUT THAT SMILE...
TUG
DAD...
I'M SO SORRY... FOR EVERY-THING.

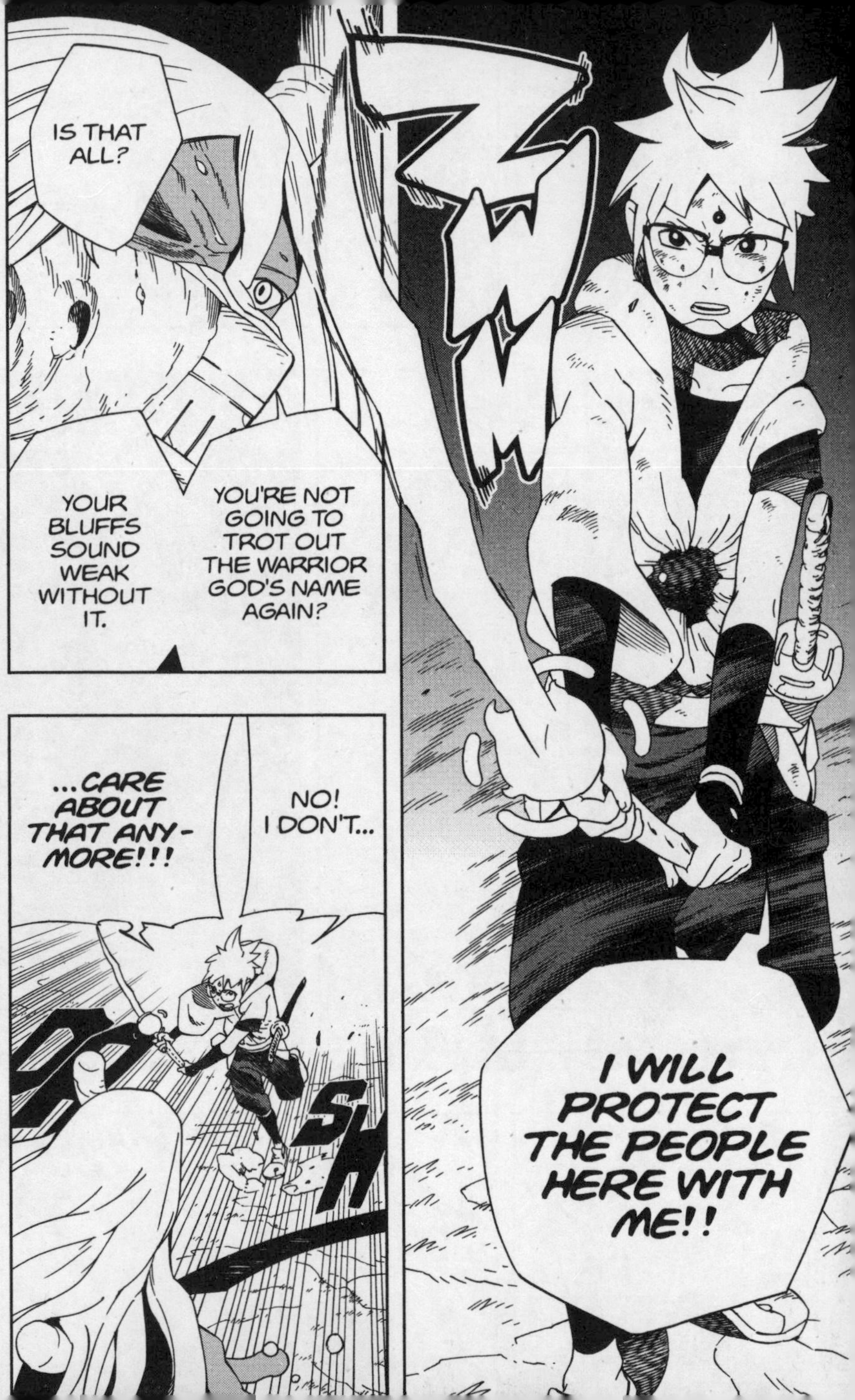
I WILL PROTECT THE PEOPLE HERE WITH ME!!
IS THAT ALL?
YOU'RE NOT GOING TO TROT OUT THE WARRIOR GOD'S NAME AGAIN?
YOUR BLUFFS SOUND WEAK WITHOUT IT.
NO! I DON'T...
...CARE ABOUT THAT ANY-MORE!!!
SH

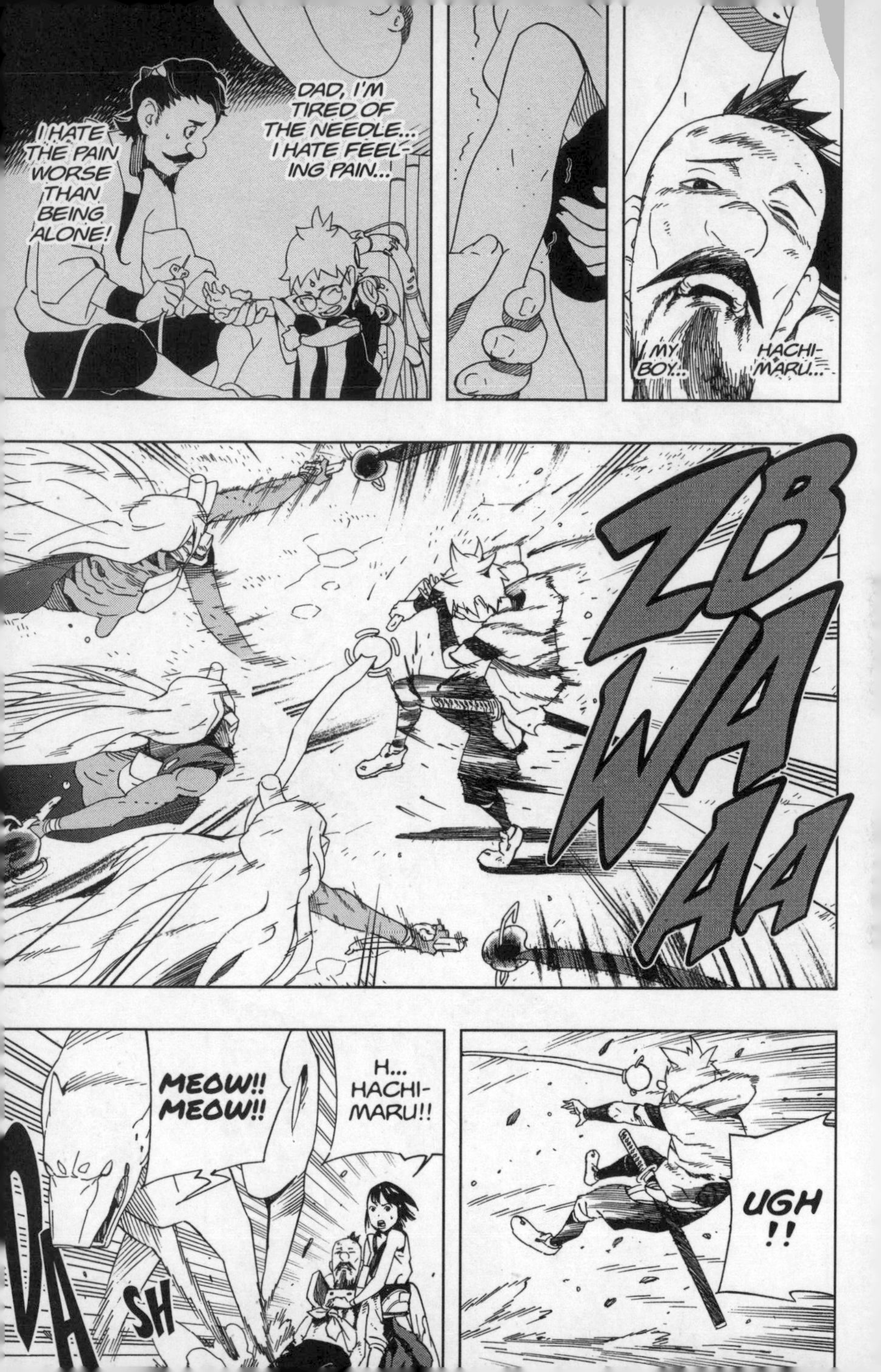
HACHI-MARU...
MY BOY...
DAD, I'M TIRED OF THE NEEDLE... I HATE FEEL-ING PAIN...
I HATE THE PAIN WORSE THAN BEING ALONE!
ZBAWAAA
UGH!!
H... HACHI-MARU!!
MEOW!! MEOW!!
DASH

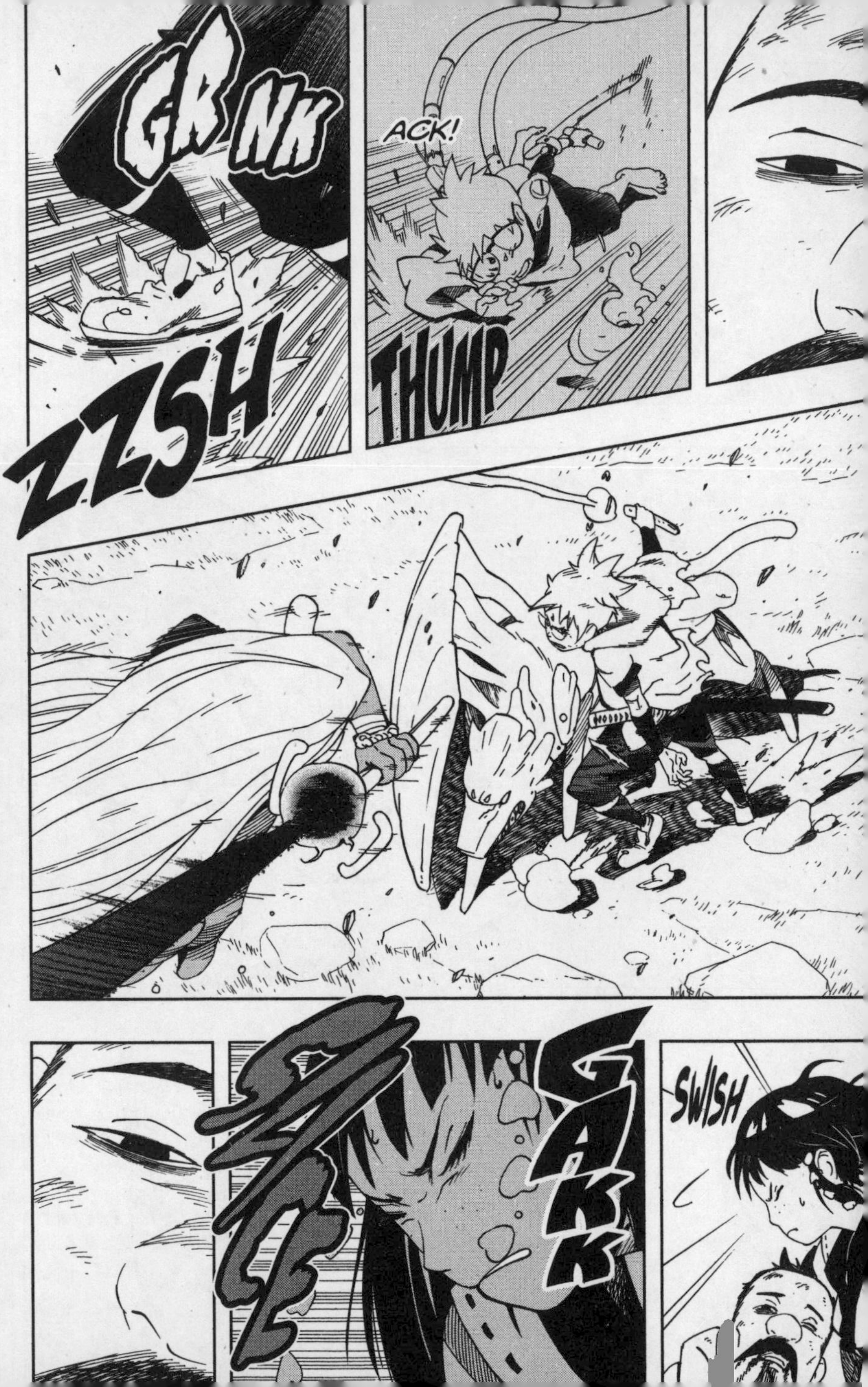
ACK!
THUMP
ZZSH
SWISH

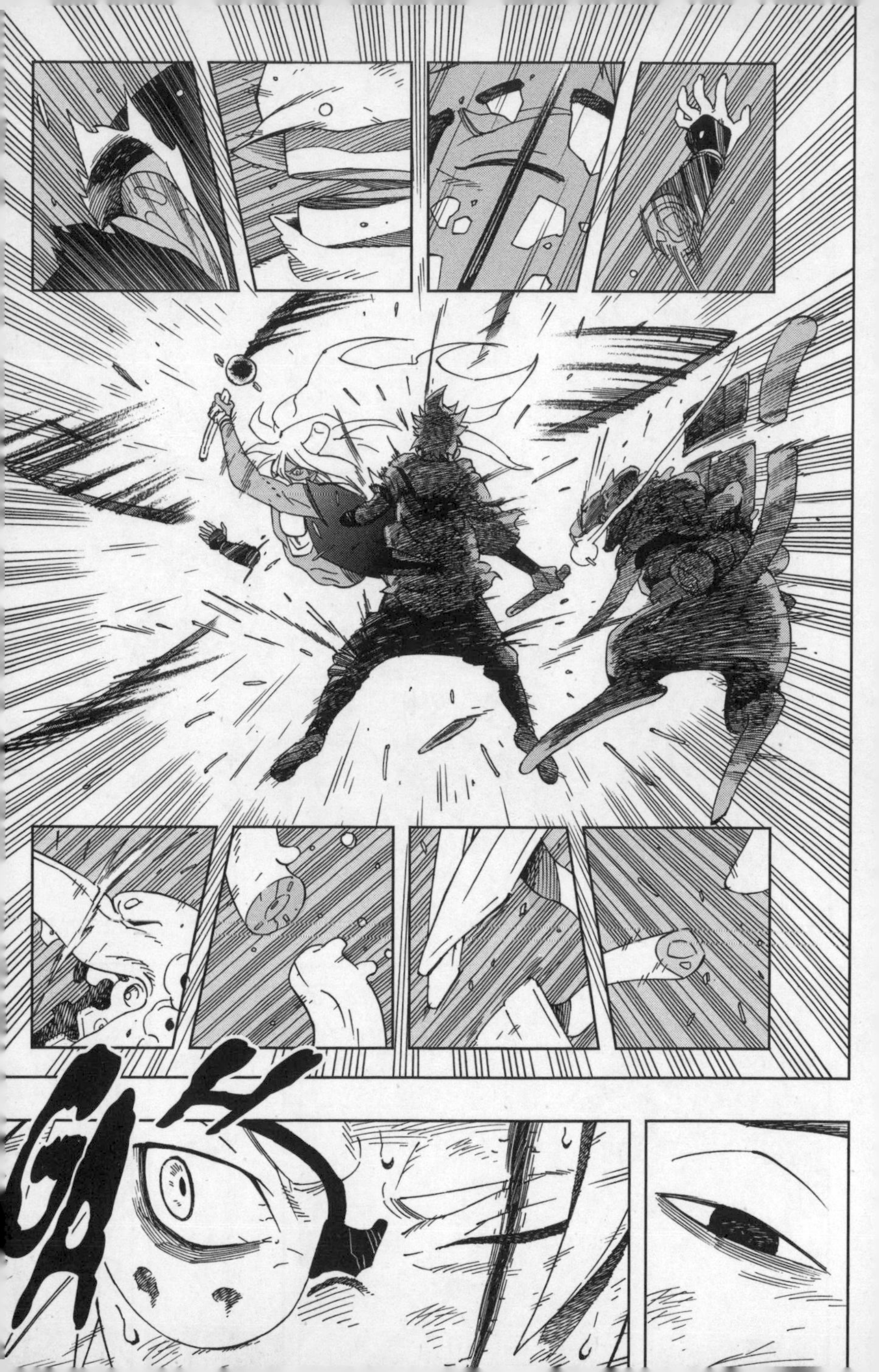
GAH

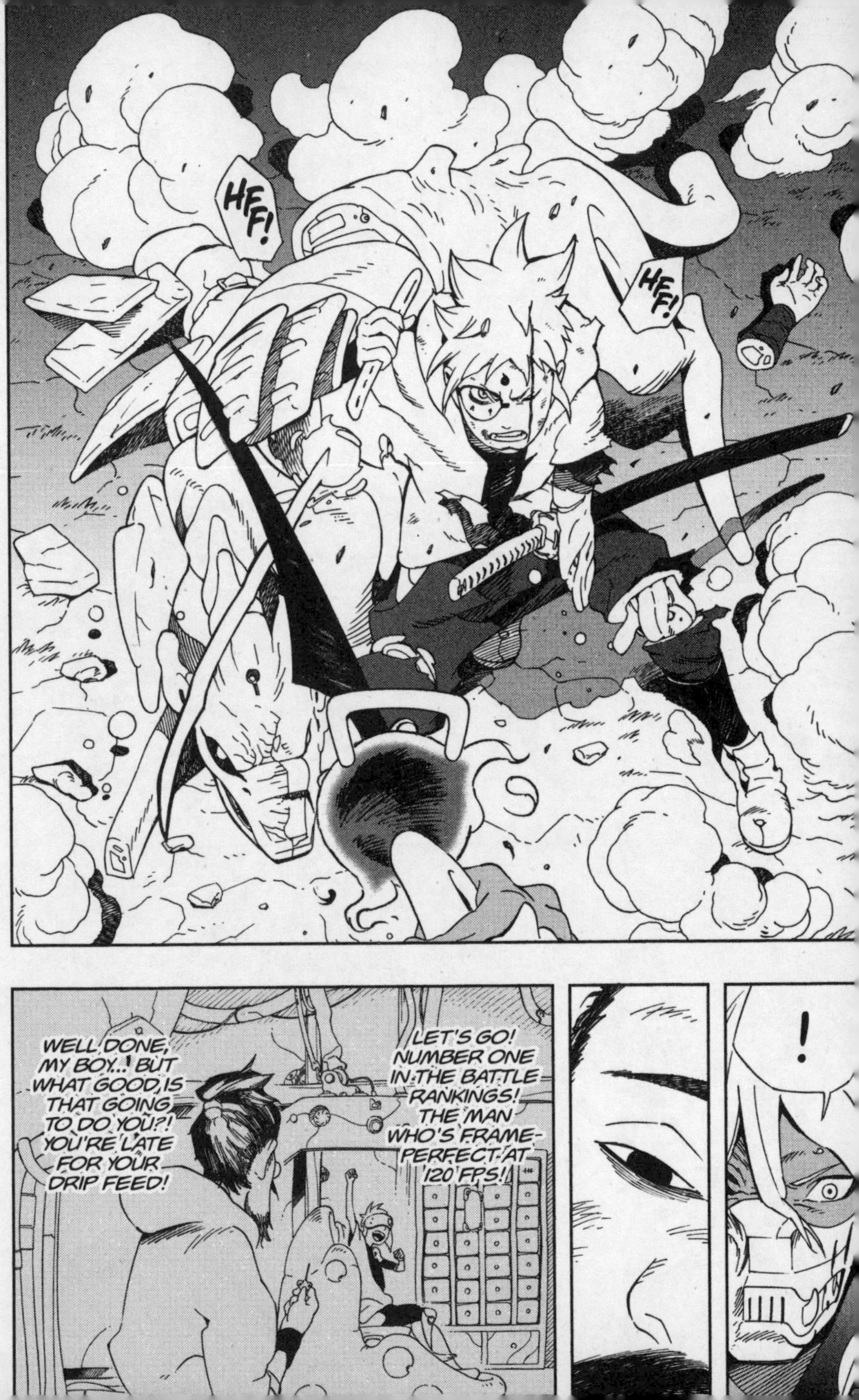
HFF!
HFF!
!
LET'S GO! NUMBER ONE IN THE BATTLE RANKINGS! THE MAN WHO'S FRAME-PERFECT AT 120 FPS!
WELL DONE, MY BOY...! BUT WHAT GOOD IS THAT GOING TO DO YOU?! YOU'RE LATE FOR YOUR DRIP FEED!

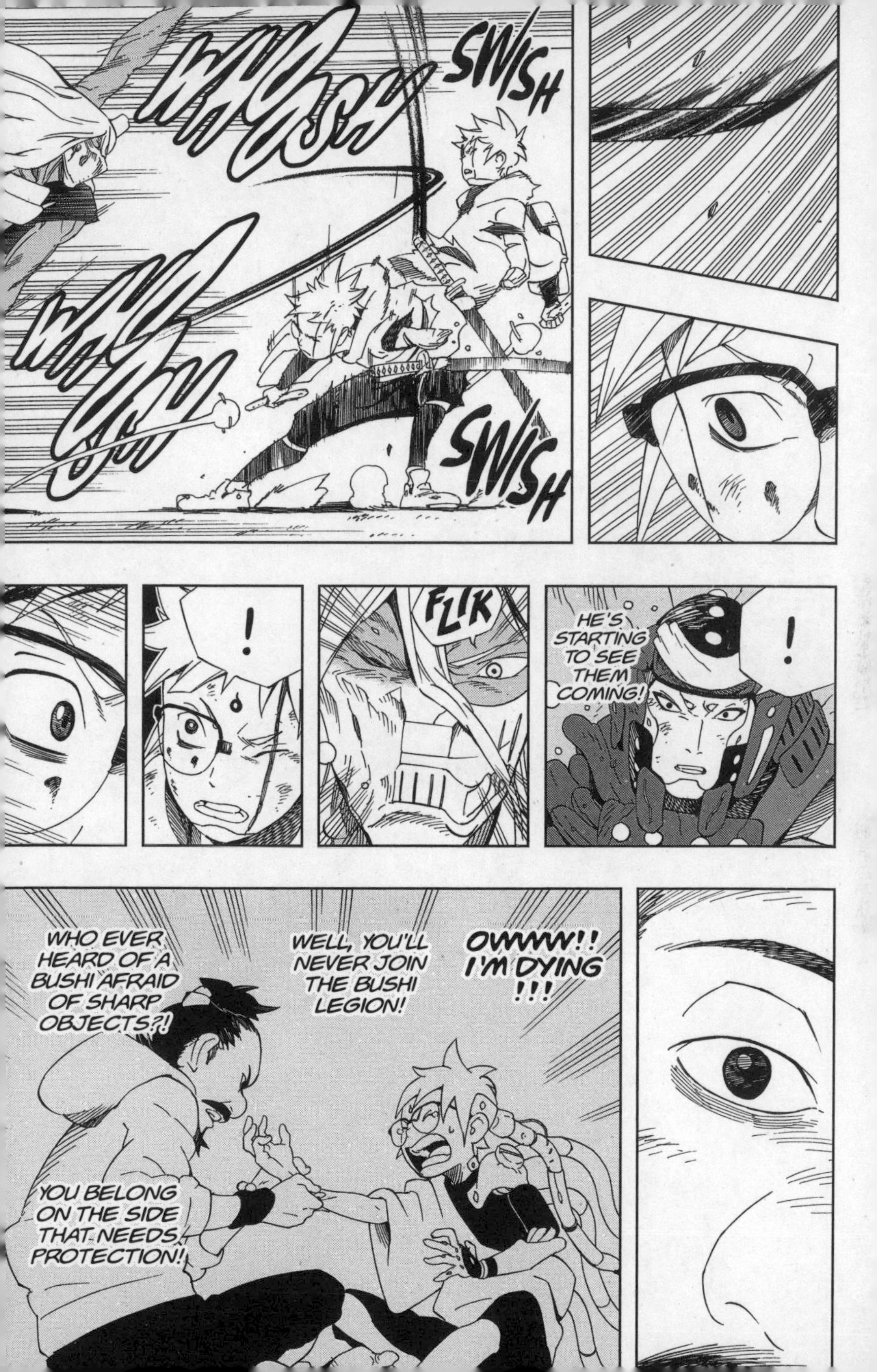
SWISH
SWISH
!
HE'S STARTING TO SEE THEM COMING!
FLIK
!
OWWW!! I'M DYING!!!
WELL, YOU'LL NEVER JOIN THE BUSHI LEGION!
WHO EVER HEARD OF A BUSHI AFRAID OF SHARP OBJECTS?!
YOU BELONG ON THE SIDE THAT NEEDS PROTECTION!

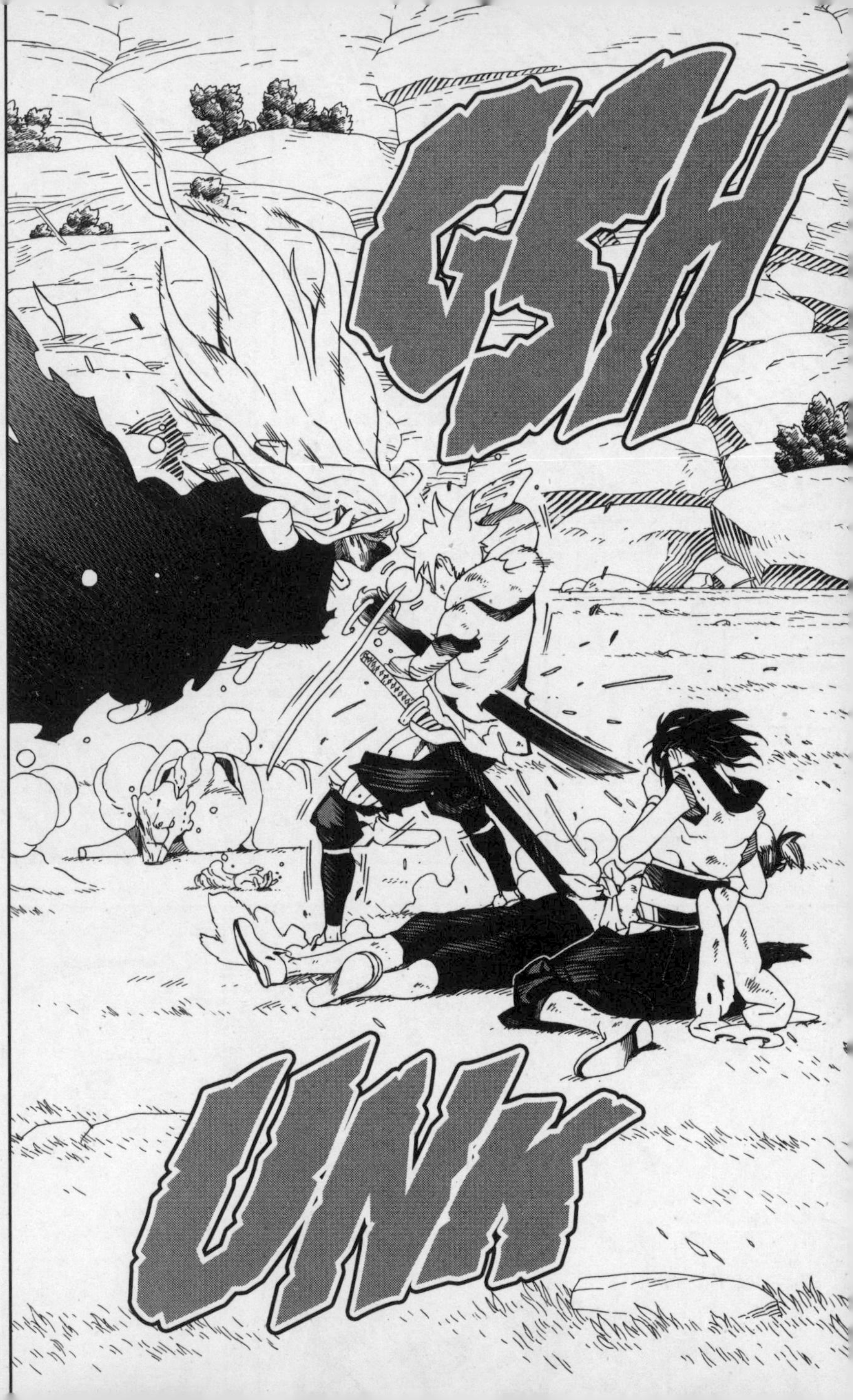
GSH
UNK

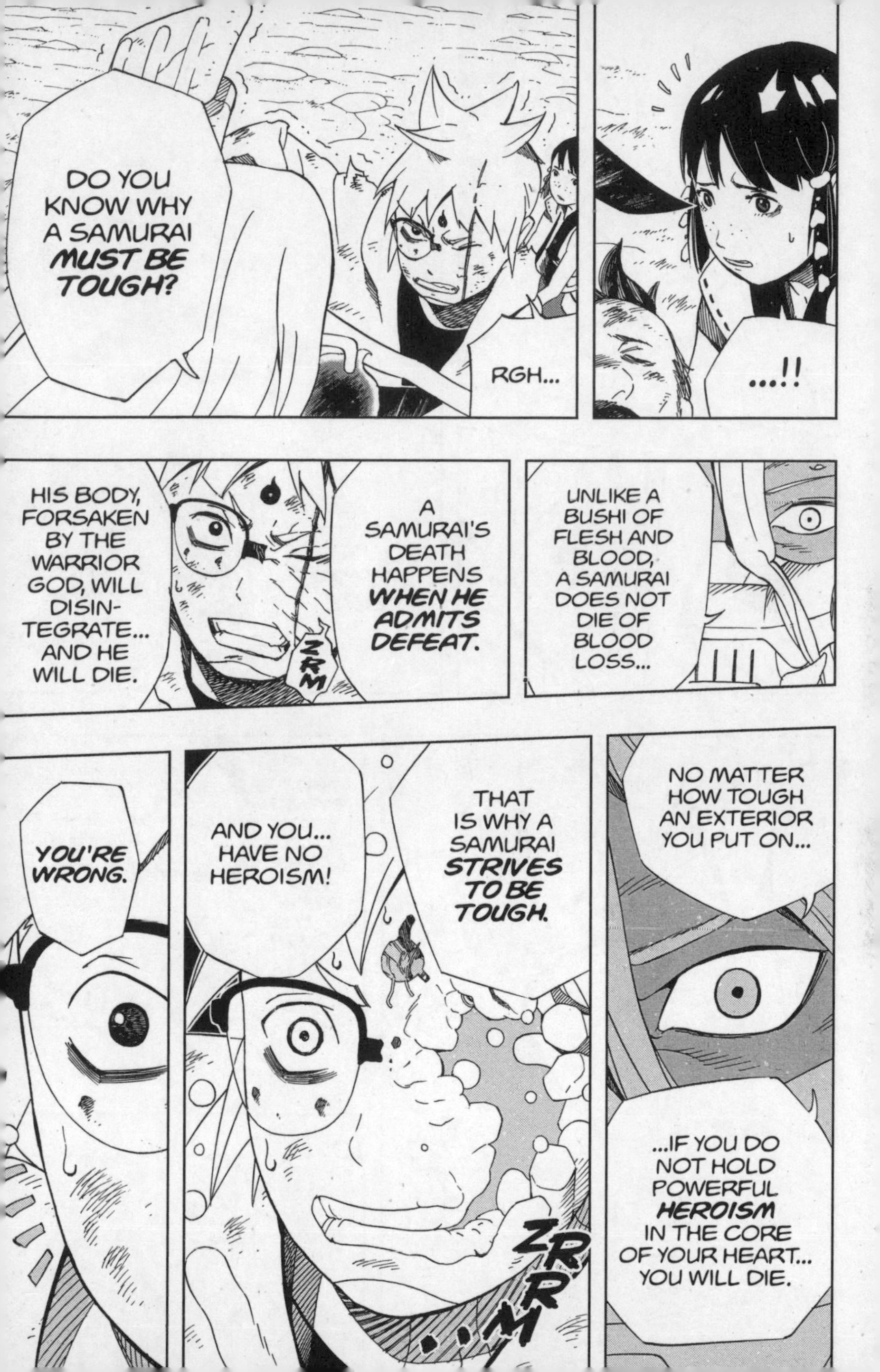
...!!
DO YOU KNOW WHY A SAMURAI *MUST BE TOUGH?*
RGH...
UNLIKE A BUSHI OF FLESH AND BLOOD, A SAMURAI DOES NOT DIE OF BLOOD LOSS...
A SAMURAI'S DEATH HAPPENS *WHEN HE ADMITS DEFEAT.*
HIS BODY, FORSAKEN BY THE WARRIOR GOD, WILL DISIN-TEGRATE... AND HE WILL DIE.
ZRM
NO MATTER HOW TOUGH AN EXTERIOR YOU PUT ON...
...IF YOU DO NOT HOLD POWERFUL *HEROISM* IN THE CORE OF YOUR HEART... YOU WILL DIE.
THAT IS WHY A SAMURAI *STRIVES TO BE TOUGH.*
AND YOU... HAVE NO HEROISM!
ZRRRM
YOU'RE WRONG.

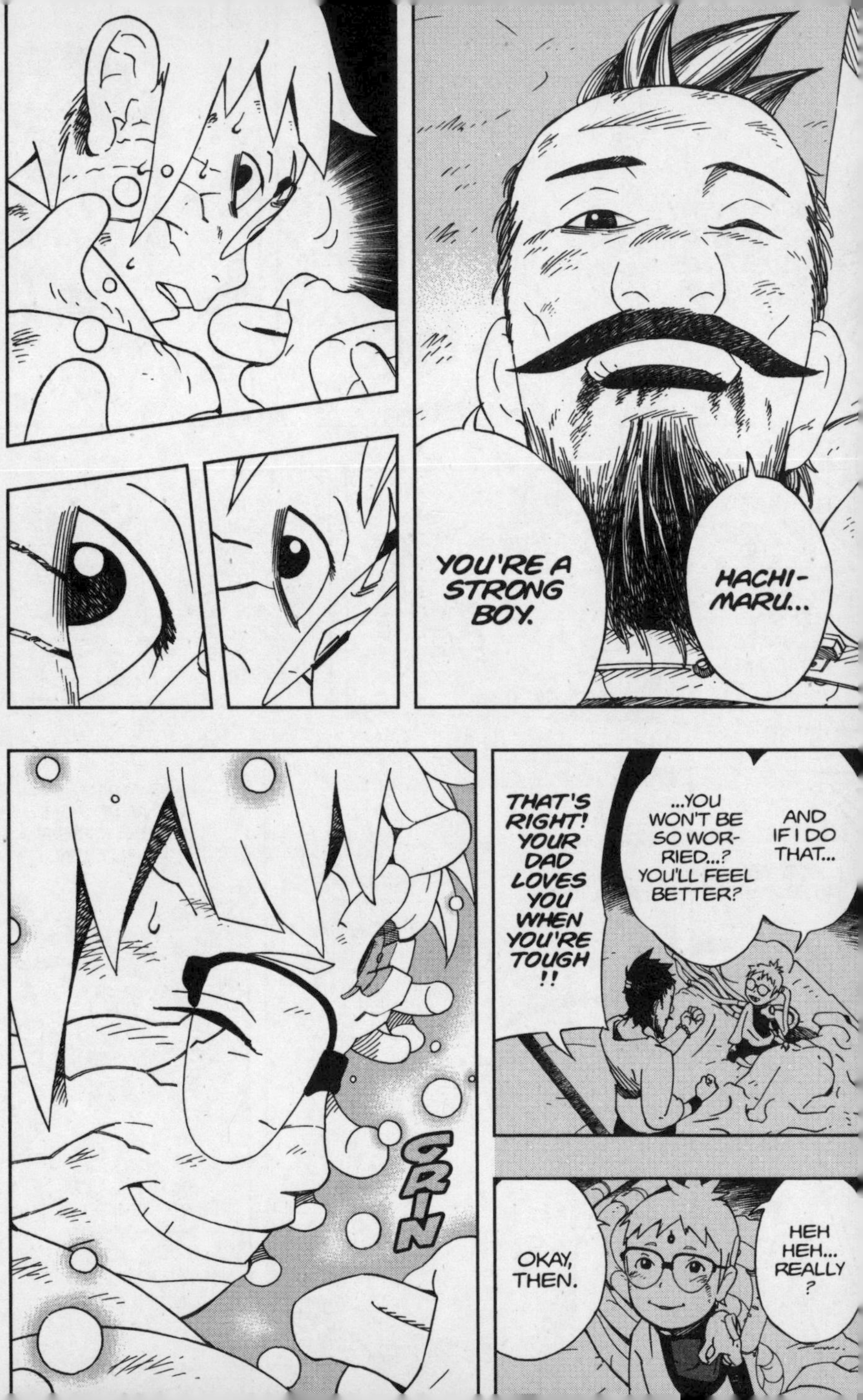
HACHI-MARU...
YOU'RE A STRONG BOY.
AND IF I DO THAT...
...YOU WON'T BE SO WOR-RIED...? YOU'LL FEEL BETTER?
THAT'S RIGHT! YOUR DAD LOVES YOU WHEN YOU'RE TOUGH!!
HEH HEH... REALLY?
OKAY, THEN.
GRIN

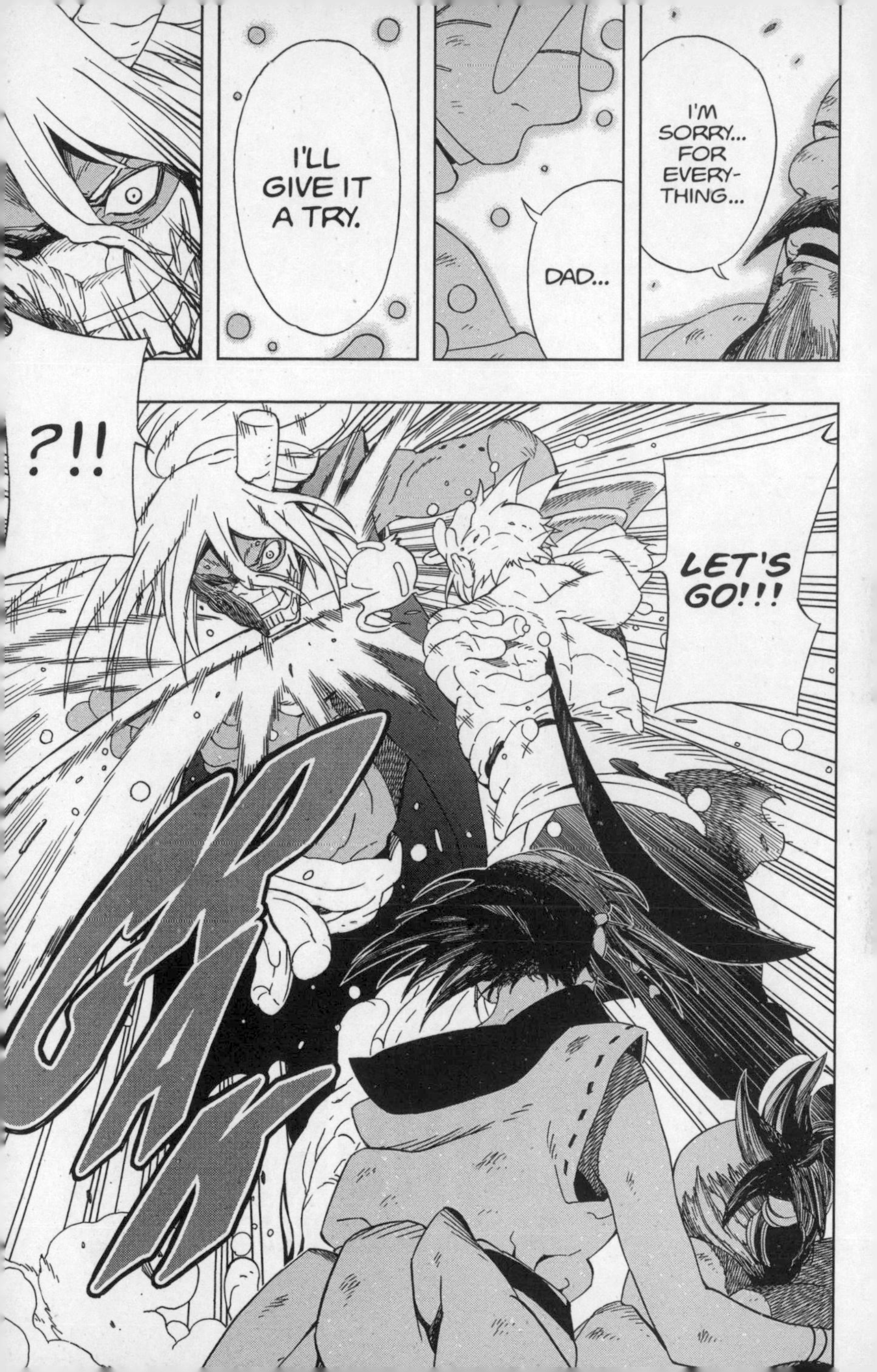
I'M SORRY... FOR EVERY-THING...
DAD...
I'LL GIVE IT A TRY.
LET'S GO!!!
?!!

SAMURAI 8
THE TALE OF HACHIMARU

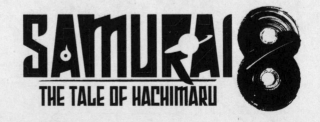

CHAPTER 13: I SAW A HERO

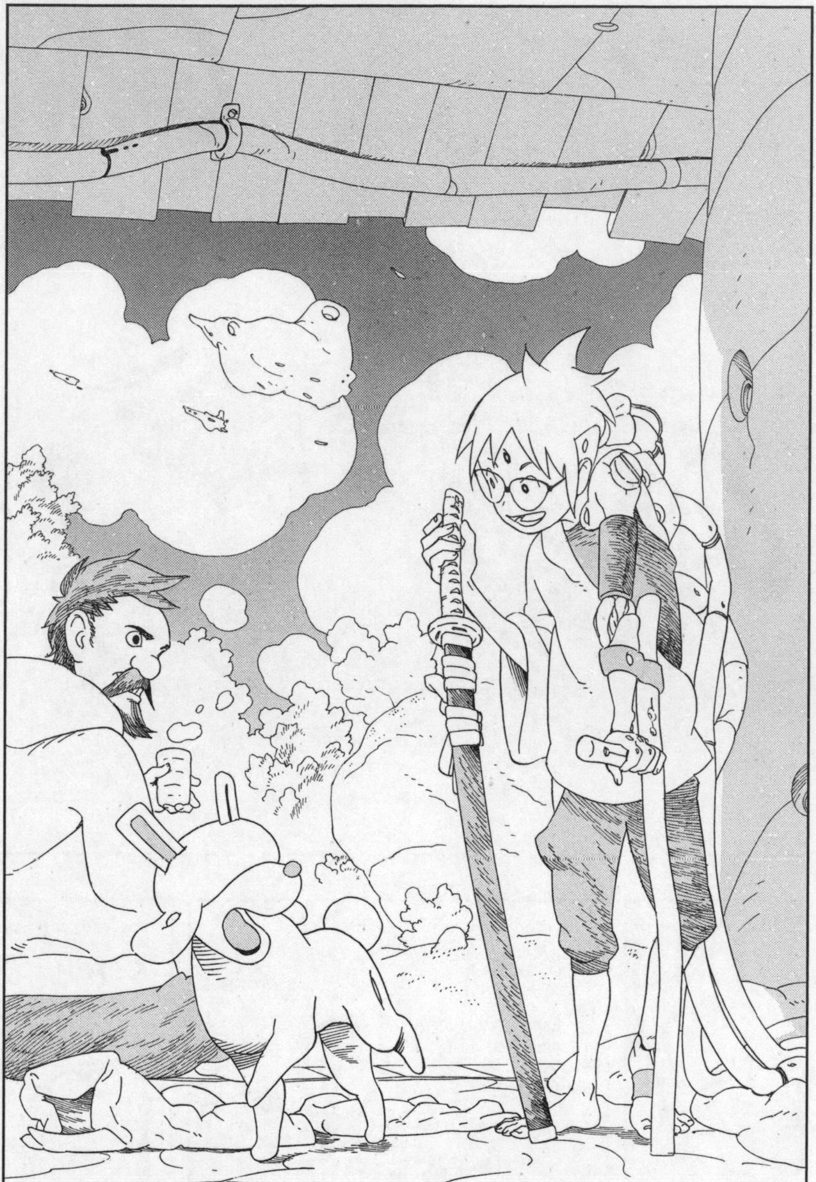

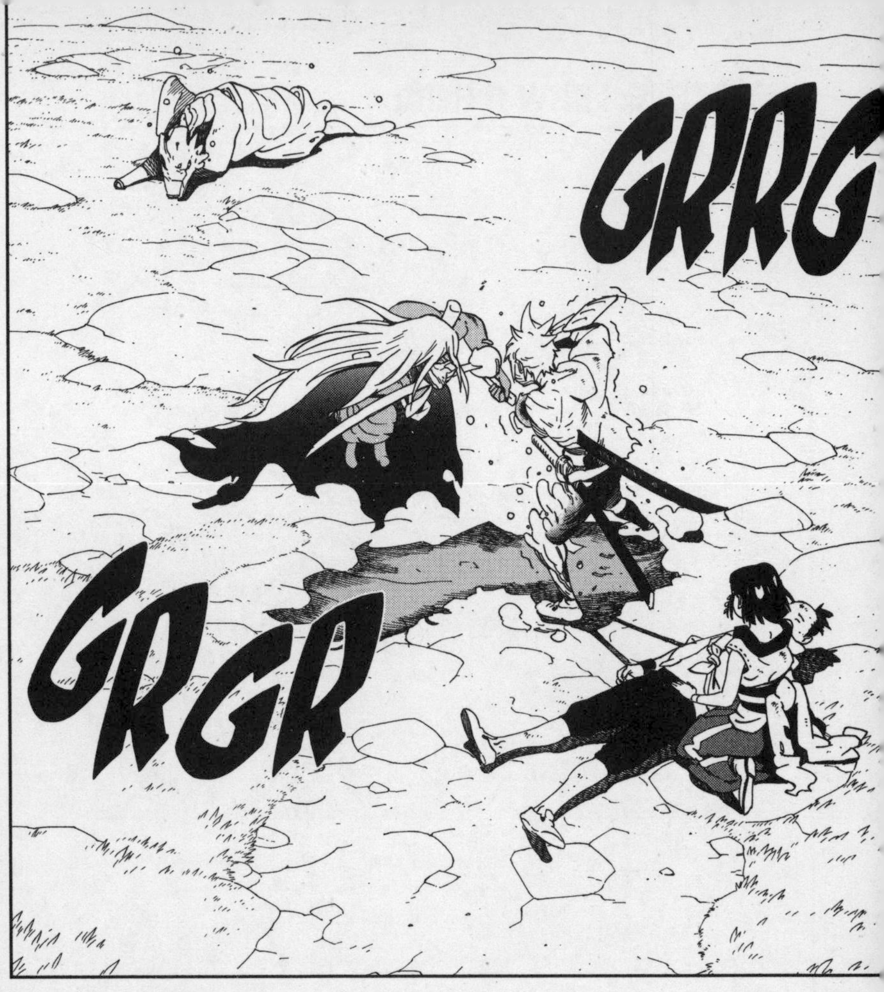
GRRG
GRGR
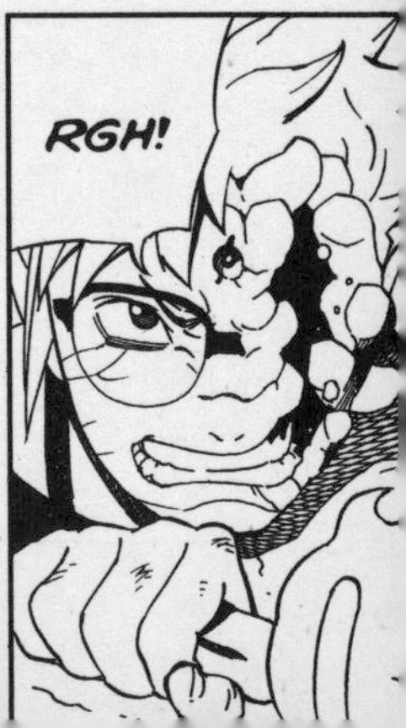
RGH!
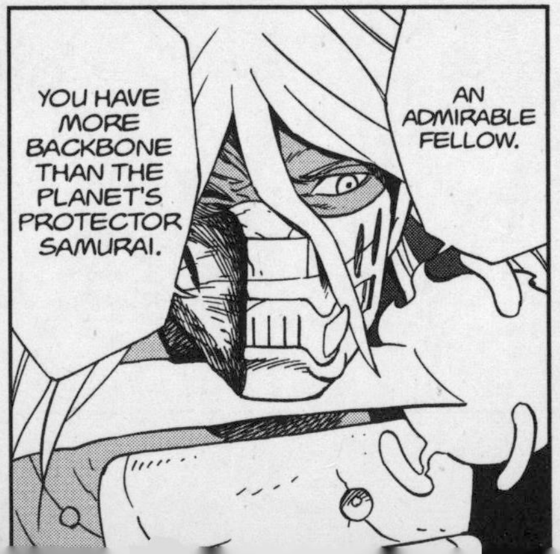
AN ADMIRABLE FELLOW.
YOU HAVE MORE BACKBONE THAN THE PLANET'S PROTECTOR SAMURAI.
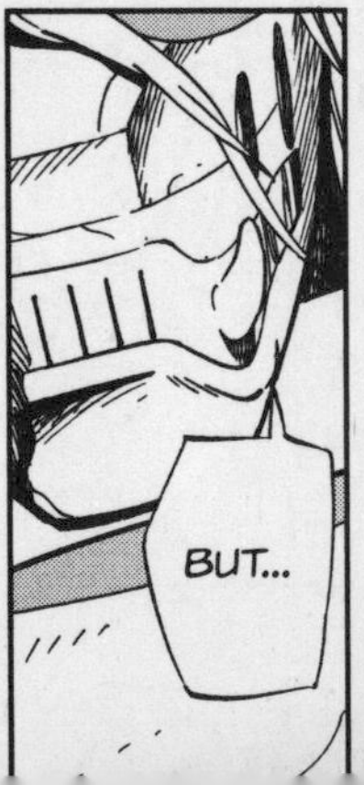
BUT...

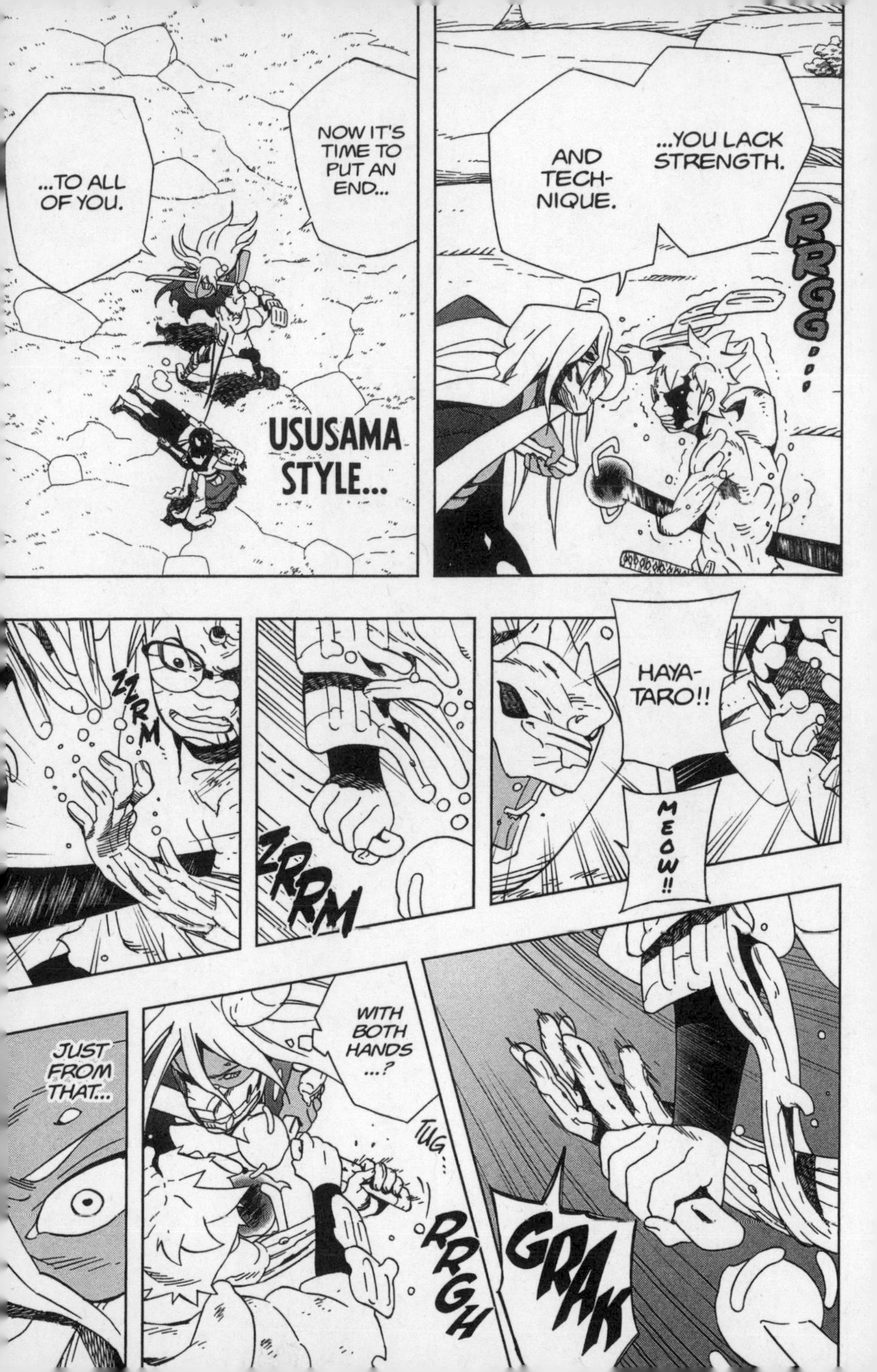
...YOU LACK STRENGTH.
AND TECH-NIQUE.
RRGG...
NOW IT'S TIME TO PUT AN END...
...TO ALL OF YOU.
USUSAMA STYLE...
HAYA-TARO!!
MEOW!!
ZRRM
ZZRM
GRAK
WITH BOTH HANDS ...?
TUG...
RRGH
JUST FROM THAT...

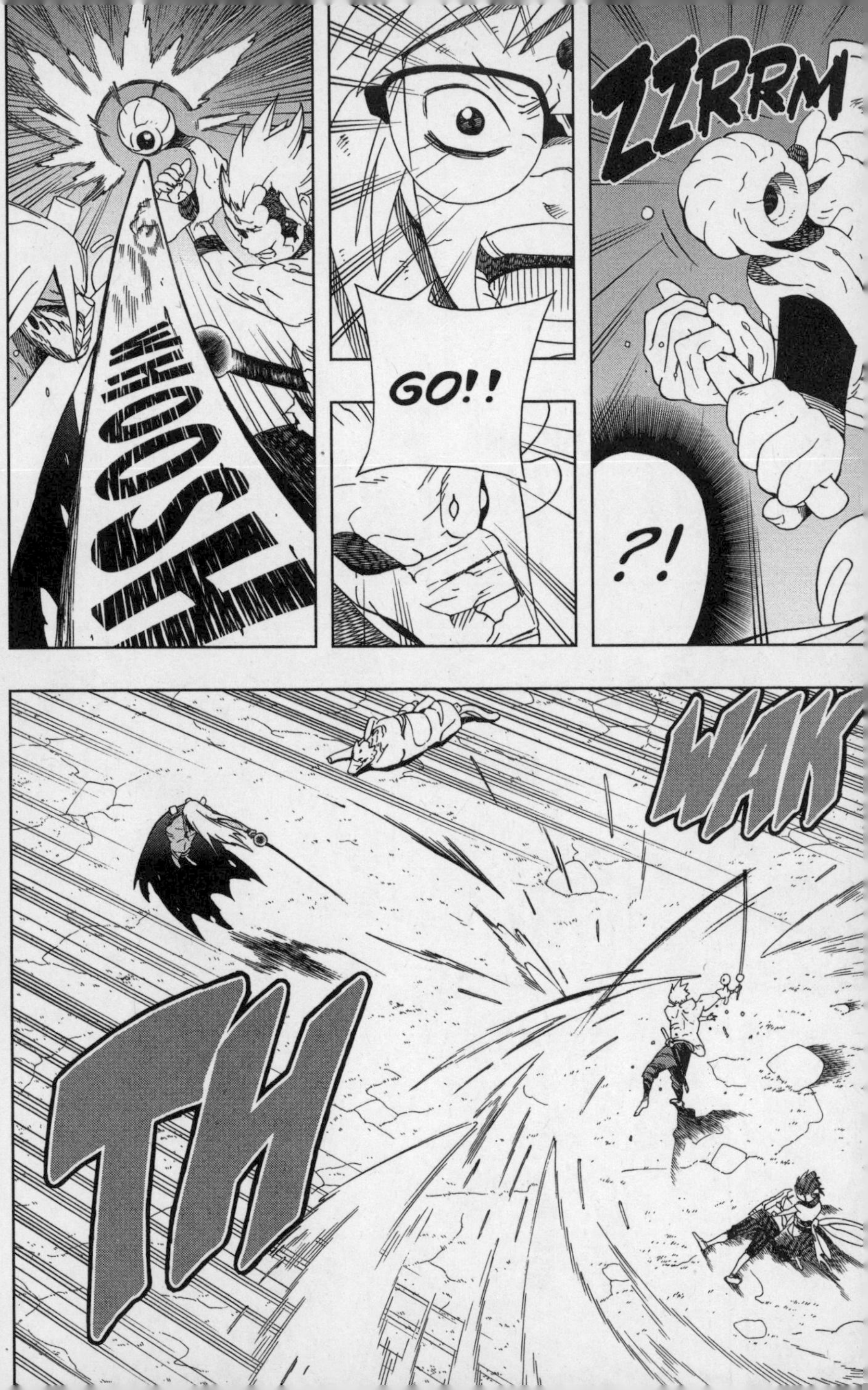
ZZRRM
?!
GO!!
WHOOSH
WAK
TH

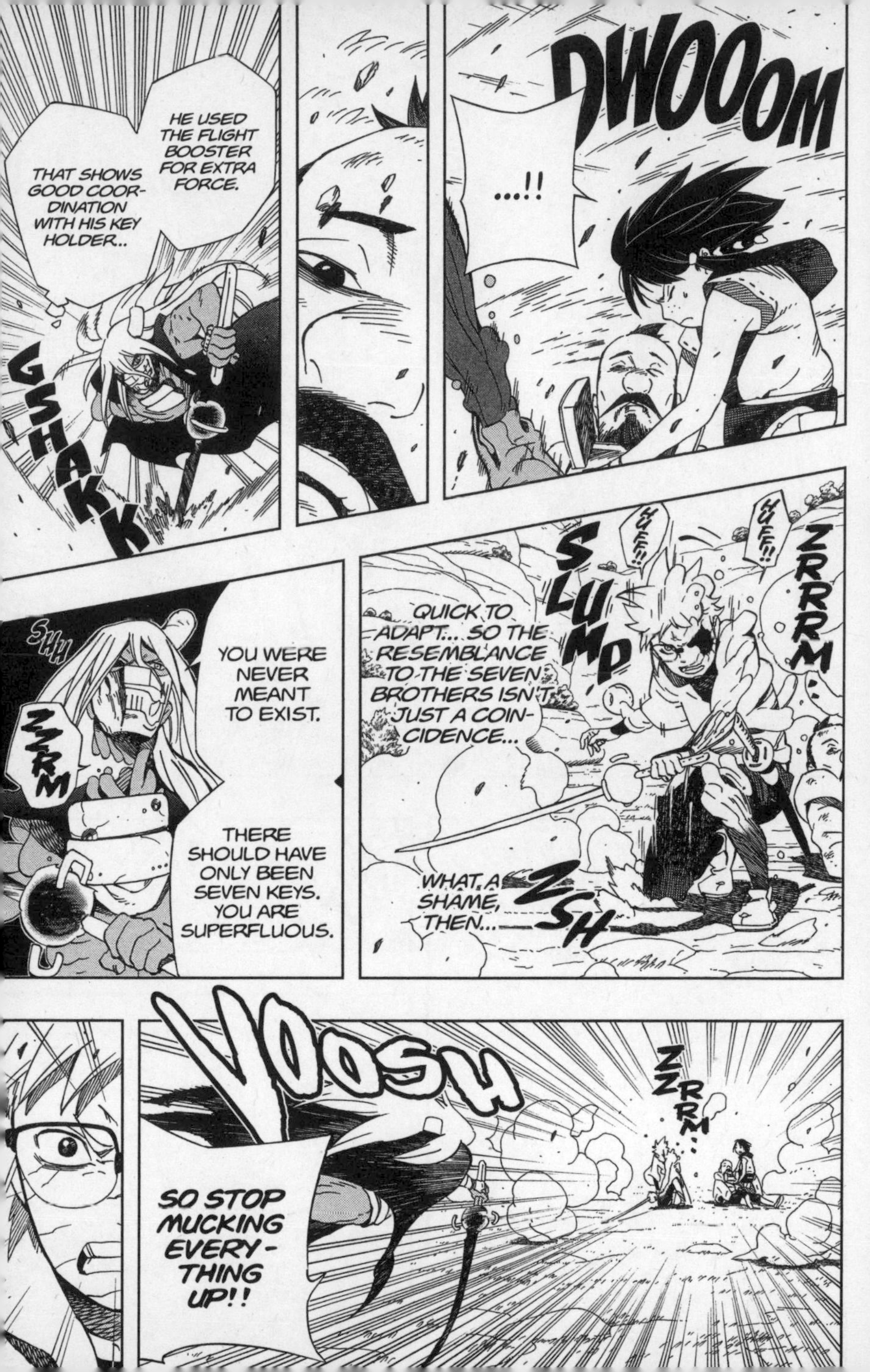
DWOOOM
...!!
HE USED THE FLIGHT BOOSTER FOR EXTRA FORCE.
THAT SHOWS GOOD COORDINATION WITH HIS KEY HOLDER..
GSHAKK
HUFF!!
HUFF!!
ZRRRM
SLUMP
QUICK TO ADAPT... SO THE RESEMBLANCE TO THE SEVEN BROTHERS ISN'T JUST A COINCIDENCE...
WHAT A SHAME, THEN...
ZSH
SHH
ZZRM
YOU WERE NEVER MEANT TO EXIST.
THERE SHOULD HAVE ONLY BEEN SEVEN KEYS. YOU ARE SUPERFLUOUS.
VOOSH
ZZRRM
SO STOP MUCKING EVERYTHING UP!!

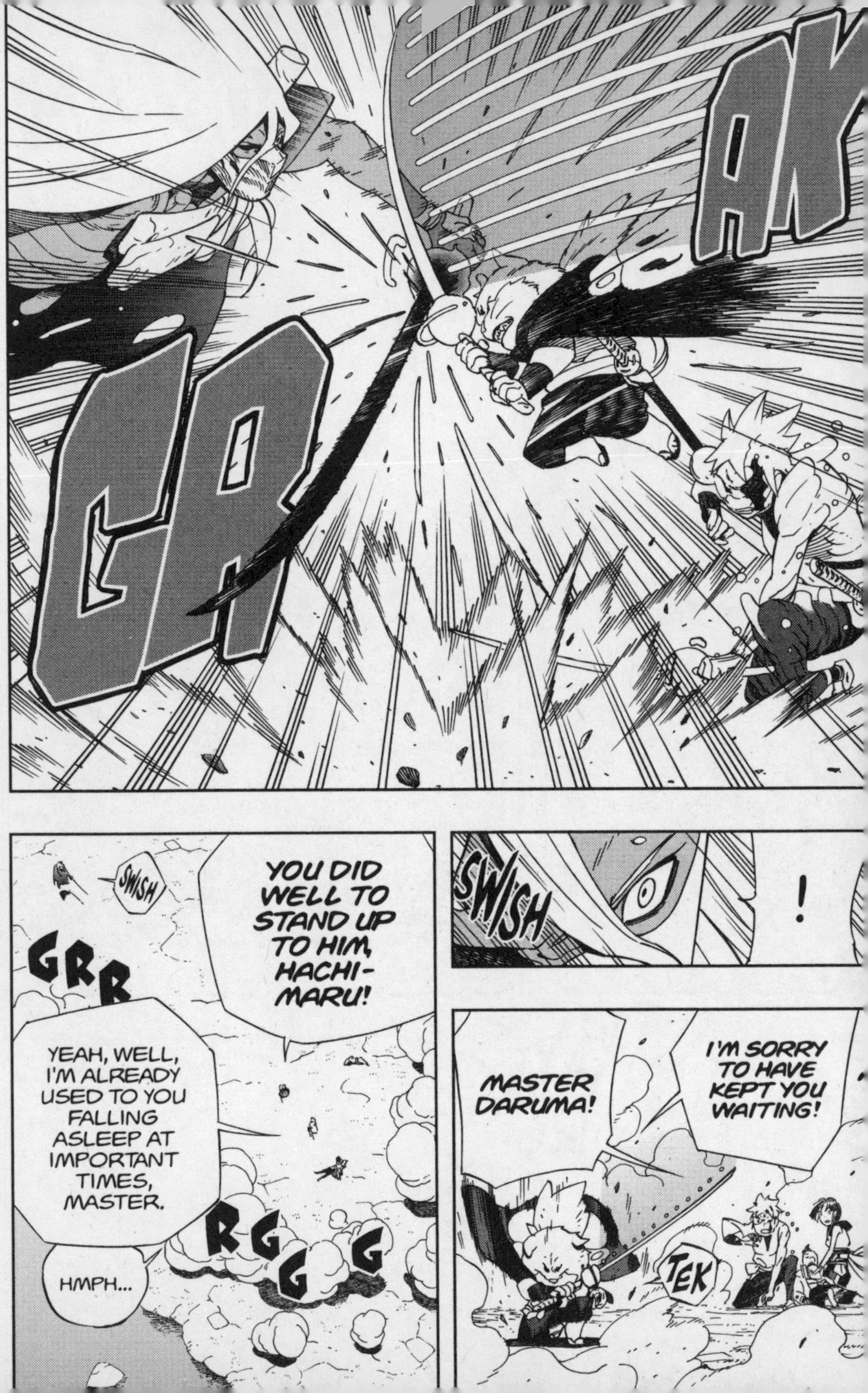
AK
GA
SWISH
!
I'M SORRY TO HAVE KEPT YOU WAITING!
MASTER DARUMA!
TEK
YOU DID WELL TO STAND UP TO HIM, HACHI-MARU!
SWISH
GRR
YEAH, WELL, I'M ALREADY USED TO YOU FALLING ASLEEP AT IMPORTANT TIMES, MASTER.
RGGG
HMPH...

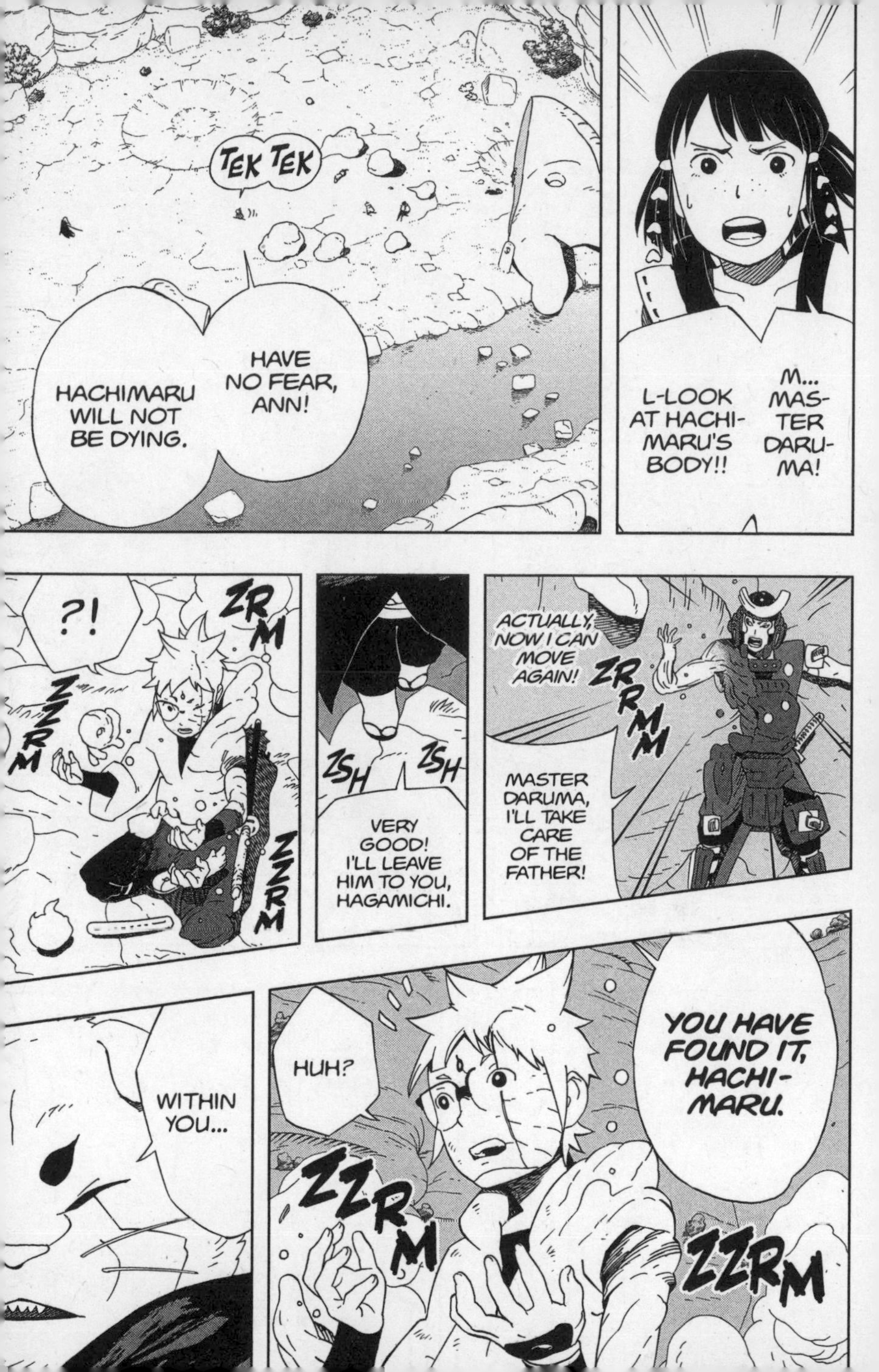
M... MASTER DARUMA!
L-LOOK AT HACHIMARU'S BODY!!
TEK TEK
HAVE NO FEAR, ANN!
HACHIMARU WILL NOT BE DYING.
ACTUALLY, NOW I CAN MOVE AGAIN!
ZRRMM
MASTER DARUMA, I'LL TAKE CARE OF THE FATHER!
ZSH ZSH
VERY GOOD! I'LL LEAVE HIM TO YOU, HAGAMICHI.
?!
ZRM
ZZRM
ZZRM
ZZRM
YOU HAVE FOUND IT, HACHIMARU.
HUH?
ZZRM
ZZRM
WITHIN YOU...

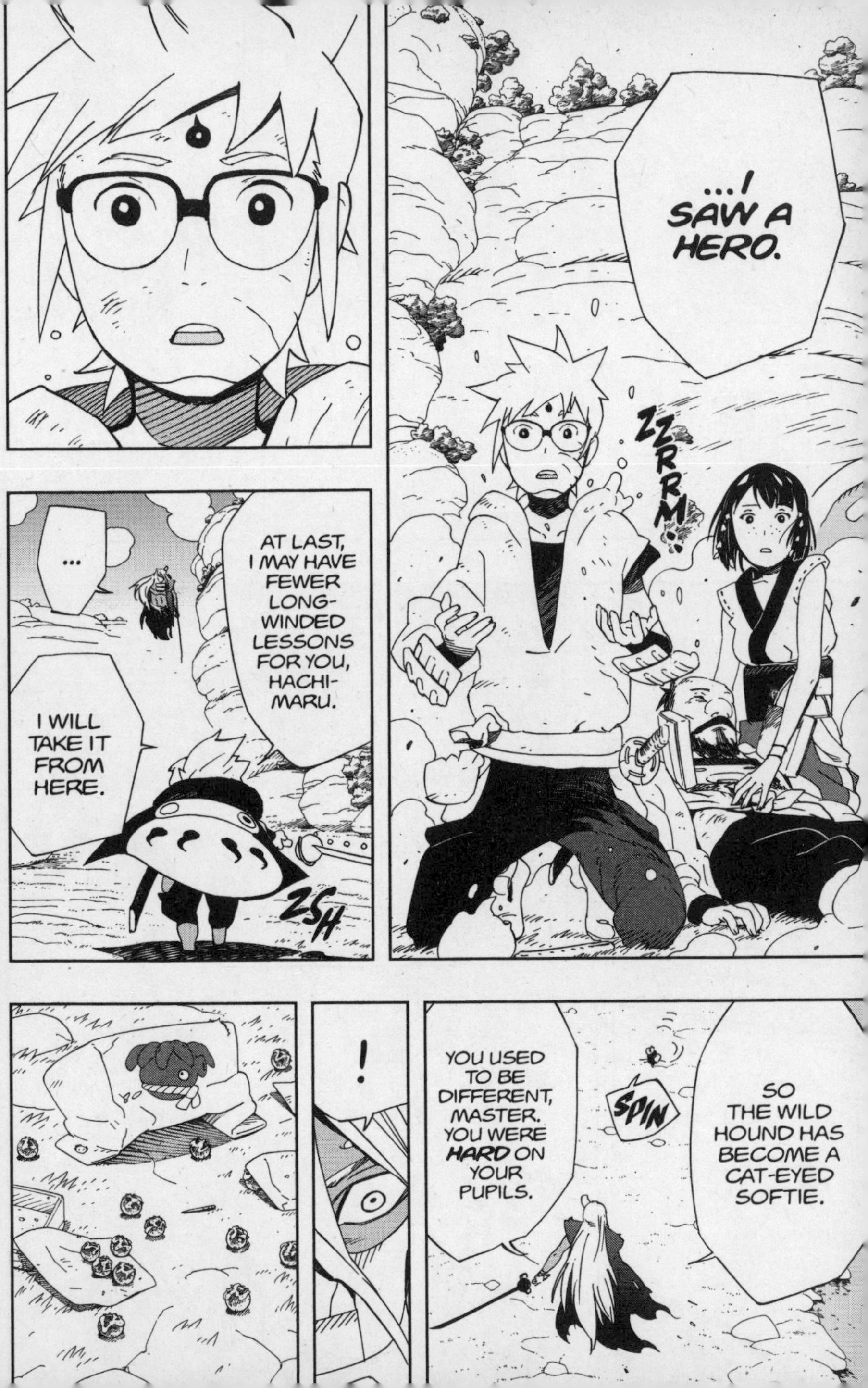
...I SAW A HERO.
ZZRRM
AT LAST, I MAY HAVE FEWER LONG-WINDED LESSONS FOR YOU, HACHI-MARU.
...
I WILL TAKE IT FROM HERE.
ZSH
SO THE WILD HOUND HAS BECOME A CAT-EYED SOFTIE.
SPIN
YOU USED TO BE DIFFERENT, MASTER. YOU WERE HARD ON YOUR PUPILS.
!

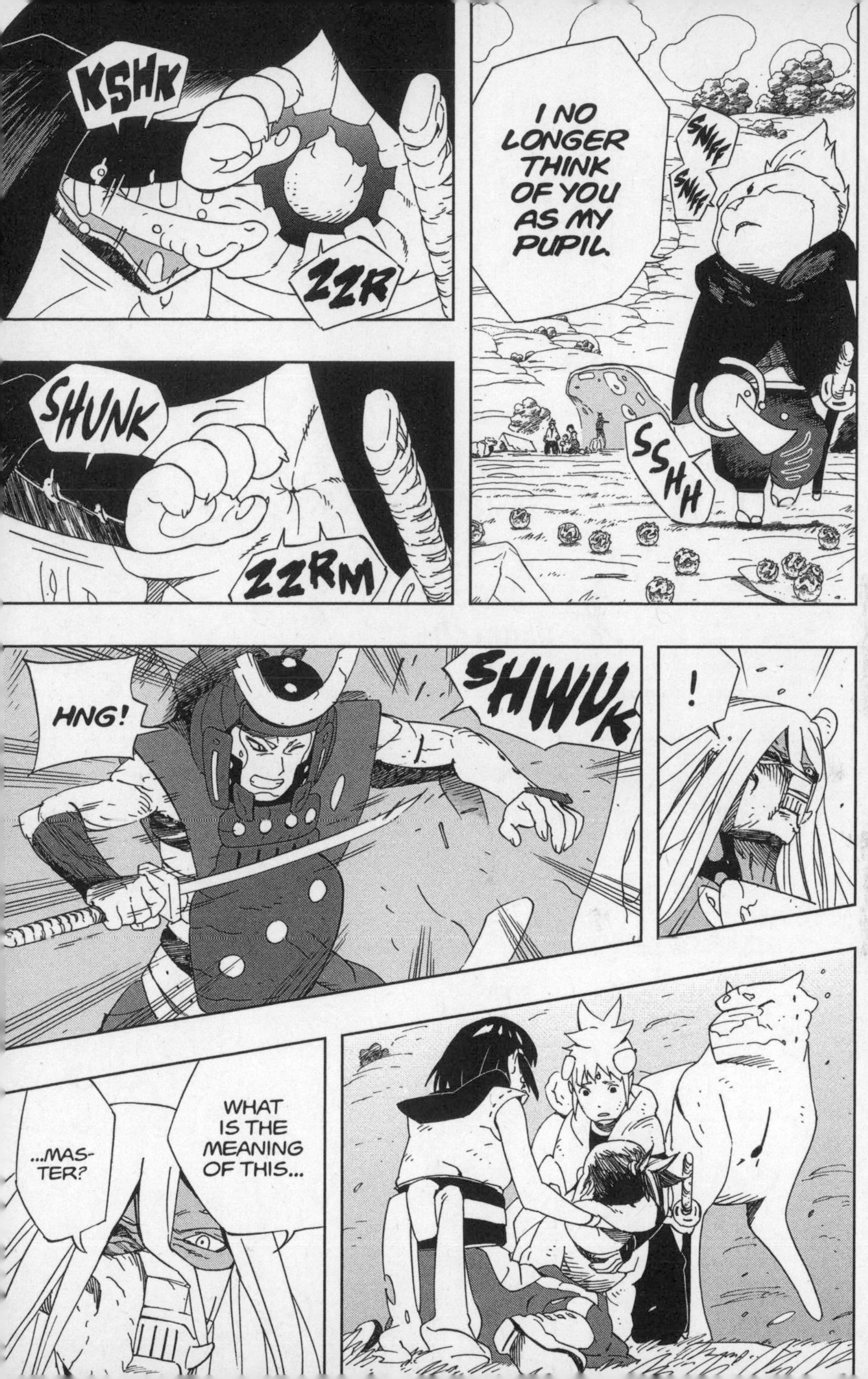

I NO LONGER THINK OF YOU AS MY PUPIL.
SNIFF
SNIFF
SSHH
KSHK
ZZR
SHUNK
ZZRM
!
SHWUK
HNG!
WHAT IS THE MEANING OF THIS...
...MASTER?

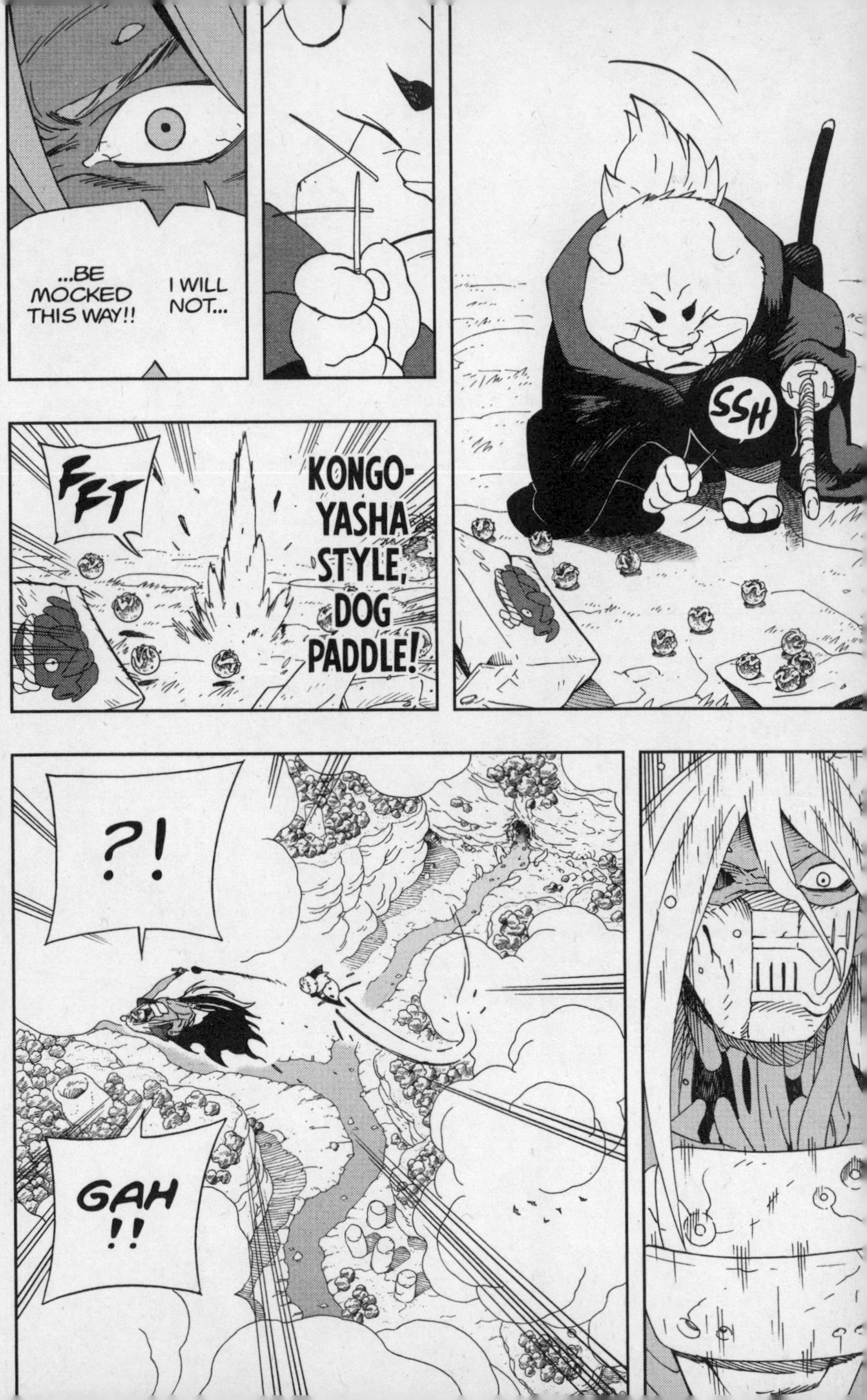
SSH
I WILL NOT...
...BE MOCKED THIS WAY!!
KONGO-YASHA STYLE, DOG PADDLE!
FFT
?!
GAH!!

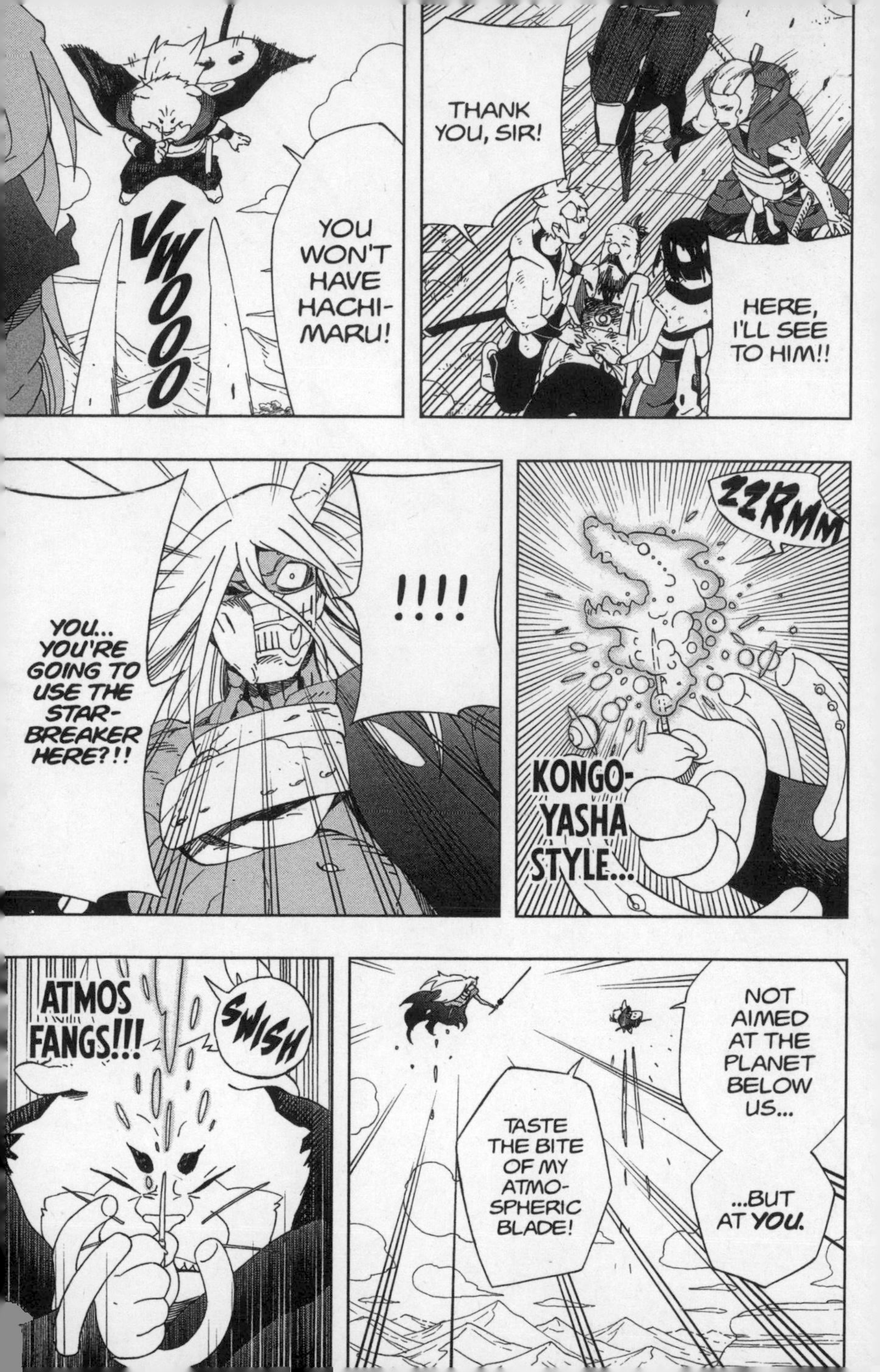
HERE, I'LL SEE TO HIM!!
THANK YOU, SIR!
YOU WON'T HAVE HACHI-MARU!
VWOOOO
ZZRMM
KONGO-YASHA STYLE...
!!!!
YOU... YOU'RE GOING TO USE THE STAR-BREAKER HERE?!!
NOT AIMED AT THE PLANET BELOW US...
...BUT AT **YOU.**
TASTE THE BITE OF MY ATMO-SPHERIC BLADE!
SWISH
ATMOS FANGS!!!

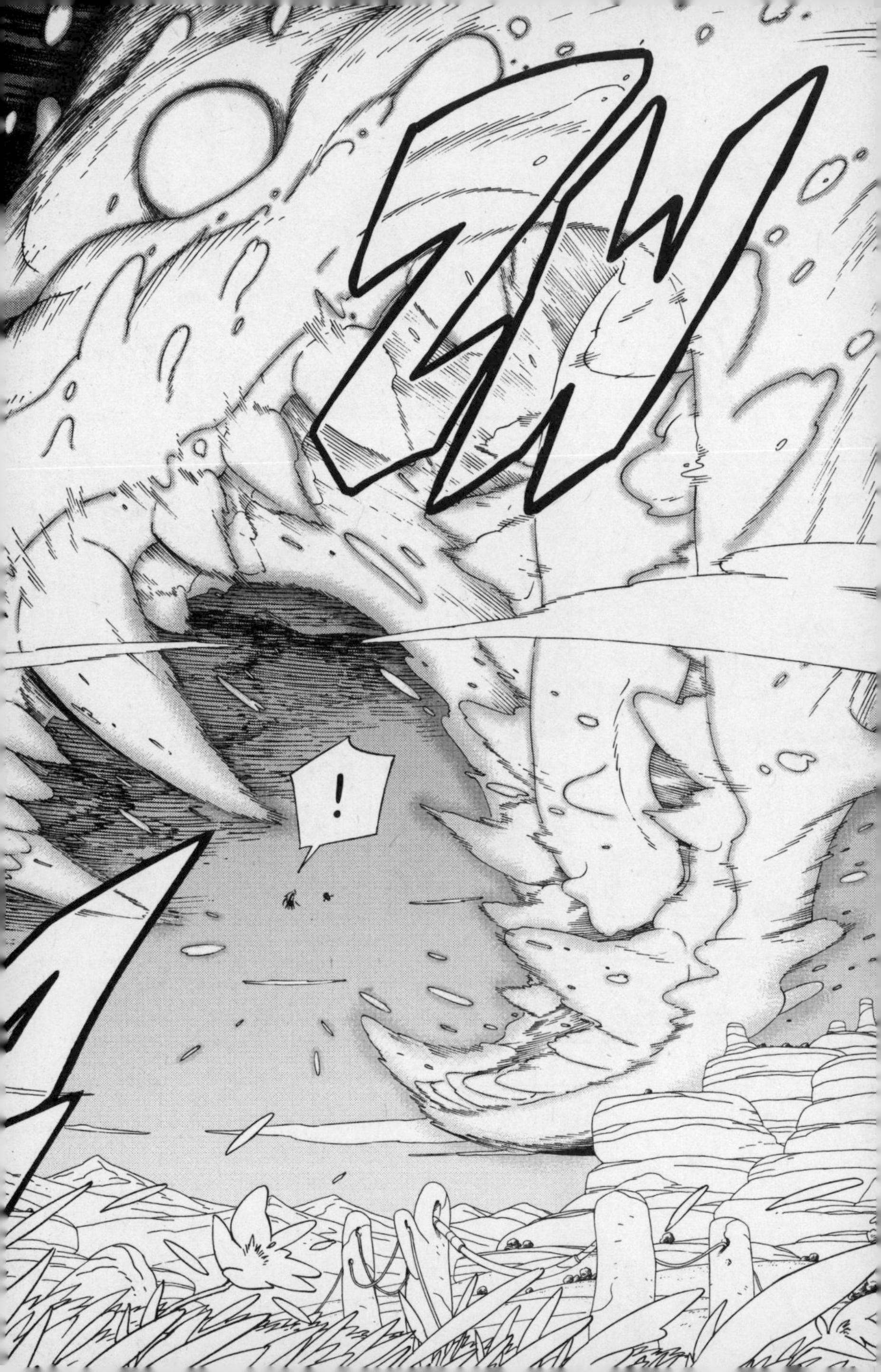
!

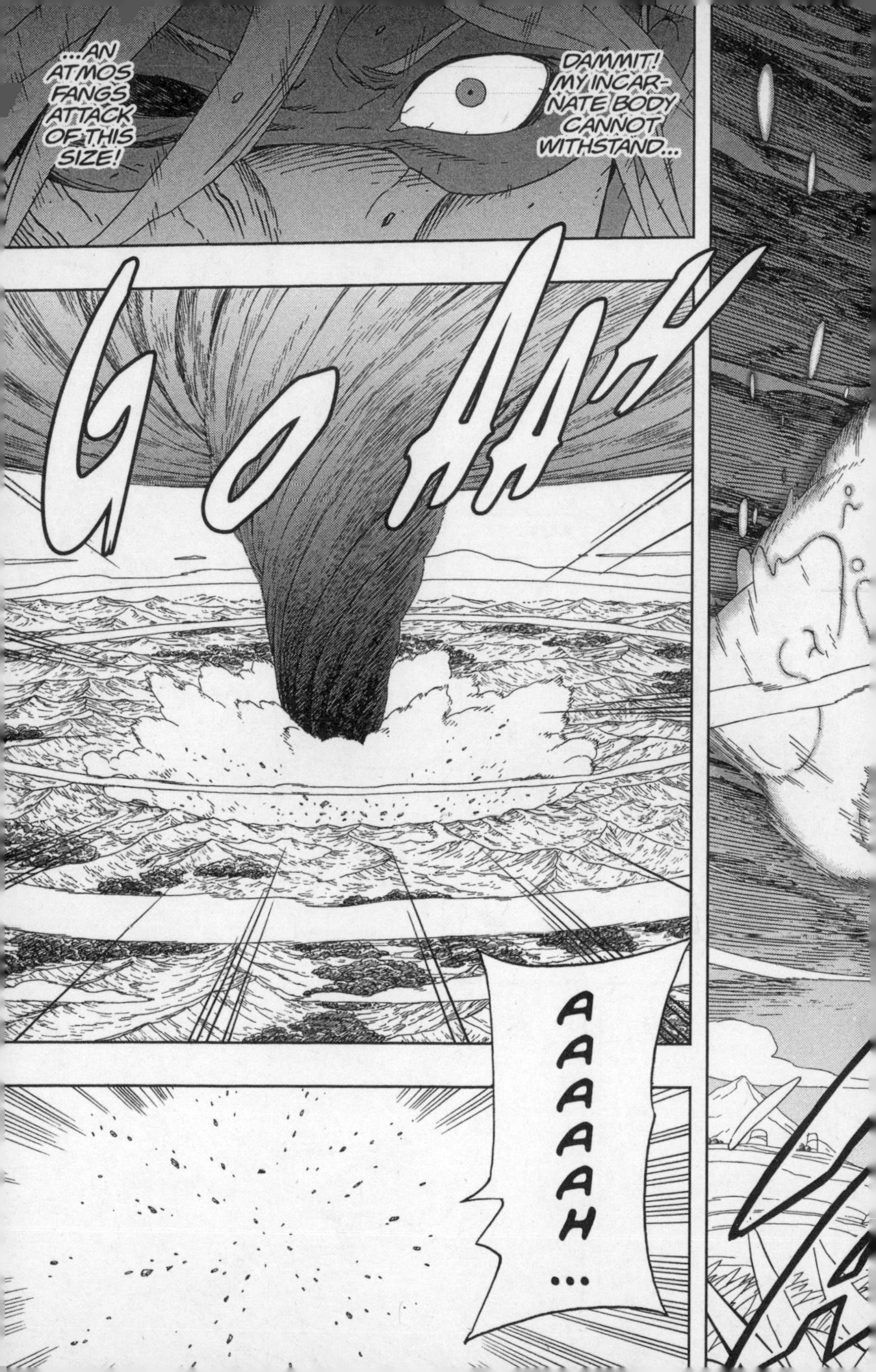
DAMMIT! MY INCARNATE BODY CANNOT WITHSTAND...
...AN ATMOS FANGS ATTACK OF THIS SIZE!
AAAAAAH...

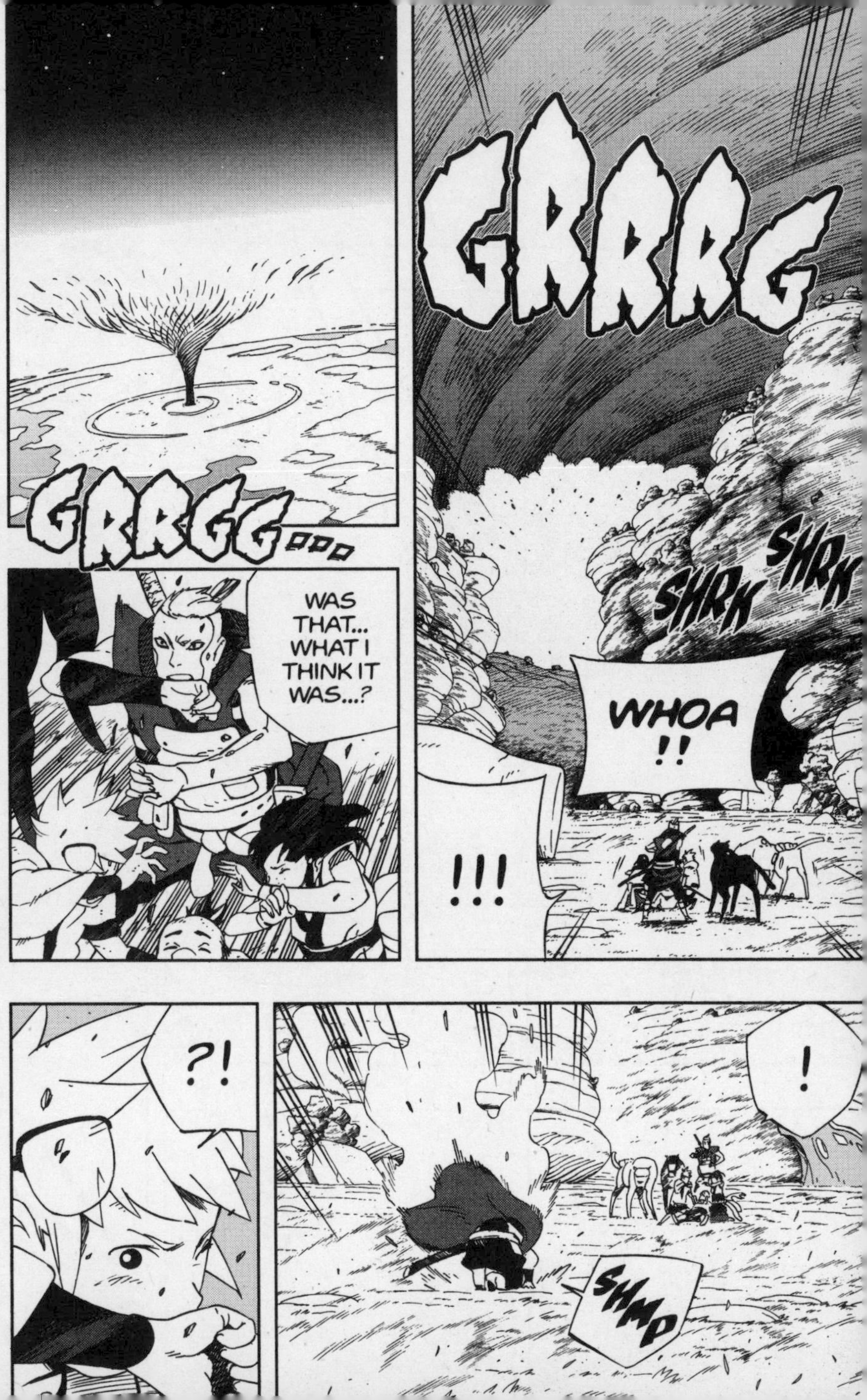
GRRRG
SHRK SHRK
WHOA !!
!!!
GRRGG...
WAS THAT... WHAT I THINK IT WAS...?
!
SHMP
?!

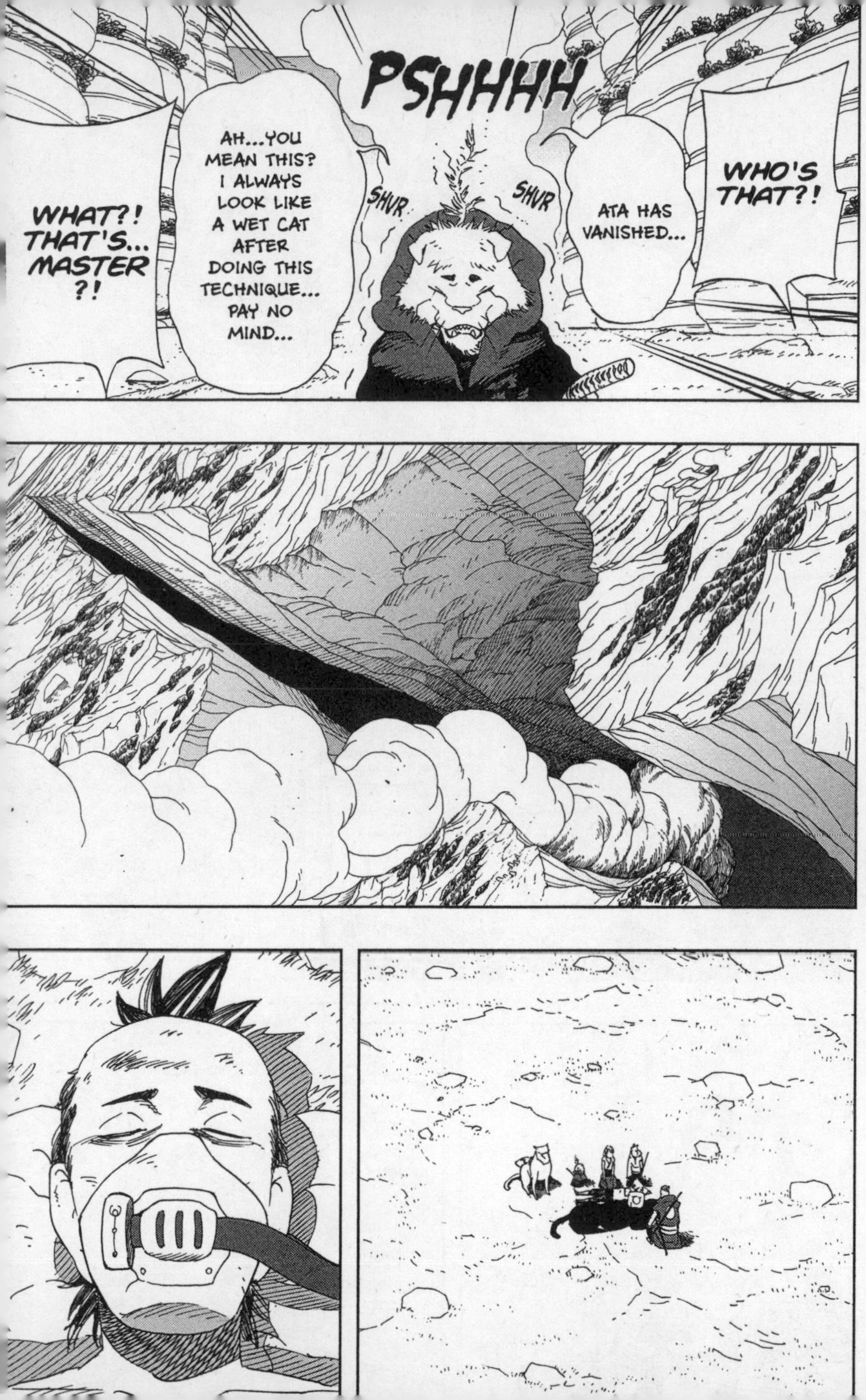
WHO'S THAT?!
PSHHHH
ATA HAS VANISHED...
SHVR
SHVR
AH...YOU MEAN THIS? I ALWAYS LOOK LIKE A WET CAT AFTER DOING THIS TECHNIQUE... PAY NO MIND...
WHAT?! THAT'S... MASTER?!

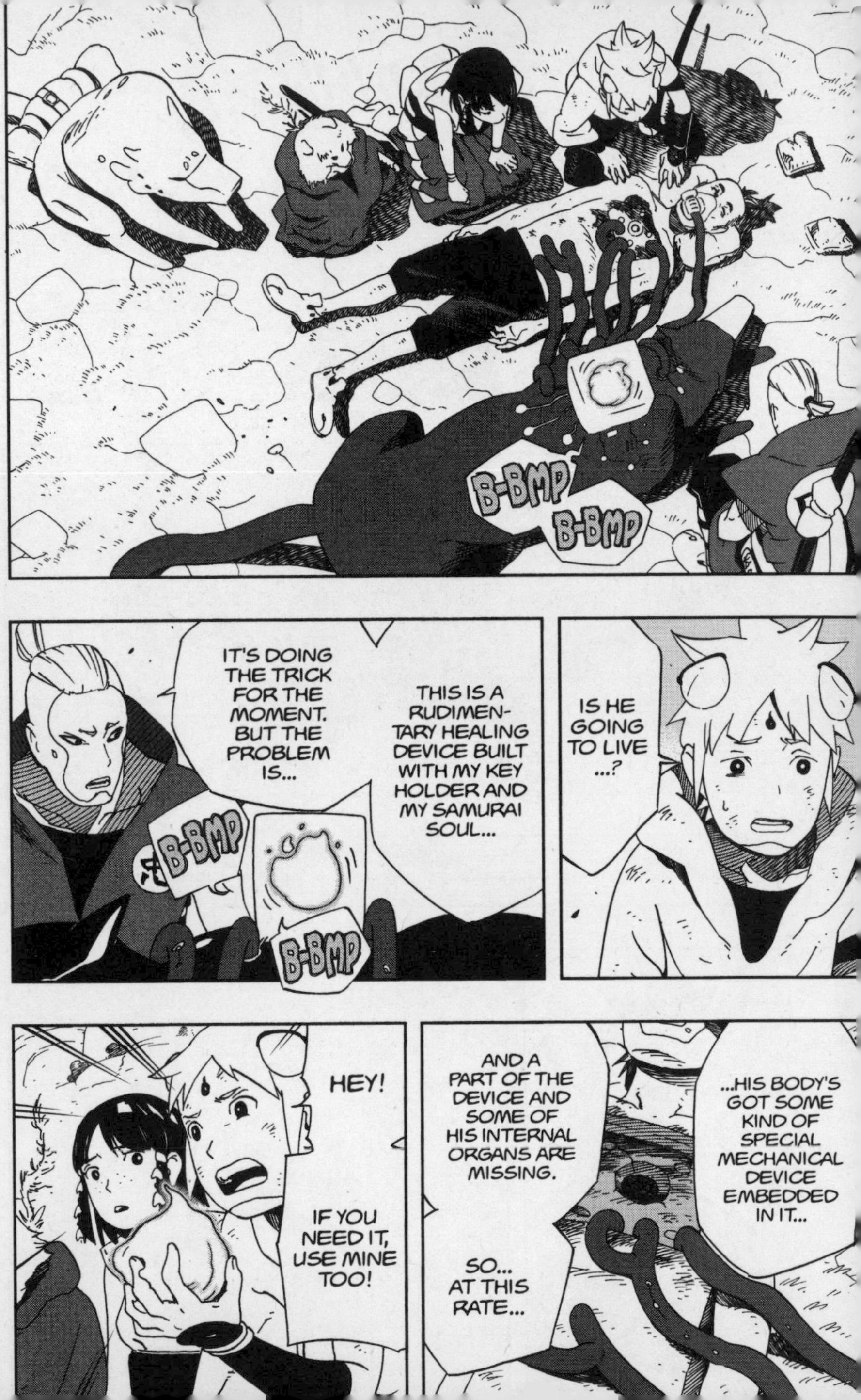
B-BMP
B-BMP
IS HE GOING TO LIVE ...?
THIS IS A RUDIMENTARY HEALING DEVICE BUILT WITH MY KEY HOLDER AND MY SAMURAI SOUL...
IT'S DOING THE TRICK FOR THE MOMENT. BUT THE PROBLEM IS...
B-BMP
B-BMP
...HIS BODY'S GOT SOME KIND OF SPECIAL MECHANICAL DEVICE EMBEDDED IN IT...
AND A PART OF THE DEVICE AND SOME OF HIS INTERNAL ORGANS ARE MISSING.
SO... AT THIS RATE...
HEY!
IF YOU NEED IT, USE MINE TOO!

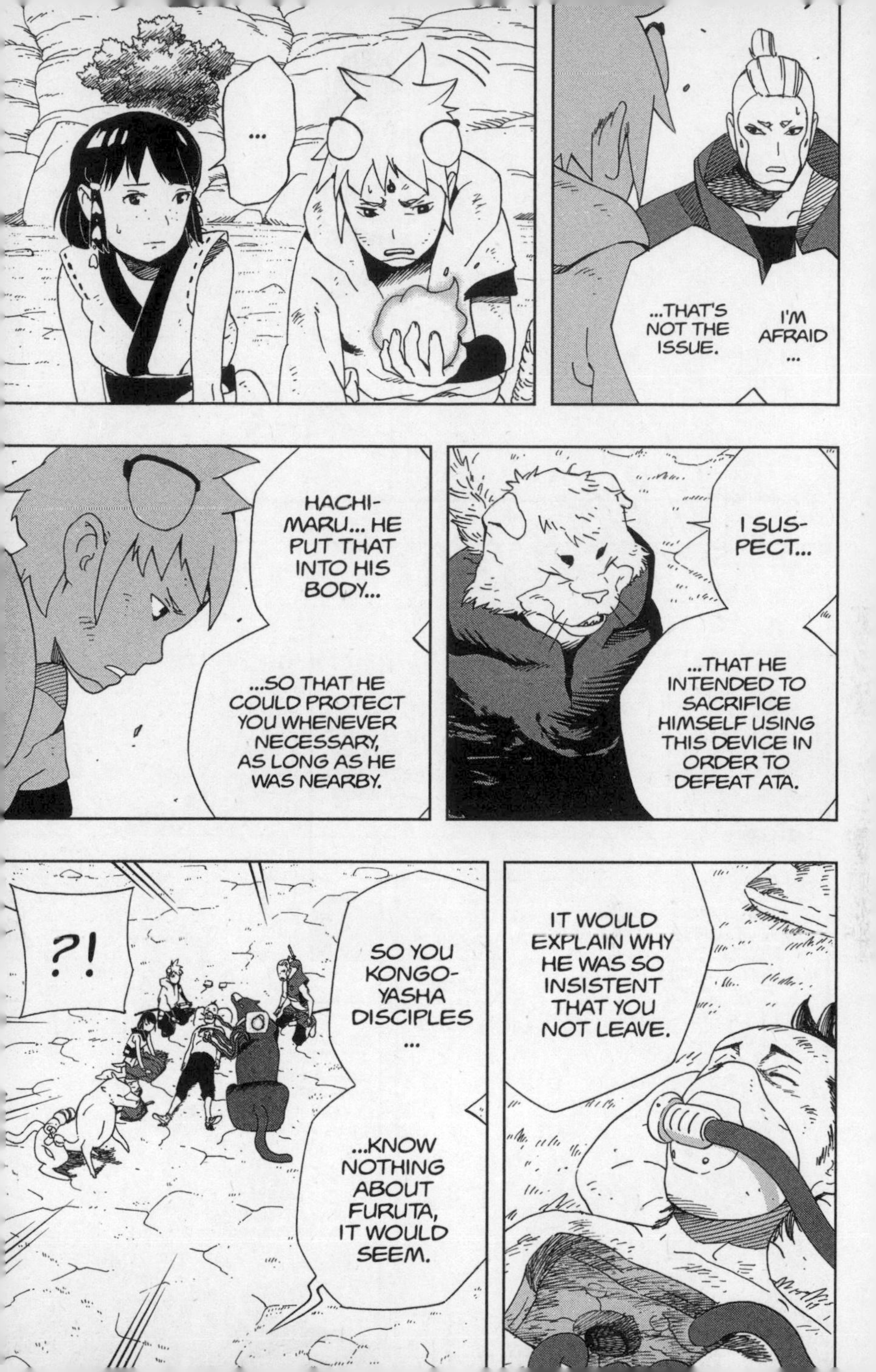
I'M AFRAID...
...THAT'S NOT THE ISSUE.
...
I SUS-PECT...
...THAT HE INTENDED TO SACRIFICE HIMSELF USING THIS DEVICE IN ORDER TO DEFEAT ATA.
HACHI-MARU... HE PUT THAT INTO HIS BODY...
...SO THAT HE COULD PROTECT YOU WHENEVER NECESSARY, AS LONG AS HE WAS NEARBY.
IT WOULD EXPLAIN WHY HE WAS SO INSISTENT THAT YOU NOT LEAVE.
SO YOU KONGO-YASHA DISCIPLES...
...KNOW NOTHING ABOUT FURUTA, IT WOULD SEEM.
?!

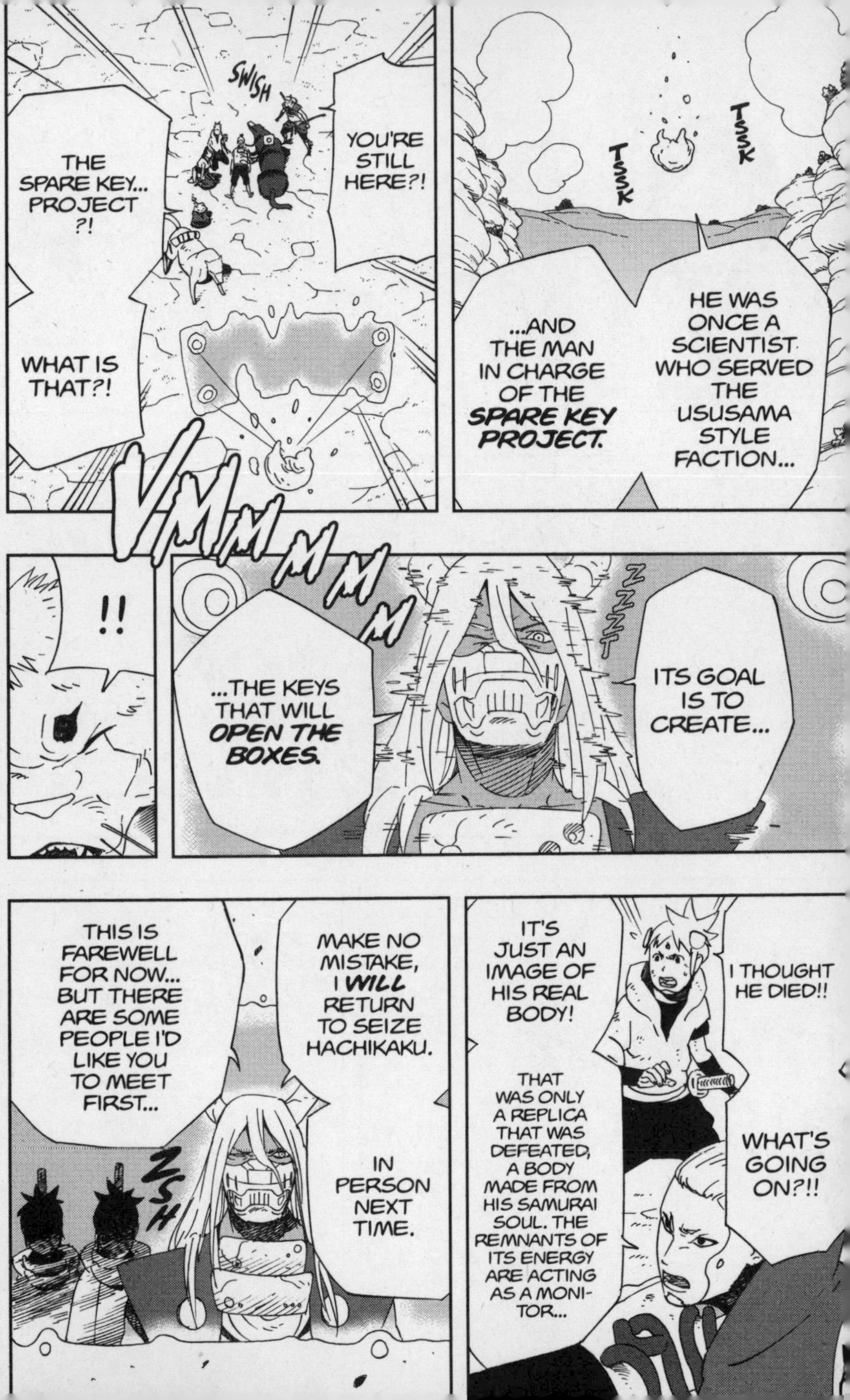
TSSK
TSSK
HE WAS ONCE A SCIENTIST WHO SERVED THE USUSAMA STYLE FACTION...
...AND THE MAN IN CHARGE OF THE SPARE KEY PROJECT.
SWISH
YOU'RE STILL HERE?!
THE SPARE KEY... PROJECT?!
WHAT IS THAT?!
VMMMMMMM
ZZZZT
ITS GOAL IS TO CREATE...
...THE KEYS THAT WILL OPEN THE BOXES.
!!
I THOUGHT HE DIED!!
IT'S JUST AN IMAGE OF HIS REAL BODY!
WHAT'S GOING ON?!!
THAT WAS ONLY A REPLICA THAT WAS DEFEATED, A BODY MADE FROM HIS SAMURAI SOUL. THE REMNANTS OF ITS ENERGY ARE ACTING AS A MONI-TOR...
MAKE NO MISTAKE, I WILL RETURN TO SEIZE HACHIKAKU.
IN PERSON NEXT TIME.
THIS IS FAREWELL FOR NOW... BUT THERE ARE SOME PEOPLE I'D LIKE YOU TO MEET FIRST...
ZSH

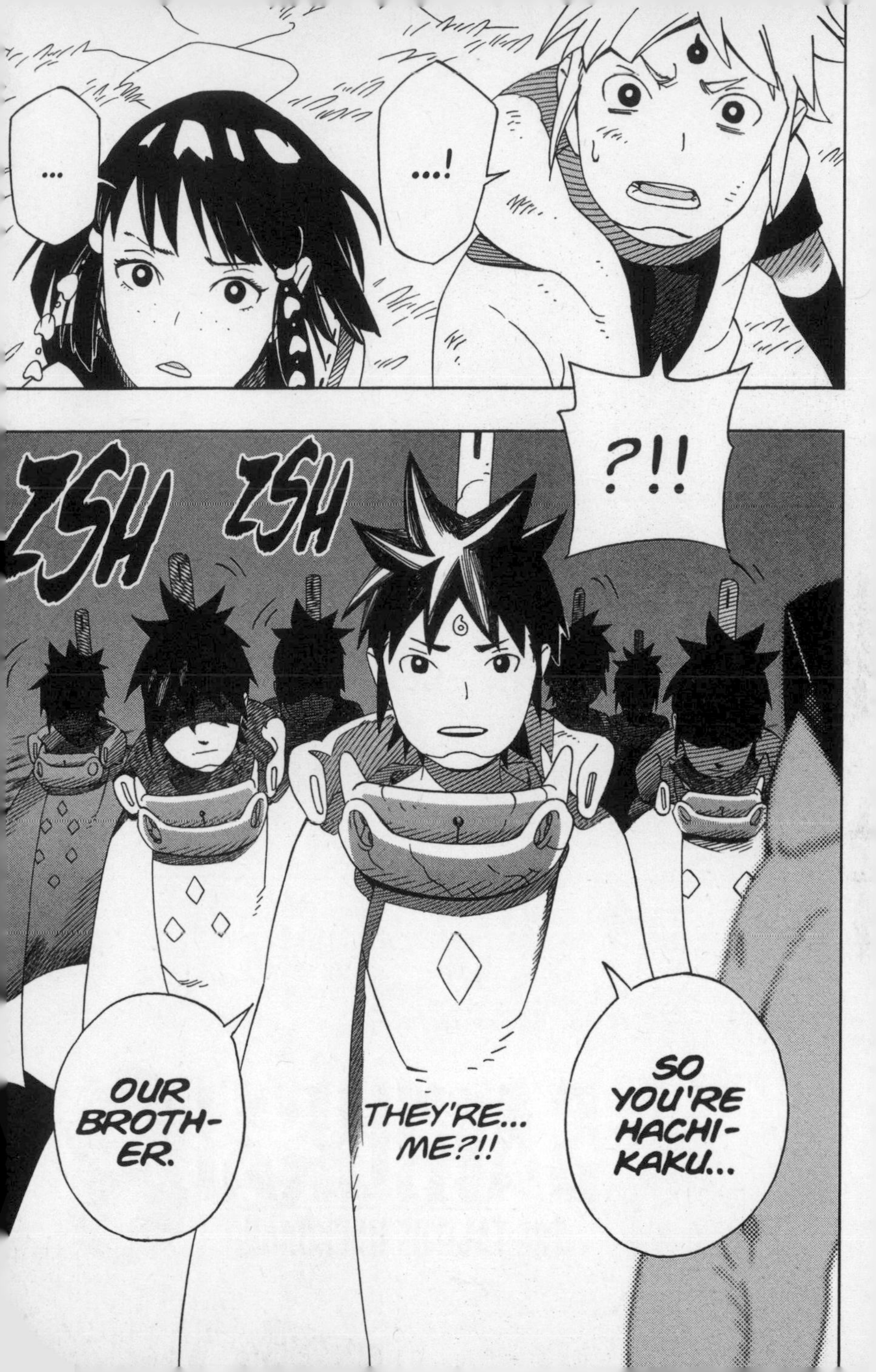
...!
...
?!!
ZSH
ZSH
SO YOU'RE HACHI-KAKU...
THEY'RE... ME?!!
OUR BROTH-ER.

SAMURAI 8

THE TALE OF HACHIMARU

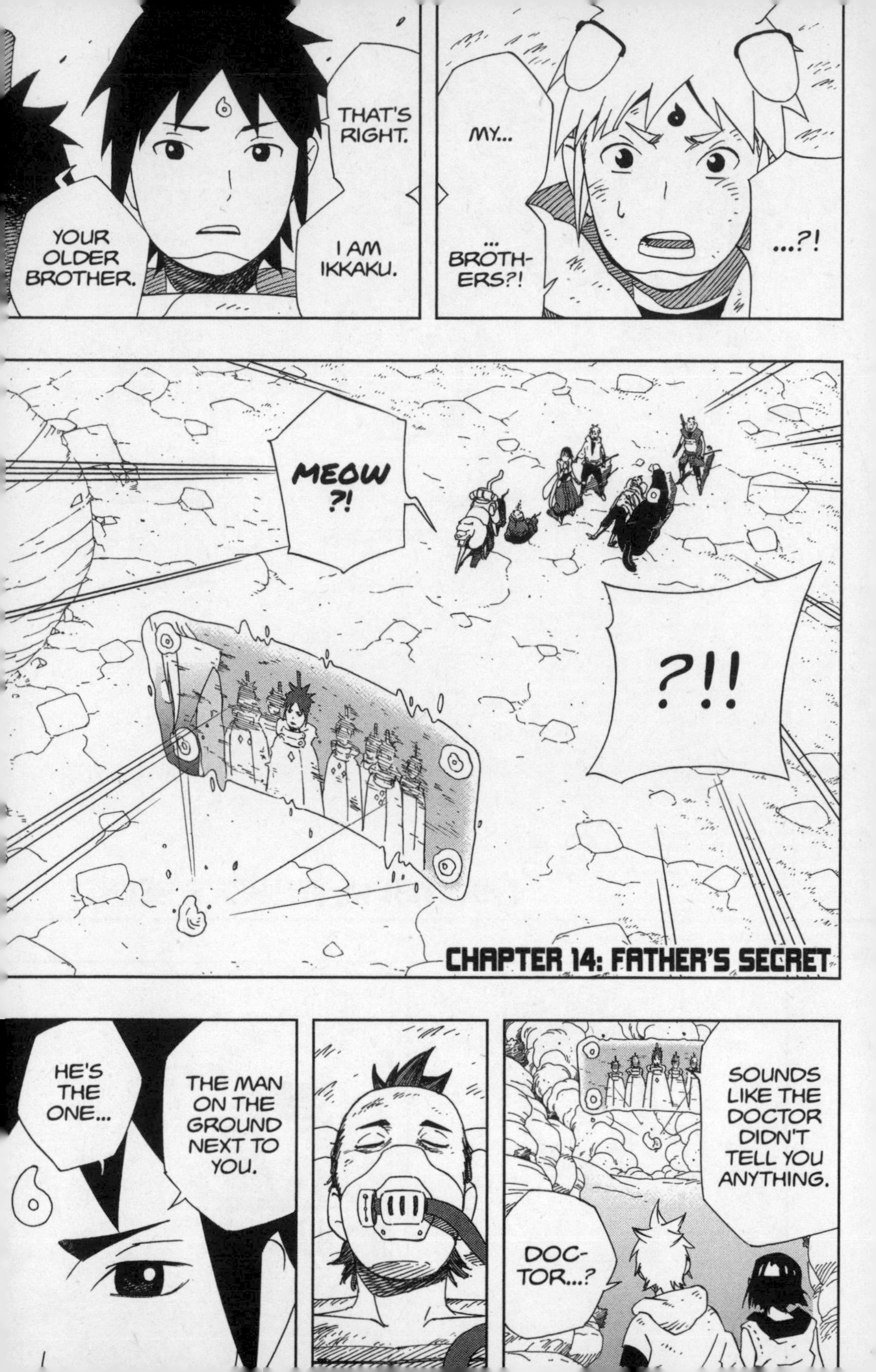
MY...
... BROTH-ERS?!
...?!
THAT'S RIGHT.
I AM IKKAKU.
YOUR OLDER BROTHER.
?!!
MEOW ?!
CHAPTER 14: FATHER'S SECRET
SOUNDS LIKE THE DOCTOR DIDN'T TELL YOU ANYTHING.
DOC-TOR...?
THE MAN ON THE GROUND NEXT TO YOU.
HE'S THE ONE...

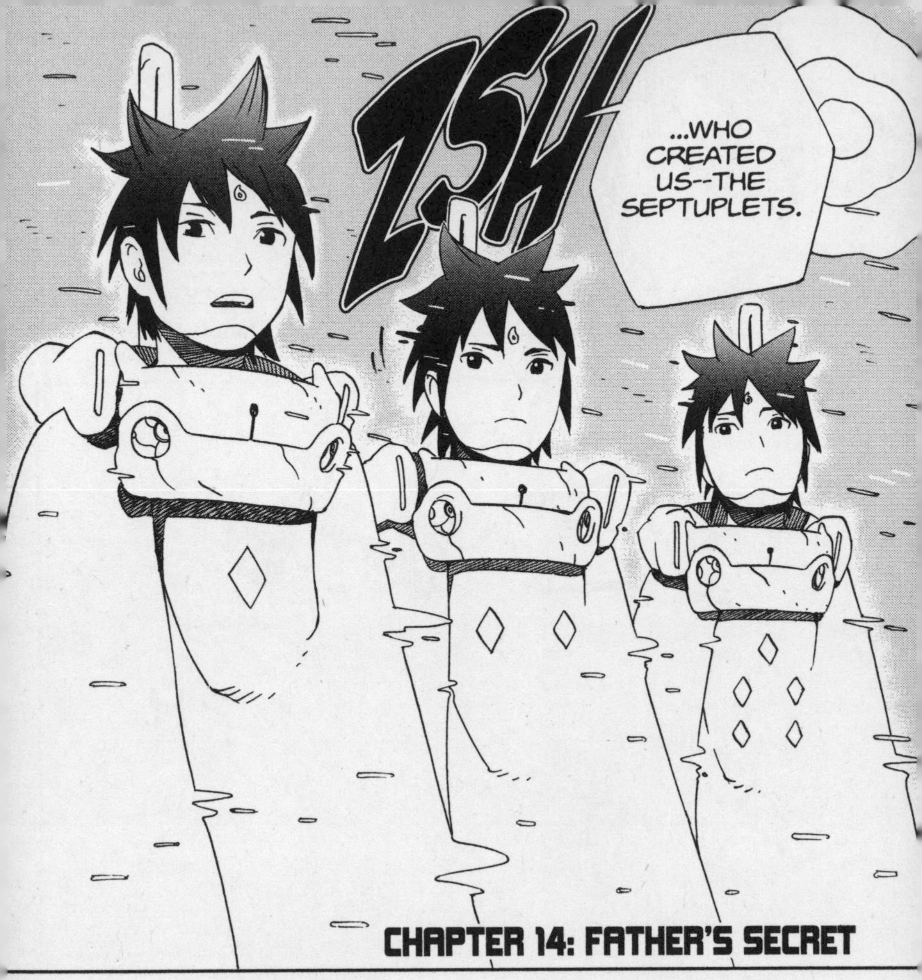
ZSH
...WHO CREATED US--THE SEPTUPLETS.

CHAPTER 14: FATHER'S SECRET

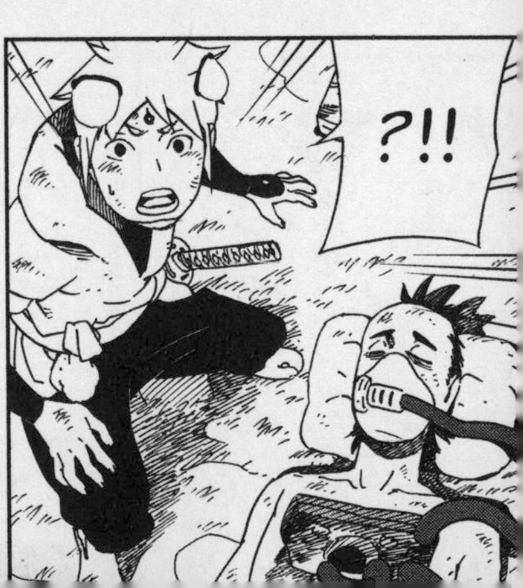
?!!

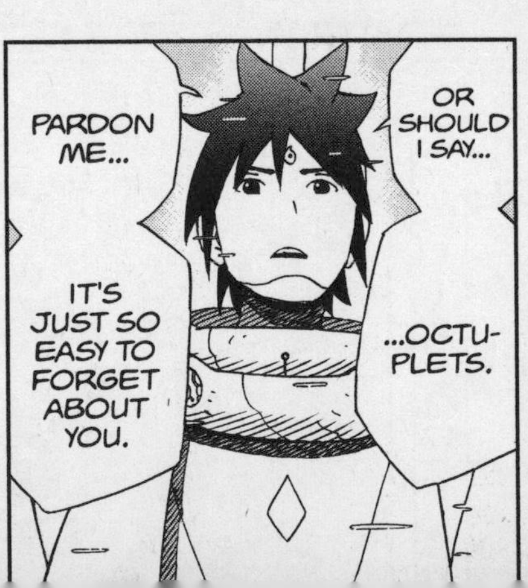
PARDON ME...
OR SHOULD I SAY...
...OCTU-PLETS.
IT'S JUST SO EASY TO FORGET ABOUT YOU.

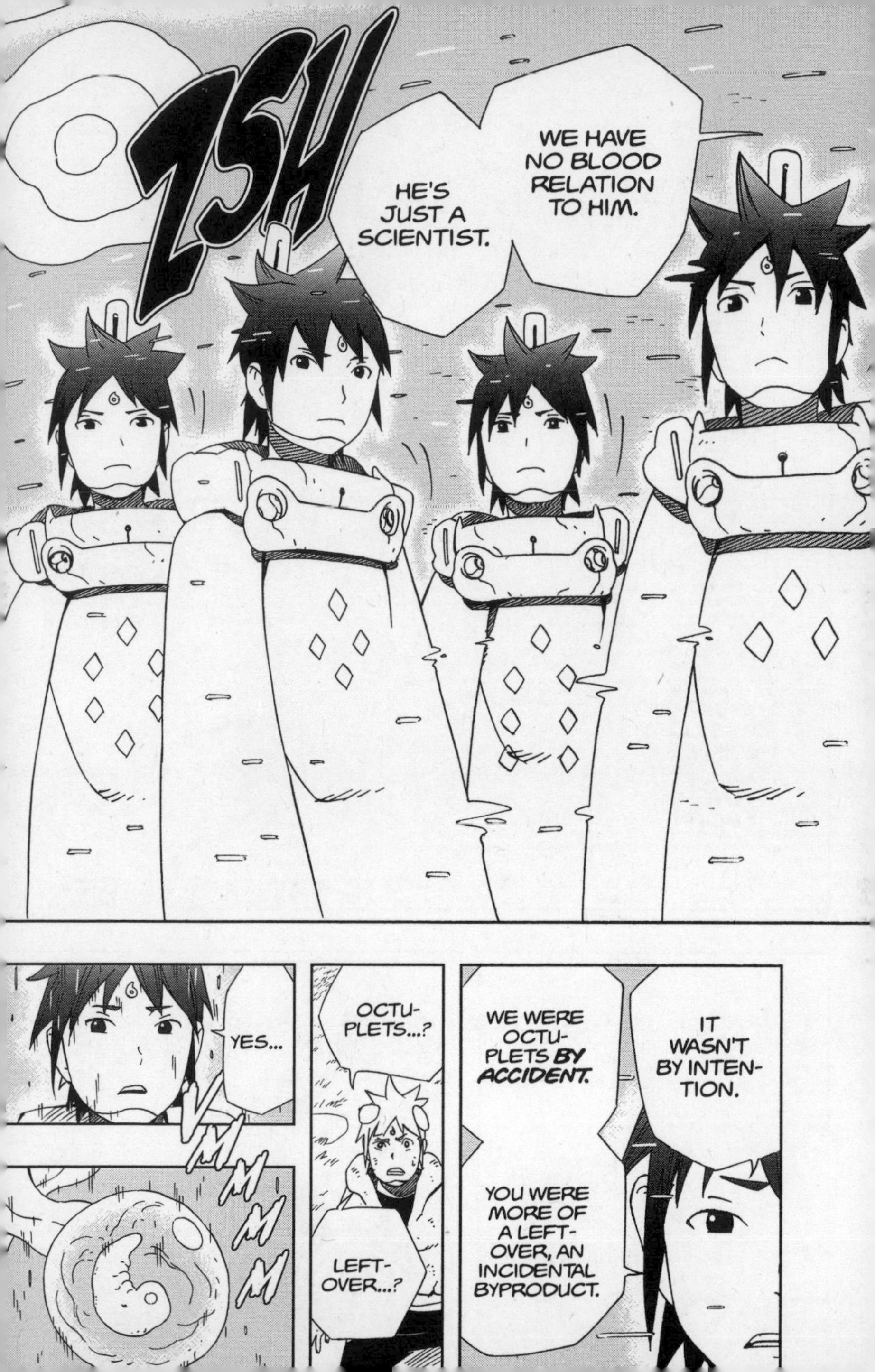
WE HAVE NO BLOOD RELATION TO HIM.
HE'S JUST A SCIENTIST.
ZSH
IT WASN'T BY INTENTION.
WE WERE OCTUPLETS **BY ACCIDENT.**
YOU WERE MORE OF A LEFTOVER, AN INCIDENTAL BYPRODUCT.
OCTUPLETS...?
LEFTOVER...?
YES...

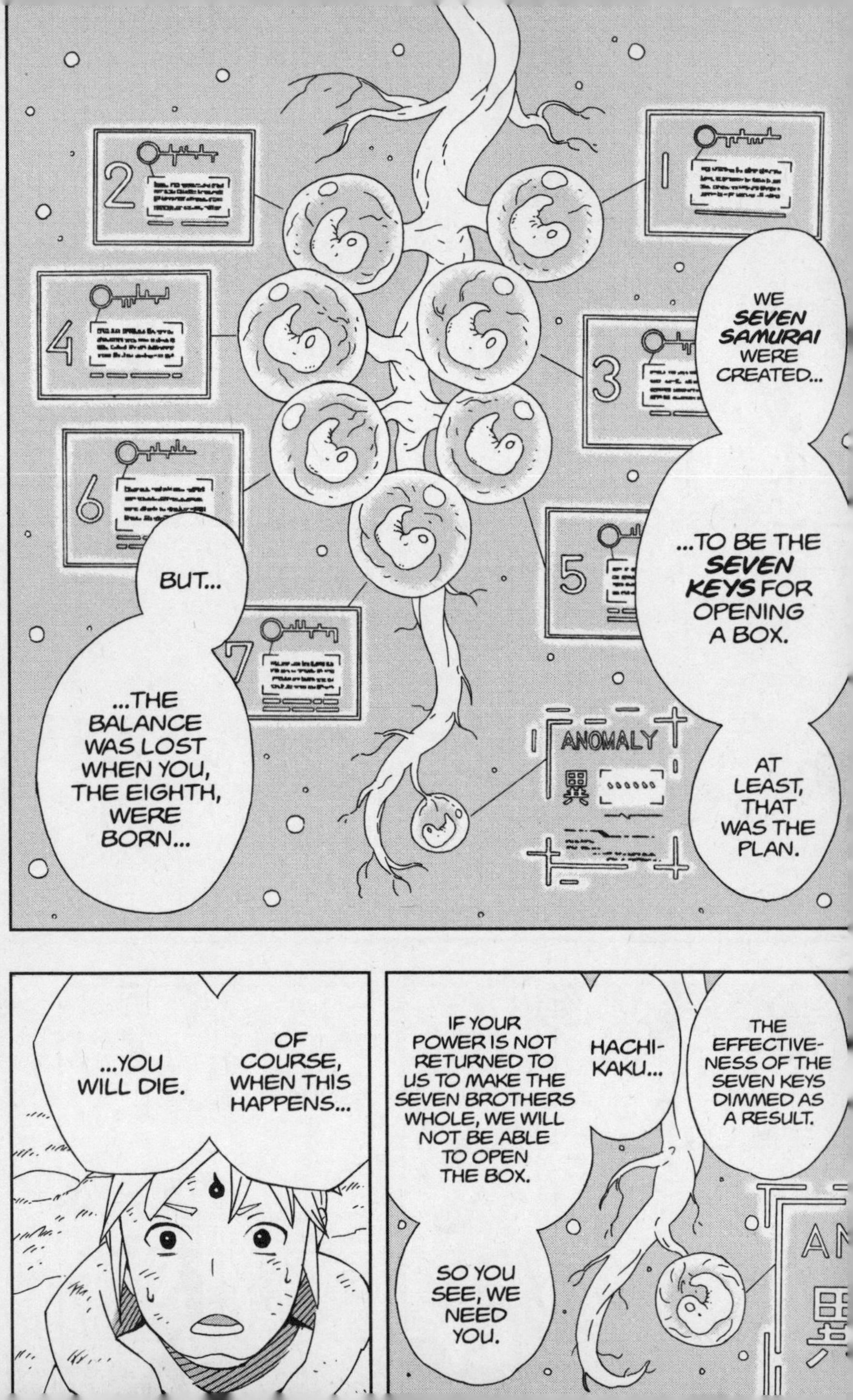
1
2
3
4
5
6
7
WE SEVEN SAMURAI WERE CREATED...
...TO BE THE SEVEN KEYS FOR OPENING A BOX.
AT LEAST, THAT WAS THE PLAN.
ANOMALY
異
BUT...
...THE BALANCE WAS LOST WHEN YOU, THE EIGHTH, WERE BORN...
THE EFFECTIVENESS OF THE SEVEN KEYS DIMMED AS A RESULT.
HACHIKAKU...
IF YOUR POWER IS NOT RETURNED TO US TO MAKE THE SEVEN BROTHERS WHOLE, WE WILL NOT BE ABLE TO OPEN THE BOX.
SO YOU SEE, WE NEED YOU.
OF COURSE, WHEN THIS HAPPENS...
...YOU WILL DIE.

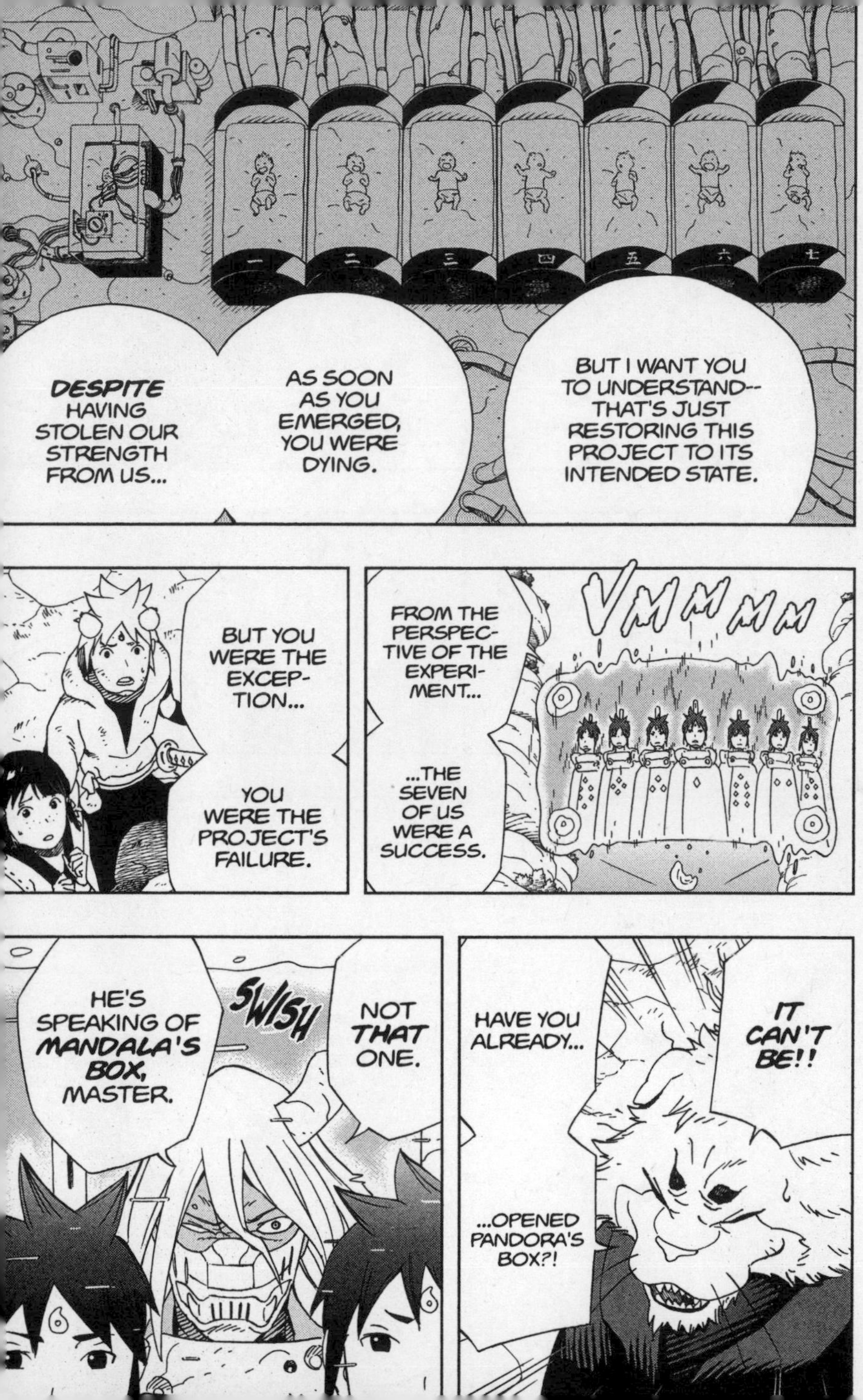
BUT I WANT YOU TO UNDERSTAND--THAT'S JUST RESTORING THIS PROJECT TO ITS INTENDED STATE.
AS SOON AS YOU EMERGED, YOU WERE DYING.
DESPITE HAVING STOLEN OUR STRENGTH FROM US...
VMMMMM
FROM THE PERSPECTIVE OF THE EXPERIMENT...
...THE SEVEN OF US WERE A SUCCESS.
BUT YOU WERE THE EXCEPTION...
YOU WERE THE PROJECT'S FAILURE.
IT CAN'T BE!!
HAVE YOU ALREADY...
...OPENED PANDORA'S BOX?!
NOT *THAT* ONE.
SWISH
HE'S SPEAKING OF *MANDALA'S BOX,* MASTER.

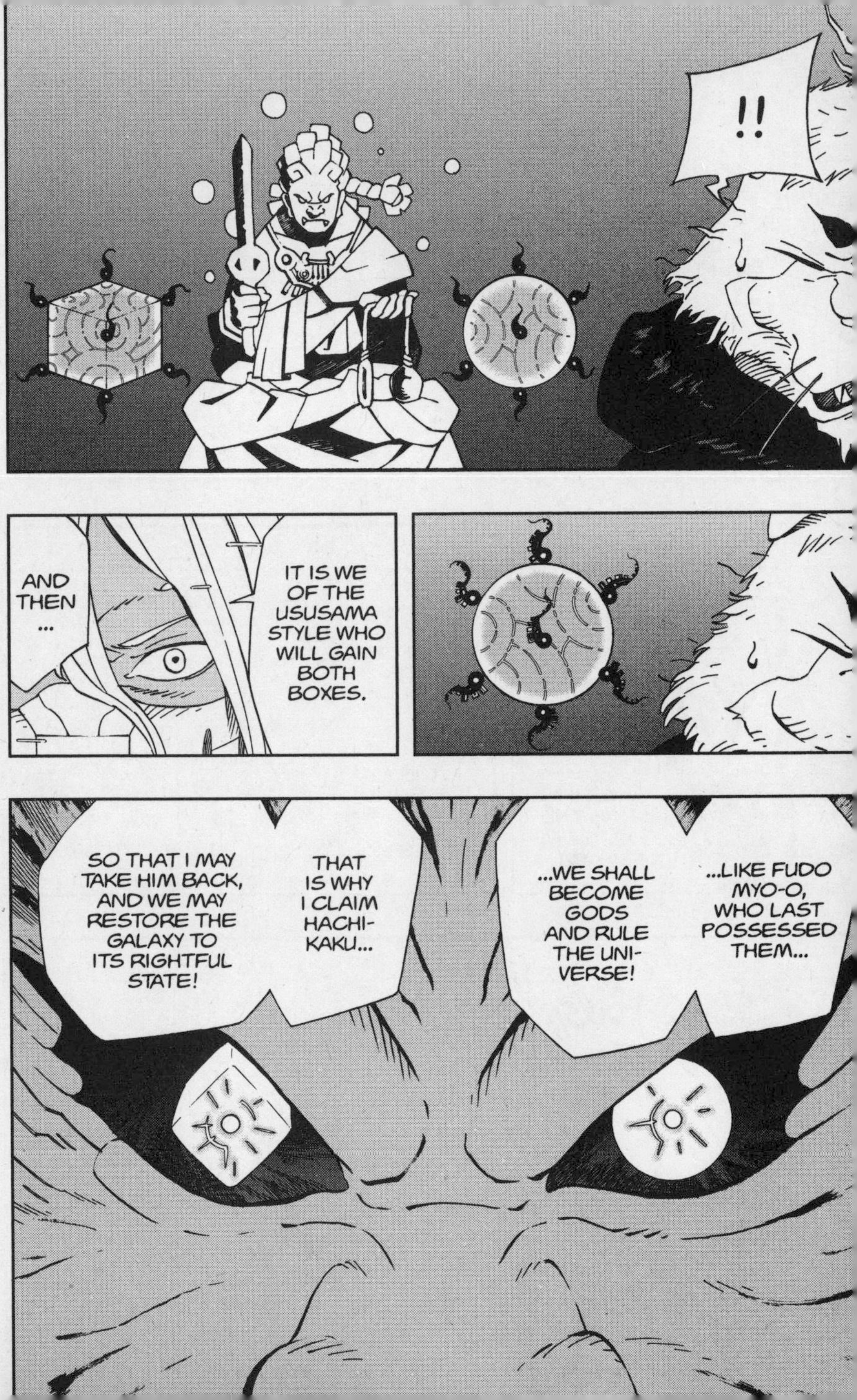
!!
IT IS WE OF THE USUSAMA STYLE WHO WILL GAIN BOTH BOXES.
AND THEN ...
...LIKE FUDO MYO-O, WHO LAST POSSESSED THEM...
...WE SHALL BECOME GODS AND RULE THE UNI-VERSE!
THAT IS WHY I CLAIM HACHI-KAKU...
SO THAT I MAY TAKE HIM BACK, AND WE MAY RESTORE THE GALAXY TO ITS RIGHTFUL STATE!

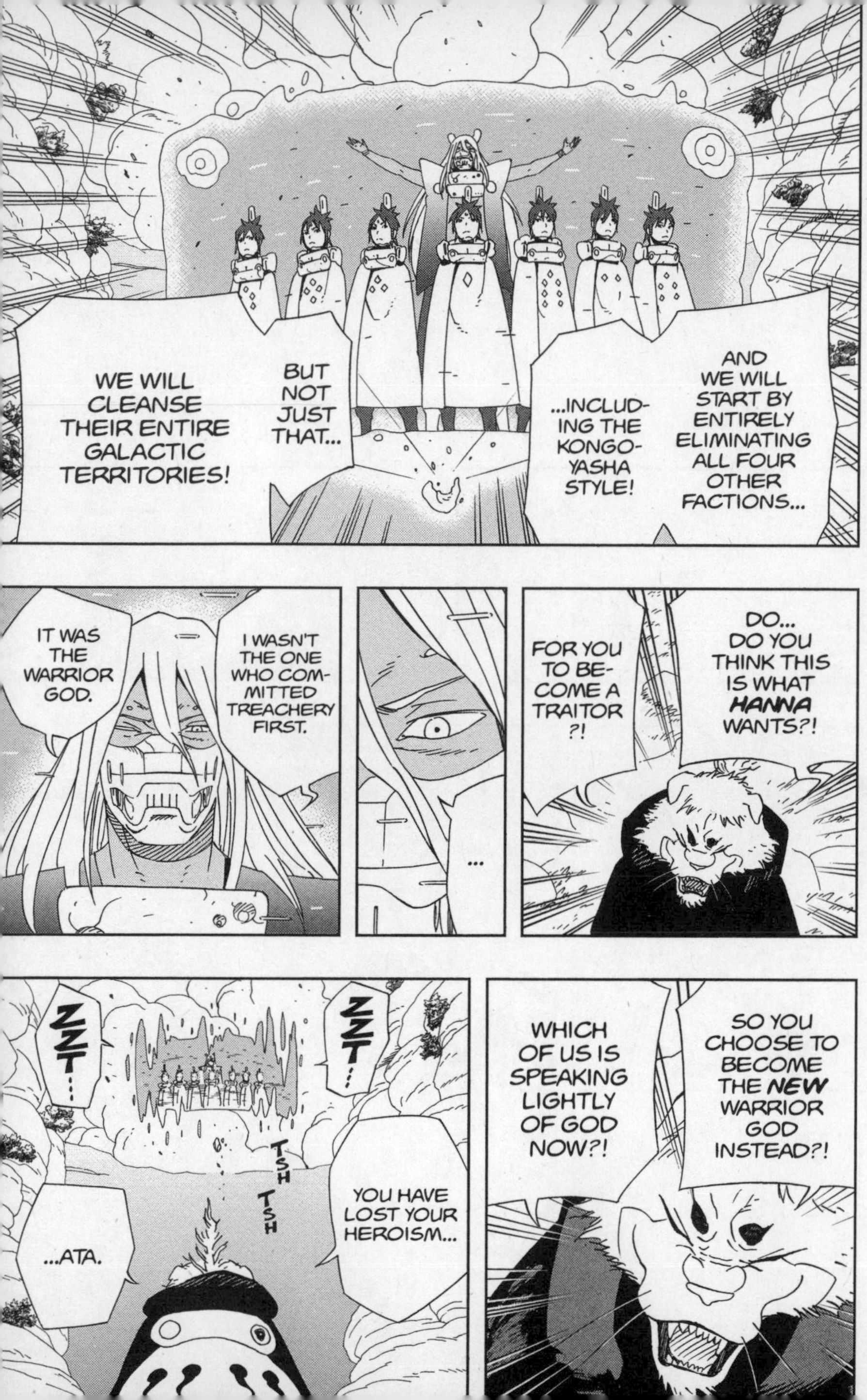
AND WE WILL START BY ENTIRELY ELIMINATING ALL FOUR OTHER FACTIONS...
...INCLUDING THE KONGO-YASHA STYLE!
BUT NOT JUST THAT...
WE WILL CLEANSE THEIR ENTIRE GALACTIC TERRITORIES!
DO... DO YOU THINK THIS IS WHAT *HANNA* WANTS?!
FOR YOU TO BECOME A TRAITOR?!
...
I WASN'T THE ONE WHO COMMITTED TREACHERY FIRST.
IT WAS THE WARRIOR GOD.
SO YOU CHOOSE TO BECOME THE *NEW* WARRIOR GOD INSTEAD?!
WHICH OF US IS SPEAKING LIGHTLY OF GOD NOW?!
ZZT...
ZZT...
TSH
TSH
YOU HAVE LOST YOUR HEROISM...
...ATA.

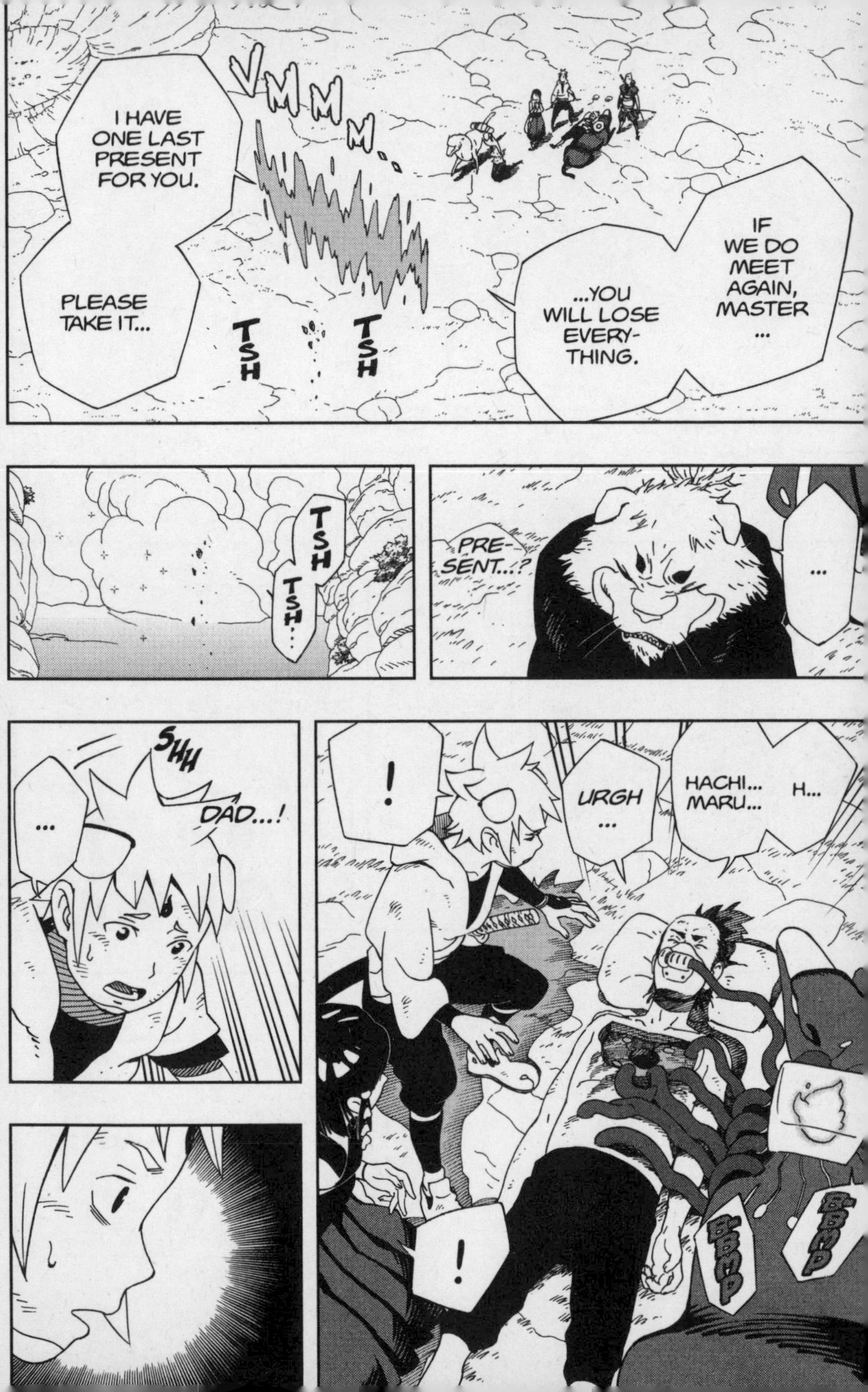
IF WE DO MEET AGAIN, MASTER ...
...YOU WILL LOSE EVERY-THING.
VMMM..
TSH
TSH
I HAVE ONE LAST PRESENT FOR YOU.
PLEASE TAKE IT...
...
PRE-SENT...?
TSH
TSH...
HACHI... MARU...
H...
URGH ...
!
!
BBMP
BBMP
SHH
DAD...!
...

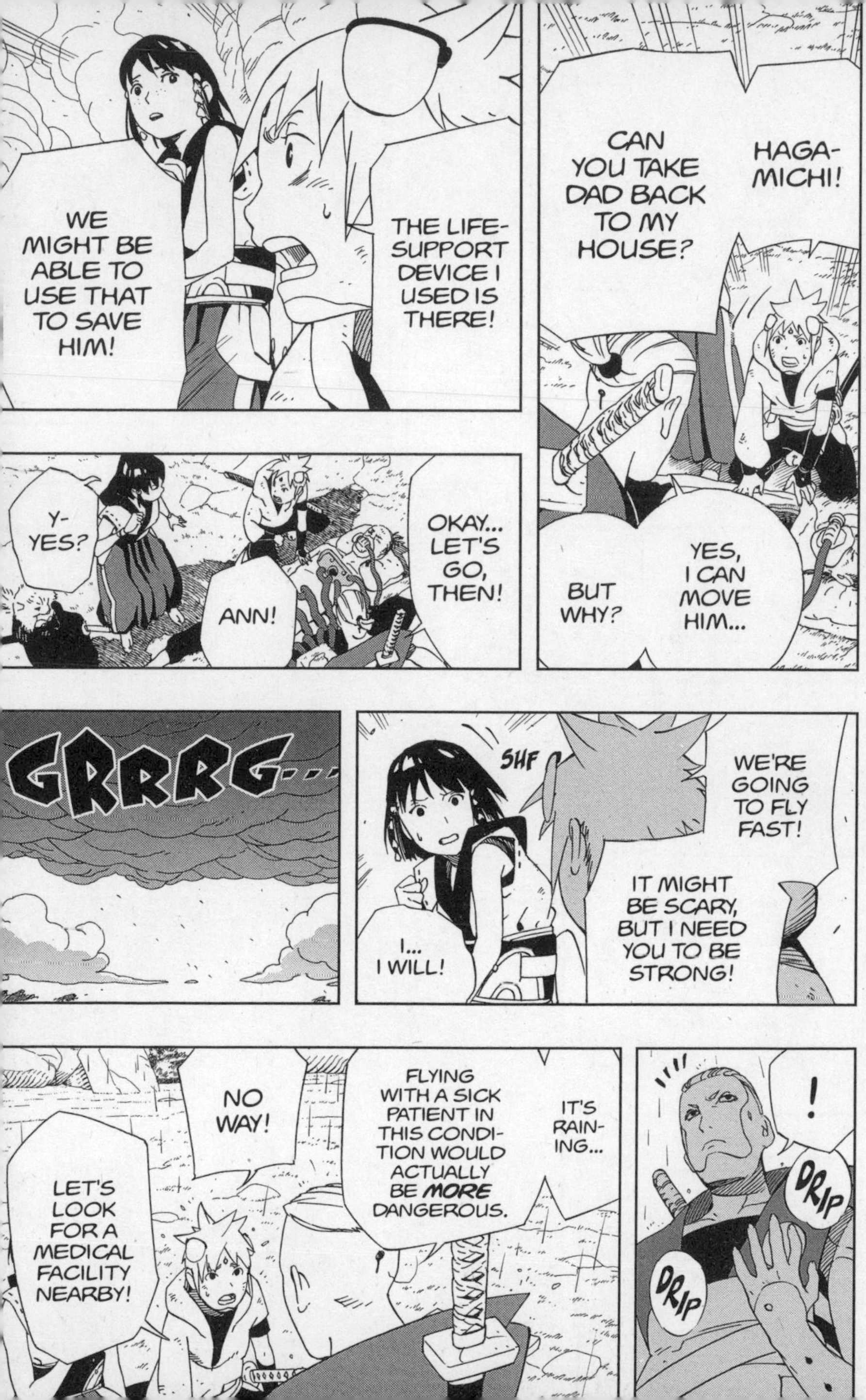
HAGA-
MICHI!
CAN YOU TAKE DAD BACK TO MY HOUSE?
YES, I CAN MOVE HIM...
BUT WHY?
THE LIFE-SUPPORT DEVICE I USED IS THERE!
WE MIGHT BE ABLE TO USE THAT TO SAVE HIM!
OKAY... LET'S GO, THEN!
ANN!
Y-YES?
SHF
WE'RE GOING TO FLY FAST!
IT MIGHT BE SCARY, BUT I NEED YOU TO BE STRONG!
I... I WILL!
GRRRG...
!
DRIP
DRIP
IT'S RAIN-
ING...
FLYING WITH A SICK PATIENT IN THIS CONDI-
TION WOULD ACTUALLY BE *MORE* DANGEROUS.
NO WAY!
LET'S LOOK FOR A MEDICAL FACILITY NEARBY!

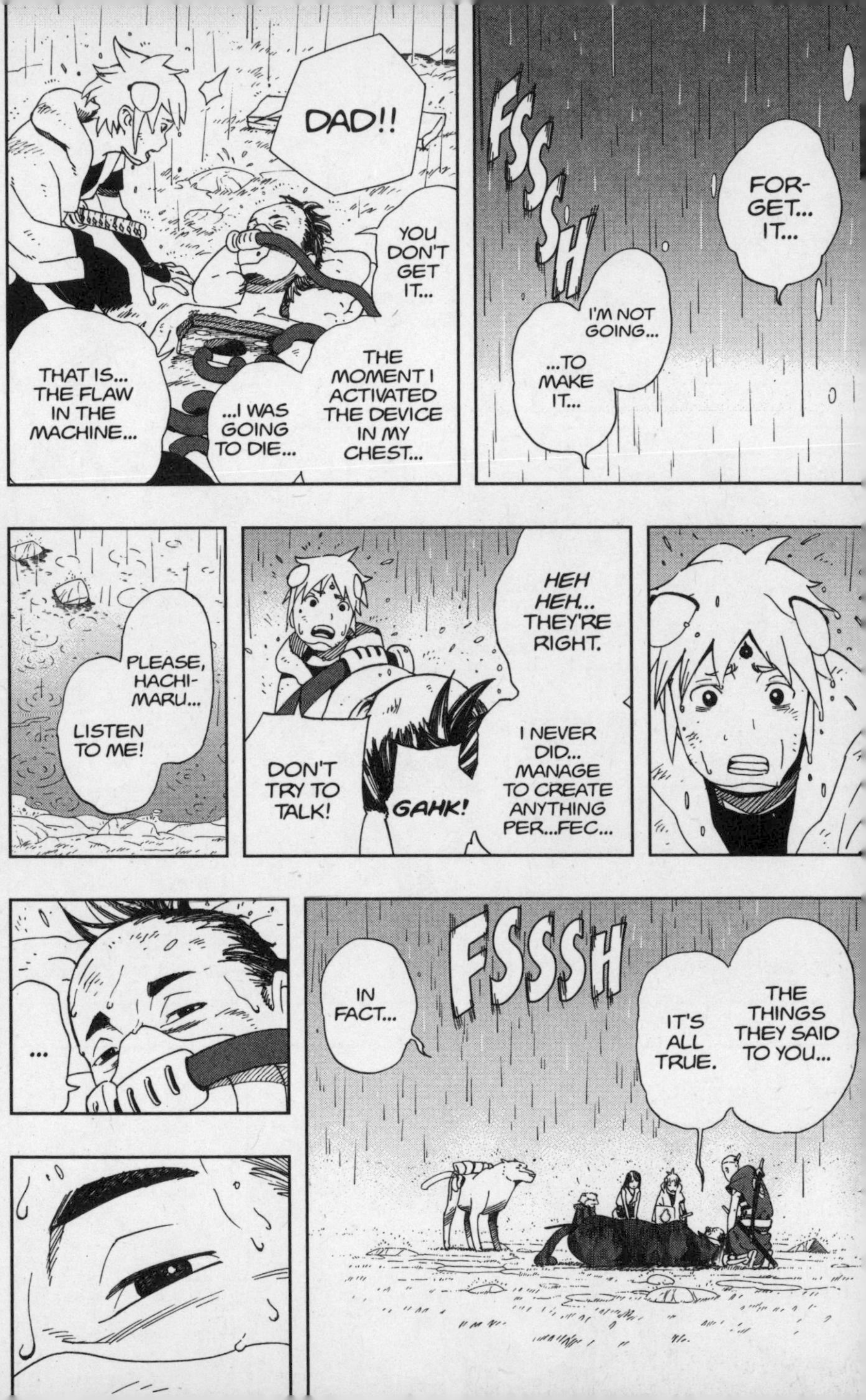
FOR-GET... IT...
FSSH
I'M NOT GOING...
...TO MAKE IT...
DAD!!
YOU DON'T GET IT...
THE MOMENT I ACTIVATED THE DEVICE IN MY CHEST...
...I WAS GOING TO DIE...
THAT IS... THE FLAW IN THE MACHINE...
HEH HEH... THEY'RE RIGHT.
I NEVER DID... MANAGE TO CREATE ANYTHING PER...FEC...
GAHK!
DON'T TRY TO TALK!
PLEASE, HACHI-MARU...
LISTEN TO ME!
THE THINGS THEY SAID TO YOU...
IT'S ALL TRUE.
FSSH
IN FACT...
...

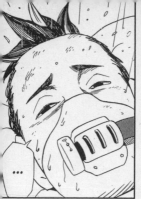

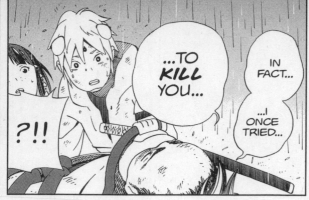

IN FACT...
...I ONCE TRIED...
...TO KILL YOU...
?!!
...
I THOUGHT THAT IF I KILLED YOU BEFORE YOUR POWER WAS RETURNED...
...TO THOSE SEPTUPLETS...
...THEY WOULDN'T BE ABLE TO OPEN THE BOXES.
BUT...
...I JUST COULDN'T DO IT.
MMF...
YOU WERE... CLINGING TO LIFE.
I WAS LONELY ...
...AND MY EXISTENCE WAS NOTHING BUT LAB EXPERIMENTS. IN THAT MOMENT...
...I FELT SOMETHING INSIDE OF ME.
A SPECIAL FEELING...
SO I LEFT.
I TOOK YOU AND FLED THE LAB...
AND THEN I CAME HERE...
...TO HIDE ON THIS PLANET ...

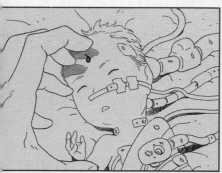

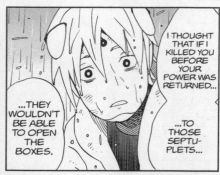

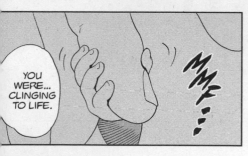

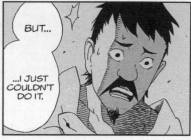

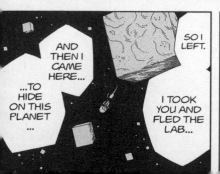

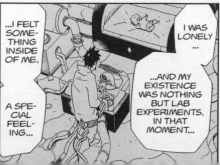

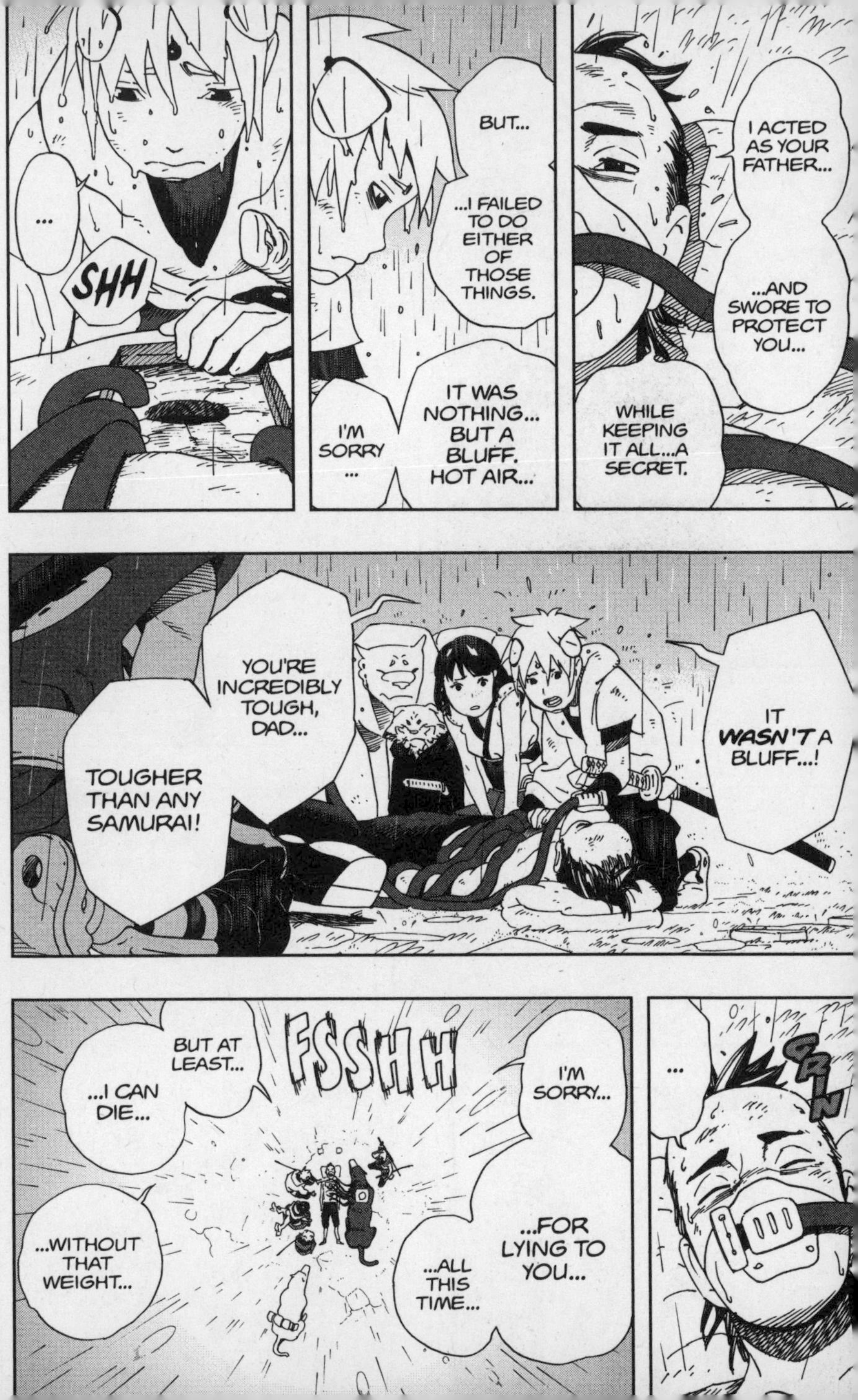
I ACTED AS YOUR FATHER...
...AND SWORE TO PROTECT YOU...
WHILE KEEPING IT ALL...A SECRET.
BUT...
...I FAILED TO DO EITHER OF THOSE THINGS.
IT WAS NOTHING... BUT A BLUFF. HOT AIR...
I'M SORRY ...
...
SHH
IT WASN'T A BLUFF...!
YOU'RE INCREDIBLY TOUGH, DAD...
TOUGHER THAN ANY SAMURAI!
...
GRIN
I'M SORRY...
...FOR LYING TO YOU...
...ALL THIS TIME...
FSSHH
BUT AT LEAST...
...I CAN DIE...
...WITHOUT THAT WEIGHT...

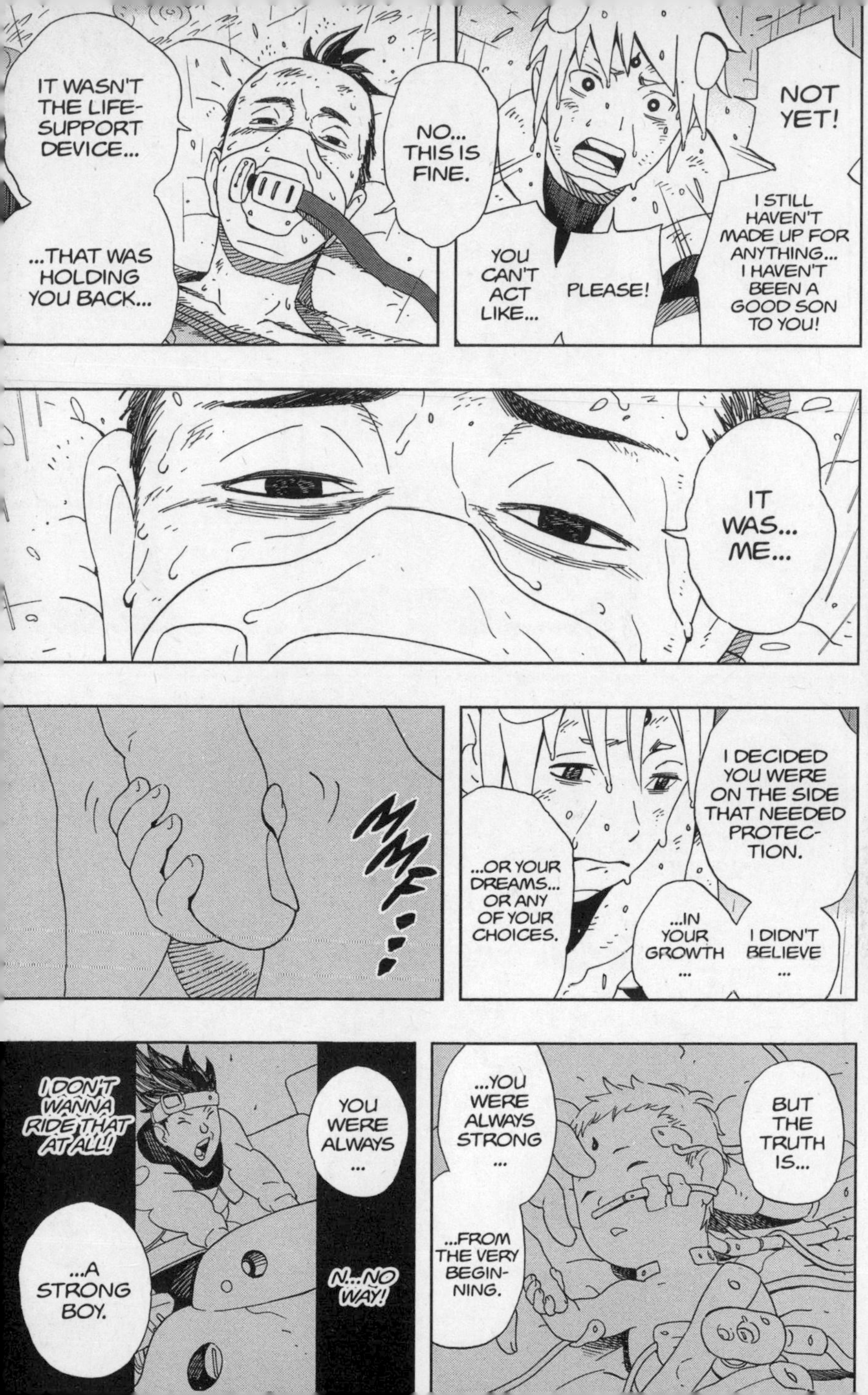
NOT YET!
I STILL HAVEN'T MADE UP FOR ANYTHING... I HAVEN'T BEEN A GOOD SON TO YOU!
PLEASE!
YOU CAN'T ACT LIKE...
NO... THIS IS FINE.
IT WASN'T THE LIFE-SUPPORT DEVICE...
...THAT WAS HOLDING YOU BACK...
IT WAS... ME...
I DECIDED YOU WERE ON THE SIDE THAT NEEDED PROTECTION.
I DIDN'T BELIEVE ...
...IN YOUR GROWTH ...
...OR YOUR DREAMS... OR ANY OF YOUR CHOICES.
MMF...
BUT THE TRUTH IS...
...YOU WERE ALWAYS STRONG ...
...FROM THE VERY BEGIN-NING.
YOU WERE ALWAYS ...
I DON'T WANNA RIDE THAT AT ALL!
N...NO WAY!
...A STRONG BOY.

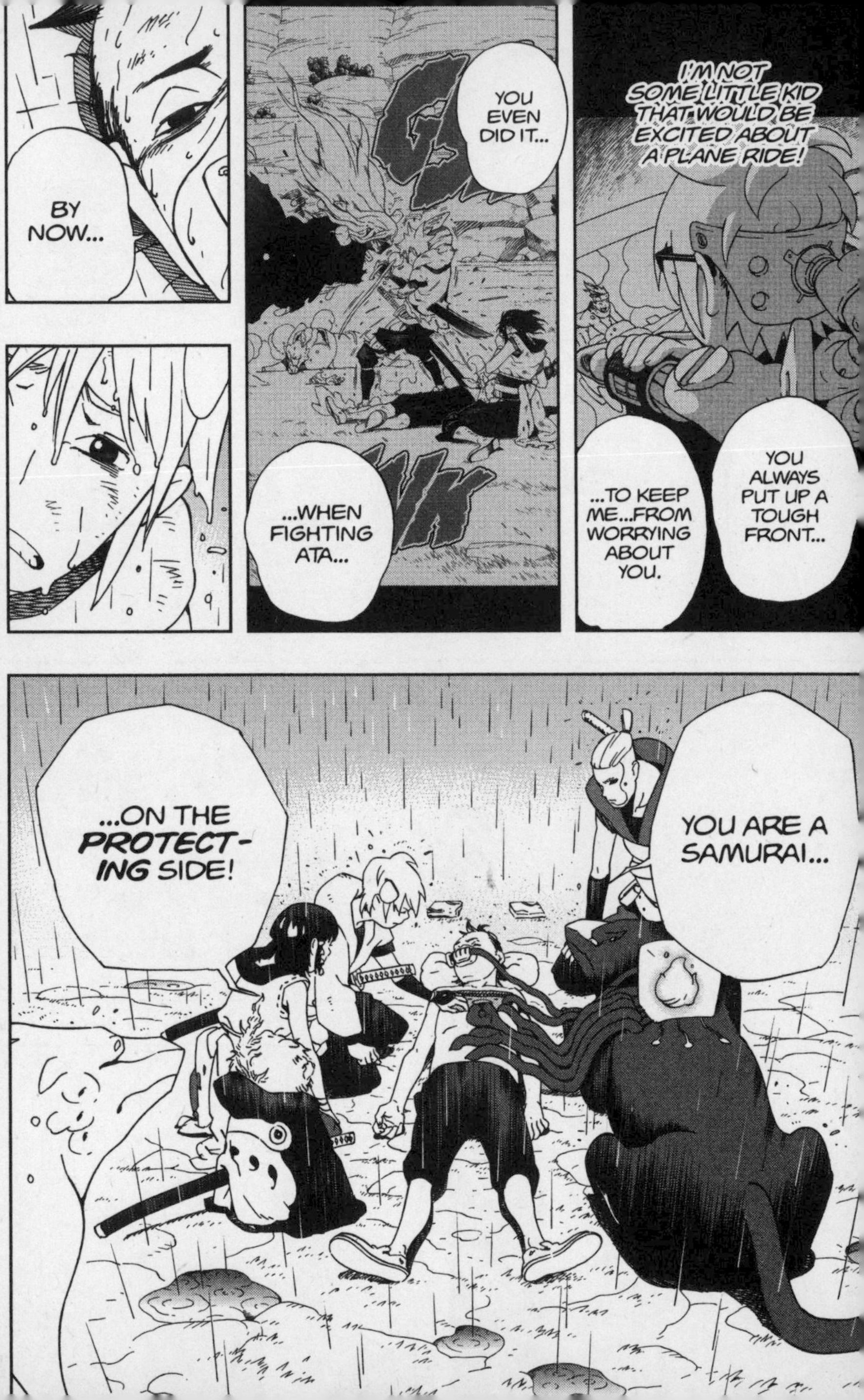
I'M NOT SOME LITTLE KID THAT WOULD BE EXCITED ABOUT A PLANE RIDE!
YOU ALWAYS PUT UP A TOUGH FRONT...
...TO KEEP ME...FROM WORRYING ABOUT YOU.
YOU EVEN DID IT...
...WHEN FIGHTING ATA...
BY NOW...
YOU ARE A SAMURAI...
...ON THE *PROTECT-ING* SIDE!

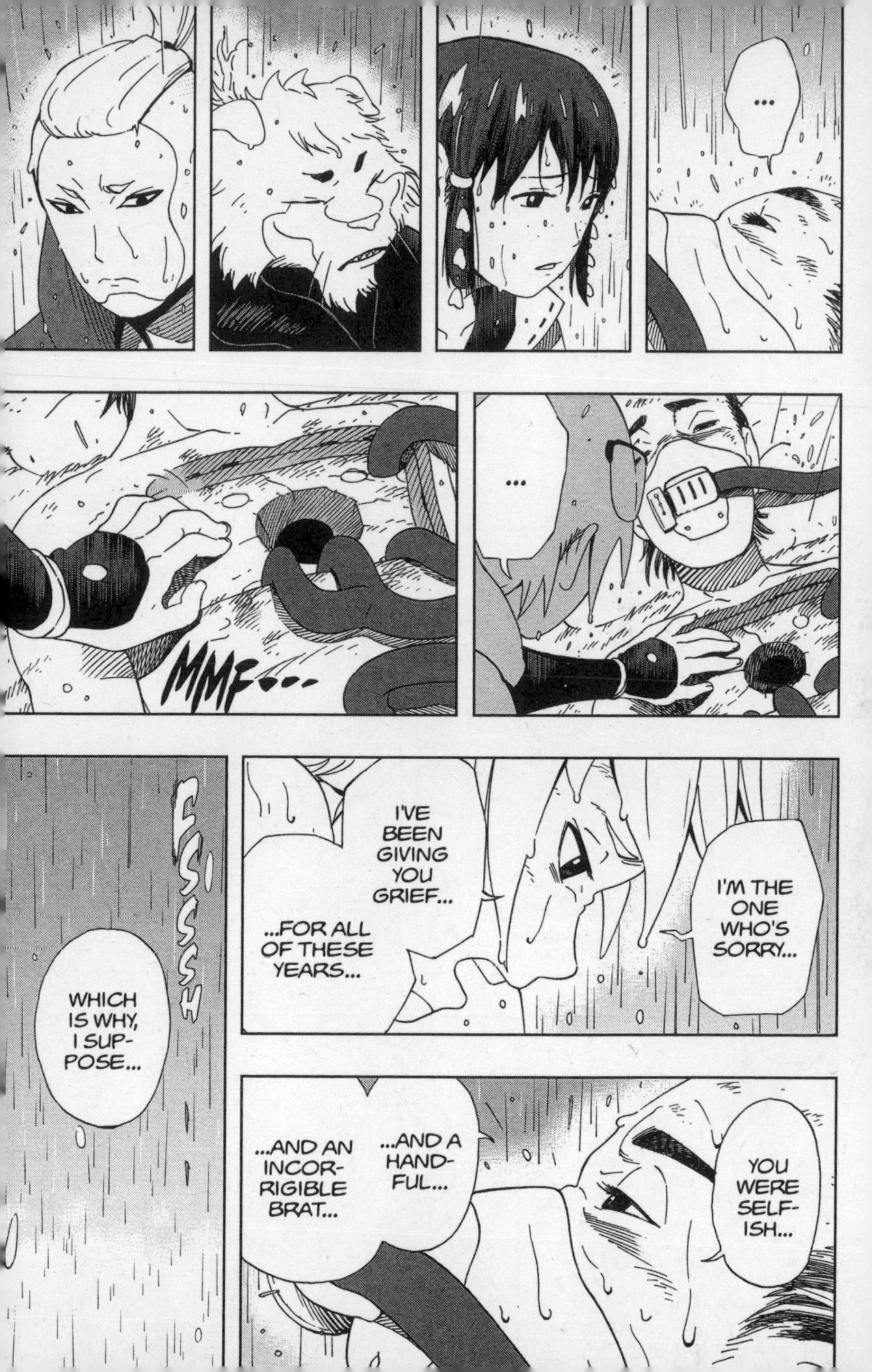
...
...
MMF...
I'M THE ONE WHO'S SORRY...
I'VE BEEN GIVING YOU GRIEF...
...FOR ALL OF THESE YEARS...
YOU WERE SELFISH...
...AND A HANDFUL...
...AND AN INCORRIGIBLE BRAT...
FSSSSH
WHICH IS WHY, I SUPPOSE...

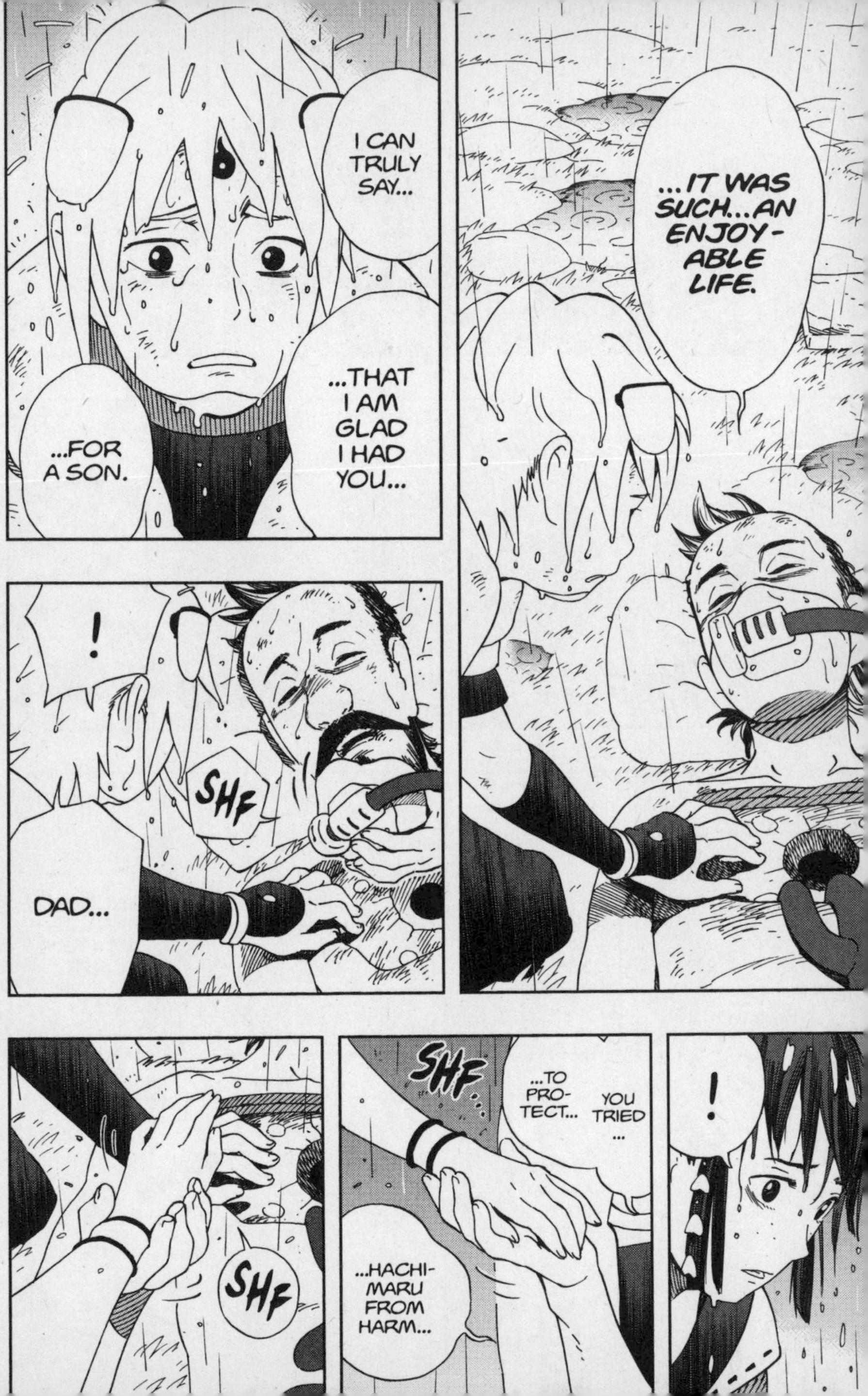
...IT WAS SUCH...AN ENJOY-ABLE LIFE.
I CAN TRULY SAY...
...THAT I AM GLAD I HAD YOU...
...FOR A SON.
!
SHF
DAD...
!
YOU TRIED ...
...TO PRO-TECT...
SHF...
...HACHI-MARU FROM HARM...
SHF

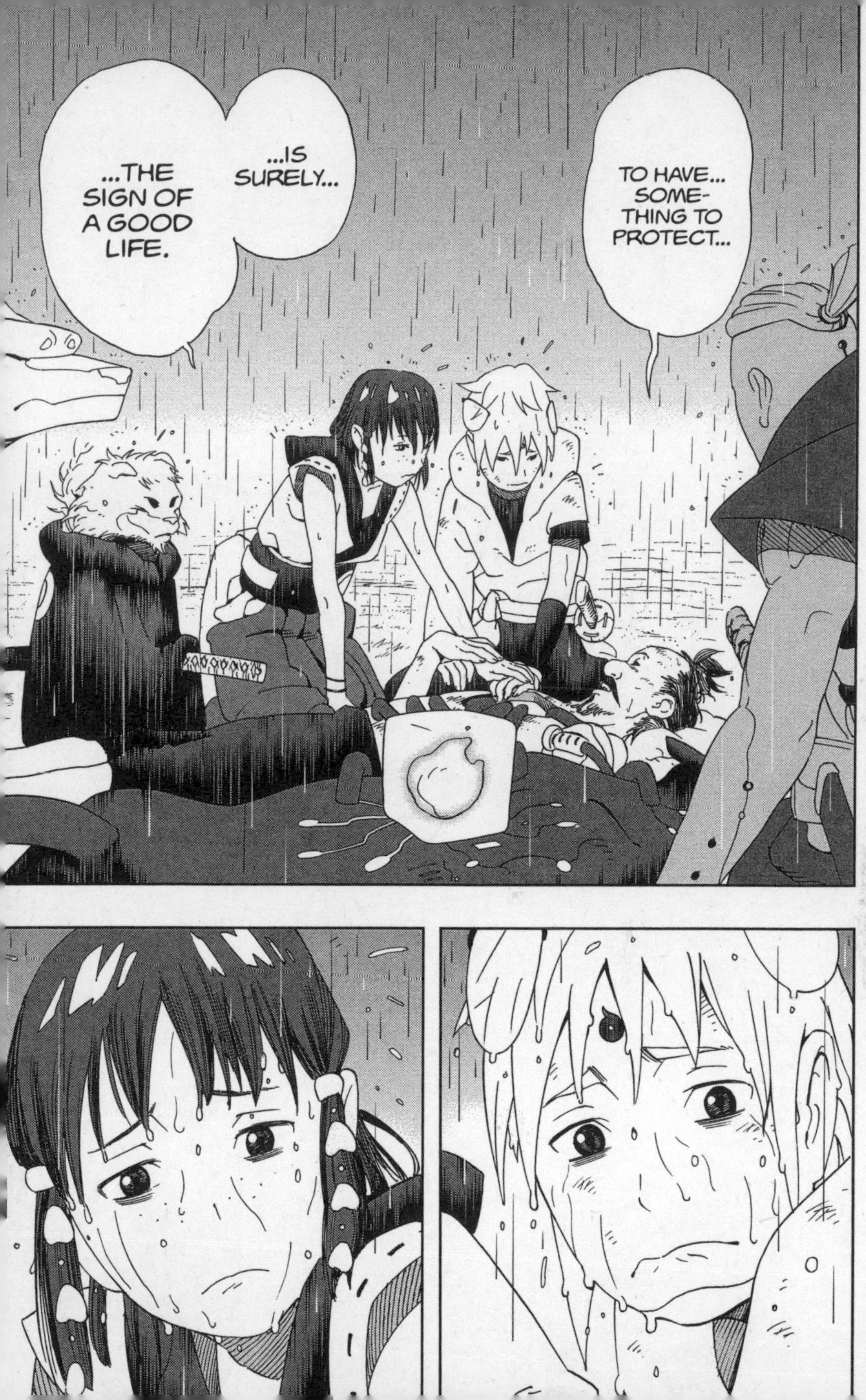
TO HAVE... SOME-THING TO PROTECT...
...IS SURELY...
...THE SIGN OF A GOOD LIFE.

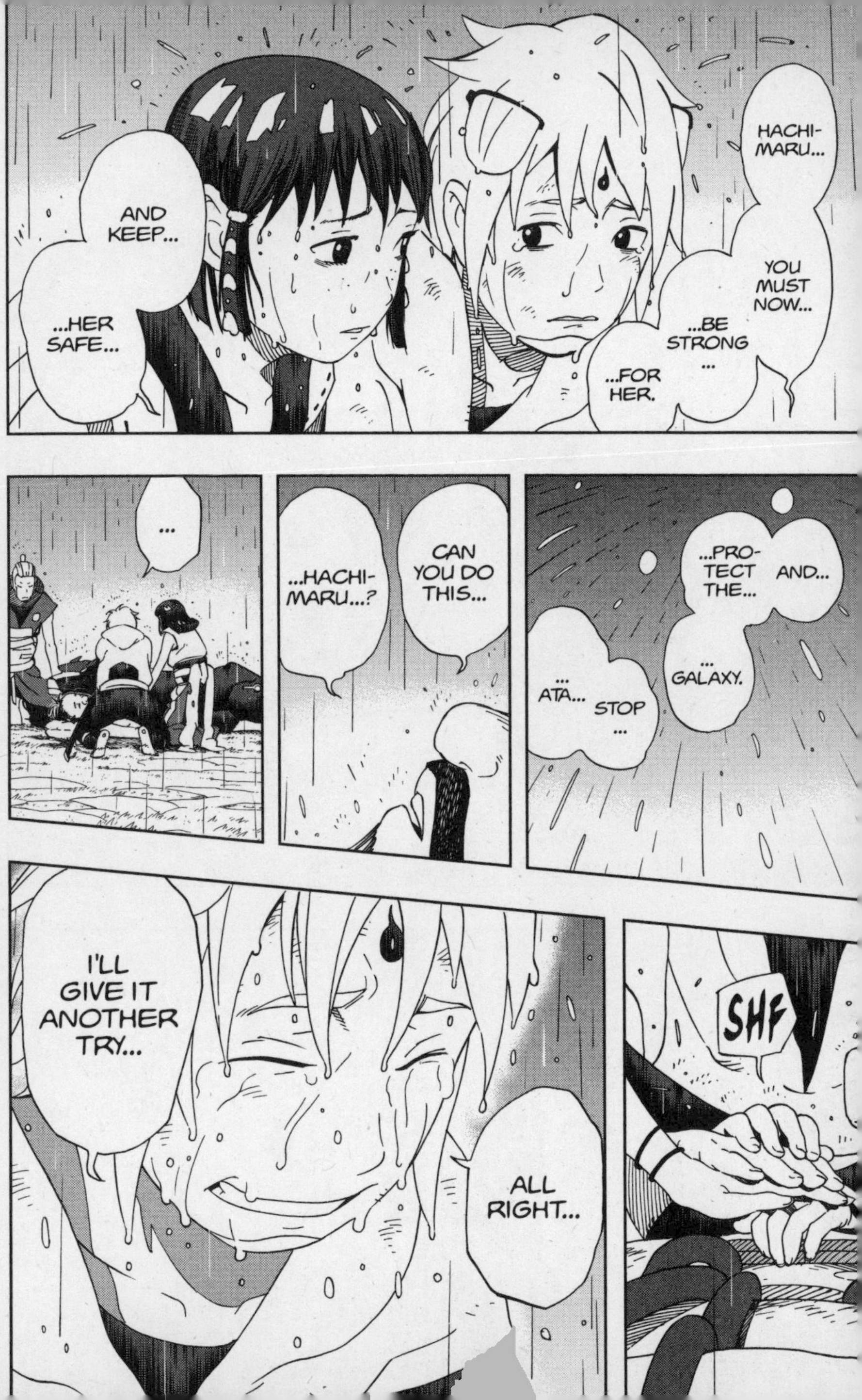
HACHI-MARU...
YOU MUST NOW...
...BE STRONG ...
...FOR HER.
AND KEEP...
...HER SAFE...
AND...
...PROTECT THE...
... GALAXY.
STOP ...
... ATA...
CAN YOU DO THIS...
...HACHI-MARU...?
...
SHF
ALL RIGHT...
I'LL GIVE IT ANOTHER TRY...

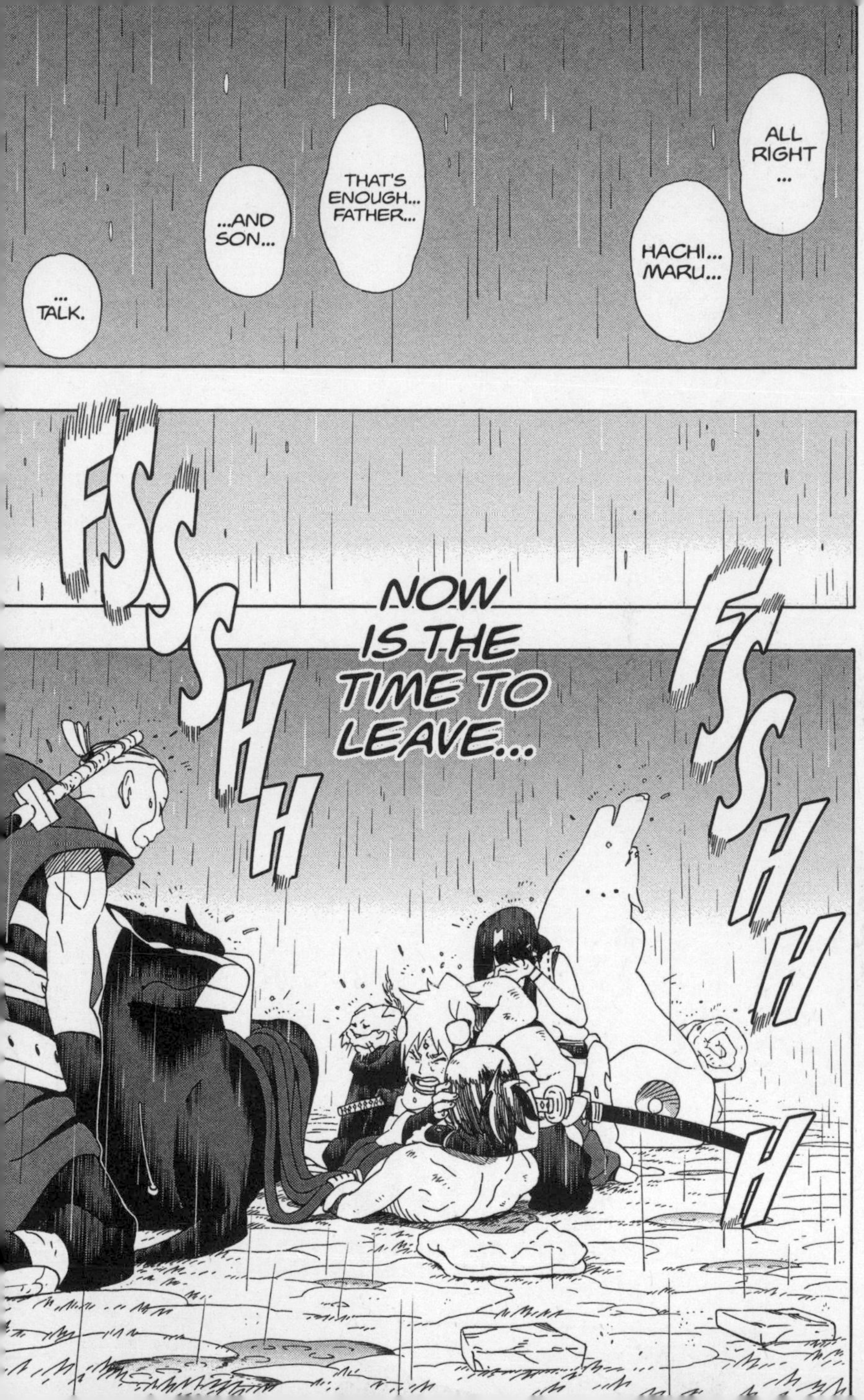
ALL RIGHT ...
HACHI... MARU...
THAT'S ENOUGH... FATHER...
...AND SON...
... TALK.
FSSHHH
NOW IS THE TIME TO LEAVE...
FSSSHH

SAMURAI 8

THE TALE OF HACHIMARU

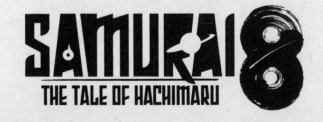

CHAPTER 15: HACHIMARU'S CALLING

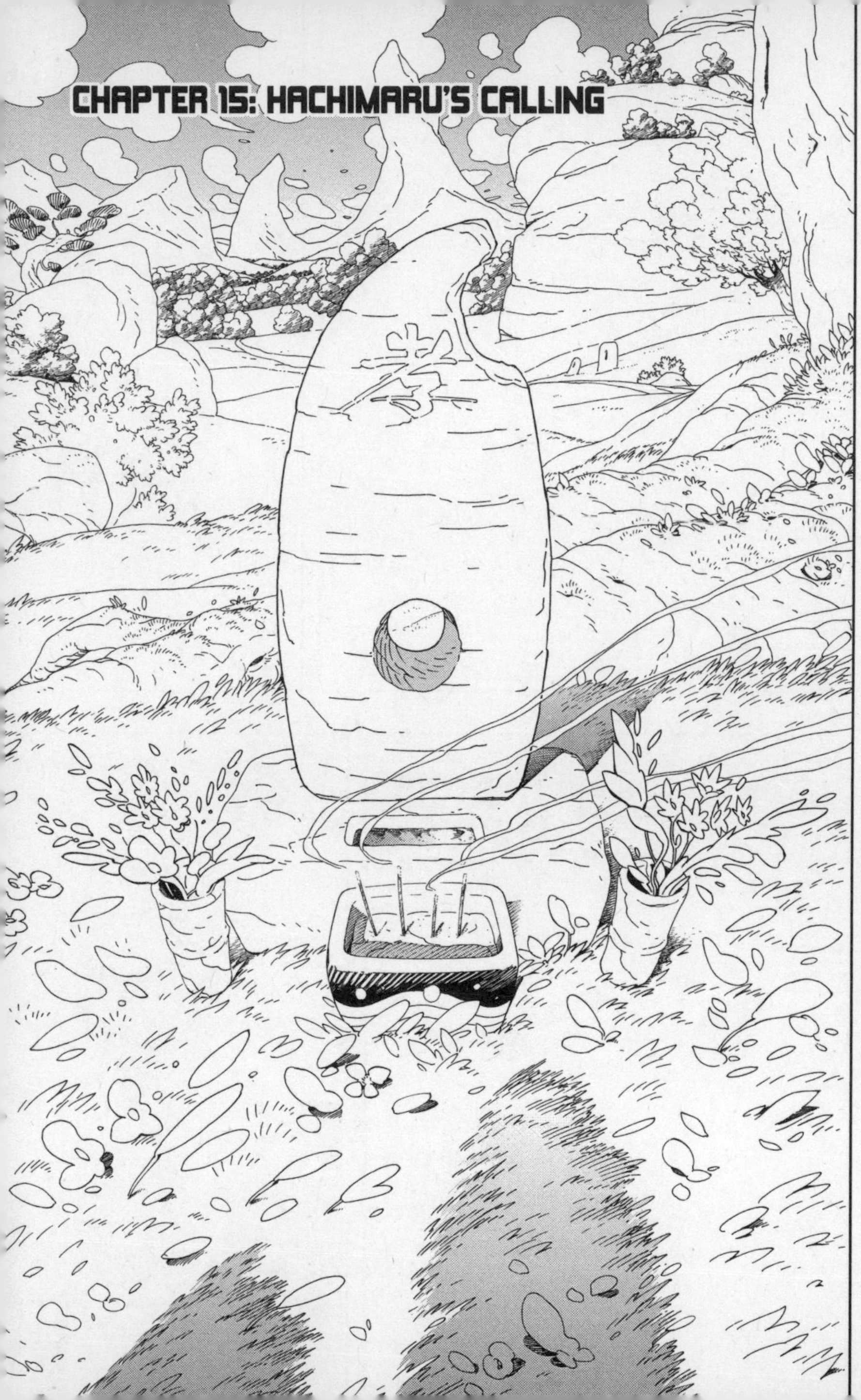

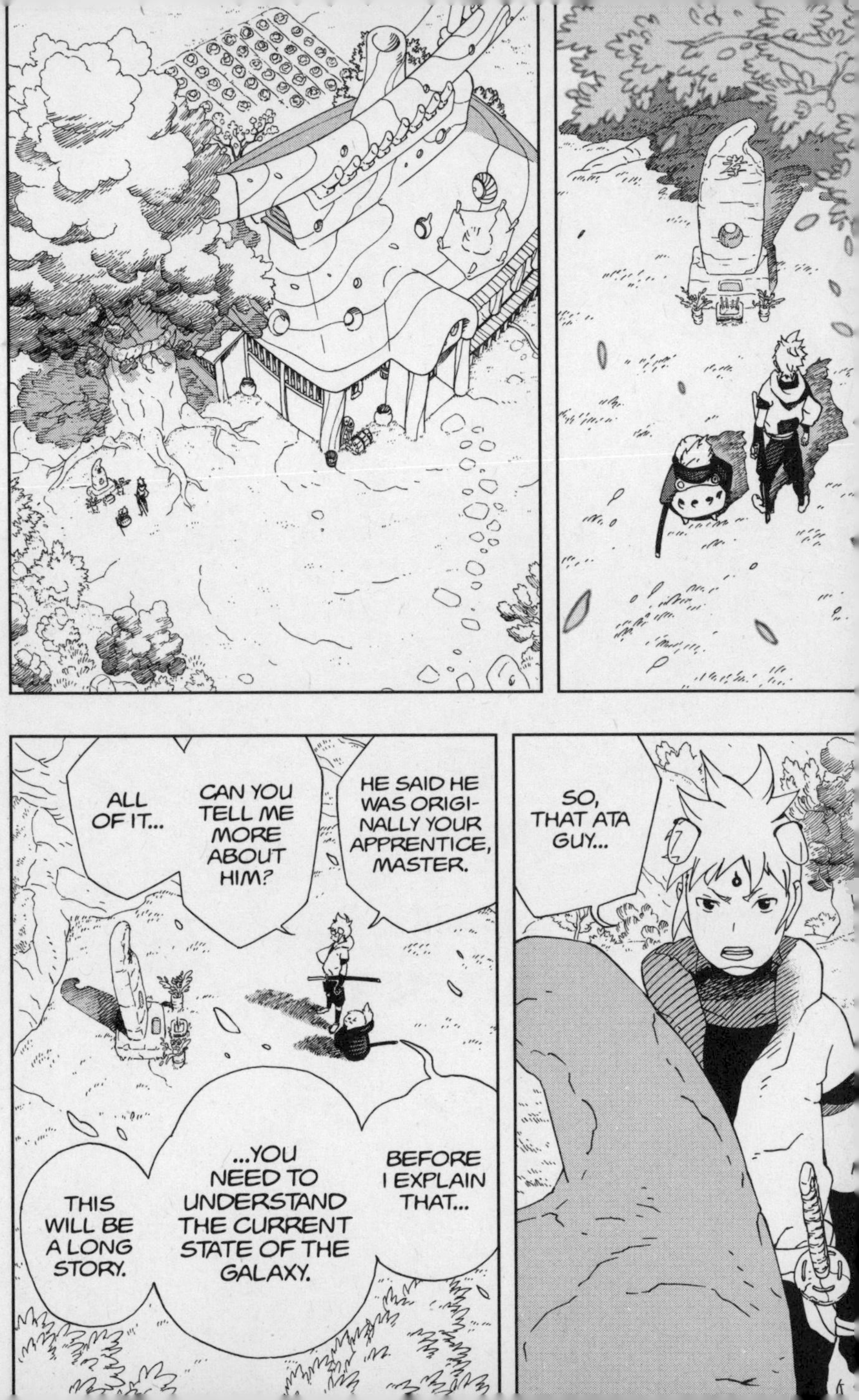
SO, THAT ATA GUY...
HE SAID HE WAS ORIGI-NALLY YOUR APPRENTICE, MASTER.
CAN YOU TELL ME MORE ABOUT HIM?
ALL OF IT...
BEFORE I EXPLAIN THAT...
...YOU NEED TO UNDERSTAND THE CURRENT STATE OF THE GALAXY.
THIS WILL BE A LONG STORY.

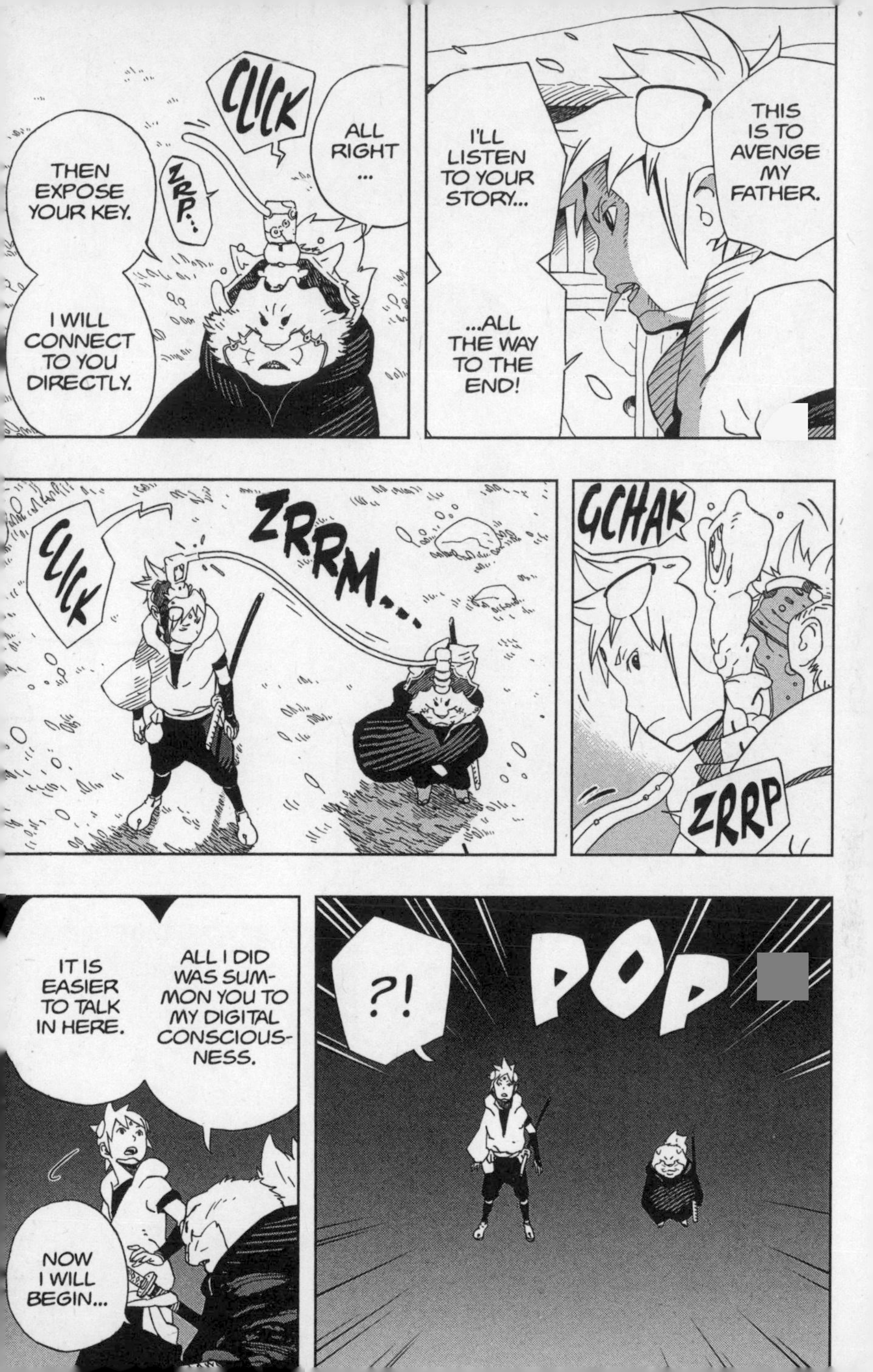
THIS IS TO AVENGE MY FATHER.
I'LL LISTEN TO YOUR STORY...
...ALL THE WAY TO THE END!
ALL RIGHT ...
CLICK
ZRP...
THEN EXPOSE YOUR KEY.
I WILL CONNECT TO YOU DIRECTLY.
GCHAK
ZRRP
ZRRM...
CLICK
POP
?!
ALL I DID WAS SUM-MON YOU TO MY DIGITAL CONSCIOUS-NESS.
IT IS EASIER TO TALK IN HERE.
NOW I WILL BEGIN...

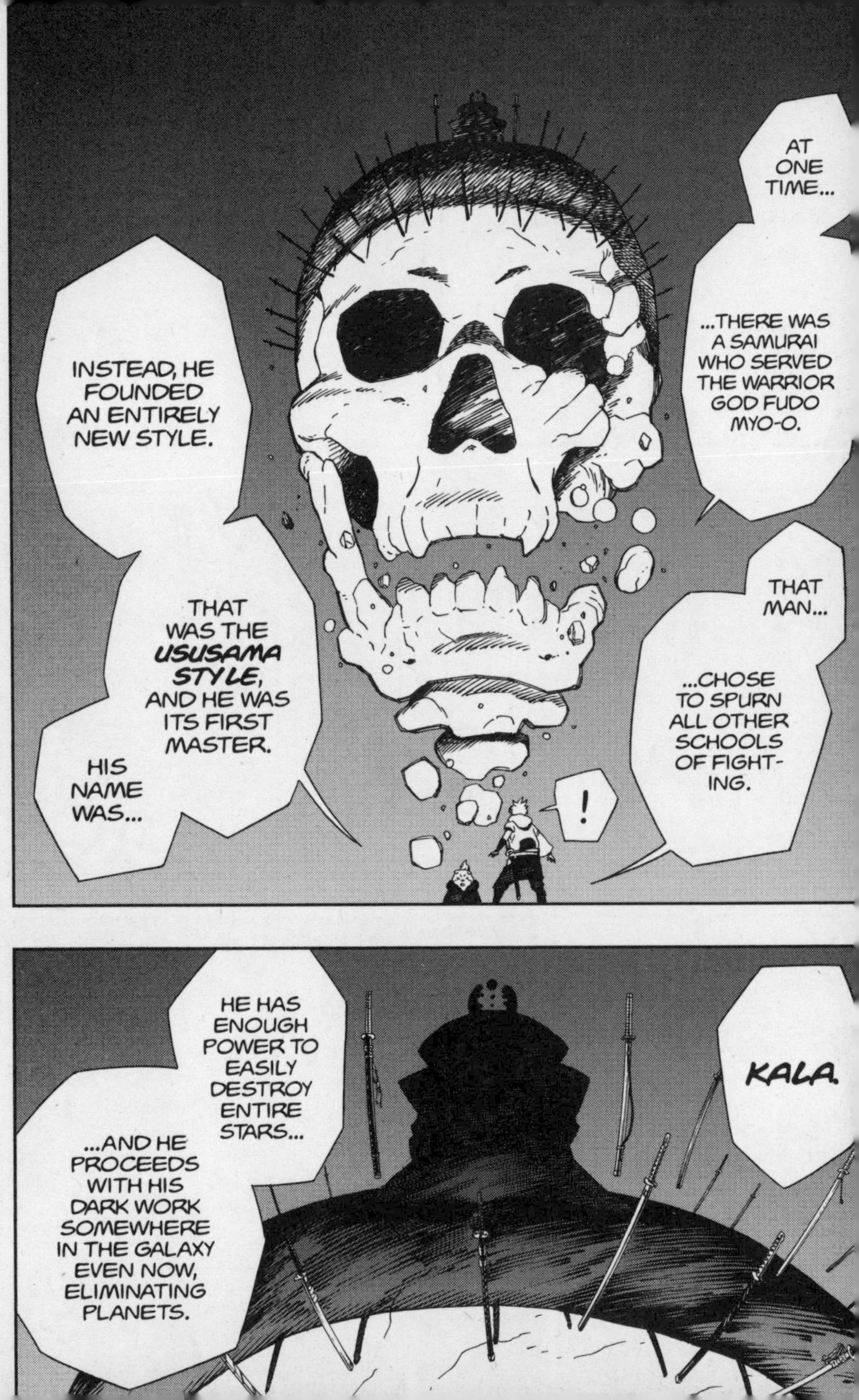
AT ONE TIME...
...THERE WAS A SAMURAI WHO SERVED THE WARRIOR GOD FUDO MYO-O.
THAT MAN...
...CHOSE TO SPURN ALL OTHER SCHOOLS OF FIGHT-ING.
!
INSTEAD, HE FOUNDED AN ENTIRELY NEW STYLE.
THAT WAS THE *USUSAMA STYLE*, AND HE WAS ITS FIRST MASTER.
HIS NAME WAS...
KALA.
HE HAS ENOUGH POWER TO EASILY DESTROY ENTIRE STARS...
...AND HE PROCEEDS WITH HIS DARK WORK SOMEWHERE IN THE GALAXY EVEN NOW, ELIMINATING PLANETS.

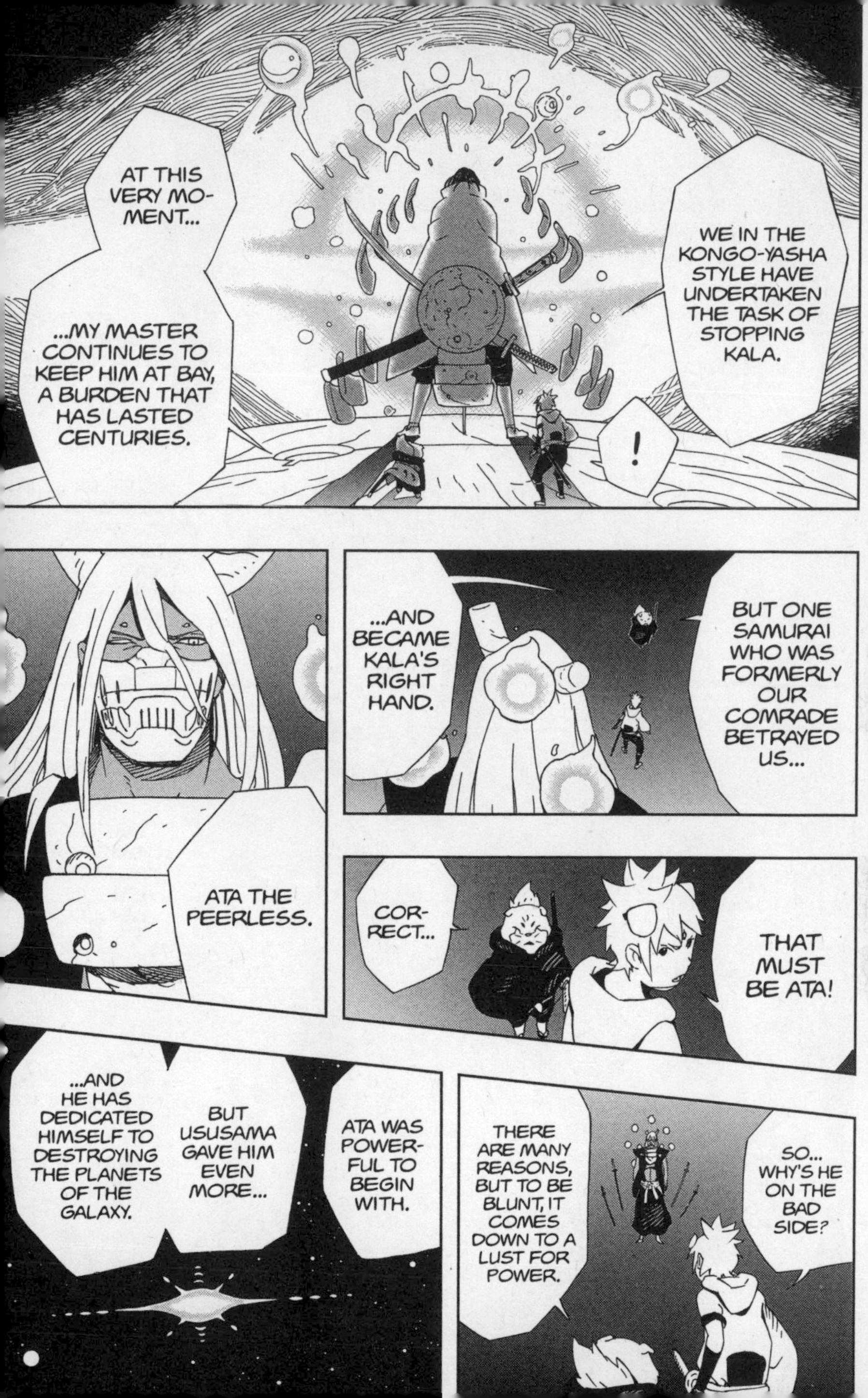
WE IN THE KONGO-YASHA STYLE HAVE UNDERTAKEN THE TASK OF STOPPING KALA.
AT THIS VERY MO-MENT...
...MY MASTER CONTINUES TO KEEP HIM AT BAY, A BURDEN THAT HAS LASTED CENTURIES.
!
BUT ONE SAMURAI WHO WAS FORMERLY OUR COMRADE BETRAYED US...
...AND BECAME KALA'S RIGHT HAND.
THAT MUST BE ATA!
COR-RECT...
ATA THE PEERLESS.
SO... WHY'S HE ON THE BAD SIDE?
THERE ARE MANY REASONS, BUT TO BE BLUNT, IT COMES DOWN TO A LUST FOR POWER.
ATA WAS POWER-FUL TO BEGIN WITH.
BUT USUSAMA GAVE HIM EVEN MORE...
...AND HE HAS DEDICATED HIMSELF TO DESTROYING THE PLANETS OF THE GALAXY.

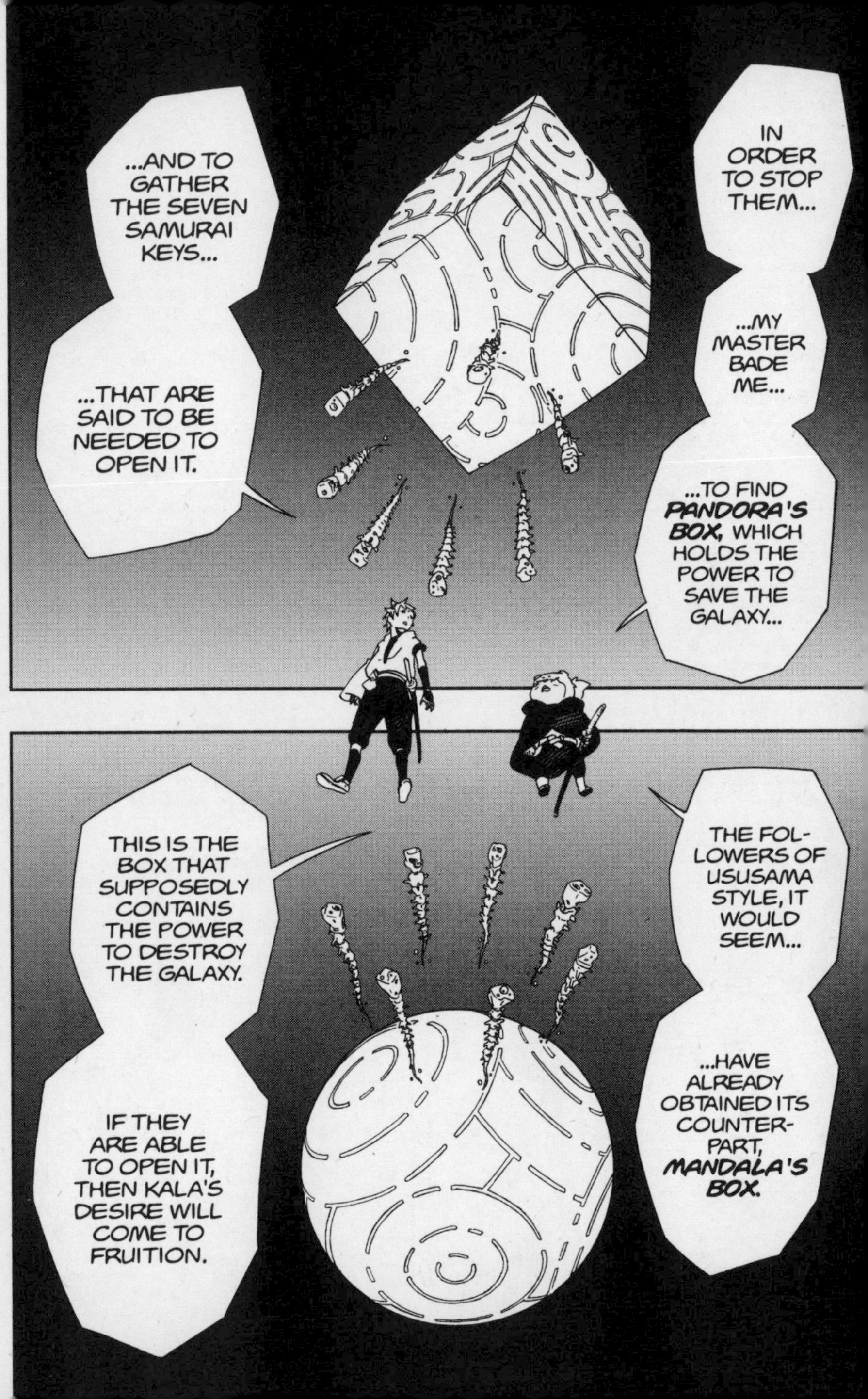

IN ORDER TO STOP THEM...
...MY MASTER BADE ME...
...TO FIND **PANDORA'S BOX,** WHICH HOLDS THE POWER TO SAVE THE GALAXY...
...AND TO GATHER THE SEVEN SAMURAI KEYS...
...THAT ARE SAID TO BE NEEDED TO OPEN IT.
THE FOL-LOWERS OF USUSAMA STYLE, IT WOULD SEEM...
...HAVE ALREADY OBTAINED ITS COUNTER-PART, **MANDALA'S BOX.**
THIS IS THE BOX THAT SUPPOSEDLY CONTAINS THE POWER TO DESTROY THE GALAXY.
IF THEY ARE ABLE TO OPEN IT, THEN KALA'S DESIRE WILL COME TO FRUITION.

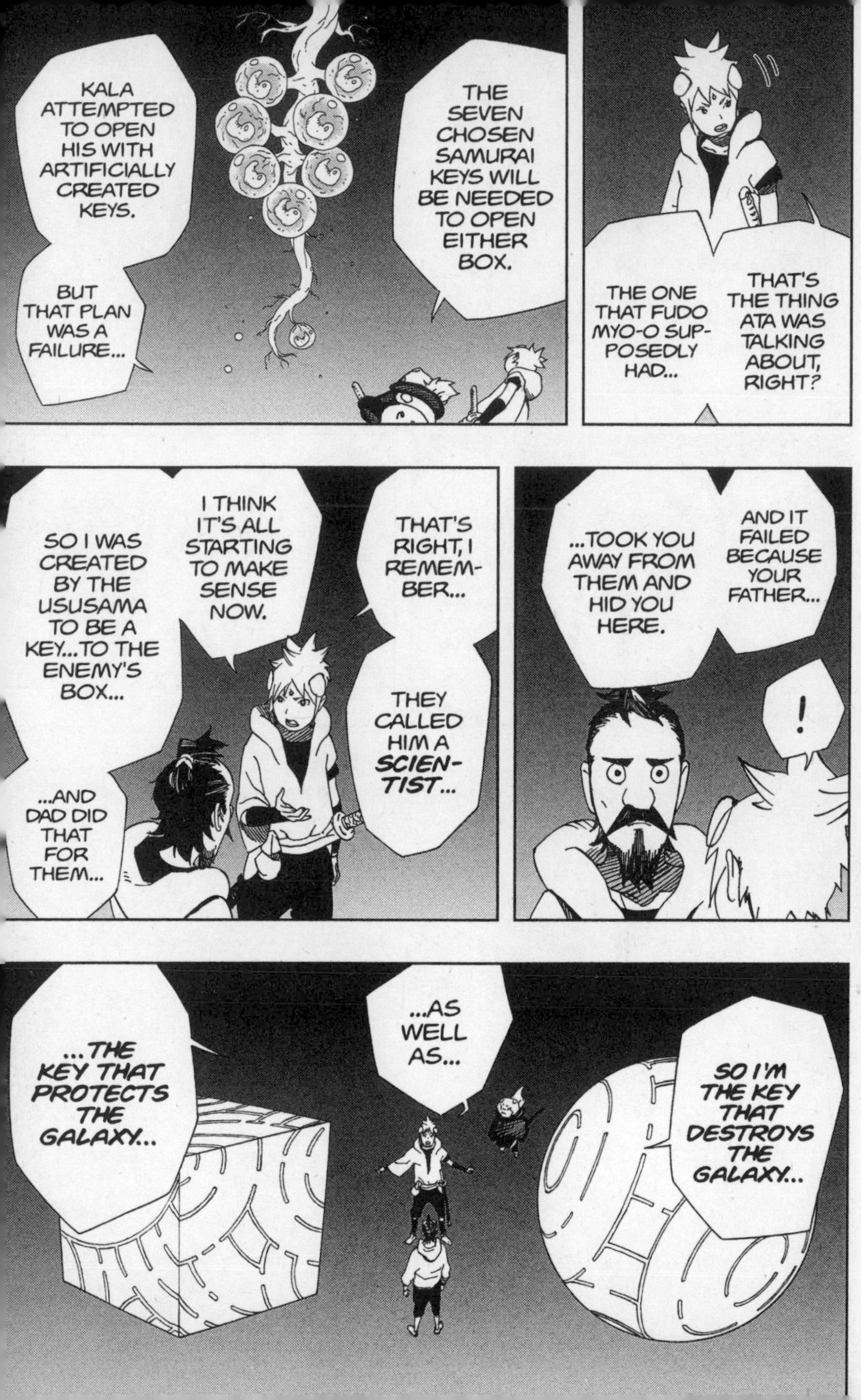
THAT'S THE THING ATA WAS TALKING ABOUT, RIGHT?
THE ONE THAT FUDO MYO-O SUP-POSEDLY HAD...
THE SEVEN CHOSEN SAMURAI KEYS WILL BE NEEDED TO OPEN EITHER BOX.
KALA ATTEMPTED TO OPEN HIS WITH ARTIFICIALLY CREATED KEYS.
BUT THAT PLAN WAS A FAILURE...
AND IT FAILED BECAUSE YOUR FATHER...
...TOOK YOU AWAY FROM THEM AND HID YOU HERE.
!
THAT'S RIGHT, I REMEM-BER...
I THINK IT'S ALL STARTING TO MAKE SENSE NOW.
SO I WAS CREATED BY THE USUSAMA TO BE A KEY...TO THE ENEMY'S BOX...
THEY CALLED HIM A *SCIEN-TIST*...
...AND DAD DID THAT FOR THEM...
SO I'M THE KEY THAT DESTROYS THE GALAXY...
...AS WELL AS...
...THE KEY THAT PROTECTS THE GALAXY...

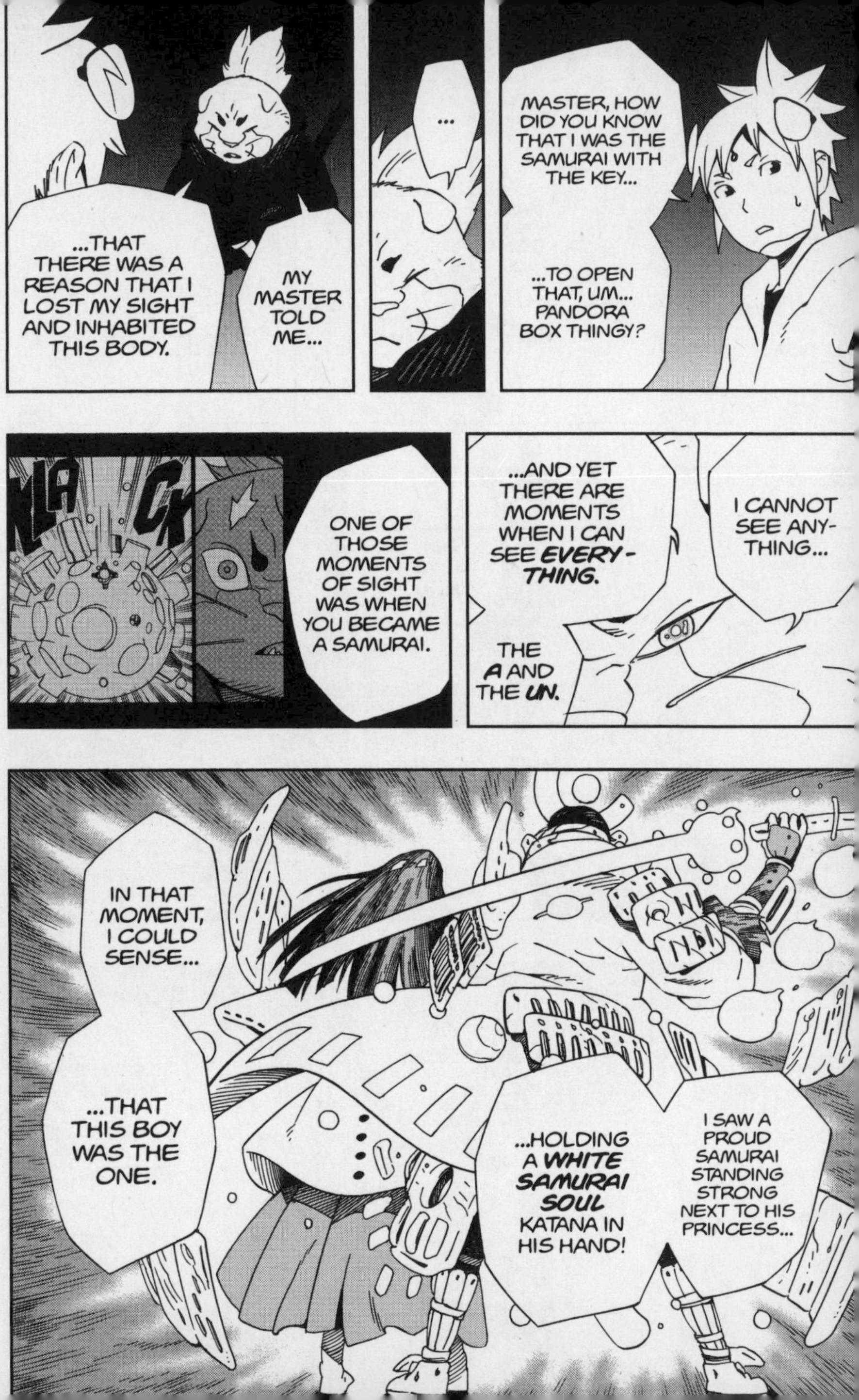
MASTER, HOW DID YOU KNOW THAT I WAS THE SAMURAI WITH THE KEY...
...TO OPEN THAT, UM... PANDORA BOX THINGY?
...
MY MASTER TOLD ME...
...THAT THERE WAS A REASON THAT I LOST MY SIGHT AND INHABITED THIS BODY.
I CANNOT SEE ANYTHING...
...AND YET THERE ARE MOMENTS WHEN I CAN SEE ***EVERYTHING.***
THE ***A*** AND THE ***UN.***
ONE OF THOSE MOMENTS OF SIGHT WAS WHEN YOU BECAME A SAMURAI.
I SAW A PROUD SAMURAI STANDING STRONG NEXT TO HIS PRINCESS...
...HOLDING A ***WHITE SAMURAI SOUL*** KATANA IN HIS HAND!
IN THAT MOMENT, I COULD SENSE...
...THAT THIS BOY WAS THE ONE.

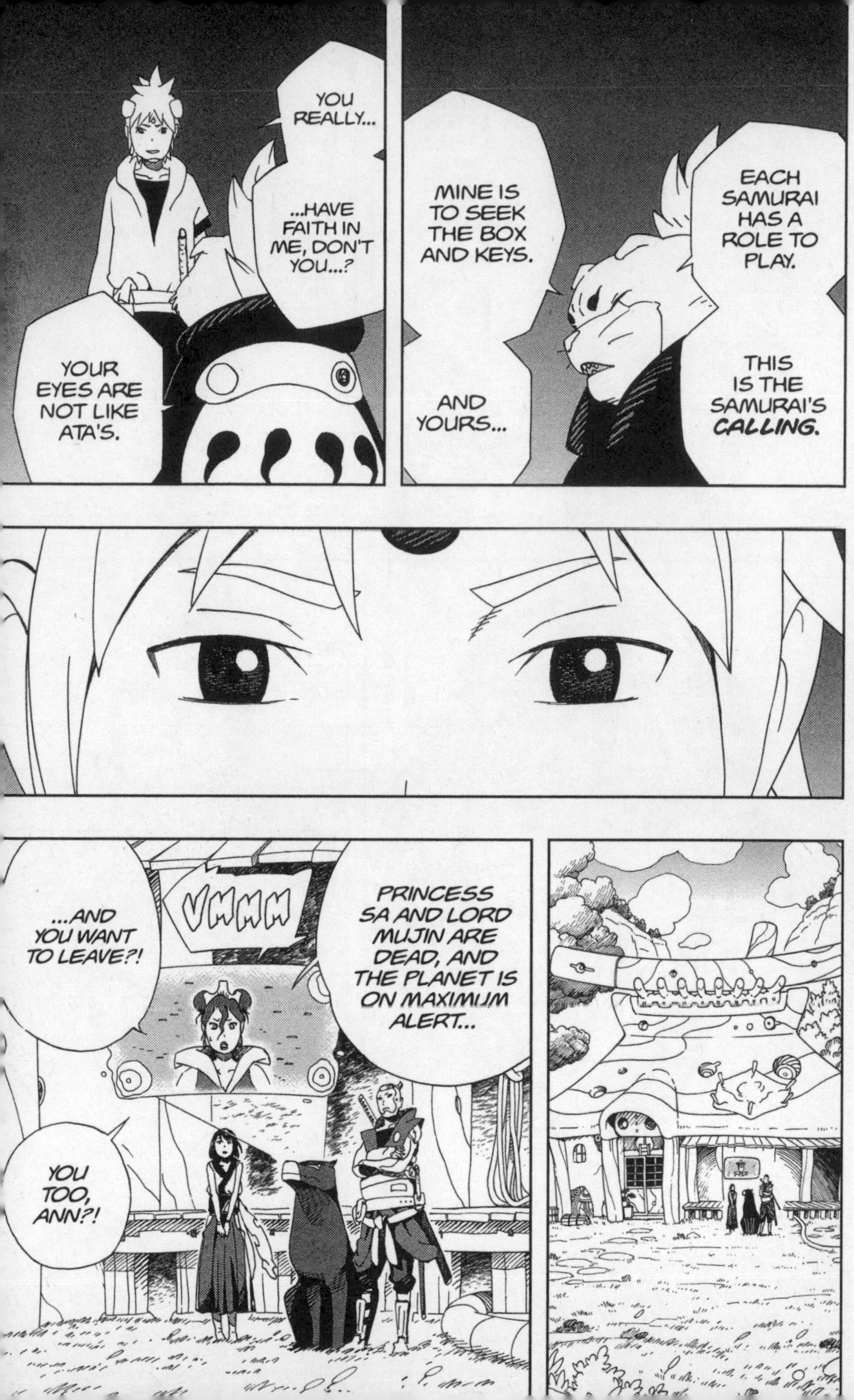

EACH SAMURAI HAS A ROLE TO PLAY.
THIS IS THE SAMURAI'S *CALLING.*
MINE IS TO SEEK THE BOX AND KEYS.
AND YOURS...
YOU REALLY...
...HAVE FAITH IN ME, DON'T YOU...?
YOUR EYES ARE NOT LIKE ATA'S.
PRINCESS SA AND LORD MUJIN ARE DEAD, AND THE PLANET IS ON MAXIMUM ALERT...
VMMM
...AND YOU WANT TO LEAVE?!
YOU TOO, ANN?!

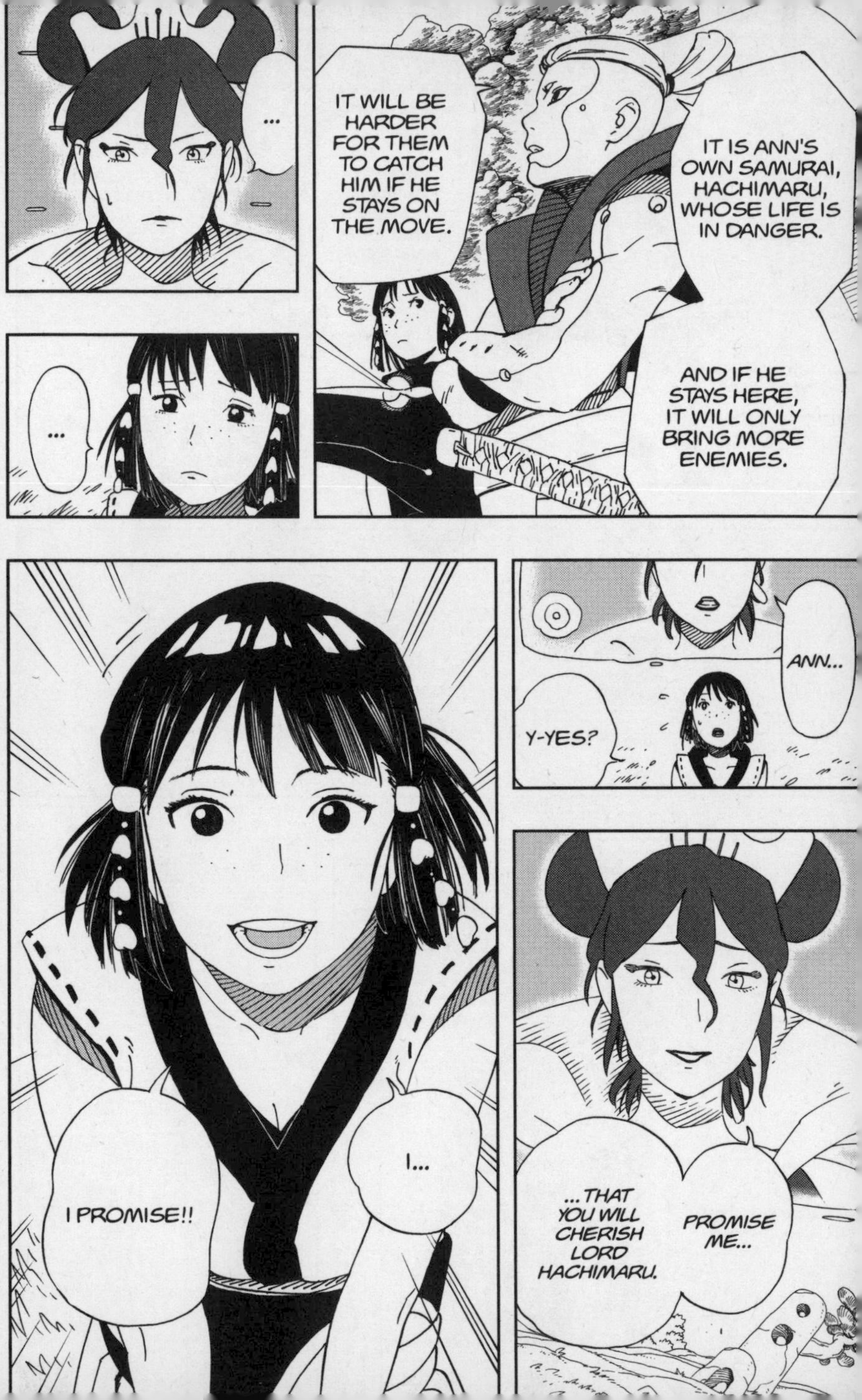
IT IS ANN'S OWN SAMURAI, HACHIMARU, WHOSE LIFE IS IN DANGER.
AND IF HE STAYS HERE, IT WILL ONLY BRING MORE ENEMIES.
IT WILL BE HARDER FOR THEM TO CATCH HIM IF HE STAYS ON THE MOVE.
...
...
ANN...
Y-YES?
PROMISE ME...
...THAT YOU WILL CHERISH LORD HACHIMARU.
I...
I PROMISE!!

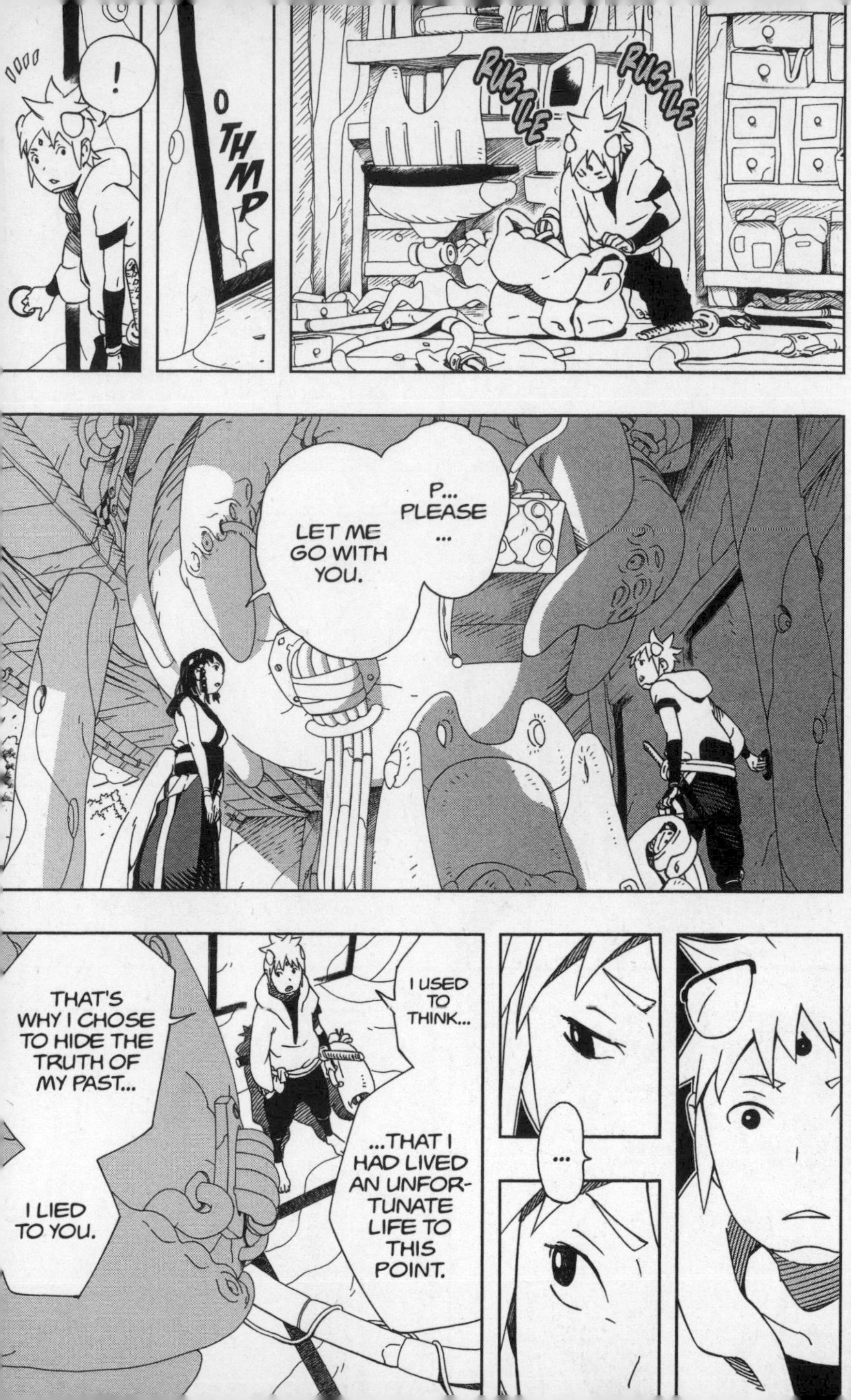
RUSTLE
RUSTLE
THMP
!
P... PLEASE ...
LET ME GO WITH YOU.
...
I USED TO THINK...
...THAT I HAD LIVED AN UNFORTUNATE LIFE TO THIS POINT.
THAT'S WHY I CHOSE TO HIDE THE TRUTH OF MY PAST...
I LIED TO YOU.

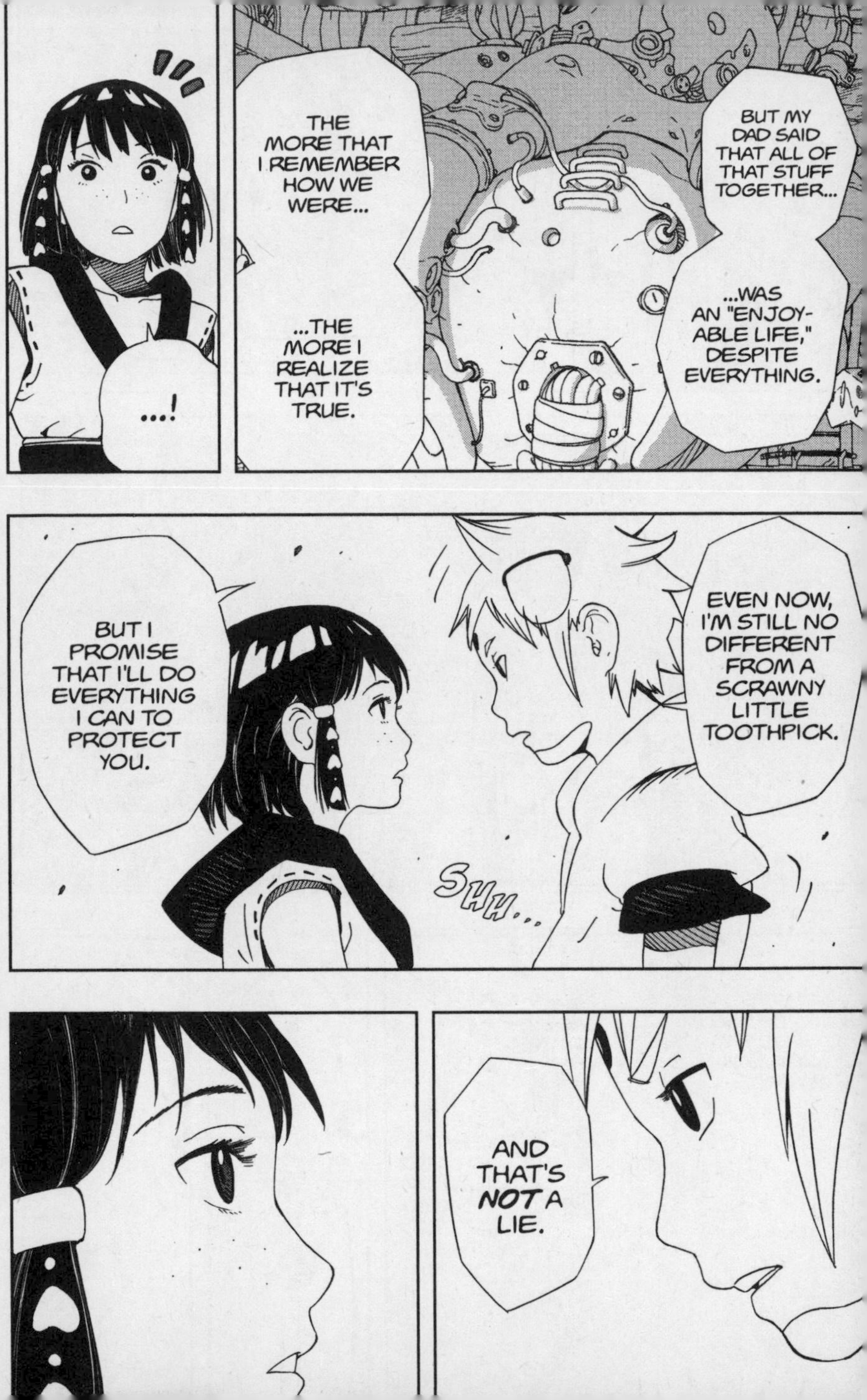
BUT MY DAD SAID THAT ALL OF THAT STUFF TOGETHER...
...WAS AN "ENJOY-ABLE LIFE," DESPITE EVERYTHING.
THE MORE THAT I REMEMBER HOW WE WERE...
...THE MORE I REALIZE THAT IT'S TRUE.
...!
EVEN NOW, I'M STILL NO DIFFERENT FROM A SCRAWNY LITTLE TOOTHPICK.
BUT I PROMISE THAT I'LL DO EVERYTHING I CAN TO PROTECT YOU.
SHH...
AND THAT'S NOT A LIE.

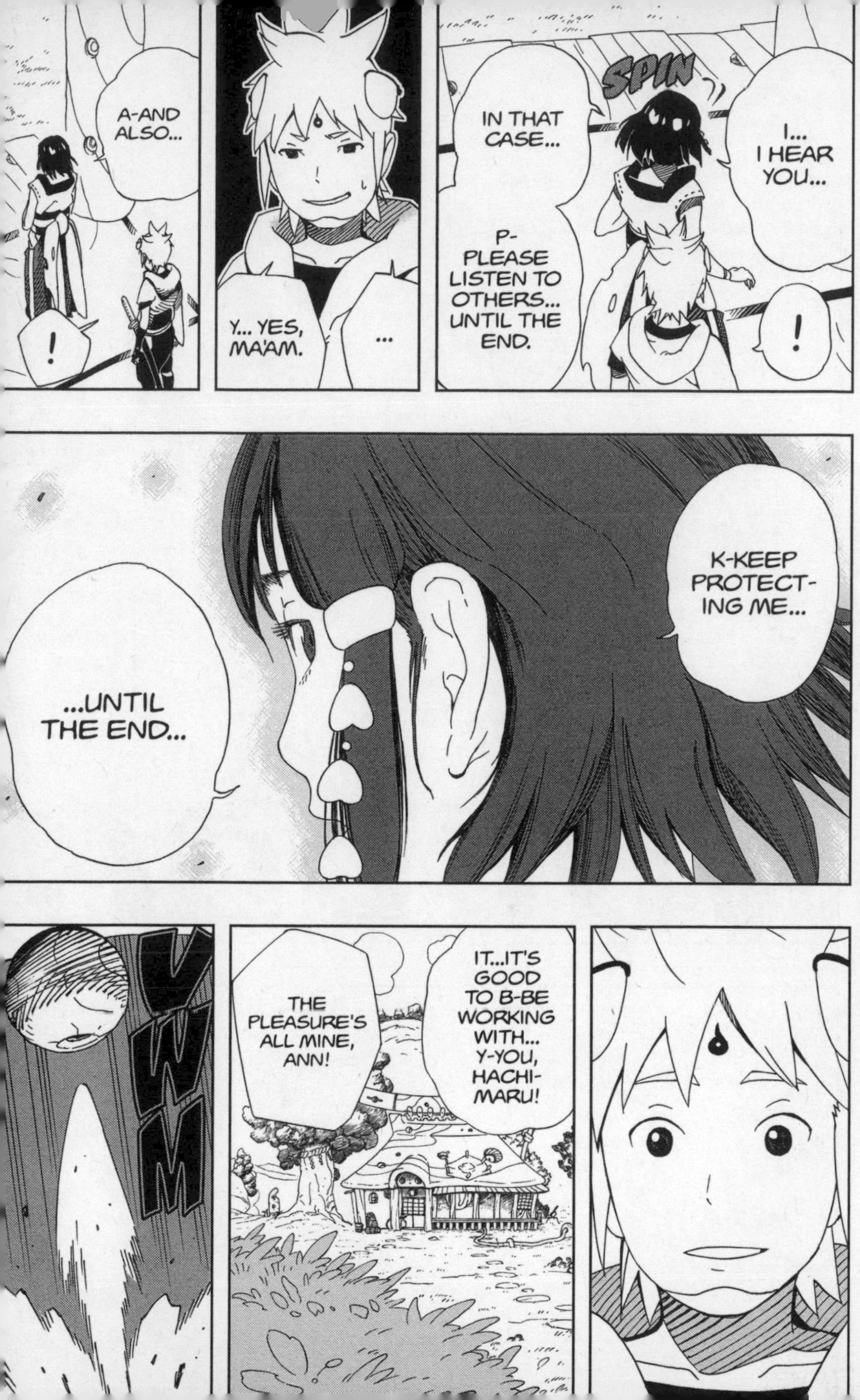
I... I HEAR YOU...
SPIN
IN THAT CASE...
!
P- PLEASE LISTEN TO OTHERS... UNTIL THE END.
Y... YES, MA'AM.
...
A-AND ALSO...
!
K-KEEP PROTECT-ING ME...
...UNTIL THE END...
IT...IT'S GOOD TO B-BE WORKING WITH... Y-YOU, HACHI-MARU!
THE PLEASURE'S ALL MINE, ANN!
VWM

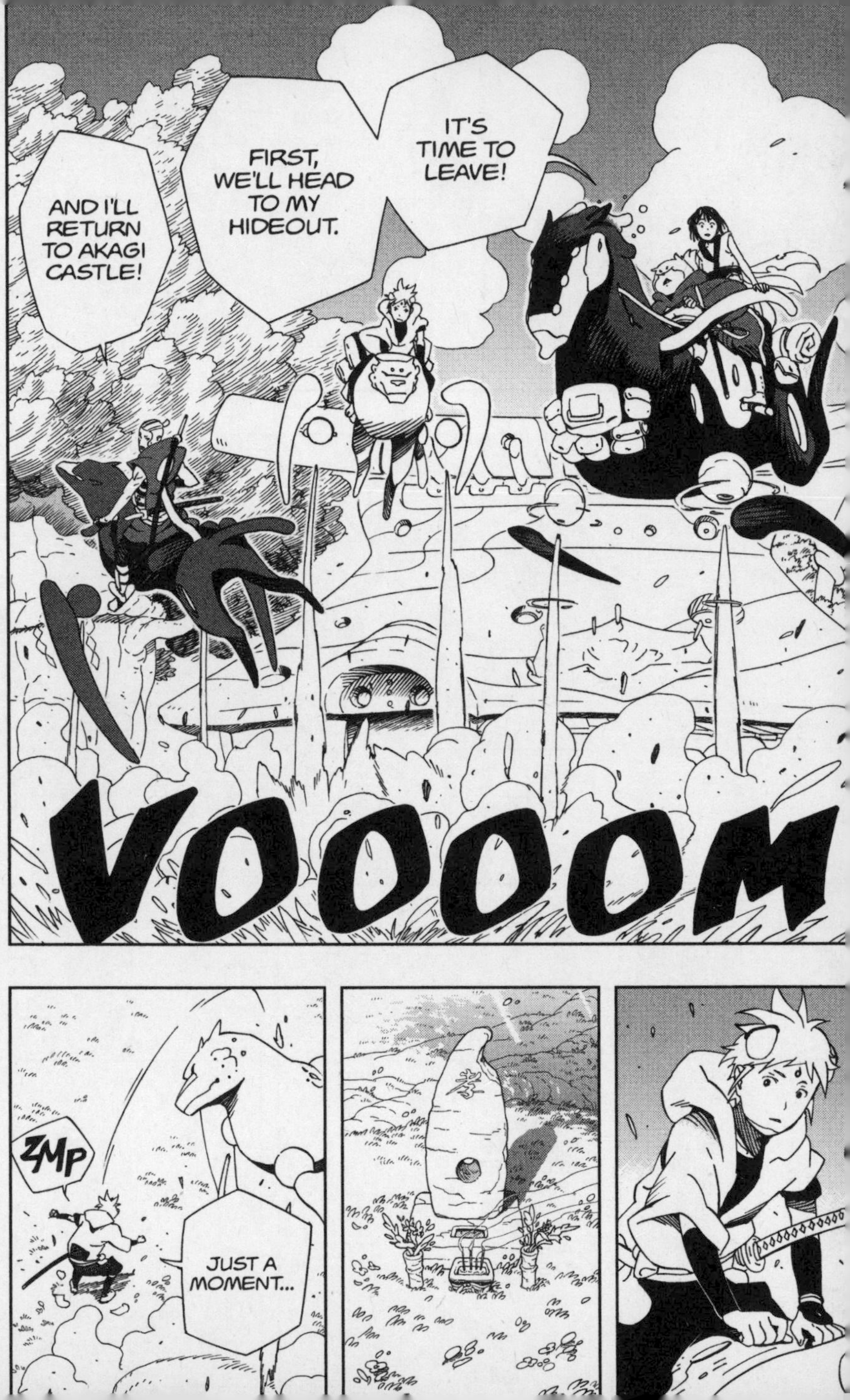
IT'S TIME TO LEAVE!
FIRST, WE'LL HEAD TO MY HIDEOUT.
AND I'LL RETURN TO AKAGI CASTLE!
VOOOOM
ZMP
JUST A MOMENT...

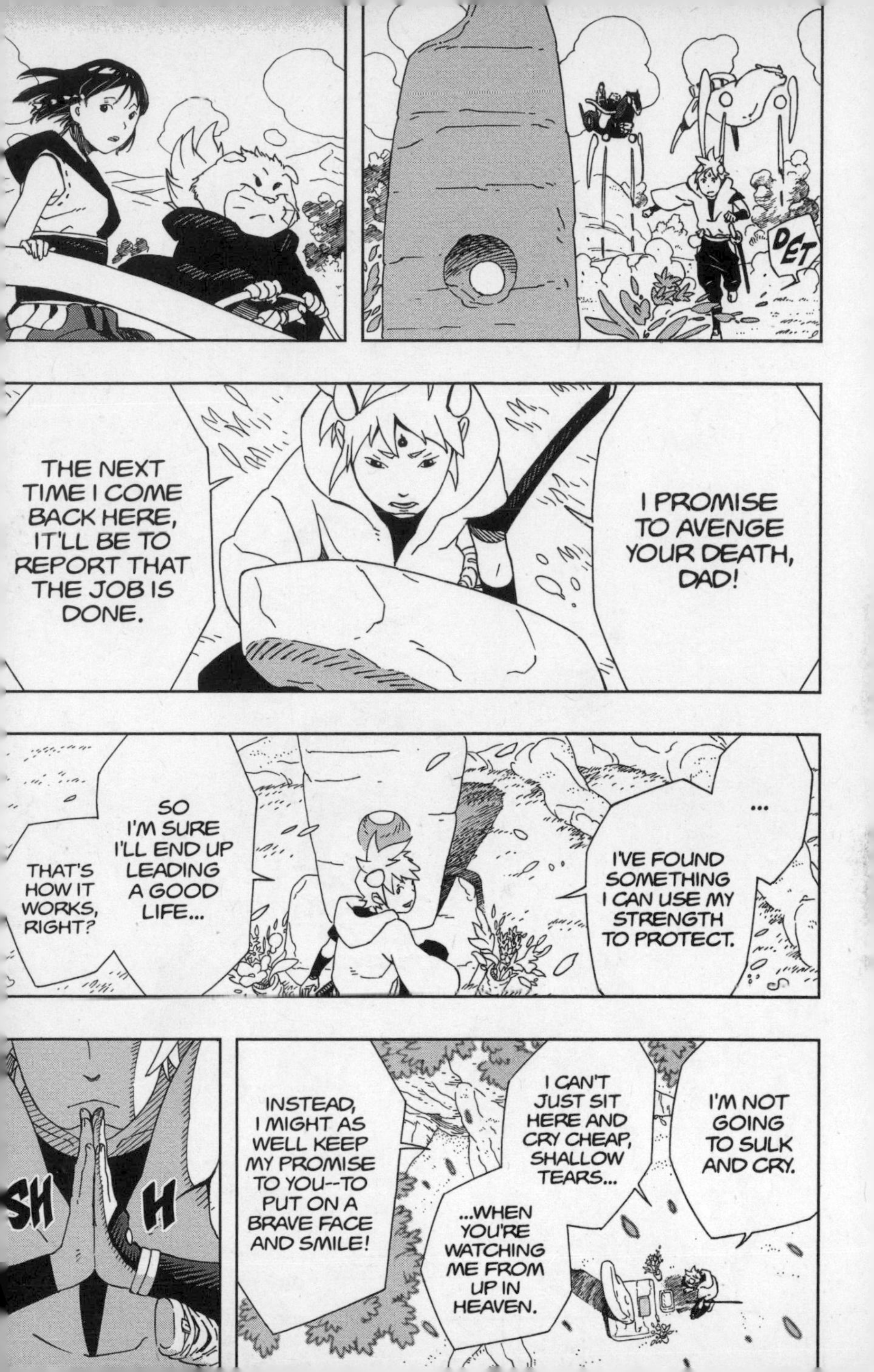
DET
I PROMISE TO AVENGE YOUR DEATH, DAD!
THE NEXT TIME I COME BACK HERE, IT'LL BE TO REPORT THAT THE JOB IS DONE.
...
I'VE FOUND SOMETHING I CAN USE MY STRENGTH TO PROTECT.
SO I'M SURE I'LL END UP LEADING A GOOD LIFE...
THAT'S HOW IT WORKS, RIGHT?
I'M NOT GOING TO SULK AND CRY.
I CAN'T JUST SIT HERE AND CRY CHEAP, SHALLOW TEARS...
...WHEN YOU'RE WATCHING ME FROM UP IN HEAVEN.
INSTEAD, I MIGHT AS WELL KEEP MY PROMISE TO YOU--TO PUT ON A BRAVE FACE AND SMILE!
SH
H

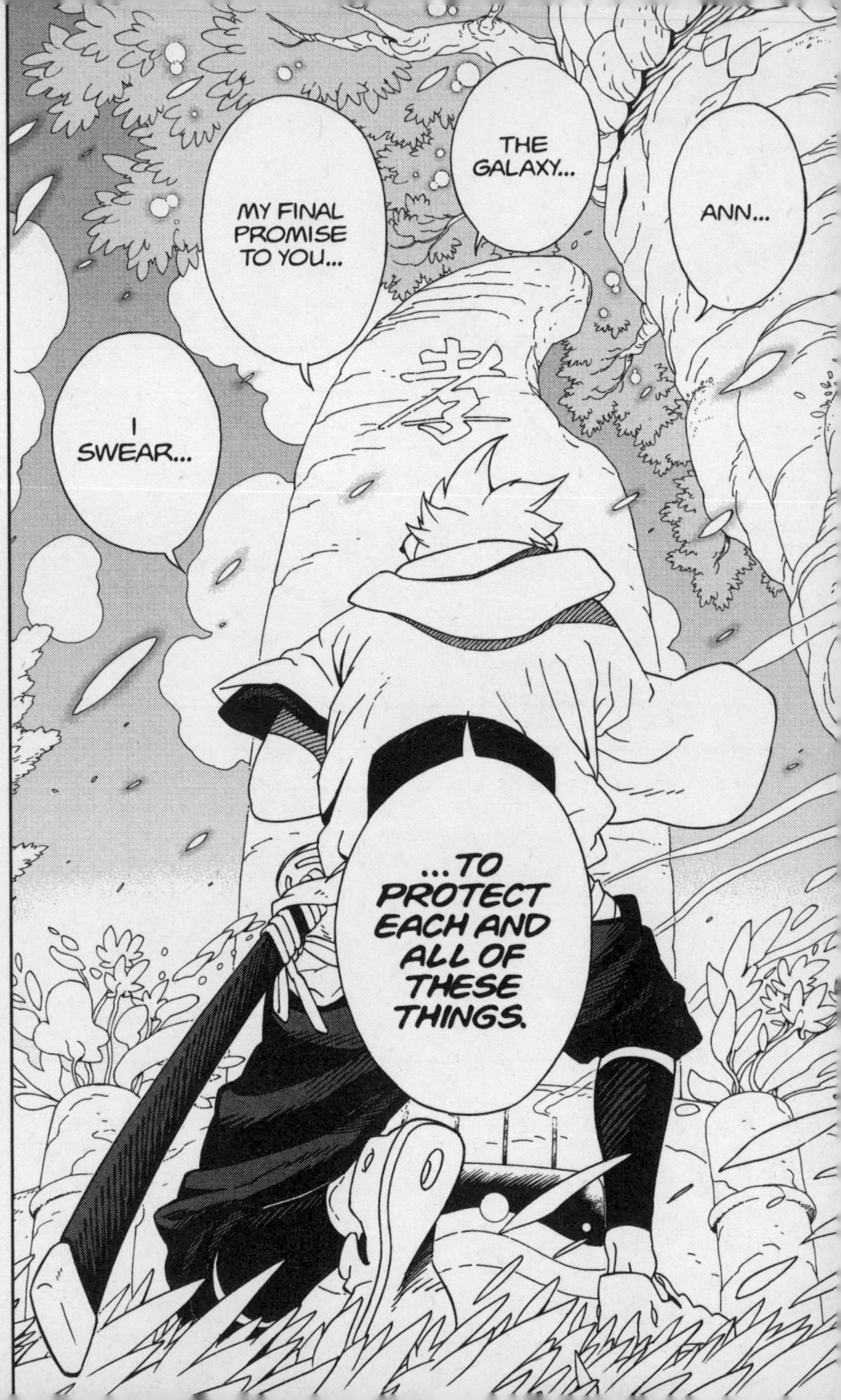
ANN...
THE GALAXY...
MY FINAL PROMISE TO YOU...
I SWEAR...
...TO PROTECT EACH AND ALL OF THESE THINGS.

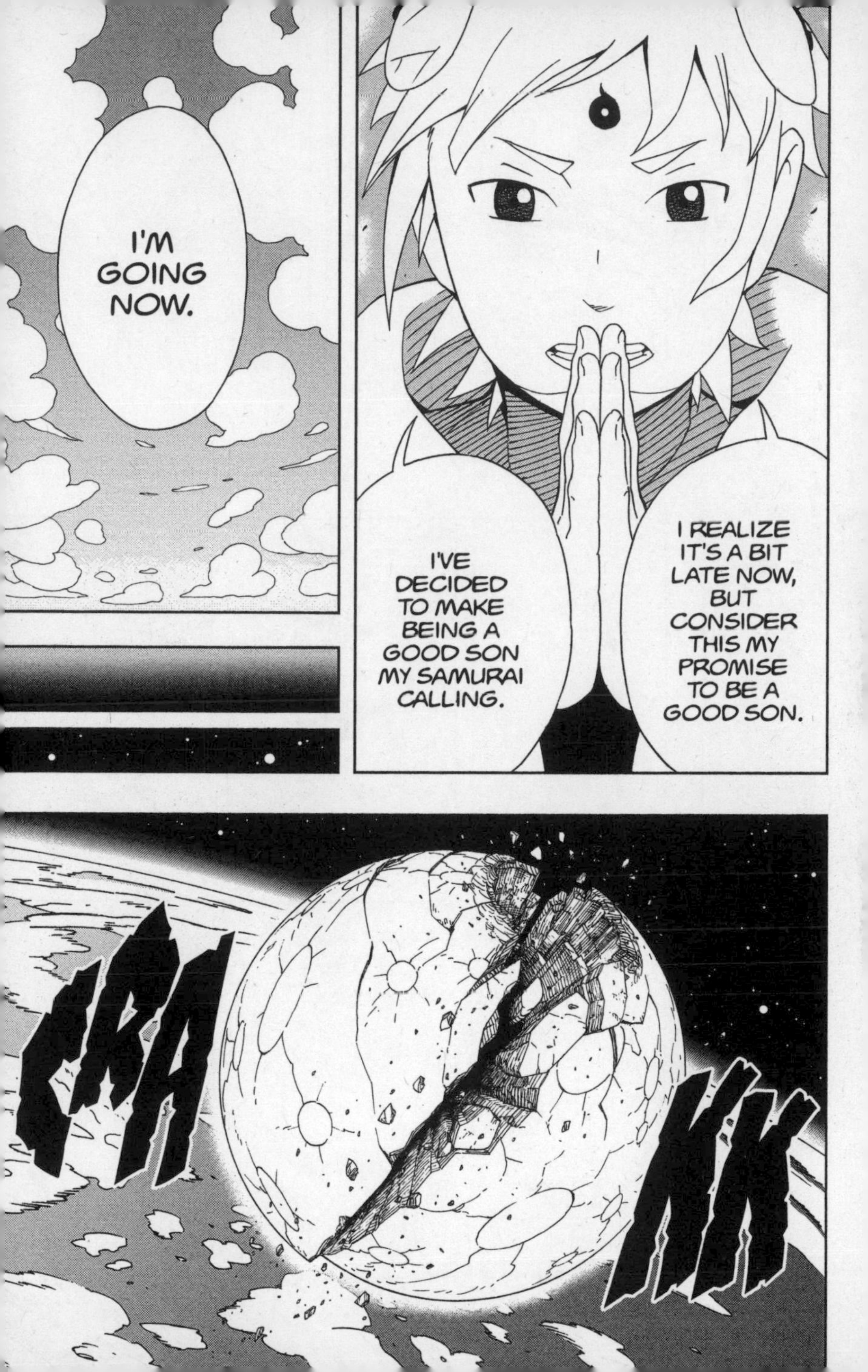
I REALIZE IT'S A BIT LATE NOW, BUT CONSIDER THIS MY PROMISE TO BE A GOOD SON.
I'VE DECIDED TO MAKE BEING A GOOD SON MY SAMURAI CALLING.
I'M GOING NOW.
CRAKK

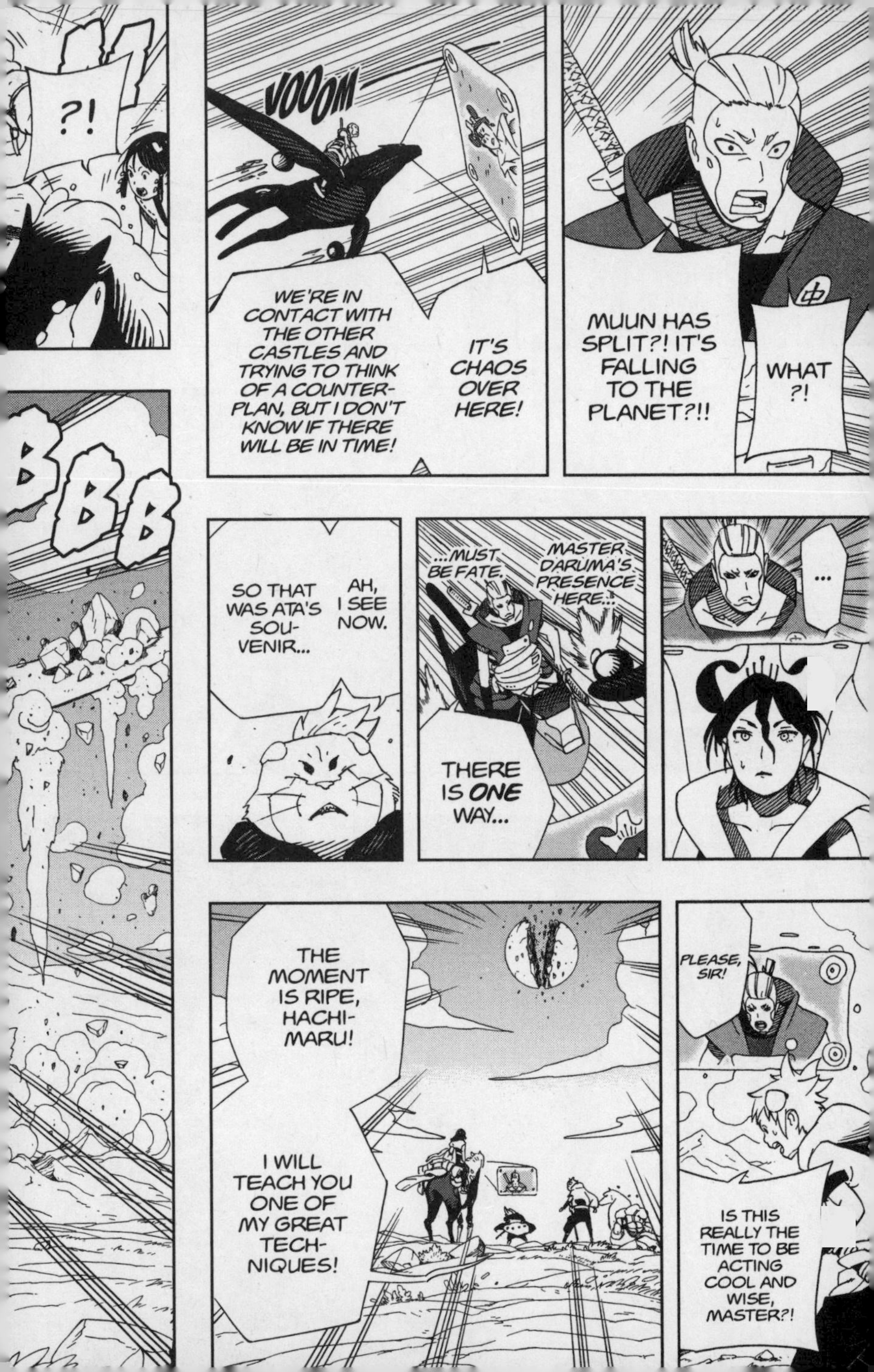
WHAT?!
MUUN HAS SPLIT?! IT'S FALLING TO THE PLANET?!!
VOOOM
IT'S CHAOS OVER HERE!
WE'RE IN CONTACT WITH THE OTHER CASTLES AND TRYING TO THINK OF A COUNTER-PLAN, BUT I DON'T KNOW IF THERE WILL BE IN TIME!
...
MASTER DARUMA'S PRESENCE HERE...
...MUST BE FATE.
THERE IS *ONE* WAY...
AH, I SEE NOW.
SO THAT WAS ATA'S SOU-VENIR...
PLEASE, SIR!
IS THIS REALLY THE TIME TO BE ACTING COOL AND WISE, MASTER?!
THE MOMENT IS RIPE, HACHI-MARU!
I WILL TEACH YOU ONE OF MY GREAT TECH-NIQUES!
?!
BBB

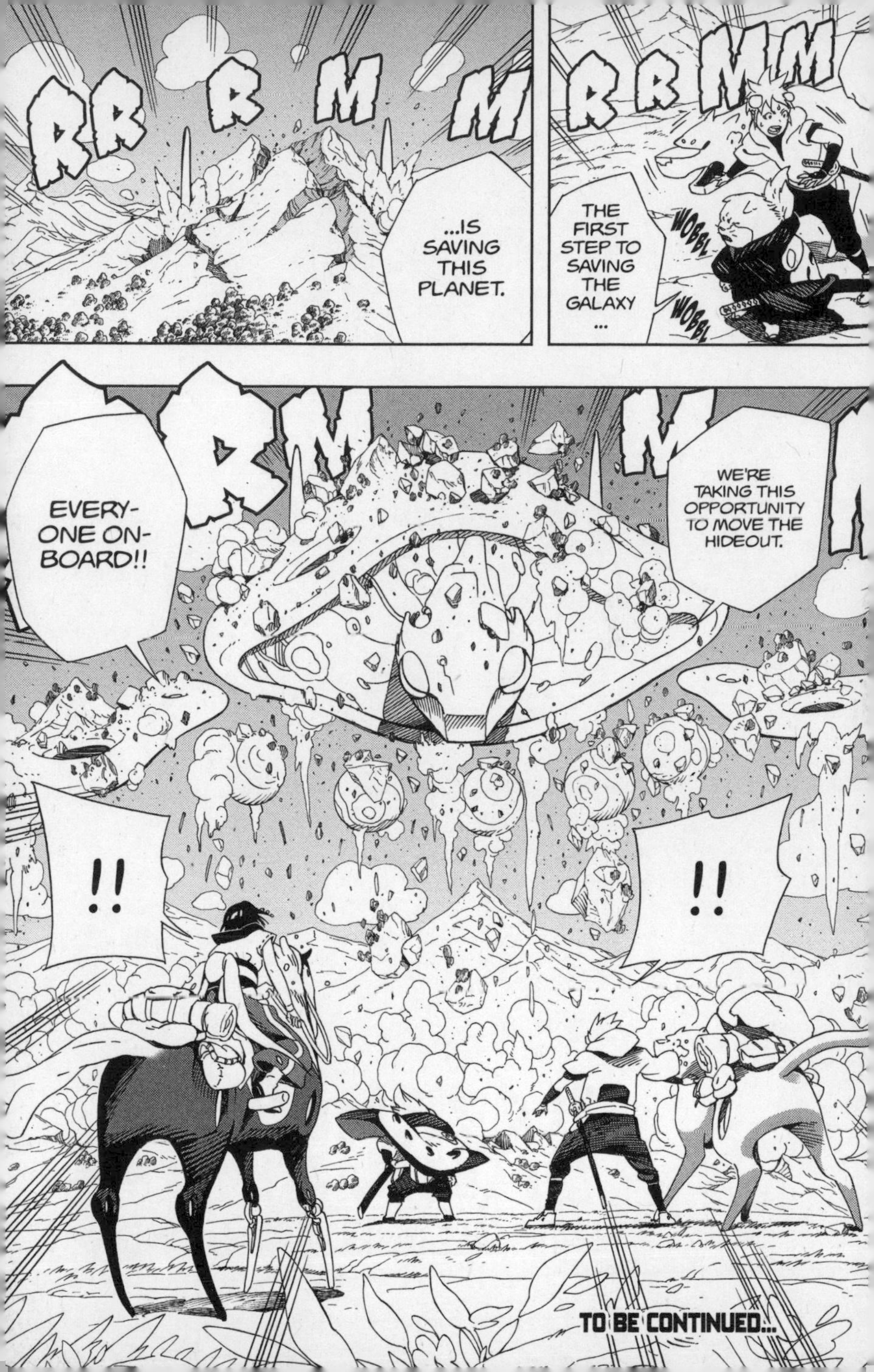
RRMM
THE FIRST STEP TO SAVING THE GALAXY ...
WOBBL
WOBBL
RRRMM
...IS SAVING THIS PLANET.
WE'RE TAKING THIS OPPORTUNITY TO MOVE THE HIDEOUT.
RM M
EVERY-ONE ON-BOARD!!
!!
!!
TO BE CONTINUED...

SAMURAI 8

THE TALE OF HACHIMARU

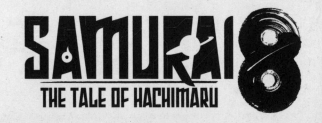

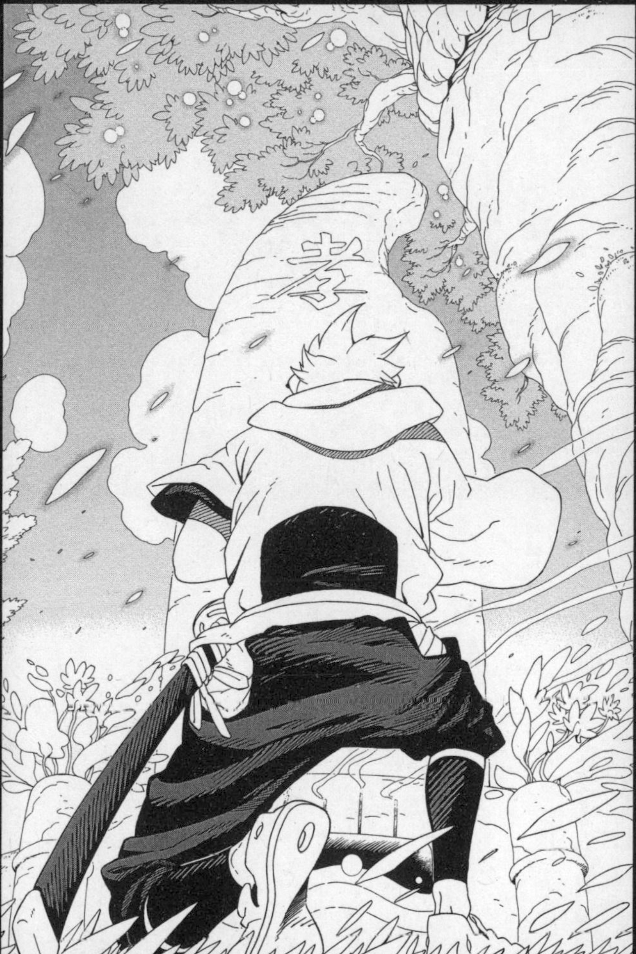
孝

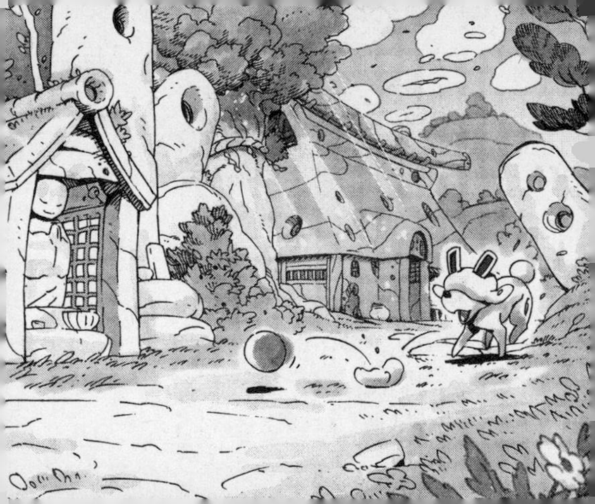

Extra Story: The Enemy's Name Is Ata

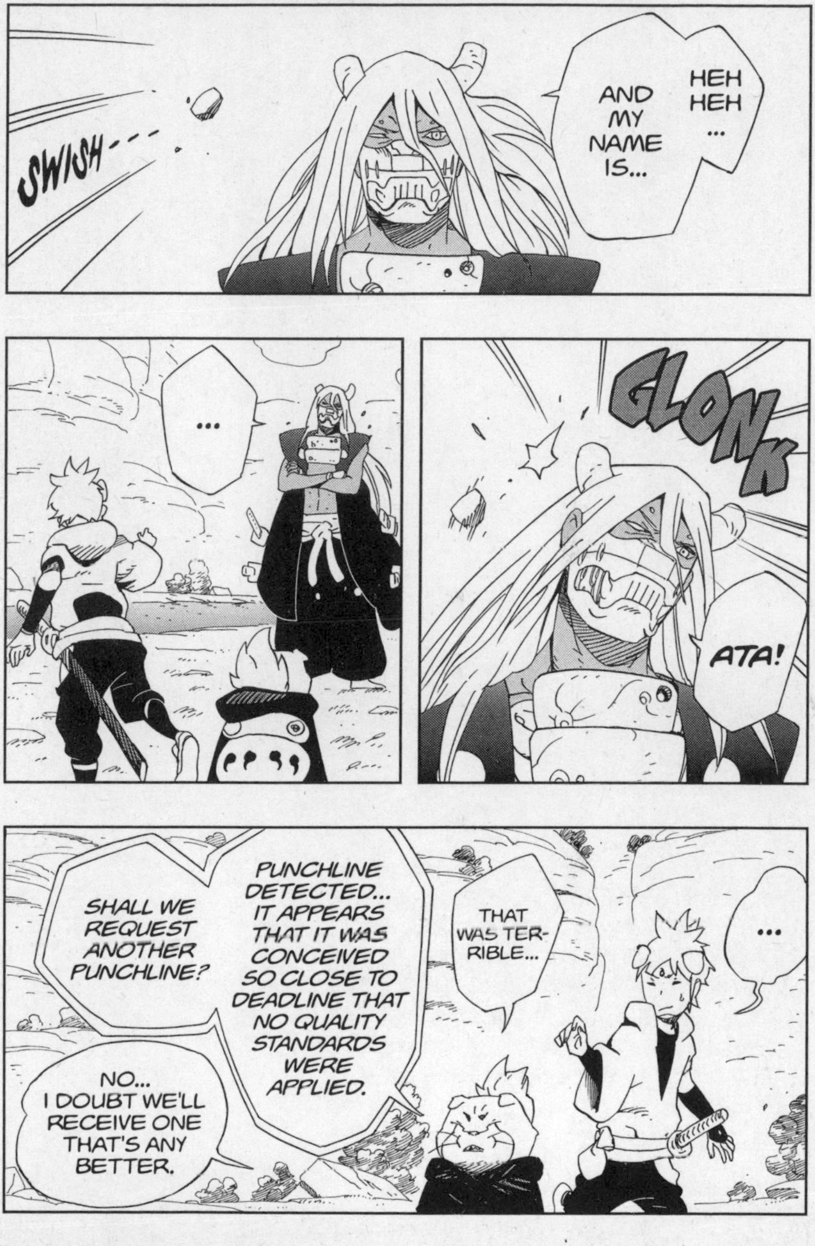
SWISH
HEH HEH...
AND MY NAME IS...
GLONK
ATA!
...
...
THAT WAS TERRIBLE...
PUNCHLINE DETECTED... IT APPEARS THAT IT WAS CONCEIVED SO CLOSE TO DEADLINE THAT NO QUALITY STANDARDS WERE APPLIED.
SHALL WE REQUEST ANOTHER PUNCHLINE?
NO... I DOUBT WE'LL RECEIVE ONE THAT'S ANY BETTER.

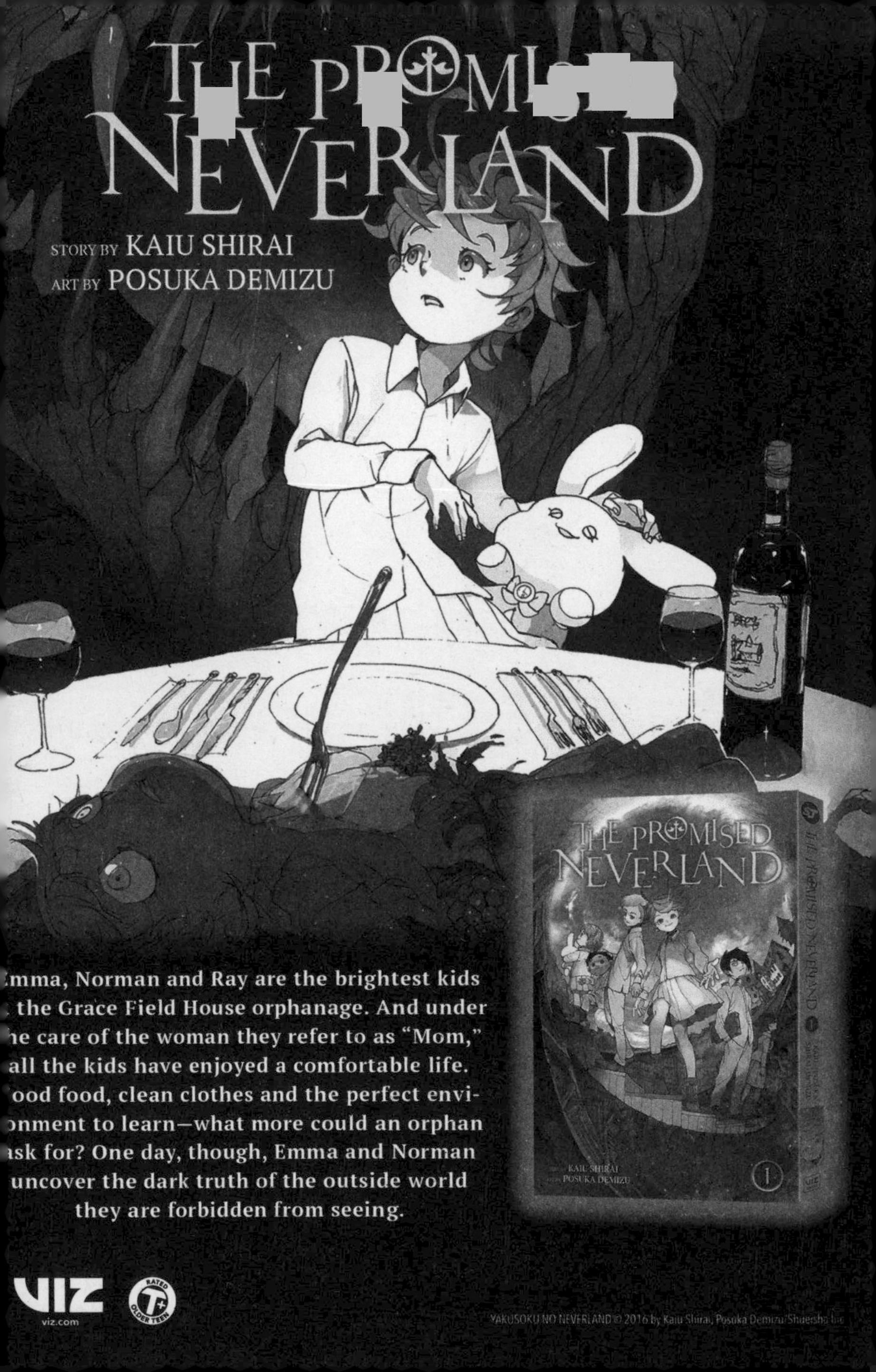
TH[redacted]E P[redacted]OMI[redacted]
NEVERLAND
STORY BY KAIU SHIRAI
ART BY POSUKA DEMIZU
:mma, Norman and Ray are the brightest kids
: the Grace Field House orphanage. And under
ıe care of the woman they refer to as "Mom,"
all the kids have enjoyed a comfortable life.
'ood food, clean clothes and the perfect envi-
onment to learn—what more could an orphan
ısk for? One day, though, Emma and Norman
uncover the dark truth of the outside world
they are forbidden from seeing.
THE PROMISED NEVERLAND
KAIU SHIRAI
POSUKA DEMIZU
1
VIZ
viz.com
RATED T+ OLDER TEEN
YAKUSOKU NO NEVERLAND © 2016 by Kaiu Shirai, Posuka Demizu/Shueisha Inc.

Dr. STONE

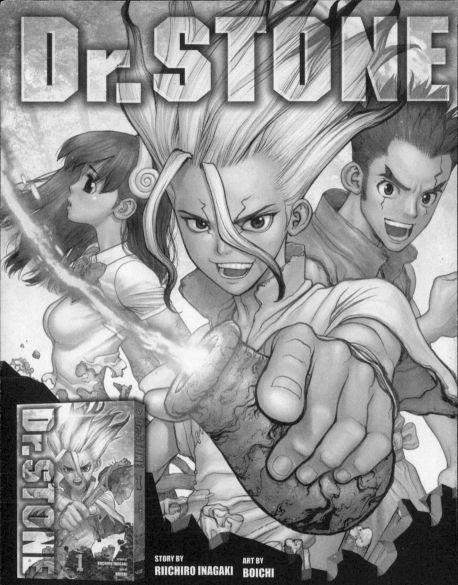

STORY BY
RIICHIRO INAGAKI

ART BY
BOICHI

One fateful day, all of humanity turned to stone. Many millennia later, Taiju frees himself from petrification and finds himself surrounded by statues. The situation looks grim—until he runs into his science-loving friend Senku! Together they plan to restart civilization with the power of science!

DR. STONE © 2017 by Riichiro Inagaki, Boichi/SHUEISHA Inc.

YOU'RE READING THE WRONG WAY!

SAMURAI 8
THE TALE OF HACHIMARU

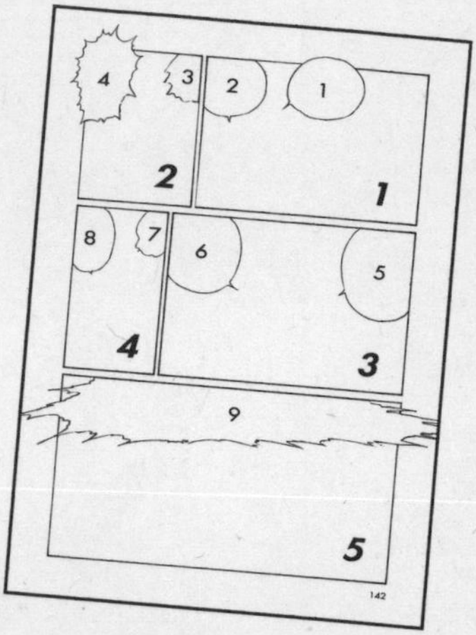

1
2
3
4
1
2
5
6
7
8
3
4
9
5
142

reads from right to left, starting in the upper-right corner. Japanese is read from right to left, meaning that action, sound effects and word-balloon order are completely reversed from English order.

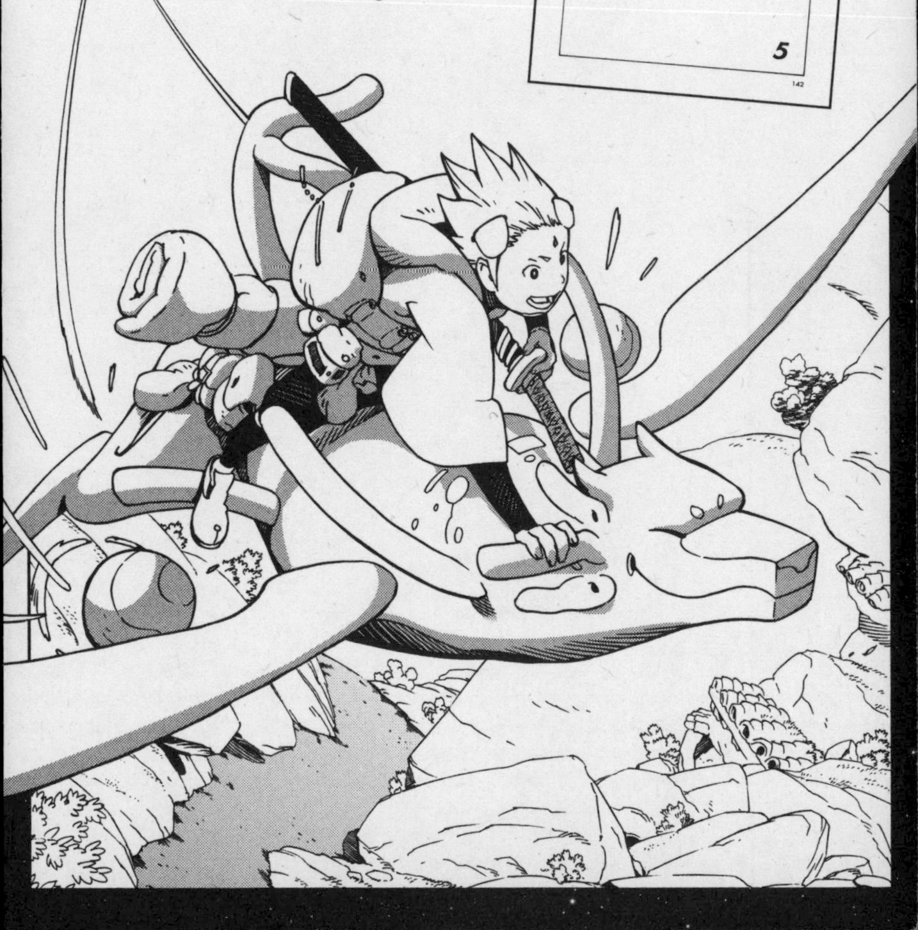

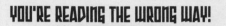